UNITED STATES CRYPTOLOGIC HISTORY

*Sources in
Cryptologic History
Number 3*

The Friedman Legacy:

A Tribute to

William and Elizebeth Friedman

Third Printing

CENTER FOR CRYPTOLOGIC HISTORY

NATIONAL SECURITY AGENCY

2006

Table of Contents

Page

Foreword v
    by David Gaddy

Biographical Sketch, William F. Friedman vii

"Six Lectures on Cryptology"
    by William F. Friedman 1

    Foreword 2
    by Frank Rowlett

    Lecture I 3
    Introduction

    Lecture II 17
    The earliest attempts at cryptography, from the invention of the art
    of writing to Bacon's "Bi-literarie" cipher.

    Lecture III 35
    The cryptosystems used by the British Regulars and by the Colonials
    during the period of the American Revolution. This is followed by a
    brief explanation of the cryptanalytic nature of the initial breaks in the
    solution of the ancient Egyptian hieroglyphic writing.

    Lecture IV 55
    Cryptology in the Civil War.

    Lecture V 91
    Cryptology from the end of the Civil War to the end of World War I.

    Lecture VI 133
    Cryptology from the end of World War I to the end of World War II.
    The emphasis has been placed upon communications security (COM-
    SEC), not only because in five preceding lectures the emphasis was
    placed very largely upon communications intelligence (COMINT), but

also because, in the final analysis, COMSEC, though not as spectacular as COMINT, is really more vital to national security.

Appendix I 173

Appendix II 177

Bibliography [for Friedman lectures] 183

"The Legendary William F. Friedman"
    by Lambros Callimahos 185

"Breaking Codes Was This Couple's Lifetime Career"
    by James R. Chiles 195

In Memoriam: Elizebeth Smith Friedman
    205

Index 209

Foreword

To term this modest collection *The Friedman Legacy* requires both explanation and apologia. Of Friedman, as of Wren, it might well be said, "If you seek his monument, look around you" at the giant and far-flung corporate entity that represents American cryptology today. But a most tangible and rewarding form of his legacy for many of us has long been his "Lectures." First published within NSA in 1963, after serialization in a journal five years earlier, they were republished two years later by his first recruit into government service and the first commandant of the National Cryptologic School, the eminent cryptologist Frank Rowlett. In his Foreword to that edition, Mr. Rowlett described the lectures as ". . . the history of Cryptology [as] recorded by the most prominent pioneer in the application of scientific principles to the field – one who, without question, laid the foundation for our modern concepts. It is hoped that both new and old employees may be inspired with a feeling of belonging to a profession that abounds in drama and fascination and that has had a profound impact on history."

The sense of what one might term "the romance of cryptology" continues to adhere: Director Vice Admiral W.O. Studeman, introducing the 1990 Cryptologic History Symposium in NSA's William F. Friedman Auditorium, referred affectionately and with a hint of awe to "this magical [MAGIC-al?] place." That mystique, derived from an appreciation of the privilege of service to the nation in a largely anonymous but most rewarding profession, in company with a rare breed of men and women, must be rediscovered with each new generation. As tools and techniques become less personal, as individual accomplishment is more difficult to discern, it comes to depend increasingly on awareness of the past – the heritage, the traditions, the symbols, of the Friedman era, when a tiny unit of Army civilians and their uniformed Navy counterparts began a revolution – and the ability to find equally satisfactory modern equivalents, to become part of a continuum.

In making *The Friedman Lectures* again available to the professional community, several related papers have been included to give the newcomer a fuller appreciation of Friedman and his fellow cryptanalyst and lifemate, Elizebeth: the recollections of his colleague and amanuensis, Lambros Callimahos, Guru and Caudillo of the Dundee Society (parochial humor that must be separately explained to the newcomer), a tribute to Elizebeth on the occasion of her death, and an appreciation of the two from a fellow laborer in the vineyard – these, with the Lectures, we have been bold to style *The Friedman Legacy*.

David W. Gaddy
Chief
Center For Cryptologic History
[1992]

Biographical Sketch

WILLIAM FREDERICK FRIEDMAN (1891-1969), the dean of modern American cryptologists, was the most eminent pioneer in the application of scientific principles to cryptology and laid the foundation for present-day cryptologic concepts. Born in Kishinev, Russia, on 24 September 1891, he was brought to the United States in 1892; married Elizebeth Smith in May 1917; fathered a son, John, and a daughter, Barbara. He retired from the National Security Agency in 1955 after thirty-five years of service with U.S. cryptologic activities. Mr. Friedman died at his home in Washington, D.C., on 2 November 1969.

B.S. (genetics), Cornell University, 1914; Research Fellow, New York State Experiment Station, Geneva, N.Y., 1914; Graduate Student and Instructor in Genetics, Cornell University, 1914-1915; Director, Department of Genetics, Riverbank Laboratories, Geneva, Ill., 1915-1916; Director, Departments of Ciphers and Genetics, Riverbank Laboratories, 1916-1918; 1st lieutenant, serving in Code and Cipher Solving Section, G-2, General Headquarters, American Expeditionary Forces (GHQ AEF), Chaumont, France, 1918-1919 (retired as lieutenant vcolonel, USAR, 1951); Director, Department of Ciphers, Riverbank Laboratories, 1919-1920; Cryptographer, Office of the Chief Signal Officer (OCSigO), Washington, D.C., 1921; Chief Cryptographer, U.S. Signal Corps, 1922-1929; Cryptanalyst, War Department, 1930-1942; Director, Communications Research, Signal Intelligence Service, later Army Security Agency, 1942-1947; Chief, Communications Research Section, Army Security Agency, 1947-1949; Cryptologic Consultant, Army Security Agency, 1949; Research Consultant, Armed Forces Security Agency, 1949-1951; Research Consultant, National Security Agency, 1951-1954; Special Assistant to the Director, NSA, 1954-1955 (retirement); Member, NSA Scientific Advisory Board, 1954-1969; Special Consultant, National Security Agency, 1955-1969.

For his many contributions to the security of his country, he received the War Department Medal for Exceptional Civilian Service (1944), the Presidential Medal for Merit (1946), the Presidential National Security Medal (1955), and a special congressional award of $100,000 for inventions and patent in the field of cryptology (1956). For their contributions to literature, he and Mrs. Friedman received the Fifth Annual Shakespeare Award in 1958 from the American Shakespeare Festival Theater and Academy for their book *The Shakespearean Ciphers Examined*.

Mr. Friedman was a member of Sigma Xi, the Cosmos Club, the U.S. Naval Institute, and the Shakespeare Association of America. He was listed in *Who's Who in America* and *American Men of Science*.

Author of many classified books and brochures, technical treatises and articles on cryptologic subjects; articles in the *Signal Corps Bulletin* (1925-1940); Riverbank Publications on Cryptology (1918-1922), the more important of which are "Several Machine Ciphers and their Solution," "The Index of Coincidence and Its Applications to Cryptography," and "Applications of the Science of Statistics to Cryptography," *Elements of Cryptanalysis* (1923); technical papers and reports published by the Office of the Chief Signal Officer and by the Signal Intelligence Service (1935-1945), among which may be mentioned "The Principles of Indirect Symmetry of Position in Secondary Alphabets and their Application in the Solution of Polyalphabetic Substitution Ciphers," "American Army Field Codes in the American Expeditionary Forces in the First World War" (1942); "Field Codes used by the German Army during the World War," and "Analysis of a Mechanico-Electrical Cryptograph"; *Encyclopedia Britannica* article "Codes and Ciphers (Cryptology)," 1927 (revised 1954); Military Cryptanalytics, *Parts I & II* (with L. Callimahos); "The Cryptologist Looks at Shakespeare"; *The Shakespearean Ciphers Examined*, coauthor with his wife Elizebeth Smith Friedman (Folger Shakespeare Prize, 1955); "Acrostics, Anagrams, and Chaucer," *Philological Quarterly*, 1959; "Jacques Casanova, Cryptologist," in *Casanova Gleanings*, Nice, France, 1961.

**William & Elizebeth
The Riverbank
Years**

The Friedman home in Washington, DC

**William & Elizebeth
The Later Years**

Six Lectures on Cryptology

by

William F. Friedman

Foreword

These six lectures by Mr. William F. Friedman, dean of American cryptologists, were prepared in order to have the history of cryptology recorded by the most eminent pioneer in the application of scientific principles to the field – one who, without question, laid the foundation for our modern concepts. It is hoped that both new and old employees may be inspired with a feeling of belonging to a profession that abounds in drama and fascination and that has had a profound impact on history. The lectures, published for the first time in 1963,* are now [1965] being reprinted to meet a continuing demand for an authoritative history of our craft.

Frank B. Rowlett
Commandant, National Cryptologic School

* Editor's Note: The Friedman lectures were also serialized in the *NSA Technical Journal* from 1959 to 1961.

Lecture I

The objective of this series of lectures is to create an awareness of the background, development, and manner of employment of a science that is the basis of a vital military offensive and defensive weapon known as CRYPTOLOGY, a word that comes from the Greek *kryptos*, meaning secret or hidden, plus *logos*, meaning knowledge or learning. Cryptology will be specifically defined a little later; at the moment, however, I'm sure you know that it has to do with secret communications.

Let me say at the outset of these lectures that I may from time to time touch upon matters that are perhaps essentially peripheral or even irrelevant to the main issues, and if a defense is needed for such occasional browsing along the byways of the subject, it will be that long preoccupation with any field of knowledge begets a curiosity, the satisfaction of which is what distinguishes the dedicated professional from the person who merely works just to gain a livelihood in whatever field he happens to find himself a job. That's not much fun, I'm afraid. By the way, a British writer, James Agate, defines a professional as the man who can do his job even when he doesn't feel like doing it; an amateur as a man who can't do his job even when he does feel like doing it. This is pretty tough on the gifted amateur, and I for one won't go all the way with Agate's definition. There are plenty of instances where gifted amateurs have done and discovered things to the chagrin and red-facedness of the professionals.

Coming back now to the main thoroughfare after the foregoing brief jaunt along a byway, I may well begin by telling you that the science of cryptology has not always been regarded as a vital military offensive and defensive weapon, or even as a weapon in the first place. Here I am reminded of a story in a very old book on cryptography. The story is probably apocryphal, but it's a bit amusing, and I give it for what it's worth.

It seems that about two thousand years ago there lived a Persian queen named Semiramis, who took an active interest in cryptology. She was in some respects an extraordinarily unpleasant woman, and we learn without surprise that she met with an untimely death. She left behind her instructions that her earthly remains were to be placed in a golden sarcophagus within an imposing mausoleum, on the outside of which, on its front stone wall, there was to be graven a message, saying

> Stay, weary traveller! If thou art footsore, hungry, or in need of money - Unlock the riddle of the cipher graven below, And thou wilt be led to riches beyond all dreams of avarice!

Below this curious inscription was a cryptogram, a jumble of letters without meaning or even pronounceability. For several hundred years the possibility of sudden wealth served as allure to many experts who tried very hard to decipher the cryptogram. They were all without success, until one day there appeared on the scene a long-haired, bewhiskered, and bespectacled savant who after working at the project for a considerable length of time, solved the cipher, which gave him detailed instructions for finding a secret entry into the tomb. When he got inside, he found an instruction to open the sarcophagus, but he had to solve several more cryptograms, the last one of which may have involved finding the correct combination to a five-tumbler combination lock – who knows? Well, he solved that one too, after a lot of work, and this enabled him to open the sarcophagus, inside which he found a box. In the box was a message, this time in plain language, and this is what it said:

> O, thou vile and insatiable monster! To disturb these poor bones!
> If thou hast learned something more useful than the art of deciphering,
> Thou wouldst not be footsore, hungry, or in need of money!

I'm frank to confess that many times during my forty-year preoccupation with cryptology, and generally near the middle and the end of each month, I have felt that good old Queen Semiramis knew what she was talking about. However, earning money is only a part of the recompense for working in the cryptologic field, and I hope that most of you will find out sooner or later what some of these other recompenses are, and what they can mean to you.

If Queen Semiramis thought there are other things to learn that are more useful than the art of deciphering, I suppose we'd have to agree, but we are warranted in saying, at least, that there isn't any question about the importance of the role that cryptology plays in modern times: all of us are influenced and affected by it, as I hope to show you in a few minutes.

I shall begin by reading from a source you'll all recognize – *Time*, the issue of 17 December 1945. I will preface the reading by reminding you that by that date World War II was all over – or at least V-E and V-J days had been celebrated some months before. Some of you may be old enough to remember very clearly the loud clamor on the part of certain vociferous members of Congress, who had for years been insisting upon learning the reasons why we had been caught by surprise in such a disastrous defeat as the Japanese had inflicted upon us at Pearl Harbor. This clamor had to be met, for these congressmen contended that the truth could no longer be hushed up or held back because of an alleged continuing need for military secrecy, as claimed by the administration and by many Democratic senators and representatives. The war was over – wasn't it? – Republican senators and representatives insisted. There had been investigations – a half dozen of them – but all except one were TOP SECRET. The Republicans wanted – and at last they got what they desired – a grand finale joint congressional investigation that would all be completely open to the public. No more secrets! It was spectacular. Not only did the congressional inquiry bring into the open every detail and exhibit uncovered by its own lengthy hearings, but it also disclosed to America and *to the whole world* everything that had been said and shown at all the previous Army and Navy investigations. Most of the information that was thus disclosed had been, and much of it still was, TOP SECRET; yet all of these precious secrets became matters of public information as a result of the congressional investigation.

There came a day in the congressional hearings when the Chief of Staff of the United States Army at the time of the Pearl Harbor attack, five-star general George C. Marshall, was called to the witness stand. He testified for several long, long days, eight of them in all. Toward the end of the second day of his ordeal, he was questioned about a letter it had been rumored he'd written to Governor Dewey in the autumn of 1944 during the presidential campaign. The letter was about codes. With frozen face, General Marshall balked at disclosing the whole letter. He pleaded most earnestly with the committee not to force him to disclose certain of its contents, but to no avail. He had to bow to the will of the majority of the committee. I shall now read from *Time* a bit of information that may be new to many of my listeners, especially to those who were too young in December 1945 to be delving into periodical literature or to be reading any pages of the daily newspaper other than those on which the comics appear.

Said *Time*:

U.S. citizens discovered last week that perhaps their most potent secret weapon of World War II was not radar, not the VT fuse, not the atom bomb, but a harmless little machine which cryptographers had painstakingly constructed in a hidden room in Washington. With this machine, built after years of trial and error, of inference and deduction, cryptographers had duplicated the decoding devices used in Tokyo. Testimony before the Pearl Harbor Committee had already shown that the machine, known as 'Magic', was in use long before December 7, 1941, and had given ample warning of the Jap's sneak attack, if only U.S. brass hats had been smart enough to realize it. Now, General Marshall continued the story of "Magic's" magic:

1. It had enabled a relatively small U.S. Force to intercept a Jap invasion fleet, win a decisive victory in the Battle of the Coral Sea, thus saving Australia and New Zealand.
2. It had directed U.S. submarines unerringly to the sea lanes where Japanese convoys would be passing.
3. It had given the U.S. full advance information on the size of the Jap forces advancing on Midway, enabled our Navy to concentrate ships which otherwise might have been 3,000 miles away, thus set up an ambush which proved to the the turning-point victory of the Pacific war.
4. By decoding messages from Japan's Ambassador Oshima in Berlin, often reporting interviews with Hitler, it had given our forces invaluable information on *German* war plans.

Time goes on to give more details of that story, to which I may later return, but I can't leave this citation of what cryptology did toward our winning of World War II without telling you that the account given by *Time* of the achievements of *Magic* makes it appear that all the secret intelligence gained from our reading Japanese messages was obtained by using that "harmless little machine" that *Time* said was used in Tokyo by the Japanese Foreign Office. I must correct that error by explaining first that *Magic* was not the name of the machine but a term used to describe the intelligence material to which the machine, among other sources, contributes and then by telling you that the secret information we obtained that way had little to do with those portions of the *Magic* material that enabled our navy to win such spectacular battles as those of the Coral Sea and Midway, and to waylay Japanese convoys. The naval parts of *Magic* were nearly all obtained from Japanese naval messages by our own very ingenious U.S. Navy cryptanalysts. At that time, I may tell those of you who are new, the army and navy had separate but cooperating cryptologic agencies and activities; the United States Air Force was not yet in existence as an autonomous and separate component of the armed forces; and work on Japanese, German, and Italian air force communications was done by army cryptanalysts, admirably assisted by personnel of what was then known as the Army Air Corps.

It is hardly necessary to tell you how carefully the *Magic* of World War II was guarded before, during, and after the war until the congressional inquiry brought most of it out in the open. Some remaining parts of it are still very carefully guarded. Even the fact of the existence of *Magic* was known to only a very few persons at the time of Pearl Harbor – and that is an important element in any attempt to explain why we were caught by surprise by the Japanese at Pearl Harbor in a devastating attack that crippled our navy for many months. Let me read a bit from page 261 of the Report of the Majority of the Joint Congressional Investigation of the attack:

> The *Magic* intelligence was pre-eminently important and the necessity for keeping it confidential cannot be overestimated. However, so closely held and top secret was this intelligence that it appears that the fact that the Japanese codes had been broken was regarded as of more importance than the information obtained from decoded traffic.

Time says, in connection with this phase of the story of Magic during World War II:

> So priceless a possession was Magic that the U.S. high command lived in constant fear that the Japs would discover the secret, change their code machinery, force U.S. cryptographers to start all over again.

Now I don't want to overemphasize the importance of communications intelligence in World War II, but I think it warranted to read a bit more of what is said about its importance in the Report of the Majority. The following is from p. 232:

> ... all witnesses familiar with Magic material throughout the war have testified that it contributed enormously to the defeat of the enemy, greatly shortened the war, and saved many thousands of lives.

General Chamberlin, who was General MacArthur's operations officer, or G-3, throughout the war in the Pacific, has written: "The information G-2, that is, the intelligence staff, gave me in the Pacific Theater alone saved us many thousands of lives and shortened the war by no less than two years." We can't put a dollars-and-cents value on what our possession of COMINT meant in the way of saving lives; but we can make a dollars-and-cents estimate of what communications intelligence meant by shortening the war by two years, and the result of that estimate is that it appears that $1.00 spent for that sort of intelligence was worth $1,000 spent for other military activities and materials.

In short, when our commanders had that kind of intelligence in World War II, they were able to put what small forces they had at the right place, at the right time. But when they didn't have it – and this happened, too – their forces often took a beating. Later on we'll note instances of each type.

I hope I've not tried your patience by such a lengthy preface to the real substance of this series of lectures; let's get down to brass tacks. For those of you who come to the subject of cryptology for the first time, a few definitions will be useful, in order that what I shall be talking about may be understood without question. Agreement on basic terminology is always desirable in tackling any new subject. In giving you the definitions, there may be a bit of repetition because we shall be looking at the same terms from somewhat different angles.

First, then, what is cryptology? Briefly, we may define it as the doctrine, theory, or branch of knowledge that treats of hidden, disguised, or secret communications. You won't find the word in a small dictionary. Even *Webster's Unabridged* defines it merely as "secret or enigmatical language"; and in its "Addenda Section," which presumably contains new or recently coined words, it is defined merely as "the study of cryptography." Neither of these definitions is broad or specific enough for those who are going to delve somewhat deeply into this science.

Cryptology has two main branches: the first is *cryptography* or, very briefly, the science of preparing secret communications and the second is cryptanalysis or the science of solving secret communications. Let's take up cryptography first, because as a procedure it logically precedes cryptanalysis: before solving anything, there must be something to solve.

Cryptography is that branch of cryptology that deals with the various means, methods, devices, and machines for converting messages in ordinary, or what we call plain language, into secret language, or what we call cryptograms. Here's a picture of one of the most famous cryptograms in history. (See fig. 1.) It was the solution of this cryptogram that resulted in bringing America into World War I on the side of the Allies on 6 April 1917, just about six weeks after it was solved. I'll tell you about it later in this series.

Cryptography also includes the business of reconverting the cryptograms into their original plain-language form, by a direct reversal of the steps followed in the original transformation. This implies that the persons involved in both of these bits of business, those at the enciphering and sending end, and those at the receiving and deciphering end, have an understanding of what procedures, devices, and so on, will be used and exactly how – down to the very last detail. The what and the how of the business constitutes what is generally referred to as the key. The key may consist of a set of rules, alphabets, procedures, and so on; it may also consist of an ordinary book that is used as a source of keys; or it may be a specialized book, called a codebook. That cryptogram I just showed you was made by using a book – a German codebook.

To *encrypt* is to convert or transform a plain-text message into a cryptogram by following certain rules, steps, or processes constituting the key or keys and agreed upon in advance by the correspondents, or furnished them by higher authority.

To *decrypt* is to reconvert or to transform a cryptogram into the original equivalent plaintext message by a direct reversal of the encrypting process, that is, by applying to the cryptogram the key or keys, usually in a reverse order, employed in producing it.

A person who encrypts and decrypts messages by having in his possession the necessary keys is called a *cryptographer or a cryptographic clerk.*

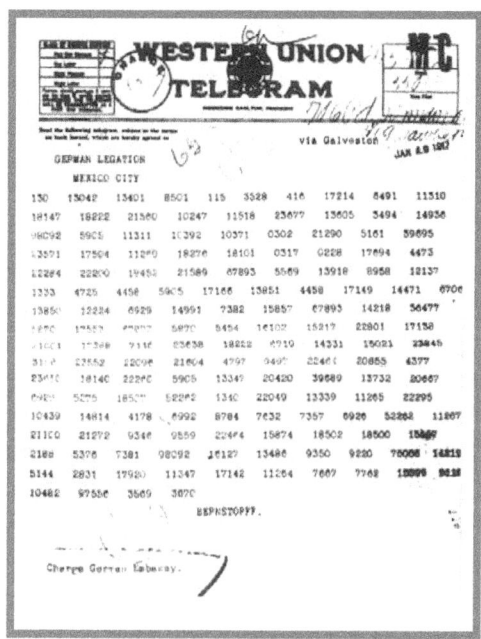

Fig. 1 The Zimmermann Telegram

Encrypting and decrypting are accomplished by means collectively designated as codes and ciphers. Such means are used for either or both of two purposes: (1) secrecy and (2) economy. Secrecy usually is far more important in diplomatic and military cryptography than economy, but it is possible to combine secrecy and economy in a single system. Persons technically unacquainted with cryptology often talk about "cipher codes," a term that I suppose came into use to differentiate the term "code" as used in cryptology from the connotations, for example, the Napoleonic Code, a traffic code, a building code, a code of ethics, and so on. Now, in cryptology, there is no such thing as a "cipher code." There are codes and there are ciphers, and we might as well learn right off the differences between them, so that we get them straightened out in our minds before proceeding further.

In ciphers, or in cipher systems, cryptograms are produced by applying the cryptographic treatment to individual *letters* of the plaintext messages, whereas in codes or in code systems, cryptograms are produced by applying the cryptographic treatment generally to entire *words, phrases, and sentences* of the plaintext messages. More specialized meanings of the terms will be explained in detail later, but in a moment I'll show you an example of a cryptogram in cipher and one in code.

A cryptogram produced by means of a cipher system is said to be in cipher and is called a *cipher message*, or sometimes simply a cipher. The act or operation of encrypting a cipher message is called *enciphering*, and the enciphered version of the plain text, as well as the act or process itself, is often referred to as the *encipherment*. A cryptographic clerk who performs the process serves as an *encipherer*. The corresponding terms applicable to the decrypting cipher messages are deciphering, decipherment, decipherer.

A cryptogram produced by means of a code system is said to be in code and is called a *code message*. The text of the cryptogram is referred to as *code text*. This act or operation of encrypting is called *encoding*, and the encoded version of the plain text, as well as the act or process itself, is referred to as the encodement. The clerk who performs the process serves as an *encoder*. The corresponding terms applicable to the decrypting of code messages are decoding, decodement, and decoder. A clerk who encodes and decodes messages by having in his possession the pertinent codebooks is called a *code clerk*.

Technically, there are only two distinctly different types of treatment that may be applied to written plain text to convert it into a cipher, yielding two different classes of ciphers. In the first, called *transposition*, the letters of the plain text retain their original identities and merely undergo some change in the relative positions, with the result that the original text becomes unintelligible. Here's an authentic example of a transposition cipher; I call it authentic because it was sent to President Roosevelt, and the Secret Service asked me to decipher it (fig. 2). Imagine my chagrin when I had to report that it says "Did you ever bite a lemon?" In the second, called *substitution*, the letters of the plain text retain their original relative positions but are replaced by other letters with different sound values, or by symbols of some sort, so that the original text becomes unintelligible.

Nobody will quarrel with you very hard if you wish to say that a code system is nothing but a specialized form of substitution; but it's best to use the word "code" when a codebook is involved, and to use "substitution cipher" when a literal system of substitution is used.

It is possible to encrypt a message by a substitution method and then to apply a transposition method to the substitution text, or vice versa. Combined transposition-substitution ciphers do not form a third class of ciphers; they are only

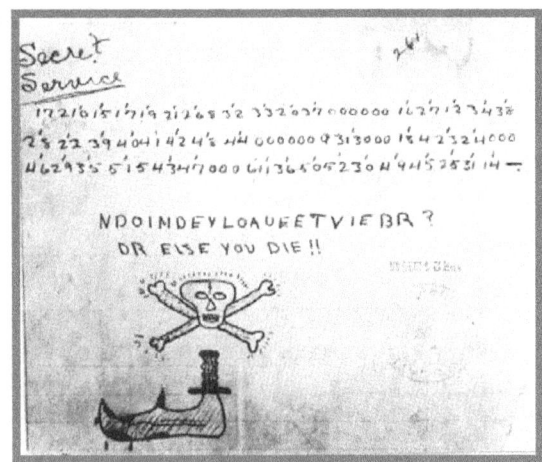

Fig. 2

occasionally encountered in military cryptography. Applying a cipher to code groups is a very frequently used procedure, and we'll see cases of that too.

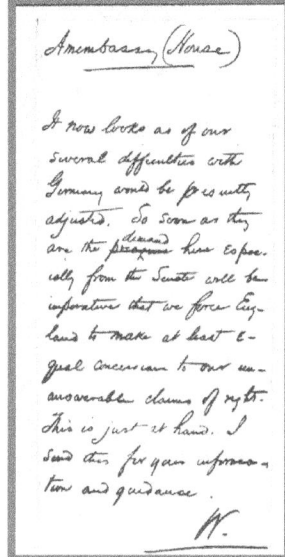

Ambassador (House)

It now looks as if our several difficulties with Germany would be presently adjusted. So soon as they are the demand here especially from the Senate will be imperative that we force England to make at least equal concession to our unanswerable claims of right. This is just at hand. I send this for your information and guidance.

W.

Fig. 3

39608 — 33391 — 37200-
67906 - 32040 - 22114 - 52927
12726 - Zodiak - 65092 - 29004 - 72
20885 - 68613 - 54058 - 43336 - 496
46352 - 22643 - 65062 - 42217 - 178
47156 - Zenobio - 36858 - 66908 - 497
58436 - 17288 - 16137 - 59957 - 327
24556 - 17503 - 39195 - 44120 - 426
22662 - 17686 - 47124 - 41126 - 7010
44885 -

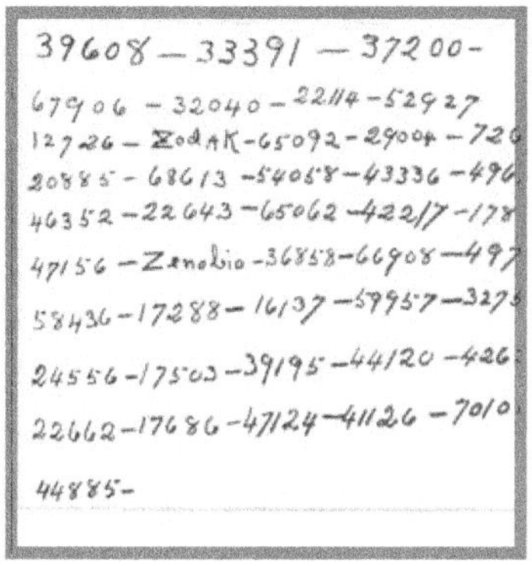

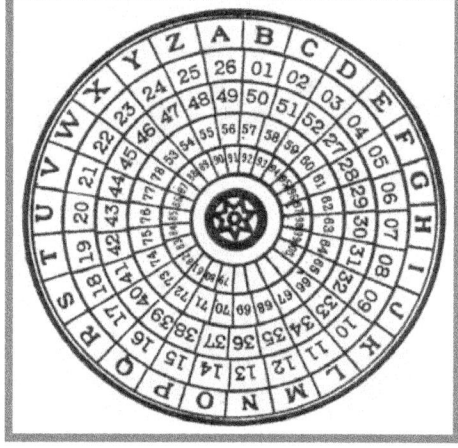

Fig. 4

Fig. 5

Now for an example of a cryptogram in code. In figure 3 is a plaintext message in the handwriting of President Wilson to his special emissary in London, Colonel House. Contained in figure 4 is the cryptogram after the plain text was encoded by Mrs. Wilson. The president himself then typed out the final message on his own typewriter, for transmission by the Department of State. It would appear that President Wilson lacked confidence in the security of the Department of State's methods – and maybe with good reason, as may be seen in the following extract from a letter dated 14 September 1914 from the president to Ambassador Page in London: "We have for some time been trying to trace the leaks, for they have occurred frequently, and we are now convinced that our code is in possession of persons at intermediary points. We are going to take thoroughgoing measures." Perhaps one of the measures was that the president got himself a code of his own. I must follow this up some day.

A cipher device is a relatively simple mechanical contrivance for encipherment and decipherment, usually hand-operated or manipulated by the fingers, for example, a device with concentric rings of alphabets, manually powered. In figure 5 is an example – a cipher device with such rings. I'll tell you about it later. A cipher machine is a relatively complex apparatus or mechanism for encipherment and decipherment, usually equipped with a typewriter keyboard and generally requiring an external power source. Modern cryptology, following the trend in mechanization and automation in other fields, now deals largely with cipher machines, some highly complicated. Figure 6 shows an example of a modern cipher machine with keyboard and printing mechanism.

One of the expressions that uninformed laymen use, but that you must never use, is "*the* German code," or "*the* Japanese code," or "the Navy cipher," and the like. When you hear this sort of expression, you may put the speaker down at once as a novice. There are literally hundreds of different codes and ciphers in simultaneous use by every large and important government or service, each suited to a special purpose; or where there is a multiplicity of systems of the same general nature, the object is to prevent a great deal of traffic being encrypted in the same key, thus overloading the system and making it vulnerable to attack by methods and procedures to be mentioned in broad terms in a few moments.

The need for secrecy in the conduct of important affairs has been recognized from time immemorial. In the case of diplomacy and organized warfare, this need is especially important in regard to communications. However, when such

Fig.6. TSEC/KL-7 Cipher Machine (U.S.)

communications are transmitted by electrical means, they can be heard or, as we say, *intercepted*, and copied by unauthorized persons, usually referred to collectively as *the enemy*. The protection resulting from all measures designed to deny to the enemy information of value that may be derived from the interception and study of such communications is called *communications security* or, for short, COMSEC.

In theory, any cryptosystem except one, to be discussed in due time, can be attacked and "broken," i.e., solved, if enough time, labor, and skill are devoted to it, and if the volume of traffic in that system is large enough. This can be done even if the general system and the specific key are unknown at the start. You will remember that I prefaced my statement any cryptosystem can be solved by saying "in theory," because in military operations theoretical rules usually give way to practical considerations.

That branch of cryptology that deals with the principles, methods, and means employed in the *solution or analysis* of cryptosystems is called *cryptanalytics*. The steps and operations performed in applying the principles of cryptanalytics constitute *cryptanalysis*. To cryptanalyze a cryptogram is to solve it by cryptanalysis. A person skilled in the art of cryptanalysis is called a *cryptanalyst*, and a clerk who assists in such work is called a *cryptanalytic clerk*.

Information derived from the organized interception, study, and analysis of the enemy's communications is called *communications intelligence* or, for short, COMINT. Let us take careful note that COMINT and COMSEC deal with communications. Although no phenomenon is more familiar to us than that of communication, the fact of the matter is that this magic word means many things to many people. A definition of communication that is broad enough for our purposes would be that communication deals with intelligent *messages* exchanged between intelligent beings. This implies that human beings and human operators are involved in the preparation, encryption, transmission, reception, decryption, and recording of messages that at some stage or stages are in written form and in some stage or stages are in electrical form as signals of one sort or another. But in recent years there have come into prominence and importance electrical signals that are not of the sort I've just indicated. They do not carry "messages" in the usual sense of the word; they do not convey from one human being to another an intelligible sequence of words and an intelligible sense. I refer here to electrical or electronic signals such as are employed in homing or directional beacons, in radar, in telemetering or recording data of an electrical or electronic nature at a distance, and so on. Information obtained from a study of enemy electronic emissions of these sorts is called *electronic intelligence* or, for short, ELINT. COMINT and ELINT comprise SIGINT, that is, *signals intelligence*. Cryptology is the science that is concerned with all these branches of secret signaling.

In this series of lectures we shall be concerned only with COMSEC and COMINT, leaving for others and for other times the subject of ELINT. This means that we shall deal with communications or *messages*.

Communication may be conducted by any means susceptible of ultimate interpretation by one of the five senses, but those most commonly used are seeing and hearing. Aside from the use of simple visual and auditory signals for communication over relatively short distances, the usual method of communication between or among individuals separated from another by relatively long distances involves, at one stage or another, the act of writing or of speaking over a telephone.

Privacy or secrecy in communication by telephone can be obtained by using equipment that affects the electrical currents involved in telephony, so that the conversations can be understood only by persons provided with suitable equipment properly arranged for the purpose. The same thing is true in the case of facsimile transmission (i.e., the electrical transmission of ordinary writing, pictures, drawings, maps). Even today there are already simple forms of enciphered television transmissions. Enciphered facsimile is called *cifax*; enciphered telephony, *ciphony*; and enciphered television, *civision*. However, these lectures will not deal with these electrically and cryptanalytically more complex forms of cryptology. We shall stick to enciphered or encrypted writing – which will be hard enough for most of us.

Writing may be either visible or invisible. In the former, the characters are inscribed with ordinary writing materials and can be seen with the naked eye; in the latter, the characters are inscribed by means or methods that make the writing invisible to the naked eye. Invisible writing can be prepared with certain chemicals called sympathetic or secret inks, and in order to "develop" such writing, that is, make it visible, special processes must usually be applied. Shown in figure 7 is an interesting example – the developed secret-ink message that figured in an $80,000,000 suit won by two American firms against the German government after World War I sabotage was proved, There are also methods of producing writing that is invisible to the naked eye because the characters are of microscopic size, thus requiring special microscopic and photographic apparatus to enlarge such writing enough to make it visible. Here's an example – a code message in a space not much larger than the head of a pin (fig. 8). A simple definition of secret writing would be to say that it comprises invisible writing and unintelligible visible writing.

There is one additional piece of basic information that it is wise to call to your attention before we proceed much further, and I'll begin by stating that the greatest and the most powerful instrument or weapon ever forged and improved by man in his long struggle for emancipation from utter dependence upon his own environment is the weapon of literacy – a mastery of reading and writing; and the most important invention, the one that made the weapon of literacy practical, was the invention of the alphabet. It is therefore a rather striking anomaly that we should now come to the study of another weapon – a counterweapon to the weapon of literacy – the weapon of secrecy, the basic intent of which is to thwart the weapon that man struggled so long to forge. Secrecy is applied to make writing more difficult and the reading of the writing very difficult, if not impossible.

Perhaps this is a good place to do a bit of theorizing about this matter of secrecy and what it implies.

Every person who enciphers a piece of writing, a message, or a text of any kind, for the purpose of hiding something or keeping something secret, does so with the idea that some other person, removed from him in distance, or time, or both, is intended to decipher the writing or message and thus uncover the secret that was so hid

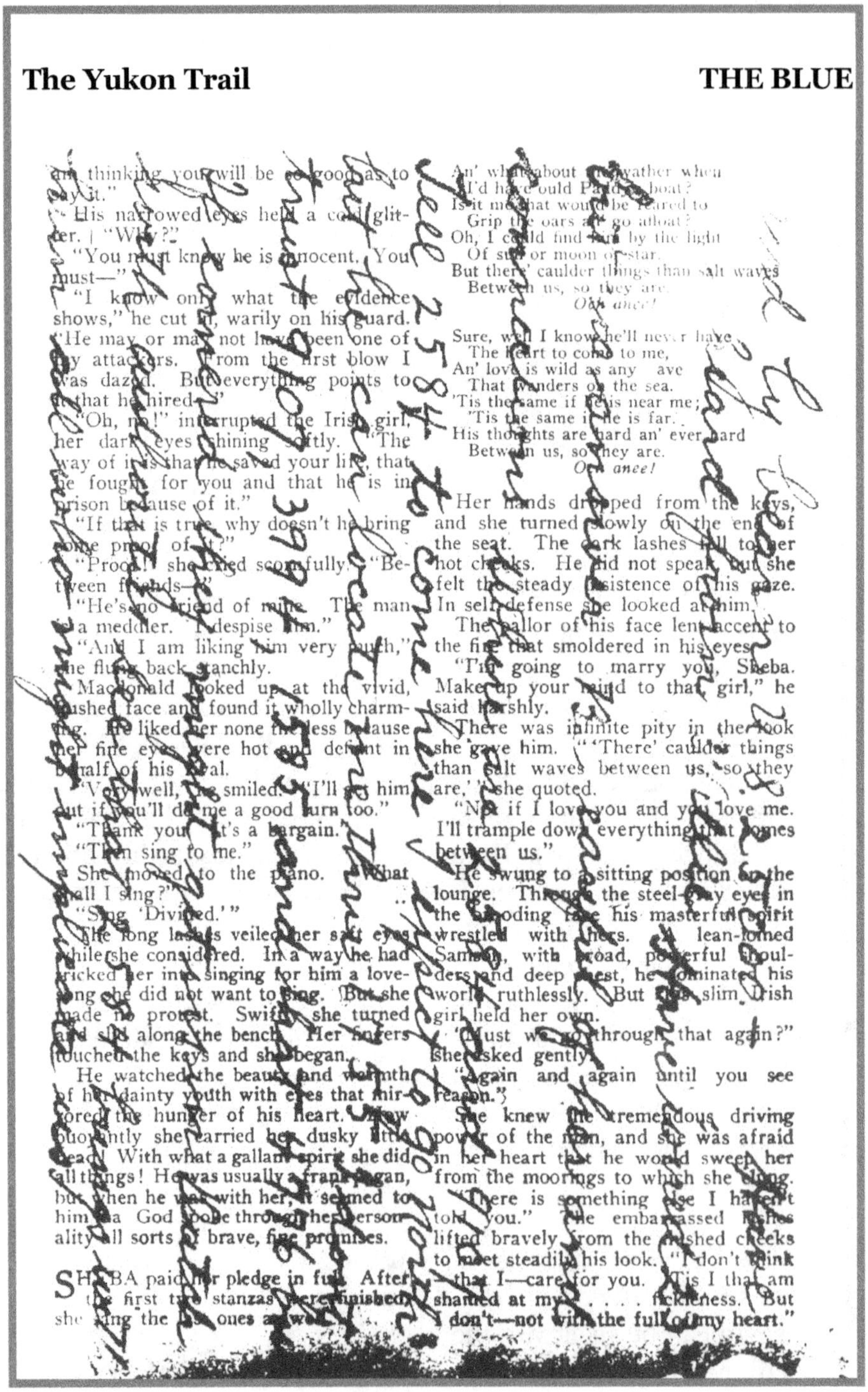

The Yukon Trail   **THE BLUE**

thinking you will be so good as to say it."

His narrowed eyes held a cold glitter. "Why?"

"You must know he is innocent. You must—"

"I know only what the evidence shows," he cut in, warily on his guard. "He may or may not have been one of my attackers. From the first blow I was dazed. But everything points to it that he hired—"

"Oh, no!" interrupted the Irish girl, her dark eyes shining softly. "The way of it is that he saved your life, that he fought for you and that he is in prison because of it."

"If that is true, why doesn't he bring some proof of it?"

"Proof!" she cried scornfully. "Between friends—"

"He's no friend of mine. The man is a meddler. I despise him."

"And I am liking him very much," she flung back stanchly.

Macdonald looked up at the vivid, flushed face and found it wholly charming. He liked her none the less because her fine eyes were hot and defiant in behalf of his rival.

"Very well, he smiled. "I'll get him out if you'll do me a good turn too."

"Thank you. It's a bargain."

"Then sing to me."

She moved to the piano. "What shall I sing?"

"Sing 'Divided.'"

The long lashes veiled her soft eyes while she considered. In a way he had tricked her into singing for him a love-song she did not want to sing. But she made no protest. Swiftly she turned and slid along the bench. Her fingers touched the keys and she began.

He watched the beauty and warmth of her dainty youth with eyes that mirrored the hunger of his heart. How buoyantly she carried her dusky little head! With what a gallant spirit she did all things! He was usually a frank pagan, but when he was with her, it seemed to him as God spoke through her personality all sorts of brave, fine promises.

SHEBA paid her pledge in full. After the first two stanzas were finished, she sang the last ones as well.

An' what about the wather when I'd haveould Paddy's boat?
Is it me that would be feared to
Grip the oars an' go afloat?
Oh, I could find him by the light
Of sun or moon or star.
But there' caulder things than salt waves
Between us, so they are.
Och anee!

Sure, well I know he'll never have
The heart to come to me,
An' love is wild as any wave
That wanders on the sea.
'Tis the same if he is near me;
'Tis the same if he is far.
His thoughts are hard an' ever hard
Between us, so they are.
Och anee!

Her hands dropped from the keys, and she turned slowly on the end of the seat. The dark lashes fell to her hot cheeks. He did not speak, but she felt the steady insistence of his gaze. In self-defense she looked at him. The pallor of his face lent accent to the fire that smoldered in his eyes.

"I'm going to marry you, Sheba. Make up your mind to that girl," he said harshly.

There was infinite pity in the look she gave him. "'There' caulder things than salt waves between us, so they are,'" she quoted.

"Not if I love you and you love me. I'll trample down everything that comes between us."

He swung to a sitting position on the lounge. Through the steel-gray eyes in the brooding face his masterful spirit wrestled with hers. A lean-loined Samson, with broad, powerful shoulders and deep chest, he dominated his world ruthlessly. But this slim Irish girl held her own.

"Must we go through that again?" she asked gently.

"Again and again until you see reason."

She knew the tremendous driving power of the man, and she was afraid in her heart that he would sweep her from the moorings to which she clung. "There is something else I haven't told you." The embarrassed flushes lifted bravely from the flushed cheeks to meet steadily his look. "I don't think that I—care for you. 'Tis I that am shamed at my . . . . fickleness. But I don't—not with the full of my heart."

Fig. 7

den. A person may possess a certain piece of knowledge that he does not wish to forget, but that he is nevertheless unwilling to commit to open writing, and therefore he may jot it down in cryptic form for himself to decipher later, when or if the information is needed. The most widely known example of such a cryptogram is found in Edgar Allan Poe's romantic tale "The Gold Bug." That sort of usage of cryptography, however, is unusual. There are also examples of the use of cipher writing to establish priority of discovery, as did the astronomers Galileo and Huygens. I suppose I should at least mention another sort of cryptic writing famous in literary history, the diaries of persons such as Samuel Pepys and William Byrd. These are commonly regarded as being "in cipher," but they were actually written in a more or less private shorthand and can easily be read without the help of cryptanalysis. In figure 9 is shown a page of Pepys' diary.

Now there can be no logical reason, point, or purpose in taking the time and trouble to encipher anything unless it is expected that some other person is to decipher the cipher some time in the future. This means that there must exist some very direct, clear-cut and unambiguous relationship between the enciphering and deciphering operations. Just what such a relationship involves will be dealt with later, but at this moment all that it is necessary to say is that in enciphering there must be rules that govern or control the operations, that these rules must admit of no uncertainty or ambiguity, and that they must be susceptible of being applied with undeviating precision, since otherwise it will be difficult or perhaps impossible for the decipherer to obtain the correct answer when he reverses the processes or steps followed in the encipherment.

This may be a good place to point out that a valid or authentic cryptanalytic solution cannot be considered as being merely what the cryptanalyst thinks or says he thinks the cryptogram means, nor does the solution represent an opinion of the cryptanalyst. Solutions are valid only

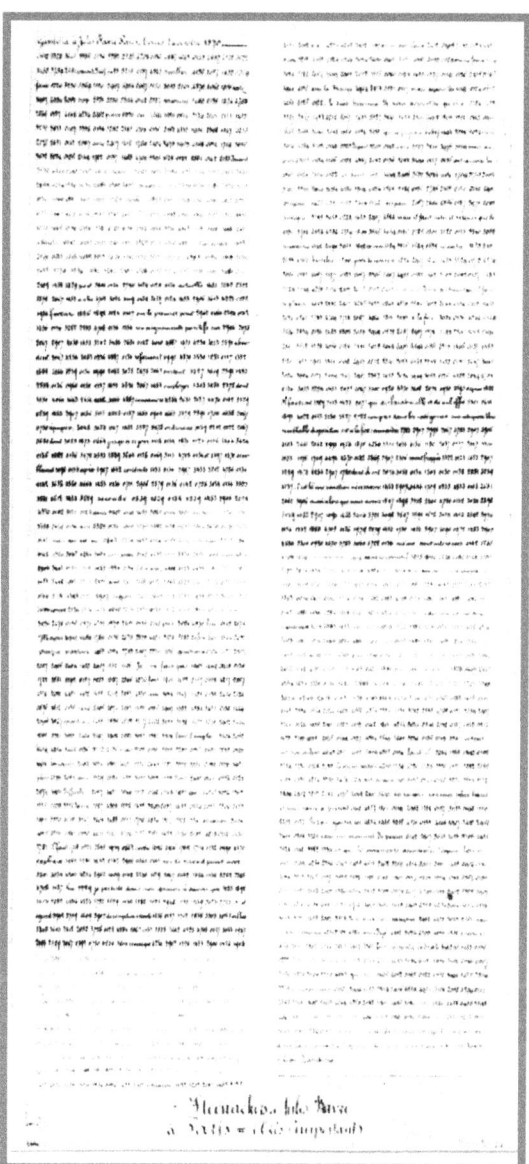

Fig. 8

insofar as they are objective and susceptible of demonstration or proof employing scientifically acceptable methods or procedures. It should hardly be necessary to indicate that the validity of the results achieved by cryptanalytic studies of authentic cryptograms rests upon the same sure and well-established scientific foundations, and is reached by the same sort of logic as are the discoveries, results, or "answers" achieved by any other scientific studies, namely, observation, hypothesis, deduction, induction, and confirmatory experiment. Implied in what I have just said is the tacitly understood and now rarely explicitly

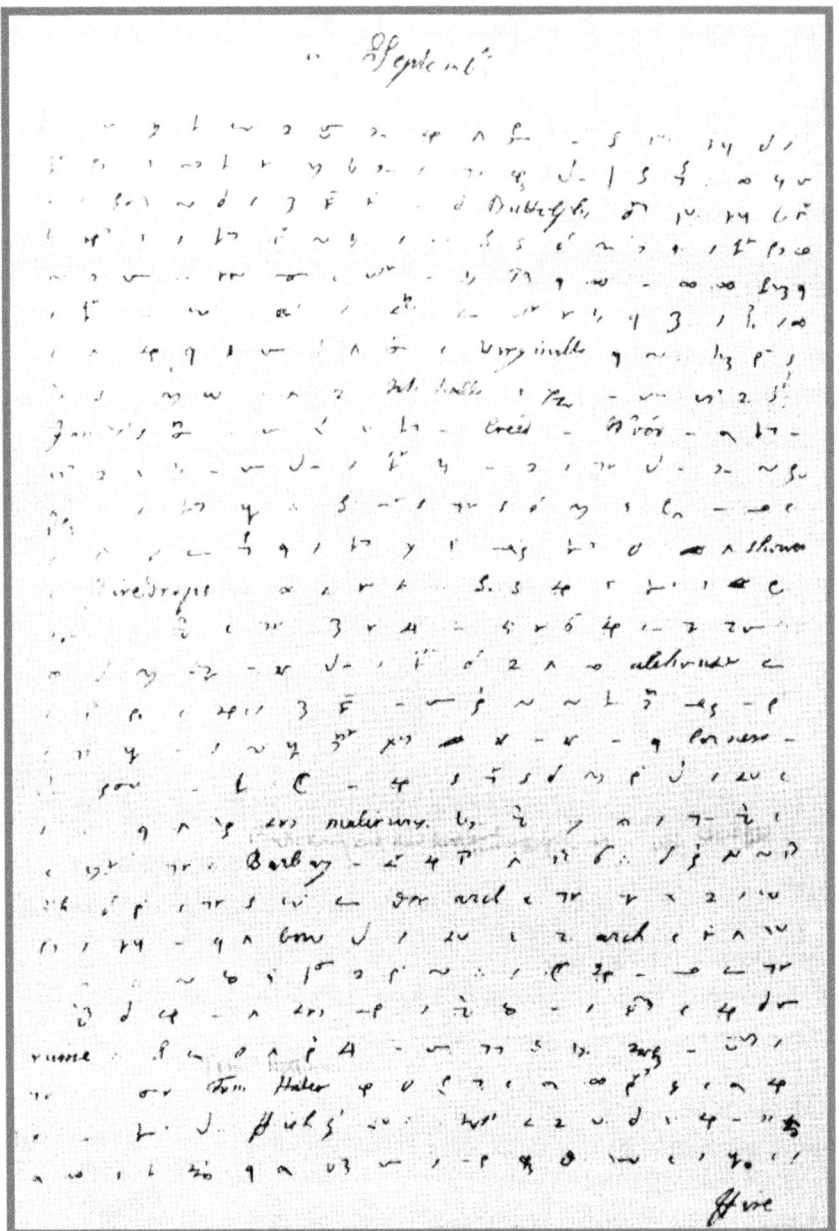

Fig. 9

stated assumption that two or more equally competent and, if necessary, specially qualified investigators, each working independently upon the same material, will achieve identical or practically identical results.

Cryptology is usually and properly considered to be a branch of mathematics, although Francis Bacon considered it also a branch of grammar and what we now call linguistics. Mathematical and statistical considerations play an ever-increasing and prominent role in practical cryptology, but don't let my statement of this point frighten those of you who have not had much formal instruction in these subjects. We have excellent cryptologists who have never studied more than arithmetic, and some of our best ones would hide if you were to go searching for mathematicians around here. What is needed is the ability to reason logically, as the mathematician sometimes does, and this ability is found in the most curious sorts of persons and places. So those of you who are frightened by the words mathematics and statistics take heart – you're not nearly so badly off as you may fear.

But now to return to the main theme, the place mathematics occupies in cryptology, let me say that just as the solution of mathematical problems leaves no room for the exercise of divination or other mysterious mental or psychic powers, so a valid solution to a cryptogram must leave no room for the exercise of such powers. In cryptologic science there is one and only one valid solution to a cryptogram, just as there is but one correct solution or "solution set" to any problem in mathematics. But perhaps I've already dwelt on this point too long; in any case, we'll come back to it later, when we come to look at certain types of what we may call pseudociphers.

In the next lecture I'm going to give you a brief glimpse into the background or history of cryptology, which makes a long and interesting story that has never been told accurately and in detail. The history of communications security, that is, of cryptography, and the history of communications intelligence, that is, of cryptanalysis, which are but opposite faces of the same coin, deserve detailed treatment, but I am dubious that this sort of history will ever be written because of the curtain of secrecy and silence that officially surrounds the whole field of cryptology. *Authentic* information on the background and development of these vital matters having to do with the security of a nation is understandably quite sparse.

But in the succeeding lectures I'll try my best to give you authentic information, and where there's conjecture or doubt I'll so indicate. I must add, however, that in this series I'm going to have to omit many highly interesting episodes and bits of information, not only because these lectures are of low classification, but also because we won't and can't for security considerations go beyond a certain period in cryptologic history. Nevertheless, I hope that you won't be disappointed and that you'll learn certain things of great interest and importance, things to remember if you wish to make cryptology your vocation in life.

Lecture II

As I said at the close of the preceding lecture, a bit of history is always useful in introducing a subject belonging to a special and not too well-known field; therefore, I'll proceed with some historical information about cryptology, which, as you learned before, comprises two closely related sciences, namely, cryptography and cryptanalysis. I will repeat and emphasize that they are but opposite faces of the same valuable coin; progress in one inevitably leads to progress in the other, and to be efficient in cryptology you must know something about each of them.

Cryptography and cryptanalysis probably go back to the dawn of the invention and development of the art of writing itself. In fact, there is reason for speculating as to which came first – the invention of writing or the invention of cryptography; it's somewhat like the question about which came first – the hen or the egg. It is possible that some phases of cryptography came before the art of writing had advanced very far.

I've mentioned the art of writing. As in the case of other seemingly simple questions – such as "why is grass green?" – when we are asked to define writing, we can't find a very simple answer, just because the answer isn't at all simple. Yet, Breasted, the famous University of Chicago historian and Orientalist, once said: "The invention of writing and of a convenient system of records on paper has had a greater influence in uplifting the human race than any other intellectual achievement in the career of man." There has been, in my humble opinion, no greater invention in all history. The invention of writing formed the real beginning of civilization. As language distinguishes man from other animals, so writing distinguishes civilized man from the barbarian. To put the matter briefly, writing exists only in a civilization, and a civilization cannot exist without writing. Let me remind you that animals and insects do communicate – there's no question about that; but writing is a thing peculiar to man and found only as a phenomenon in which man – and no animal or insect – engages. Mankind lived and functioned for an enormous number of centuries before writing was discovered, and there is no doubt that writing was preceded by articulate speech for eons – but civilization began only when men got the idea of and invented the art of writing. In Western or Occidental civilization, writing is, in essence, a means of representing the sounds of what we call speech or spoken language. Other systems of writing were and some still are handicapped by trying to represent things and ideas by pictures. I'm being a bit solemn about this great invention because I want to impress upon you what our studies in cryptology are really intended to do, namely, to defeat the basic or intended purpose of that great invention: instead of recording things and ideas for the *dissemination* of knowledge, we want and strive our utmost to prevent this aim from being realized, *except among our own brethren and under certain special circumstances*, for the purpose of our mutual security, our self-preservation. And that's important.

Writing is a comparatively new thing in the history of mankind. No complete system of writing was used before about 3500 B.C.

Ordinary writing, the sort of writing you and I use, is perhaps an outgrowth or development of picture writing or rebus writing, which I'm sure most of you enjoyed as children. A rebus contains features of both ordinary and cryptographic writing; you have to "decrypt" the significance of some of the symbols, combine single letters with syllables, pronounce the word that is represented by pictures, and so on. Figure 10 is an example that I have through the courtesy of the Bell Telephone

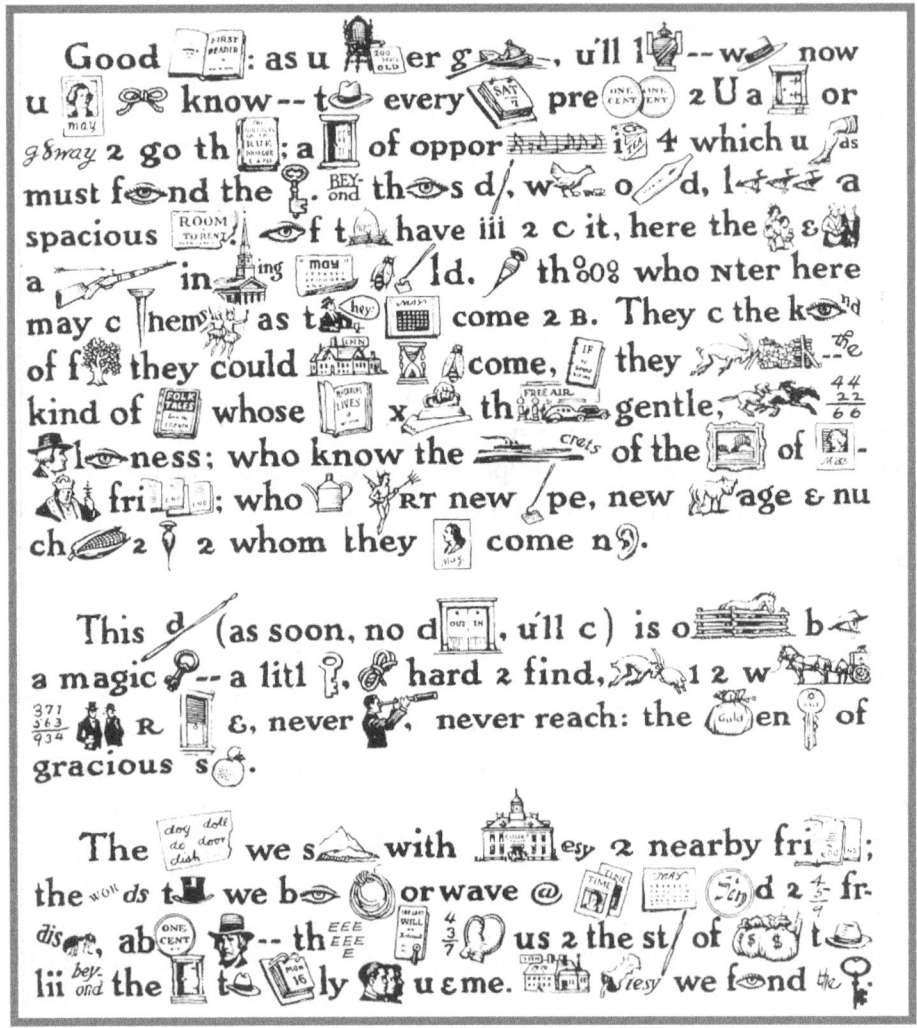

Fig. 10

Laboratories. See how much of it you can make out in half a minute.

From rebus writing there came in due course alphabetic writing, and let me say right now that the invention of the alphabet – which apparently happened only once in the history of mankind, in some Middle East Semitic region, in or near the Palestine-Syria area, then spread throughout the whole of the European continent, and finally throughout most of the world – is Western man's greatest, most important, and most far-reaching invention because it forms the foundation of practically all our written and printed knowledge, except that in Chinese. The great achievement of the invention of the alphabet was certainly not the creation of the signs or symbols. It involved two brilliant ideas. The first was the idea of representing merely the *sounds* of speech by symbols, that is, the idea of what we may call *phoneticization*; the second was the idea of adopting a system in which, roughly speaking, each speech sound is denoted or represented by one and only one symbol. Simple as these two ideas seem to us *now*, the invention was apparently made, as I've said, only once, and the inventor or inventors of the alphabet deserve to be ranked among the greatest benefactors of mankind. It made possible the recording of the memory of mankind in our libraries, and from that single invention have come all past and present alphabets. Some of the greatest of men's achievements we are now apt to take for granted; we seldom give them

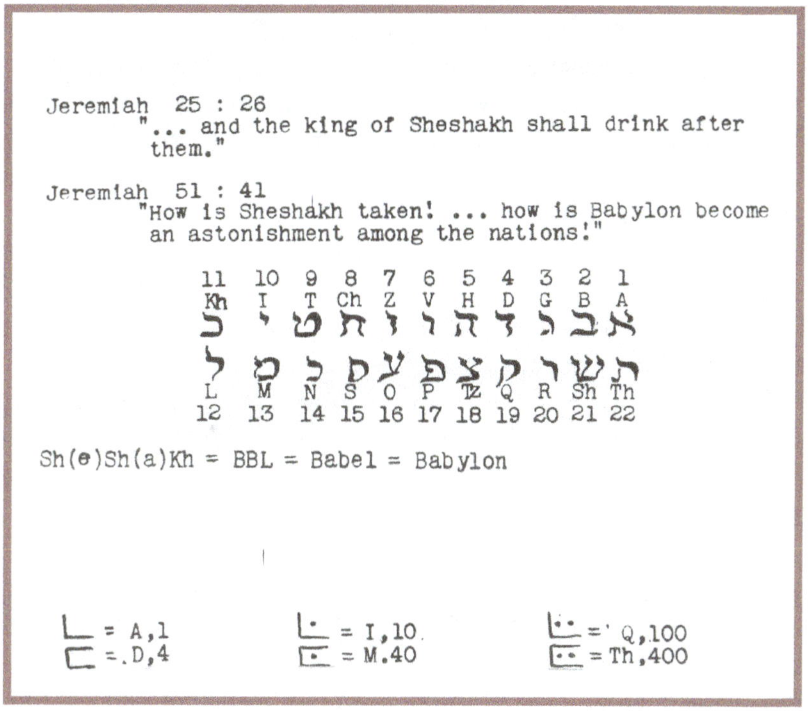

```
Jeremiah  25 : 26
    "... and the king of Sheshakh shall drink after
    them."

Jeremiah  51 : 41
    "How is Sheshakh taken! ... how is Babylon become
    an astonishment among the nations!"
```

```
 11  10   9   8   7   6   5   4   3   2   1
 Kh   I   T   Ch  Z   V   H   D   G   B   A
  כ   י   ט   ח   ז   ו   ה   ד   ג   ב   א
  ל   מ   נ   ס   ע   פ   צ   ק   ר   ש   ת
  L   M   N   S   O   P   Tz  Q   R   Sh  Th
 12  13  14  15  16  17  18  19  20  21  22

Sh(e)Sh(a)Kh = BBL = Babel = Babylon
```

```
 L = A,1        L· = I,10       L·· = Q,100
 ⌐ = D,4        ⌐· = M,40       ⌐·· = Th,400
```

Fig. 11

any thought. The invention of the art of writing and the invention of the alphabet are two such achievements, and they are worth pondering upon. Where would we be without them? Note that among living languages Chinese presents special problems not only for the cryptologist but also for the Chinese themselves. No Sinologist knows all the 80,000 or so Chinese symbols, and it is also far from easy to master merely the 9,000 or so symbols actually employed by Chinese scholars. How far more simple it is to use only twenty to twenty-six symbols! Since Chinese is a monosyllabic language, it seems almost hopeless to try to write Chinese by the sort of mechanism used in an alphabetic polysyllabic language; attempts along these lines have been unsuccessful, and the difficulties in memorizing a great many Chinese characters, account for the fact that even now only about ten percent of the Chinese people can read or write to any significant degree. The spread of knowledge in Chinese is thereby much hampered.

We find instances of ciphers in the Bible. In Jeremiah 25:26, occurs this expression: "And the King of Sheshakh shall drink after them." Also, again in Jeremiah 51:41: "How is Sheshakh taken!" Well, for perhaps many years that name "Sheshakh" remained a mystery, because no such place was known to geographers or historians. But then it was discovered that if you write the twenty-two letters of the Hebrew alphabet in two rows, – eleven in one row and eleven in the other, as in figure 11, you set up a substitution alphabet whereby you can replace letters by those standing opposite them. For example, "shin" is represented by "beth" or vice versa, so that "Sheshakh" translates "Babel," which is the old name of "Babylon." Hebrew then did not have and still doesn't have vowels; they must be supplied. This is an example of what is called ATHBASH writing, that is, where aleph, the first letter is replaced by teth, the last letter; beth, the second letter, by shin, the next-to-the-last, etc. By sliding the second row of letters one letter each time there are eleven different cipher alphabets available for use. The old Talmudists went in for cryptography to a considerable extent. Incidentally, in mentioning the Bible, I will add that Daniel, who, after Joseph in Genesis, was an early interpreter of dreams and therefore one of the first psychoanalysts, was also the first cryptanalyst. I say that he was an early psychoanalyst because you will remember that he interpreted Nebuchadnezzar's dreams. In the Bible's own words, "Nebuchadnezzar dreamed dreams, wherewith his spirit was troubled, and sleep brake from him." But, unfortunately, when he woke up he just couldn't remember those troublesome dreams. One morning he called for his wise men, magicians, astrologers, and Chaldean sorcerers and asked them to interpret the dream he'd had during the preceding night. "Well, now, tell us the dream and we'll try to interpret it," they said. To which King Nebuchadnezzar exclaimed, "The thing is gone from me. I don't remember it. But it's part of your job to find that out, too, and interpret it. And if you can't tell me what the dream was, and interpret it, things will happen to you." What the king asked was a pretty stiff assignment, of course, and it's no wonder they failed to make good, which irked Nebuchadnezzar no end. Kings had a nasty habit of chopping your head off in those days if you failed or made a mistake, just as certain arbitrary and cruel despots are apt to do even in modern times for more minor infractions, such as not following the Party Line. So in this case it comes as no surprise to learn that Nebuchadnezzar passed the word along to destroy all the wise men of Babylon, among whom was one of the wise men of Israel, named Daniel. Well, when the king's guard came to fetch him, Daniel begged that he be given just a bit more time. Then, by some act of divination – the Bible simply says that the secret was revealed to Daniel in a night vision – Daniel was able to reconstruct the dream and then to interpret it. Daniel's reputation was made.

Some years later, Nebuchadnezzar's son Belshazzar was giving a feast, and, during the course of the feast, in the words of the Bible, "came forth fingers of a man's hand and wrote over against the candlestick upon the poster of the wall." The hand wrote a secret message. You can imagine the spinechilling scene. Belshazzar was very much upset, and just as his father did, he called for his wise men, soothsayers, Chaldean sorcerers, magicians and so on, but they couldn't read the message. Apparently they couldn't even read the cipher characters! Well, Belshazzar's queen fortunately remembered what that Israelite Daniel had done years before, and she suggested that Daniel be called in as a consultant. Daniel was called in by Belshazzar, and he succeeded in doing two things. He succeeded not only in reading the writing on the wall: "MENE, MENE, TEKEL, UPHARSIN," but also in deciphering the meaning of those strange words. His interpretation: "Mene"– "God hath numbered thy kingdom and finished it." "Tekel" – "Thou are weighed in the balances and found wanting." "Upharsin" – "Thy kingdom shall be divided and given to the Medes and Persians." Apparently the chap who did the handwriting on the wall knew a thing or two about cryptography, because he used what we call "variants," or different values, for in one case the last word in the secret writing on the wall is "Upharsin" and in the other it is "Peres"; the commentators are a bit vague as to why there are these two versions of the word in the Bible. At any rate, Babylon was finished, just as the inscription prophesied; it died with Belshazzar. I think this curious Biblical case of the use of cryptography is interesting because I don't think anybody has really found the true meaning of the sentence in secret writing, or explained why the writing on the wall was unintelligible to all of Belshazzar's wise men.

Probably the earliest reliable information on the use of cryptography in connection with an alphabetic language dates from about 900 B.C. Plutarch mentioned that from the time of Lycurgus there was in use among the Lacedemonians, or ancient Spartans, a device called the scytale. This device, which I'll explain in a moment, was definitely known to have been used in the time of Lysander, which would place it about 400 B.C. This is about the time that Aeneas Taciticus wrote his large treatise on the defense of fortification, in which there is a chapter devoted specifically to cryptography. In addition to mentioning ways of physically concealing messages, a peculiar sort of cipher disk is described. Also a method of replacing words and letters by dots is mentioned.

Figure 12 is a picture of the scytale, one of the earliest cipher devices history records.

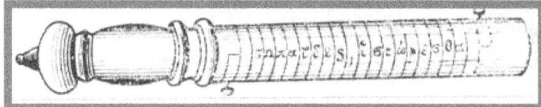

Fig. 12.

The scytale was a wooden cylinder of specific dimensions around which they wrapped spirally a piece of parchment or leather; they then wrote the message on the parchment, unwound it, and sent it to its destination by a safe courier, who handed it over to the commander for whom it was intended and who, having been provided with an identically dimensioned cylinder, would wind the strip of leather or parchment around his cylinder and thus bring together properly the letters representing the message. This diagram may not be accurate. I don't think anyone really understands the scheme. The writing was done across the edges of the parchment, according to some accounts, and not between the edges, as shown here. Incidentally, you may be interested to learn that the baton the European field marshal still carries as one of the insignia of his high office derives from this very instrument.

We don't know much about the use of cryptography by the Romans, but it is well known that Caesar used an obviously simple method; all he did was to replace each letter by the one that was fourth from it in the alphabet. For example, A would be represented by D, B by E, and so on. Augustus Caesar is said to have used the same sort of thing, only it was even more simple: each letter was replaced by the one that followed it in the alphabet. Cicero was one of the inventors of what is now called shorthand. He had a slave by the name of Tiro, who wrote Cicero's records in what are called Tironian notes. Modern shorthand is a development of Tiro's notation system.

In figure 13 we see some cipher alphabets of olden times, alphabets used by certain historical figures you'll all remember. The first cipher alpha-

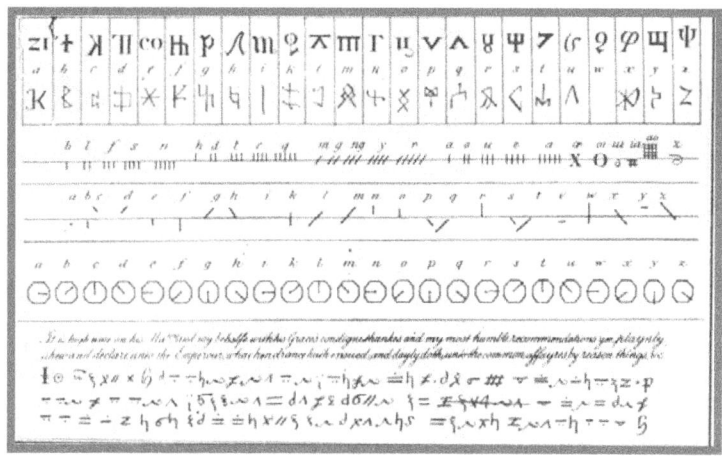

Fig. 13

bet in this figure was employed by Charlemagne, who reigned from 768 to 814 A.D. The second one was used in England during the reign of Alfred the Great, 871 to 899. The third alphabet is called Ogam Writing and was used in ancient Ireland. The alphabets below that were used much later in England: the fourth one was used by Charles the First in 1646; the fifth, the so-called "clock cipher," was used by the Marquis of Worcester in the seventeenth century; finally, the last one was used by Cardinal Wolsey in about 1524.

In the Middle Ages cryptography appears first as a method of concealing proper names, usually by the simple substitution of each letter by the next one in the alphabet, just about as Augustus Caesar did hundreds of years before. At other times the vowels were replaced by dots, without changing the consonants – a method that was used throughout Europe to about 1000 A.D., when letters began to be replaced by various signs, by other letters, by letters from another language, by runes which are found in abundance in Scandinavia, and by arbitrary symbols. Figure 14 is an example of a runic inscription on a stone that stands before Gripsholm Castle near Stockholm, Sweden. The word rune means "secret."

Within a couple of hundred years, the outlines of modern cryptography began to be formed by the secret correspondence systems employed by the

Fig. 14. A couple of old ruins

small papal states in Italy. In fact, the real beginnings of systematic, modern cryptology can be traced back to the days of the early years of the thirteenth century, when the science began to be extensively employed by the princes and chanceries of the papal states in their diplomatic relations amongst themselves and with other countries in Europe. The necessity for secret communication was first met by attempts inspired by or derived from ancient cryptography, as I've outlined so far. There was a special predilection for vowel substitution, but there appeared about this time one of the elements that was later to play a very prominent role in all cipher systems, an element we now call a *syllabary* or a *repertory*. These were lists of letters, syllables, frequently used parts of speech and words, with additions of arbitrary equivalents for the names of persons and places. There is still in existence one such syllabary and list of arbitrary equivalents that was used about 1236 A.D., and there are other examples that were used in Venice in 1350.

Among examples of ciphers in medieval cryptography is a collection of letters of the Archbishop of Naples, written between 1363 and 1365, in which he begins merely with symbol substitutions for the vowels and uses the letters that are actually vowels to serve as nulls or nonsignificant letters to throw the would-be cryptanalyst off the right track. As a final development, the high-frequency consonants *L, M, N, R,* and *S,* and all the vowels, are replaced not only by arbitrary symbols but also by other letters.

About 1378 an experienced cryptologist named Gabriele Lavinde of Parma was employed as a professional by Clement VII, and in the Vatican Library is a collection of ciphers devised and used by Lavinde about 1379. It consists of repertories in which every letter is replaced by an arbitrary symbol. Some of these ciphers also have nulls and arbitrary equivalents or signs for the names of persons and places. There is a court cipher of Mantua, dated 1395, that used this system.

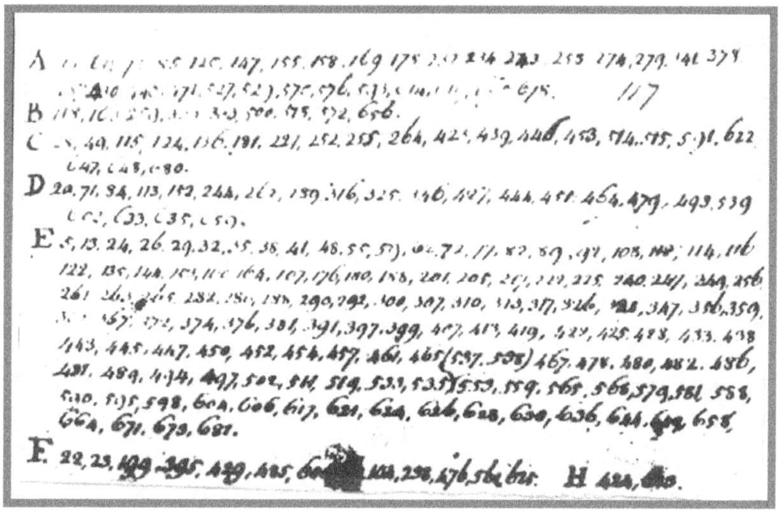

Fig. 15

At the beginning of the fifteenth century, the necessity of having variants for the high-frequency letters, especially the vowels, became obvious. Figure 15 is an alphabet of that period that is interesting because it shows that even in those early days of cryptology there was already a recognition of the basic weakness of what we call single or monoalphabetic substitution, that is, where every letter in the plaintext message is represented by another and always the same letter.

Solution of this type of cipher, as many of you may know, is accomplished by taking advantage of the fact that the letters of an alphabetic language are used with greatly differing frequencies. I don't have to go into that now because many of you, at some time or other, have read Edgar Allan Poe's "The Gold Bug" and understand the principles of that sort of analysis. It is clearly shown in the figure that the early Italian cryptographers understood the fact of varying frequencies and introduced stumbling blocks to quick and easy solution by having the high-frequency letters represented by more than a single character, or by several characters, as you can see. I will add that the earliest tract that the world possesses on the subject of cryptography, or for that matter, cryptanalysis, is that which was written in 1474 by a Neapolitan, Sicco Simonetta. He set forth the basic principles and methods of solving ciphers, simple ciphers no doubt, but he describes them and their solution in a very clear and concise form.

Cipher systems of the type I've described continued to be improved, In figure 16 is shown what we may call the first complete cipher system of this sort. There are substitution symbols for each letter; the vowels have several equivalents; there are nulls; and there is a small list of arbitrary symbols, such as those for "the pope," the word "and," the preposition "with," and so on, This cipher, dated 1411, was used in Venice, and it is typical of the ciphers used by the papal chanceries of those days.

The step remaining to be taken in the development of these ciphers was to expand the "vocabulary," that is, the list of equivalents for frequently used words and syllables, the names of persons and places, parts of speech, and so on. This step was reached in Italy during the first half of the fifteenth century and became the prototype of diplomatic ciphers used in practically all the states of Europe for several centuries. One of seventy ciphers collected in a Vatican codex and used from about 1440 to 1469 is shown in figure 17. Note that the equivalents of the plaintext items are Latin words and combinations of two and three letters and that they are listed in an order that is somewhat alphabetical but not strictly so. I suppose that by constant use the cipher clerks would learn the equivalents

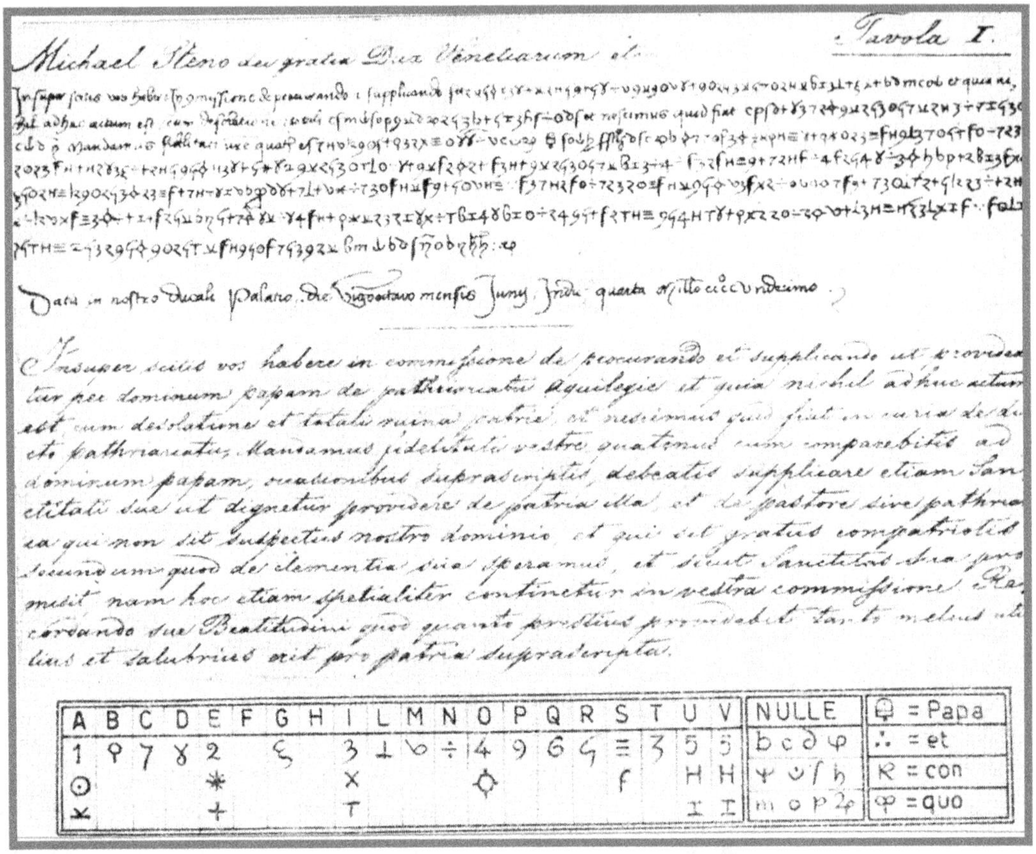

Fig. 16

almost by heart, so that an adherence to a strict alphabetic sequence either for the plaintext items or for their cipher equivalents didn't hamper their operations too much, In figure 18 there is much the same sort of arrangement, except that now the cipher equivalents seem to be digraphs, and these are arranged in a rather systematic order for ease in enciphering and deciphering. Now we have the real beginnings of what we call a one-part code, that is, the same list will serve both for encoding and decoding. These systems, as I've said, remained the prototypes of the cryptography employed throughout the whole of Europe for some centuries. The papal states used them, and as late as 1793 we find them used in France. I wish here to mention specifically the so-called King's General Cipher used in 1562 by the Spanish Court. It is shown in figure 19.

But there were two exceptional cases that show that the rigidity of cryptographic thought was now and then broken during the four centuries we have been talking about in this brief historical survey, Some of the papal ciphers of the sixteenth century and those of the French Court under Kings Louis XIII and XIV exemplify these exceptions. In the case of these French Court ciphers, we find that a French cryptologist named Antonio Rossignol, who was employed by Cardinal Richelieu, understood quite well the weaknesses of the one-part code and syllabaries. It was he who, in about 1640, introduced a new and important improvement: the idea of the two-part code or syllabary, in which for encoding a message the items in the vocabulary are listed in some systematic order, nearly always alphabetical; the code equivalents, whatever they may be, are assigned to the alphabetically listed items in random order. This means that there must be another arrangement or book for ease in decoding, in which the code equivalents are listed in systematic order, numerically or alphabetically as the case may be, and alongside each appears its meaning in the encoding arrangement, or book. The sig-

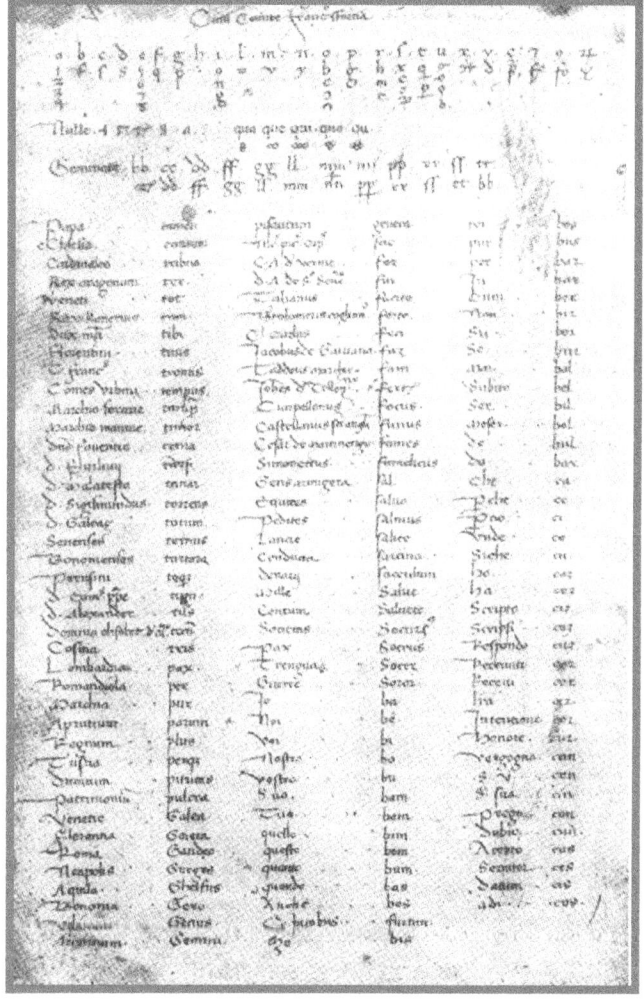

Fig. 17

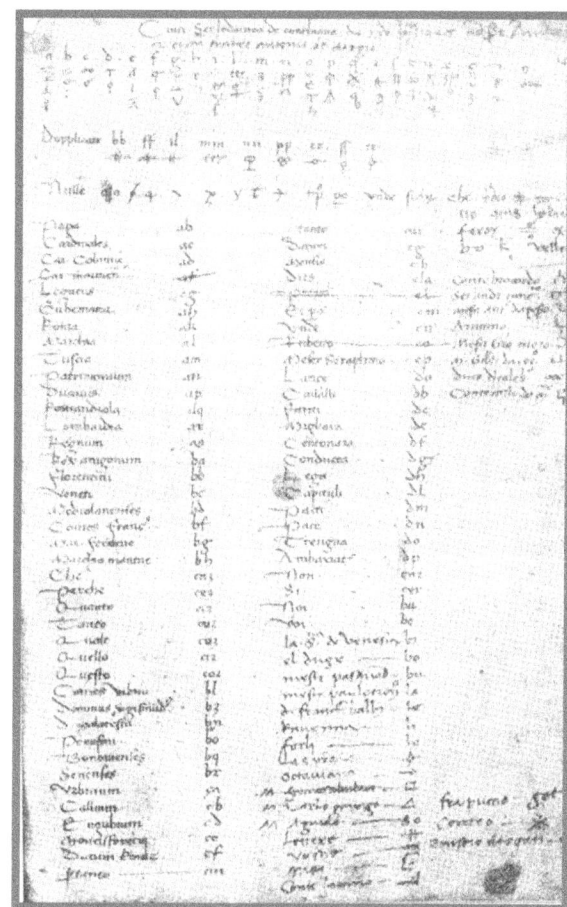

Fig. 18

nificance of this improvement you'll find out sooner or later, Codes of this sort also had variants – Rossignol was clever, indeed. One such code, found in the 1691 correspondence of Louis XIV, had about 600 items, with code groups of two and three digits. Not at all bad, for those days!

Now this sort of system would appear to be quite secure, and I suppose it was indeed so for those early days of cryptographic development – but it wasn't proof against the cleverness of British brains, for the eminent mathematician John Wallis solved messages in it in 1689. Never underestimate the British in this science – as we'll have reason to note in another lecture in this series.[1]

French cryptography under Kings Louis XV and XVI declined, reaching perhaps its lowest level under Napoleon the Great. It is a fact that in Napoleon's Russian enterprise the whole of his army used but a single codebook of only 200 groups, practically without variants, even for the high-frequency letters. Furthermore, not all the words in a message were encoded – only those that the code clerk or the writer thought were important. It's pretty clear that the Russians intercepted and read many of Napoleon's messages – this comes from categorical statements to this effect by Czar Alexander I himself. We won't be far wrong in believing that the weaknesses of Napoleon's cryptocommunications formed an important factor in Napoleon's disaster. One hundred twenty-five years later, Russian ineptitude in cryptographic communications lost them the Battle of Tannenberg and eventually knocked them out of World War I.

The other sixteenth century papal ciphers that constituted the second exception to the general similarity of cryptographic systems of those days were quite different from those I've shown you. In this exception the ciphers were monoalphabetic, shown below: You'll note that the digit 0 has two values, *A* and *T*; the digit 2 has three values, *U, V,* and *B*, and so on. There were two digits used as nulls, 1 and 8; digits with dots above them stood for words such as *qua, que, qui,* and so on,

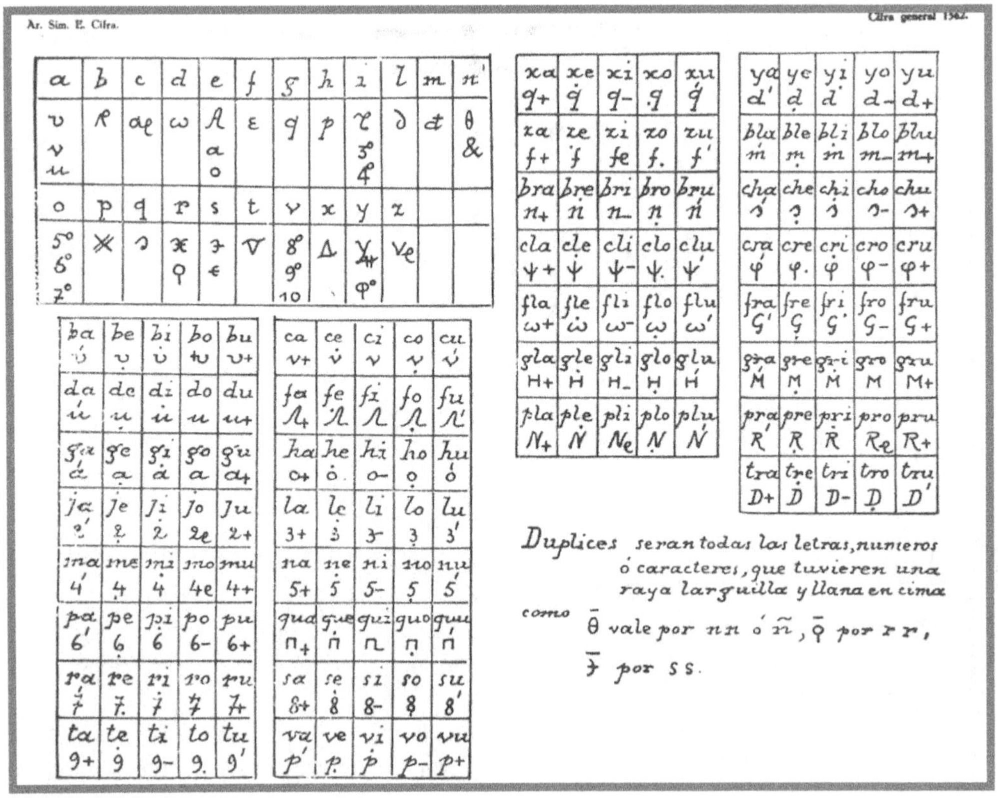

Fig. 19

CIPHER OF THE INQUISITOR OF MALTA (1585)
(From SACCO, MANUALE DE CRITTOGRAFIA, 1947)

Plain:	A,T	E,F	I,G	O,D	U,V,B	C,L,N	M,R	P,S,Z
Cipher:	0	3	5	4	2	6	9	7
Nulls:	1,8							

Plain:	qua	que	qui	quo	che	chi	non	quando	perché	et per
Cipher:	7˙	9˙	6˙	2˙	4˙	5˙	3˙	0˙	1,8˙˙	

---

but some letters had the same equivalent, so that on decipherment the context had to be used to decide which of two or more possible plaintext values was the one meant by each cipher letter. One such cipher, used by the Maltese Inquisitor in 1585, is

Page 27 shows a message and its encipherment: A bit tricky, isn't it? Many, many years later Edgar Allan Poe described a cipher of this same general type, where the decipherer must choose between two or more possible plaintext equivalents in building up his plain text, the latter guiding the choice of the right equivalent. The trouble with this sort of cipher is that you have to have pretty smart cipher clerks to operate it, and even then I imagine that in many places there would be doubtful decipherments of words. It wasn't really a practical system even in those days, but it could, if used skillfully and with only a small amount of text, give a cryptanalyst plenty of headaches. But such systems didn't last very long because of the practical difficulties in using them.

The first regular or official cipher bureau in the Vatican was established in about 1540 and in Venice at about the same time, about 100 years before a regular cipher bureau was established in France by Cardinal Richelieu. It is interesting to observe that no new or remarkable ideas for cryptosystems were developed for a couple of hundred years after the complex ones I've described as having been developed by the various papal cryptologists. One-part and two-part syllabaries and simple or complex ones with variants were in use for many decades, but later on, in a few cases, the code equivalents were superenciphered, that is, the code groups formed the text for the application of a cipher, generally by rather simple systems of additives. Governmental codes were of the two-part type and were superenciphered by the more sophisticated countries.

The first book or extensive treatise on cryptography is that by a German abbot named Trithemius, who published in 1531 the first volume of a planned monumental four-volume work. I said that he planned to publish four volumes; but he gave up after the third one, because he wrote so obscurely and made such fantastic claims that he was charged with being in league with the Devil, which was a rather dangerous association in those or even in these days. They didn't burn Trithemius, but they did burn his books. Figure 20 illustrates that the necessity for secrecy in this business was recognized from the very earliest days of cryptology, and certainly by Trithemius. Here is the sort of oath that Trithemius recommended be administered to students in the science of cryptology. All of you have subscribed to a somewhat similar oath, but we can now go further and back up the oath with a rather strict law. You've all read it, I'm sure.

We come now to some examples from more recent history. In figure 21 we see a cipher alphabet used by Mary, Queen of Scots, who reigned from 1542 to 1567 and was beheaded in 1587. In this connection it may interest you to learn that question has been raised as to whether the

```
Cipher:    4 5   1   0 2 0 4   1 4 0 9 4   8   9 5 6 2 0 4   1 0 2 5 7 4
"Plain":   O I   A   U A O     O A M O         M I C U A O   A U I P O
           D G   T   B T D     D T R D         R G L B T D   T B G S D
                     V                             N V           V Z

Plain      D I   T U T O       D A R O         M I N U T O   A V I S O

Cipher:    1     4 5 6 5 1 6 4 9 5 3 9 3 8
"Plain":   ET    O I C I   C O M I   E M E
           PER   D G L G   N D R G F R F
           PERCHE    N     L

Plain:     PER   O G N I   C O R I E R E
```

Queen was "framed" by means of this forged postscript (fig. 22) in a cipher that was known to have been used by her.

The Spanish Court under Philip II, in the years 1555-1598, used a great many ciphers, one of which is shown in figure 23. You see that it is quite complex for those early days, and yet ciphers of this sort were solved by an eminent French mathematician named Vieta, the father of modern algebra. In 1589 he became a Councilor [*sic*] of Parliament at Tours and then Privy Councillor. While in that job he solved a Spanish cipher system using more than 500 characters, so that all the Spanish dispatches falling into French hands were easily read. Philip was so convinced of the security of his ciphers that when he found the French were aware of the contents of his cipher dispatches to the Netherlands, he complained to the pope that the French were using sorcery against him. Vieta was called on the carpet and forced to explain how he'd solved the ciphers in order to avoid being convicted of sorcery, a serious offense.

The next cryptologist I want you to know something about is another Italian savant who wrote a book, published in 1563, in which he showed certain types of cipher alphabets that have come down in history and are famous as Porta's alphabets. Figure 24 is an example of the Porta Table, showing one alphabet with key letters *A* or *B*, another alphabet with key letters *C* or *D*, and so on.

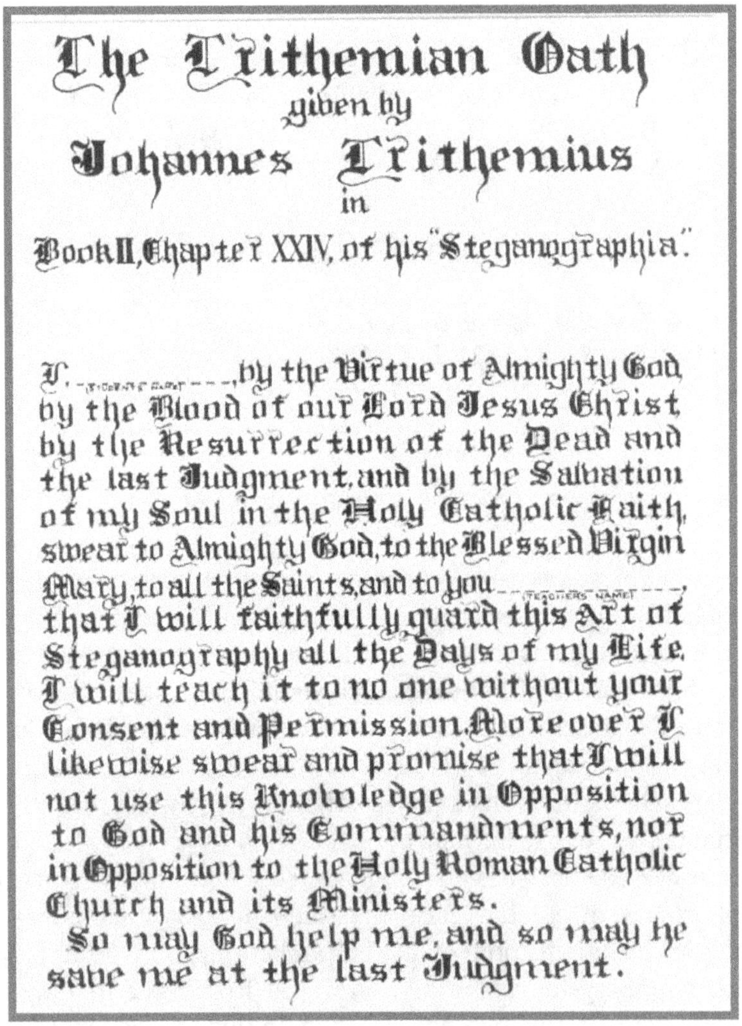
The Trithemian Oath
given by
Johannes Trithemius
in
Book II, Chapter XXIV, of his "Steganographia."

I, ______ (STUDENT'S NAME), by the Virtue of Almighty God, by the Blood of our Lord Jesus Christ, by the Resurrection of the Dead and the last Judgment, and by the Salvation of my Soul in the Holy Catholic Faith, swear to Almighty God, to the Blessed Virgin Mary, to all the Saints, and to you ______ (TEACHER'S NAME), that I will faithfully guard this Art of Steganography all the Days of my Life. I will teach it to no one without your Consent and Permission. Moreover I likewise swear and promise that I will not use this Knowledge in Opposition to God and his Commandments, nor in Opposition to the Holy Roman Catholic Church and its Ministers.

So may God help me, and so may he save me at the last Judgment.

Fig. 20

I don't want to go into exactly how the key letters are used; it is sufficient to say that even to this day cryptograms using the Porta alphabets are occasionally encountered.

That Porta's table was actually used in official correspondence is shown by figure 25, which is a picture of a table found among the state papers of Queen Elizabeth's time; it was used for communicating with the English ambassador to Spain. Porta was, in my opinion, the greatest of the old writers on cryptology. I also think he was one of the early, but by no means the first, cryptanalyst able to solve a system of keyed substitution, that is, where the key is changing constantly as the message undergoes encipherment. Incidentally, Porta was also the inventor of the photographic camera, the progenitor of which was known as the *camera obscura*.

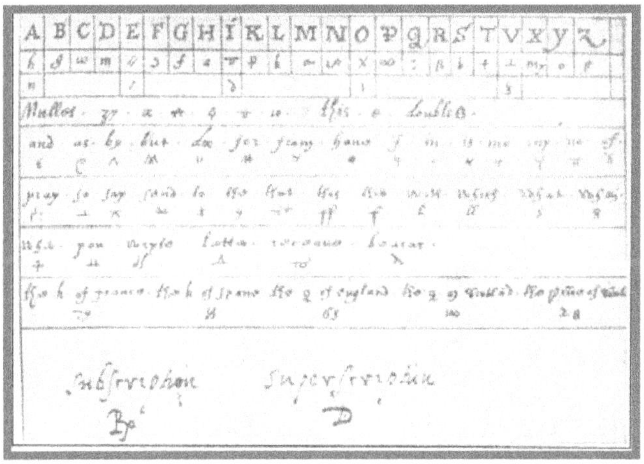

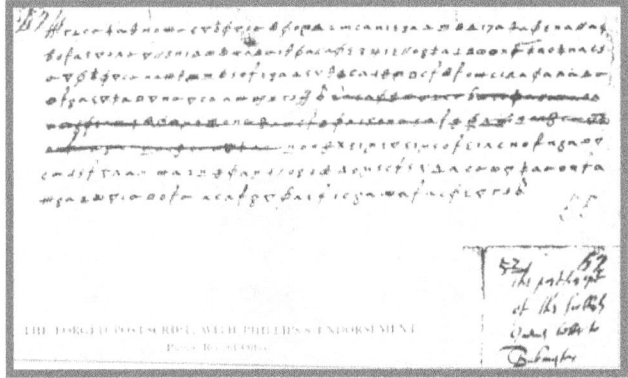

Fig. 21

Fig. 22

Figure 26 is a picture of what cryptographers usually call the Vigenère Square, the Vigenère Table, or the Vigenère Tableau. It consists of a set of twenty-six alphabets successively displaced one letter per row, with the plaintext letters at the top of the square, the key letters at the side, and the cipher letters inside. The method of using the table is to agree upon a key word, which causes the equivalents of the plaintext letters to change as the key changes. Vigenère is commonly credited with having invented that square and cipher, but he really didn't and, what's more, never said he did. His table, as it appears in his book, the first edition of which was published in 1586, is shown in figure 27. It is more complicated than as described in ordinary books on cryptology.

Figure 28 is one more example of another old official cipher. In it we can see the alphabets that could be slid up and down, as a means of changing the key. Another early official cipher is shown in figure 29. It is a facsimile of a state cipher used in Charles the First's time, in 1627, for communicating with France and Flanders. It involves coordinates, and I want you to notice that there are two complete alphabets inside it, intended to smooth out frequencies. The letters of the key words OPTIMUS and DOMINUS serve as the coordinates used to represent the letters inside the square. A third old cipher, one used by George III in 1799, is shown in figure 30.

One writer deserving special attention as a knowledgeable cryptologist in the seventeenth century, and the one with whose cipher I'll close this lecture, is Sir Francis Bacon, who invented a very useful cipher and mentioned it for the first time in his *Advancement of Learning*, published in 1604 in London. The description is so brief that I doubt whether many persons understood what he was driving at. But Bacon described it in full detail, with examples, in his great book *De Augmentis Scientiarum*, which was published almost twenty years later, in 1623, and which first appeared in an English translation by Gilbert Wats in 1640 under the title *The Advancement of Learning*. Bacon

Page 29

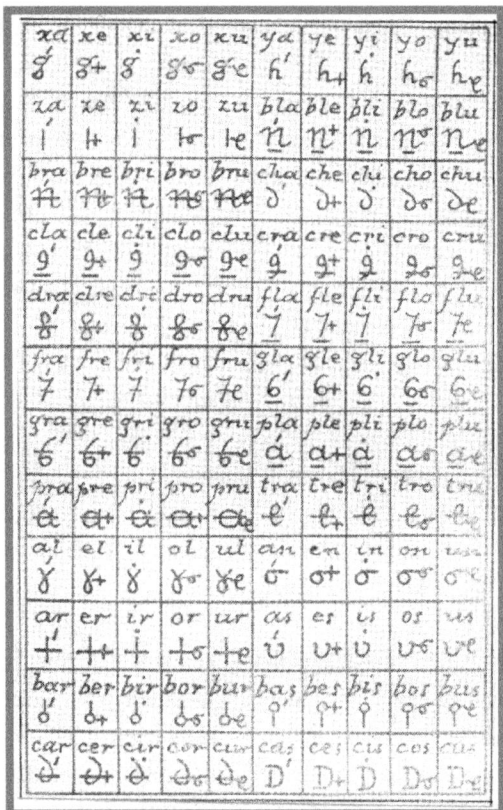

Fig. 23

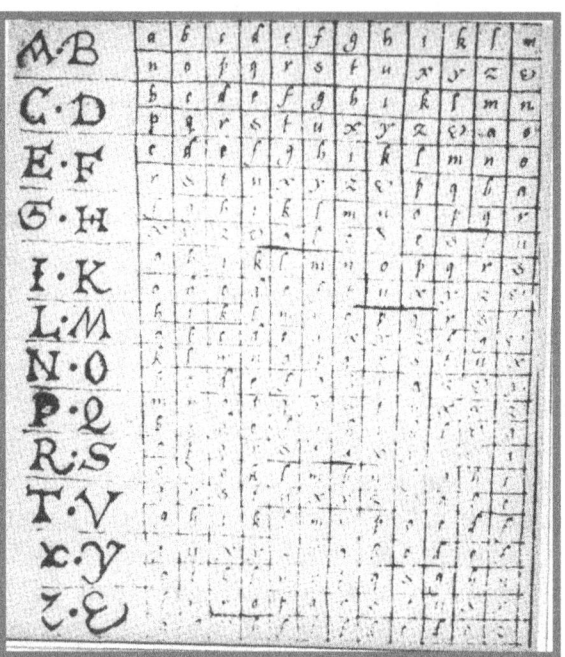

Fig. 25

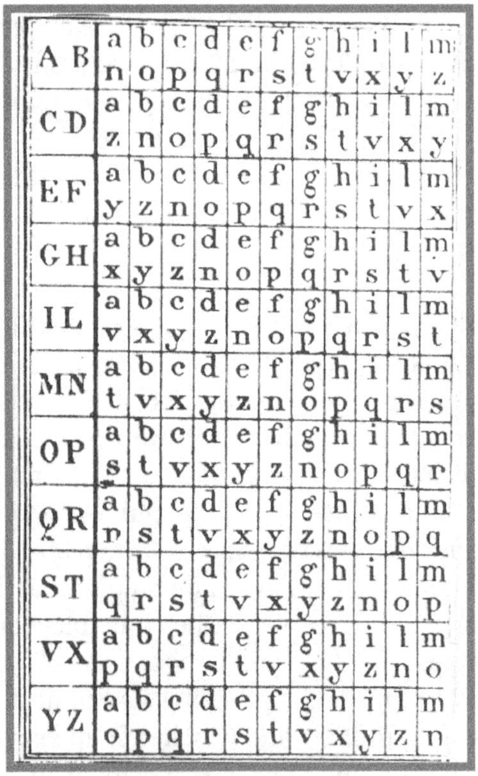

A B	a	b	c	d	e	f	g	h	i	l	m
	n	o	p	q	r	s	t	v	x	y	z
C D	a	b	c	d	e	f	g	h	i	l	m
	z	n	o	p	q	r	s	t	v	x	y
E F	a	b	c	d	e	f	g	h	i	l	m
	y	z	n	o	p	q	r	s	t	v	x
G H	a	b	c	d	e	f	g	h	i	l	m
	x	y	z	n	o	p	q	r	s	t	v
I L	a	b	c	d	e	f	g	h	i	l	m
	v	x	y	z	n	o	p	q	r	s	t
M N	a	b	c	d	e	f	g	h	i	l	m
	t	v	x	y	z	n	o	p	q	r	s
O P	a	b	c	d	e	f	g	h	i	l	m
	s	t	v	x	y	z	n	o	p	q	r
Q R	a	b	c	d	e	f	g	h	i	l	m
	r	s	t	v	x	y	z	n	o	p	q
S T	a	b	c	d	e	f	g	h	i	l	m
	q	r	s	t	v	x	y	z	n	o	p
V X	a	b	c	d	e	f	g	h	i	l	m
	p	q	r	s	t	v	x	y	z	n	o
Y Z	a	b	c	d	e	f	g	h	i	l	m
	o	p	q	r	s	t	v	x	y	z	n

Fig. 24

	A	B	C	D	E	F	G	H	I	J	K	L	M	N	O	P	Q	R	S	T	U	V	W	X	Y	Z
A	a	b	c	d	e	f	g	h	i	j	k	l	m	n	o	p	q	r	s	t	u	v	w	x	y	z
B	b	c	d	e	f	g	h	i	j	k	l	m	n	o	p	q	r	s	t	u	v	w	x	y	z	a
C	c	d	e	f	g	h	i	j	k	l	m	n	o	p	q	r	s	t	u	v	w	x	y	z	a	b
D	d	e	f	g	h	i	j	k	l	m	n	o	p	q	r	s	t	u	v	w	x	y	z	a	b	c
E	e	f	g	h	i	j	k	l	m	n	o	p	q	r	s	t	u	v	w	x	y	z	a	b	c	d
F	f	g	h	i	j	k	l	m	n	o	p	q	r	s	t	u	v	w	x	y	z	a	b	c	d	e
G	g	h	i	j	k	l	m	n	o	p	q	r	s	t	u	v	w	x	y	z	a	b	c	d	e	f
H	h	i	j	k	l	m	n	o	p	q	r	s	t	u	v	w	x	y	z	a	b	c	d	e	f	g
I	i	j	k	l	m	n	o	p	q	r	s	t	u	v	w	x	y	z	a	b	c	d	e	f	g	h
J	j	k	l	m	n	o	p	q	r	s	t	u	v	w	x	y	z	a	b	c	d	e	f	g	h	i
K	k	l	m	n	o	p	q	r	s	t	u	v	w	x	y	z	a	b	c	d	e	f	g	h	i	j
L	l	m	n	o	p	q	r	s	t	u	v	w	x	y	z	a	b	c	d	e	f	g	h	i	j	k
M	m	n	o	p	q	r	s	t	u	v	w	x	y	z	a	b	c	d	e	f	g	h	i	j	k	l
N	n	o	p	q	r	s	t	u	v	w	x	y	z	a	b	c	d	e	f	g	h	i	j	k	l	m
O	o	p	q	r	s	t	u	v	w	x	y	z	a	b	c	d	e	f	g	h	i	j	k	l	m	n
P	p	q	r	s	t	u	v	w	x	y	z	a	b	c	d	e	f	g	h	i	j	k	l	m	n	o
Q	q	r	s	t	u	v	w	x	y	z	a	b	c	d	e	f	g	h	i	j	k	l	m	n	o	p
R	r	s	t	u	v	w	x	y	z	a	b	c	d	e	f	g	h	i	j	k	l	m	n	o	p	q
S	s	t	u	v	w	x	y	z	a	b	c	d	e	f	g	h	i	j	k	l	m	n	o	p	q	r
T	t	u	v	w	x	y	z	a	b	c	d	e	f	g	h	i	j	k	l	m	n	o	p	q	r	s
U	u	v	w	x	y	z	a	b	c	d	e	f	g	h	i	j	k	l	m	n	o	p	q	r	s	t
V	v	w	x	y	z	a	b	c	d	e	f	g	h	i	j	k	l	m	n	o	p	q	r	s	t	u
W	w	x	y	z	a	b	c	d	e	f	g	h	i	j	k	l	m	n	o	p	q	r	s	t	u	v
X	x	y	z	a	b	c	d	e	f	g	h	i	j	k	l	m	n	o	p	q	r	s	t	u	v	w
Y	y	z	a	b	c	d	e	f	g	h	i	j	k	l	m	n	o	p	q	r	s	t	u	v	w	x
Z	z	a	b	c	d	e	f	g	h	i	j	k	l	m	n	o	p	q	r	s	t	u	v	w	x	y

Fig. 26

called his invention the *Biliteral Cipher*, and it is so ingenious that I think you should be told about it so that you will all fully understand it.

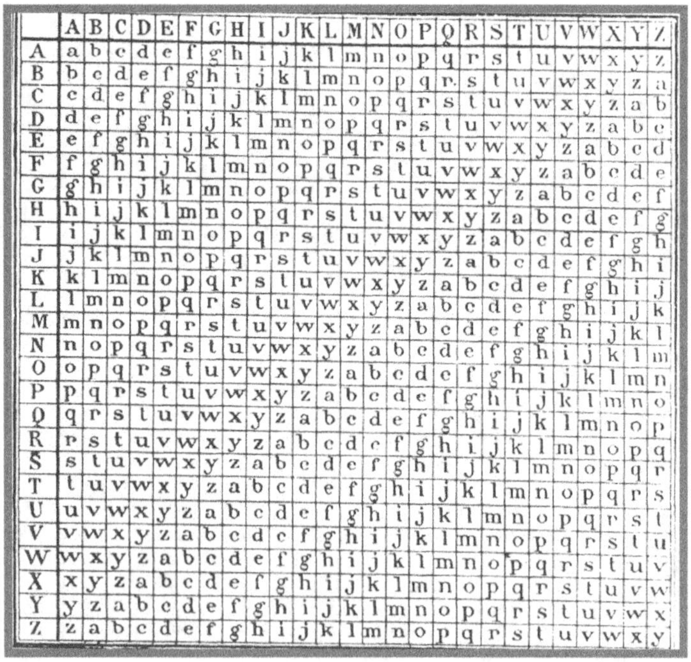

In his *De Augmentis* Bacon writes briefly about ciphers in general and says that the virtues required in them are three: "that they be easy and not labo-

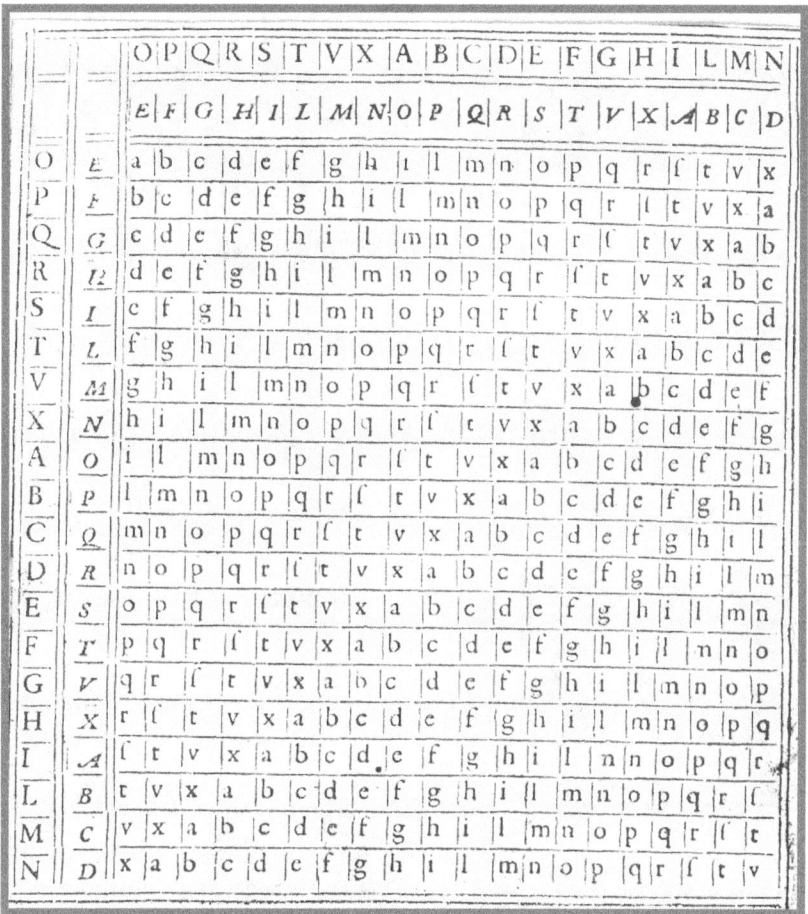

Fig. 27

rious to write; that they be safe, and impossible to be deciphered without the key; and lastly, that they be, if possible, such as not to raise suspicion or to elude inquiry." He then goes on to say: "But for avoiding suspicion altogether, I will add another contrivance, which I devised myself when I was at Paris in my early youth, and which I still think worthy of preservation." Mind you, this was forty years later! Let's consult Bacon for further details. In figure 31 we see a couple of pages of the Gilbert Wats' translation of Bacon's *De Augmentis Scientiarum*. Bacon shows what he calls "An Example of a Bi-literaire Alphabet," that is, one composed of two elements that, taken in groupings of fives, yield thirty-two permutations. You can use these permutations to represent the letters of the alphabet, says Bacon, but you need only twenty-four of them [because *I* and *J*, *U* and *V*, were then used interchangeably]. These permutations of two different things – they may be *a*'s and *b*'s, *1*'s and *2*'s, pluses and minuses, apples and oranges, anything you please – can be used to express or signify messages. Bacon was, in fact, the inventor of the binary code that forms the basis of modern electronic digital computers. Bacon gives a brief example in the word *fuge* – the Latin equivalent of our modern *scram* – as can be seen in figure 31. Figure 32 is another example, which quite obviously isn't what it appears to be – a crude picture of a castle, in which there are shaded and unshaded stones. It was drawn by a friend who was a physician, and the message conveyed by it is

> My business is to write prescriptions
> And then to see my doses taken;
> But now I find I spend my time
> Endeavoring to out-Bacon Bacon.

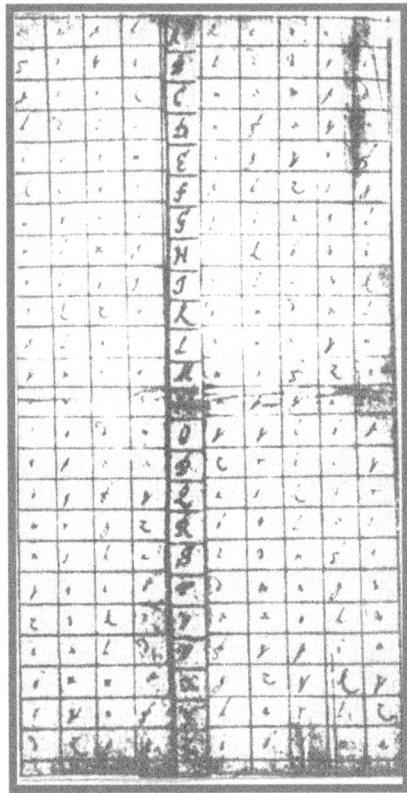

Fig. 28

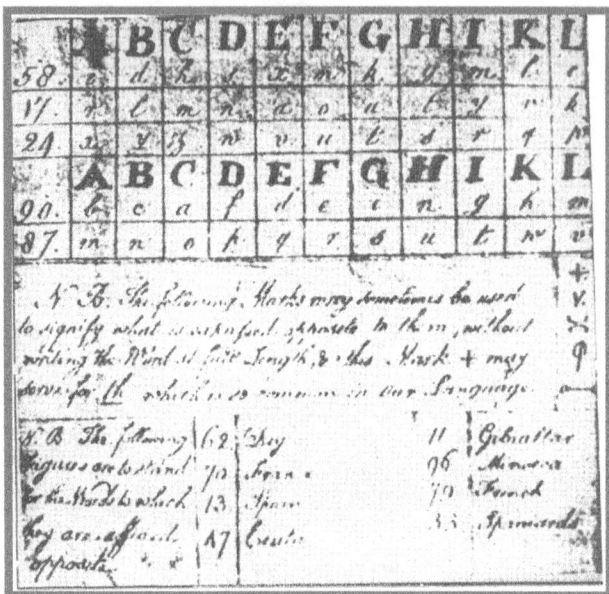

Fig. 30

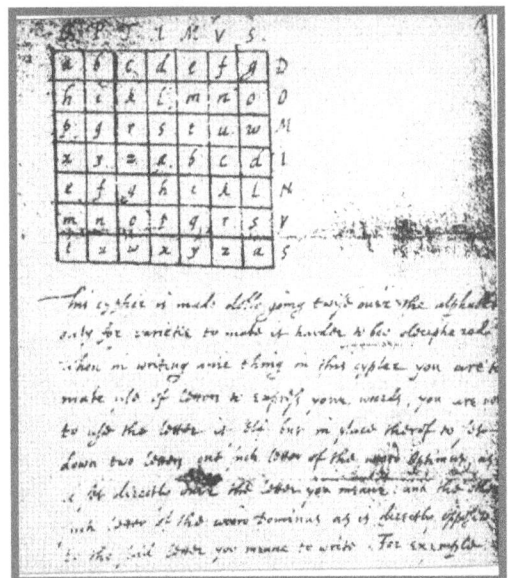

Fig. 29

So far this is simple enough – too much so, Bacon says, for the example he used in the case of the word *fuge* is patently cryptic and would not avoid suspicion under examination. So Bacon goes on to describe the next step, which is to have at hand a "Bi-formed Alphabet," that is, one in which all the letters of the alphabet, both capital and small, are represented by two slightly different forms of letters (fig. 33). Having these two different forms at hand, when you want to encipher your secret message, you write another external and innocuous message five times as long as your secret message, using the appropriate two forms of letters to correspond to the *a*'s and *b*'s representing your secret message. Here's *fuge* (fig. 34), enciphered within an external message saying "Manere te volo donec veniam," meaning "Stay where you are until I come." In other words, whereas the real message says scram, the phony one says "Stick around awhile; wait for me." Bacon gives a much longer example, the SPARTAN DISPATCH; here it is, and here's the secret message that it contains (fig. 35).

Bacon's biliteral cipher is an extremely ingenious contrivance. There can be no question whatsoever about its authenticity and utility as a valid cipher. Thousands of people have checked his long example, and they all find the same answer – the one that Bacon gives.

Figure 36 is a modern example that uses two slightly different fonts of type called Garamond and

Page 32

Imprint, which are so nearly alike that it takes good eyes to differentiate them.

The fact that Bacon invented this cipher and described it in such detail lends plausibility to a theory entertained by many persons that Bacon wrote the Shakespeare plays and that he inserted secret messages in those plays by using his cipher. If you'd like to learn more about this theory, I suggest with some diffidence that you read a book entitled *The Shakespearean Ciphers Examined.* I use the word *diffidence* because my wife and I wrote the book, which was published in late 1957 by the Cambridge University Press.

In the next lecture we'll take up cryptology as used during the period of the American Revolution by both the colonial and the British forces in America.

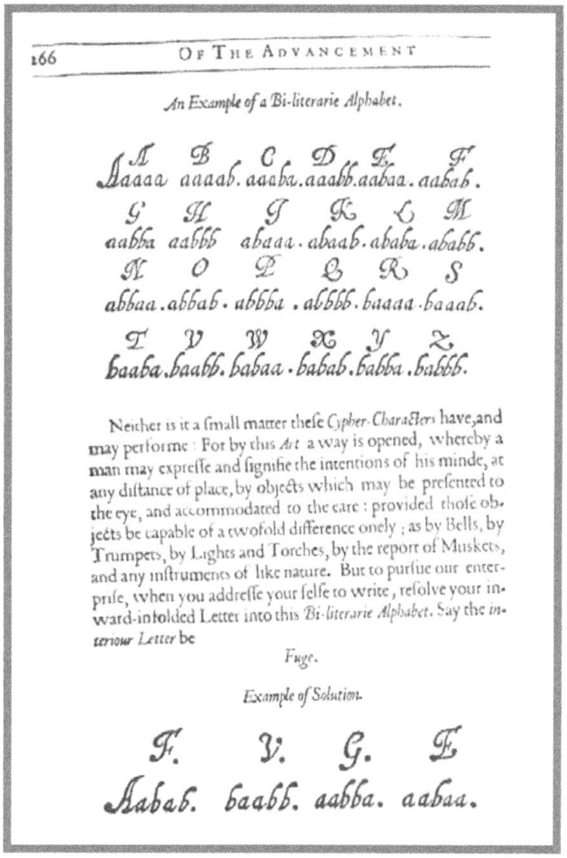
166 OF THE ADVANCEMENT

An Example of a Bi-literarie Alphabet.

A B C D E F
aaaaa. aaaab. aaaba. aaabb. aabaa. aabab.
G H I K L M
aabba. aabbb. abaaa. abaab. ababa. ababb.
N O P Q R S
abbaa. abbab. abbba. abbbb. baaaa. baaab.
T V W X Y Z
baaba. baabb. babaa. babab. babba. babbb.

Neither is it a ſmall matter theſe *Cypher-Characters* have, and may performe: For by this *Art* a way is opened, whereby a man may expreſſe and ſignifie the intentions of his minde, at any diſtance of place, by objects which may be preſented to the eye, and accommodated to the eare: provided thoſe objects be capable of a twofold difference onely; as by Bells, by Trumpets, by Lights and Torches, by the report of Muskets, and any inſtruments of like nature. But to purſue our enterpriſe, when you addreſſe your ſelfe to write, reſolve your inward-infolded Letter into this *Bi-literarie Alphabet*. Say the *interiour Letter* be

Fuge.

Example of Solution.

F. V. G. E.
aabab. baabb. aabba. aabaa.

Fig. 31

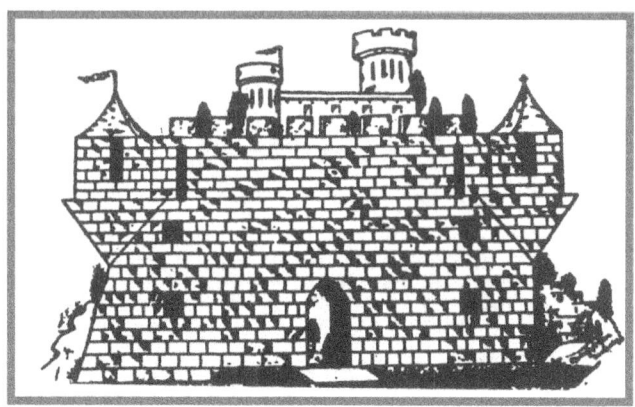

Fig. 32

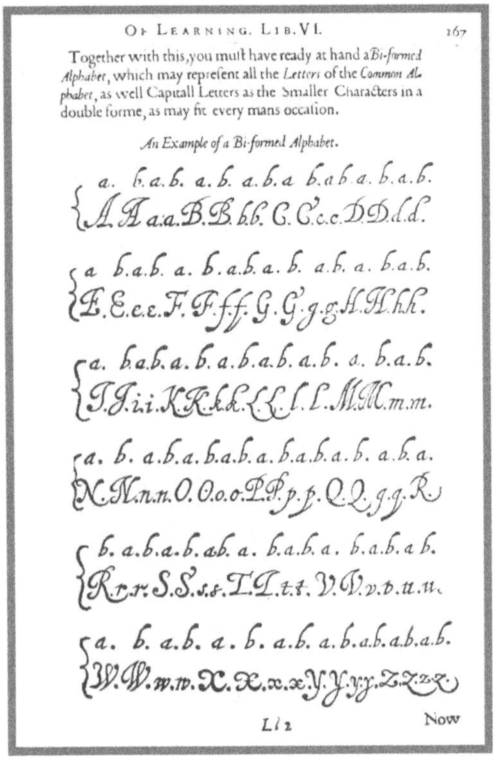

Fig. 33

OF LEARNING. LIB. VI.   167

Together with this, you must have ready at hand a *Bi-formed Alphabet*, which may represent all the *Letters* of the *Common Alphabet*, as well *Capitall Letters* as the *Smaller Characters* in a double forme, as may fit every mans occasion.

An Example of a Bi-formed Alphabet.

a. b.a.b. a. b. a.b. a. b. b.a.b.a.b.
A A a.a. B B b.b. C C c.c. D D d.d.

a b.a.b. a. b. a.b. a. b. a. b. a.b.
E E e.e. F F f.ff. G G g.g. H H h.h.

a. b.a.b. a. b. a.b. a. b. a. b.a.b.
I J. i.i. K K k.k. L L l.l. M M m.m.

a. b. a. b. a.b. a. b. a. b. a. b. a.
N N n.n. O O o.o. P P p.p. Q Q q.q. R

b. a. b. a.b. a. b. a. b. a. b.a.b.
R r.r. S S s.s. T T t.t. V V v.v. u.u.

a. b. a.b. a. b. a.b. a. b.a.b.a.b.
W W w.w. X X x.x. Y Y y.y. Z z.z

Ll 2   Now

PLATE No. 50

Fig. 34

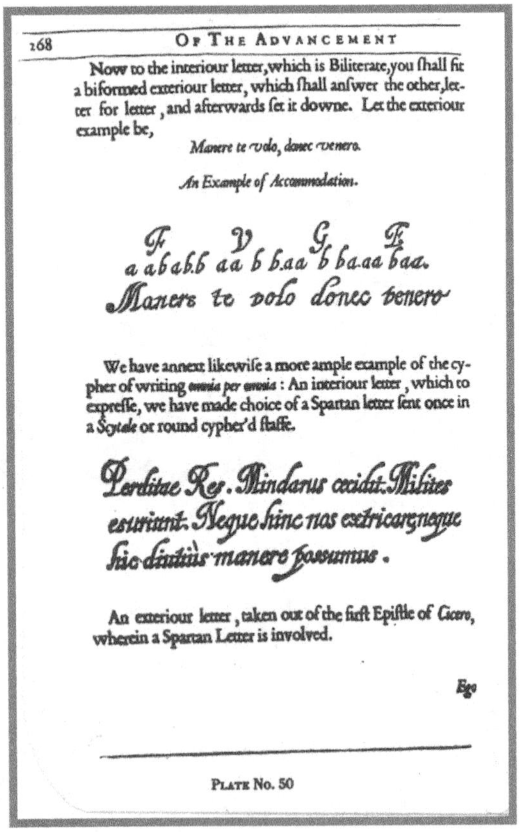

268   OF THE ADVANCEMENT

Now to the interiour letter, which is Biliterate, you shall fit a biformed exteriour letter, which shall answer the other, letter for letter, and afterwards set it downe. Let the exteriour example be,

Manere te volo, donec venero.

An Example of Accommodation.

F V G E
a aba.b.b aa b b.aa b ba.aa baa.
Manere te volo donec venero

We have annext likewise a more ample example of the cypher of writing *omnia per omnia*: An interiour letter, which to expresse, we have made choice of a Spartan letter sent once in a *Scytale* or round cypher'd staffe.

Perditae Res. Mindarus cecidit. Milites
esuriunt. Neque hinc nos extricare, neque
hic diutius manere possumus.

An exteriour letter, taken out of the first Epistle of *Cicero*, wherein a Spartan Letter is involved.

Ego

PLATE No. 50

Fig. 35

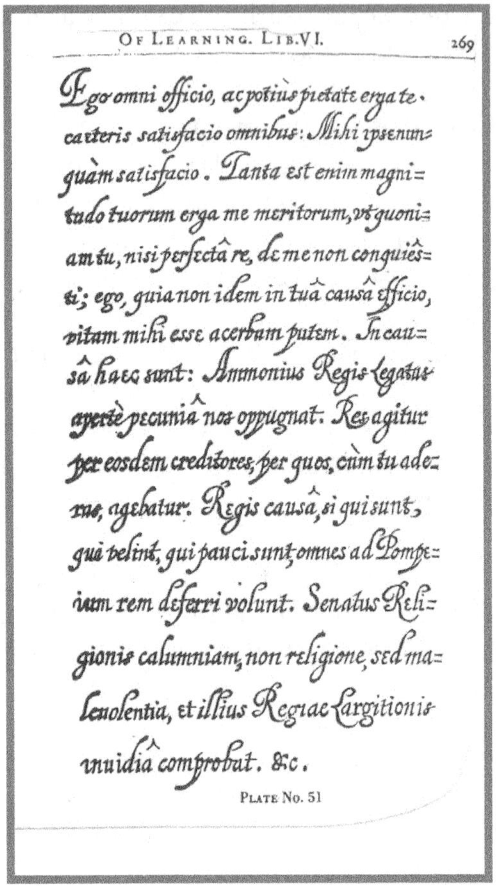

OF LEARNING. LIB. VI.   269

Ego omni officio, ac potius pietate erga te
cæteris satisfacio omnibus: Mihi ipse nun=
quam satisfacio. Tanta est enim magni=
tudo tuorum erga me meritorum, vt quoni=
am tu, nisi perfectâ re, de me non conquies=
ti; ego, quia non idem in tuâ causa efficio,
vitam mihi esse acerbum putem. In cau=
sâ hæc sunt: Ammonius Regis Legatus
aperte pecunia nos oppugnat. Res agitur
per eosdem creditores, per quos, cùm tu ade=
ras, agebatur. Regis causa, si qui sunt,
quâ velint, qui pauci sunt, omnes ad Pompe=
ium rem deferri volunt. Senatus Reli=
gionis calumniam, non religione, sed ma=
leuolentia, et illius Regiae Largitionis
inuidiâ comprobat. &c.

PLATE No. 51

Fig. 36

In all duty or rather piety towards you I satisfy every body except myself. Myself I never satisfy. For so great are the services which you have rendered me, that seeing you did not rest in your endeavours on my behalf till the thing was done, I feel as if life had lost all its sweetness, because I cannot do as much in this cause of yours. The occasions are these: Ammonius the King's ambassador openly besieges us with money: the business is carried on through the same creditors who were employed in it when you were here, &c.

Lecture III

Continuing with our survey of cryptologic history, the period of the American Revolution in U.S. history is naturally of considerable interest to us and warrants more than cursory treatment. Information regarding the codes and ciphers employed during that period has been rather sparse until quite recently, when a book entitled *Turncoats, Traitors and Heroes* by Colonel John Bakeless, AUS, was published in 1959 by Lippincott. After a good many years of research, Colonel Bakeless brought together for the first time a considerable amount of authentic information on the subject, and some of it is incorporated in this lecture.

According to Colonel Bakeless – and believe it or not – in early 1775 the British commander in chief in America, General Gage, had no code or cipher at all, nor even a staff officer who knew how to compile or devise one; he had to appeal to the commanding general in Canada, from whom he probably obtained the single substitution cipher that was used in 1776 by a British secret agent who – again, believe it or not – was General Washington's own director general of hospitals, Dr. Benjamin Church. General Washington had means for secret communication from the very beginning of hostilities, probably even before the fighting began at Lexington and Concord. If the British under General Gage were poorly provided in this respect, by the time Sir Henry Clinton took over from General Howe, who succeeded Gage, they were much better off – they had adequate or apparently adequate means for secret communication.

Are you astonished to learn that the systems used by the American colonial forces and by the British regulars were almost identical? You shouldn't be, because the language and backgrounds of both were identical. In one case, in fact, they used the same dictionary as a code book, something that was almost inevitable because there were so few English dictionaries available. Here's a list of the systems they used:

a. Simple, monoalphabetic substitution – easy to use and to change

b. Monoalphabetic substitution with variants, by the use of a long key sentence. I'll show you presently an interesting example in Benjamin Franklin's system of correspondence with the elder Dumas.

c. The Vigenère cipher with repeating key.

d. Transposition ciphers of simple sorts.

e. Dictionaries employed as code books, with and without added encipherment. Two were specially favored, Entick's *New Spelling Dictionary* and Bailey's *English Dictionary*. A couple of pages from the former are shown in figure 37. To represent a word by code equivalent, you simply indicated the page number, then whether column 1 or column 2 contained the word you wanted, and then the number of the word in the column. Thus, the word *jacket* would be represented by 178-2-2.

f. Small, specially compiled, alphabetic one-part codes of 600-700 items and code names – our old friend the syllabary, or repertory, of hoary old age, but in new dress. In some cases these were of the "one-part" or "alphabetic" type.

g. Ordinary books, such as Blackstone's *Commentaries on the Laws of England*, giving the page number, the line number, and the letter number in the line, to build up, letter-by-letter, the word to be represented. Thus, 125-12-16 would indicate

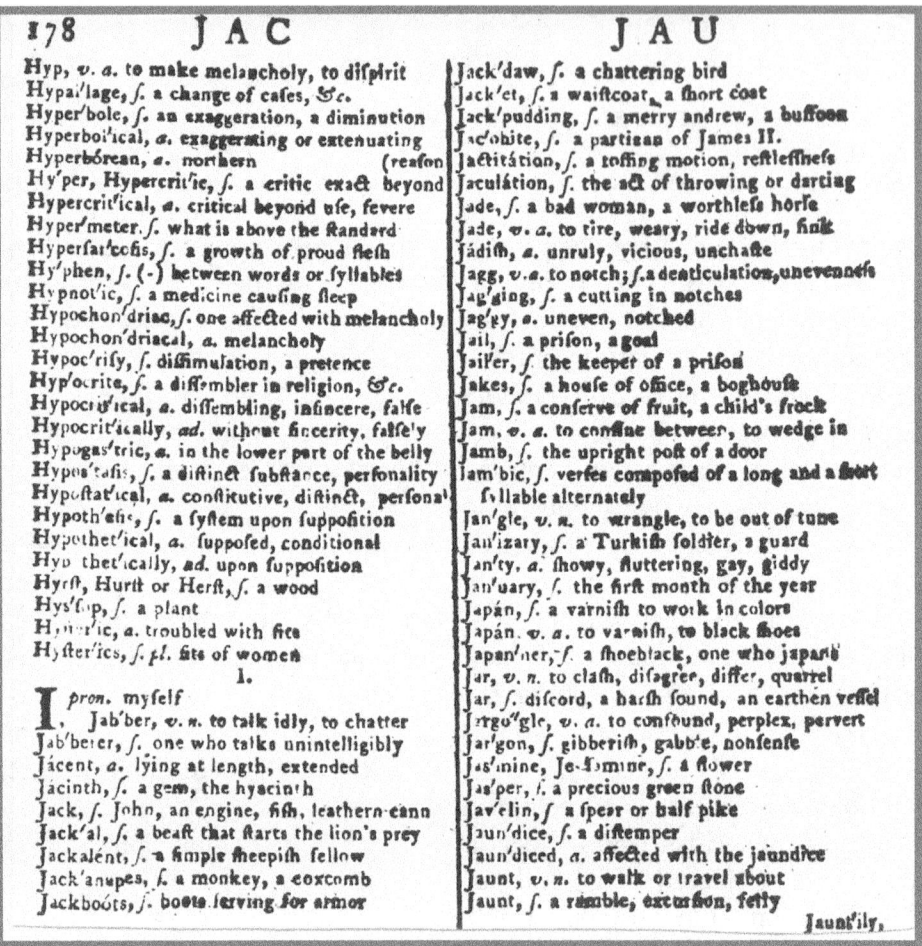

Fig. 37

the 16th letter in the 12th line on page 125; it might be the letter T.

h. Secret inks. Both the British and Americans made extensive use of this method.

i. Special designs or geometric figures, such as the one I'll show you presently.

j. Various concealment methods, such as using hollow quills of large feathers or hollowing out a bullet and inserting messages written on very thin paper. Strictly speaking, however, this sort of stratagem doesn't belong to the field of cryptology. But it's a good dodge, to be used in special cases.

In the way of ciphers a bit more complex than simple monoalphabetic substitution ciphers, the British under Clinton's command used a system described by Bakeless in the following terms:

> . . . a substitution cipher in which the alphabet was reversed, "z" becoming "a" and "a" becoming "z." To destroy frequency clues, the cipher changed in each line of the message, using "y" for "a" in the second line, "x" for "a" in the third, and so on. When the cipher clerk reached "o" in the middle of the alphabet, he started over again. A spy using this cipher did not have to carry incriminating papers, since the system was easy to remember.

The alphabets of this scheme are simple reversed standard alphabets:

```
A B C D E F G H I J K L M N O P Q R S T U V W X Y Z
Z Y X W V U T S R Q P O N M L K J I H G F E D C B A
Y X W V U T S R Q P O N M L K J I H G F E D C B A Z
X W V U T S R Q P O N M L K J I H G F E D C B A Z Y
W V U T S R Q P O N M L K J I H G F E D C B A Z Y X
V U T S R Q P O N M L K J I H G F E D C B A Z Y X W
U T S R Q P O N M L K J I H G F E D C B A Z Y X W V
T S R Q P O N M L K J I H G F E D C B A Z Y X W V U
S R Q P O N M L K J I H G F E D C B A Z Y X W V U T
R Q P O N M L K J I H G F E D C B A Z Y X W V U T S
Q P O N M L K J I H G F E D C B A Z Y X W V U T S R
P O N M L K J I H G F E D C B A Z Y X W V U T S R Q
O N M L K J I H G F E D C B A Z Y X W V U T S R Q P
```

Bakeless doesn't explain why the cipher sequences are only twelve in number – nor does the source from which he obtained the information, a note found among the *Clinton Papers* in the Clements Library at the University of Michigan.

Bakeless continues:

> Clinton also used another substitution cipher, with different alphabets for the first, second and third paragraphs. Even if an American cryptanalyst should break the cipher in one paragraph, he would have to start all over in the next. As late as 1781, however, Sir Henry was using one extremely clumsy substitution cipher, in which "a" was 51, "d" was 54, "e," 55. Finding that "a" was 51 and "d" was 54, anyone could guess (correctly) that "b" was 52, "c" 53. Somewhat more complex was his "pigpen" cipher, in which twenty-five letters of the alphabet were placed in squares. Then an angle alone would represent a letter, the same angle with a dot another letter, the same angle with two dots still another. In some cases, cryptography was used only for a few crucial words in an otherwise "clear" message, a method also favored by certain American officials.

Of the first cipher mentioned in the preceding extract, there is much more to be said. Perhaps Bakeless was limited by space considerations. In any case, I will leave that story for another time and place. As for the second cipher Bakeless mentions in the extract, I can give you the whole alphabet, for it exists among the Clinton Papers.

```
A  B  C  D  E  F  G  H  I  K  L  M
51 52 53 54 55 60 61 62 63 64 65 66
N  O  P  Q  R  S  T  U  W  X  Y  Z
67 68 69 70 71 72 73 74 75 76 77 78
```

There is no explanation why the sequence beginning with 50 stops with E-55 and then starting with F-60 goes straight on without any break to Z-78. (Remember that in those days I and J were used interchangeably, as were U and V.)

Finally, as to what Bakeless (and others) calls the "pigpen" cipher, this is nothing but the hoary old so-called "Masonic" cipher based upon the four-cross figure that can accommodate twenty-seven characters, not twenty-five, as Bakeless indicates. Letters can be inserted in the design in many different arrangements.

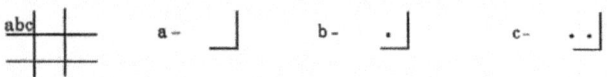

I've mentioned that code or conventional names were used to represent the names of important persons and places in these American colonial and British cryptograms of the Revolution. Here are examples selected from a list of code names prepared by the famous British spy, Major Andre, chief of intelligence under General Clinton:

For American Generals — the names of the Apostles, for instance:

General Washington was *James*
General Sullivan was *Matthew*

Names of Forts:

Fort Wyoming – *Sodom*
Fort Pitt – *Gomorrha*

Names of Cities:

Philadelphia – *Jerusalem*
Detroit – *Alexandria*

Names of Rivers and Bays:

Susquehanna – *Jordan*
Delaware – *Red Sea*

Miscellaneous:

Indians – *Pharisees*
Congress – *Synagogue*

I'm sure you've learned as school children all about the treasonable conduct of Benedict Arnold when he was in command of the American forces at West Point; but you probably don't know that practically all his exchanges of communications with Sir Henry Clinton, commander of the British forces in America, were in cipher or in invisible inks. One of Arnold's cipher messages, in which he offers to give up West Point for £20,000, is shown below, figure 38*a* being the secret version, figure 38*b*, the plain text. Arnold left a few words *en clair*, the ones he considered unimportant; for the important ones he used a dictionary as a codebook, indicating the page number, column number and line number corresponding to the position in the dictionary of the

Fig. 38a

Inclosed in a cover addressed to Mr. Anderson.

Two days since I received a letter without date or signature, informing me that S. Henry — was obliged to me for the intelligence communicated, and that he placed a full confidence in the sincerity of my intentions, &c. &c. — On the 13th instant I addressed a letter to you expressing my sentiments and expectations, viz. that the following preliminaries be settled previous to cooperating. First, that S. Henry secure to me my property, valued at ten thousand pounds sterling, to be paid to me or my heirs in case of loss; and, as soon as that shall happen, — hundred pounds per annum to be secured to me for life, in lieu of the pay and emoluments I give up, for my services as they shall deserve. — If I point out a plan of cooperation by which S. H. shall possess himself of West Point, the Garrison, &c. &c. &c. twenty thousand pounds sterling I think will be a cheap purchase for an object of so much importance. At the same time I request a thousand pounds to be paid my Agent — I expect a full and explicit answer — The 20th I set off for West Point. A personal interview with an officer that you can confide in is absolutely necessary to plan matters. In the mean time I shall communicate to our mutual Friend S—y all the intelligence in my power, until I have the pleasure of your answer.

July 15th

Moore

To the line of my letter of the 13th I did not add seven.

N.B. The postscript only relates to the manner of conveying the cypher in the letter referred to —

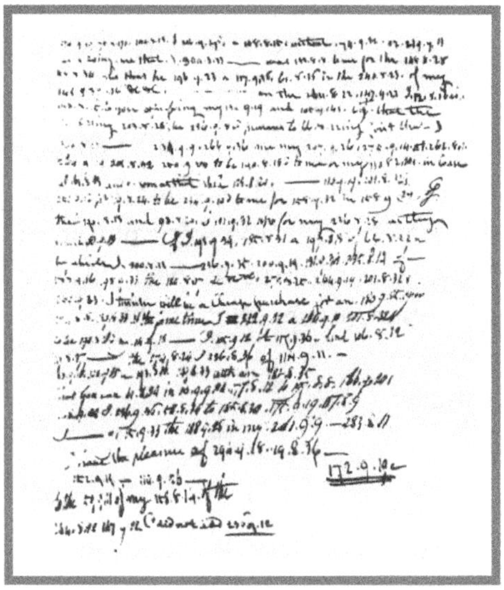

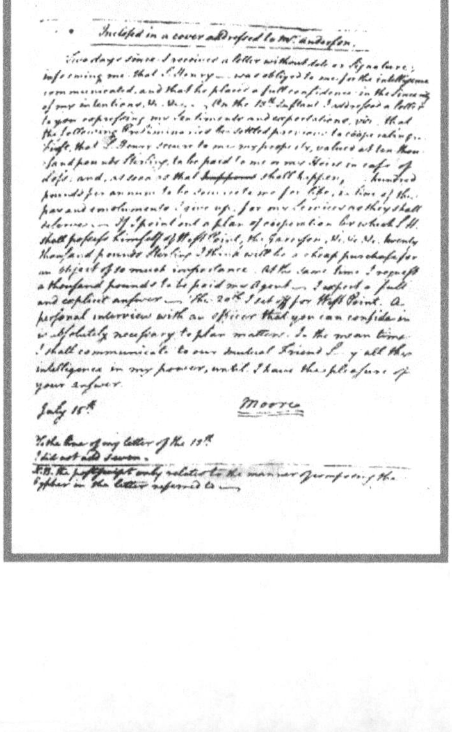

Fig. 38b

plaintext word the code group represents. Arnold added 7 to these numbers, which accounts for the fact that the first number in a code group is never less than 8, the central number is always either 8 or 9, and the third number is never less than 8 or more than 36. The significant sentence appears near the middle of the message: "If I 198-9-34, 185-8-31 a 197-8-8..." yields the plain text: lf I point out a plan of cooperation by which S.H. (Sir Henry Clinton) shall possess himself of West Point, the Garrison, etc., etc., etc., twenty thousands pound Sterling I think will be a cheap purchase for an object of so much importance." The signature 172-9-19 probably stands for the word "Moor"; Arnold's code name in these communications was "John Moore." He had also another name, "Gustavus."

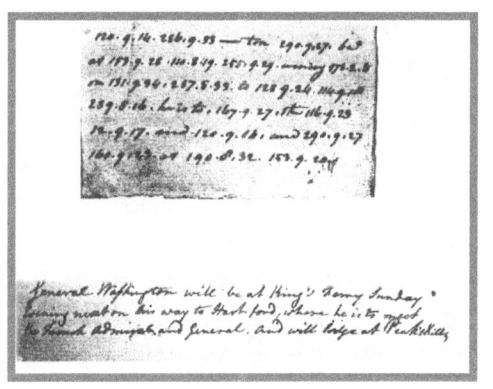

Fig. 39

Figure 39 is a message in which he gave the British information that might have led to the capture of his commander in chief, General Washington; the top shows the code message, the bottom the plain text. Arnold used the same additive as in the preceding example. Washington, however, was too smart to be ambushed – he went by a route other than the one he said he'd take.

You may find figure 40 interesting as an example of the special sort of mask or grille used by Fig. 39 Arnold and by the British in their negotiations with him. The real or significant text is written in lines outlined by an hourglass figure, and then dummy words are supplied to fill up the lines so that the entire letter apparently makes good sense. To read the secret message, you're supposed to have the same size hourglass figure that was used to conceal the secret message. In figure 40 the left-hand portion shows the "phony" message. Masks having small rectangular apertures were also used, the significant words being written so that they were disclosed when the mask was placed on the written message so as to isolate them from the non-significant words. The significant text in this example is shown in printed form to the right of the original hourglass design.

An interesting episode involving concealment of this sort is recorded by Bakeless. An urgent message from Sir Henry Clinton, dated 8 October 1777, and written on thin silk, was concealed in an oval silver ball, about the size of a rifle bullet, which was handed to Daniel Taylor, a young officer who had been promised promotion if he got through alive. The bullet was made of silver, so that the spy could swallow it without injury from corrosion. . . . Almost as soon as he started, Taylor was captured. . .. Realizing his peril too late, the spy fell into a paroxysm of terror and crying, "I am lost," swallowed the silver bullet. Administration of a strong emetic soon produced the bullet with fatal results, for Taylor was executed. "A rather heartless American joke went around," adds Bakeless, "that Taylor had been condemned 'out of his own mouth'."

We next see (fig. 41) one Benedict Arnold message that was never deciphered. It is often referred to as "Benedict Arnold's Treasonable Cow Letter." Only one example is extant; certain words have purely arbitrary meanings, as prearranged. The letter was written just two weeks before the capture of Major André.

In figure 42, we see a British cipher message of the vintage 1781. It was deciphered before finding the key, always a neat trick when or if you can do it. The key – the title page of the then current British Army List – is shown in figure 43. The numbers in the cipher text obviously refer to line numbers and letter numbers in the line of a key text, the first series of numbers, viz., 22.6.7.39.5.9.17, indicating line number 22, letter numbers 6.7.39.5.9.17 in that

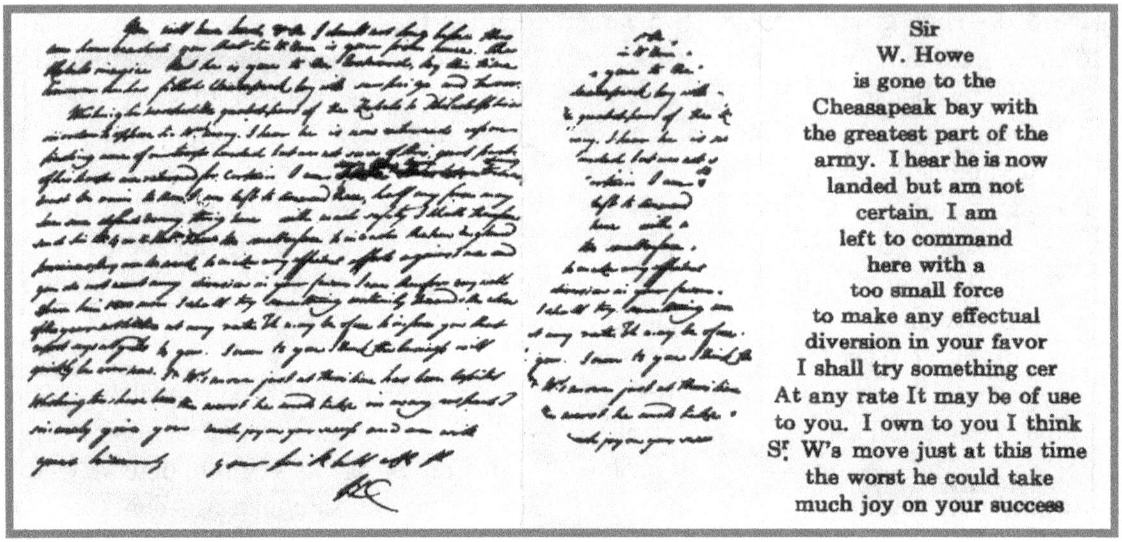

Sir
W. Howe
is gone to the
Cheasapeak bay with
the greatest part of the
army. I hear he is now
landed but am not
certain. I am
left to command
here with a
too small force
to make any effectual
diversion in your favor
I shall try something cer
At any rate It may be of use
to you. I own to you I think
S^r W's move just at this time
the worst he could take
much joy on your success

Fig. 40

Fig. 41

No. 98 -- (1781), Sep. 13

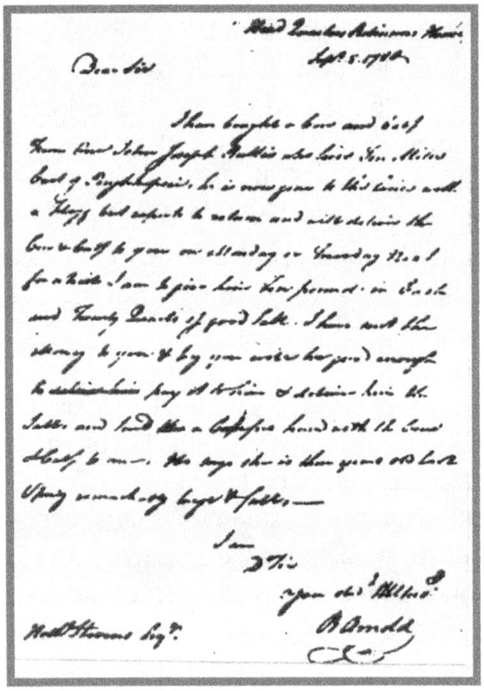

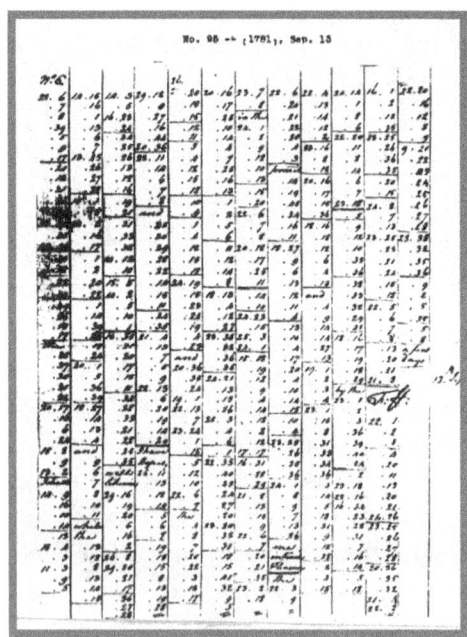

Fig. 42

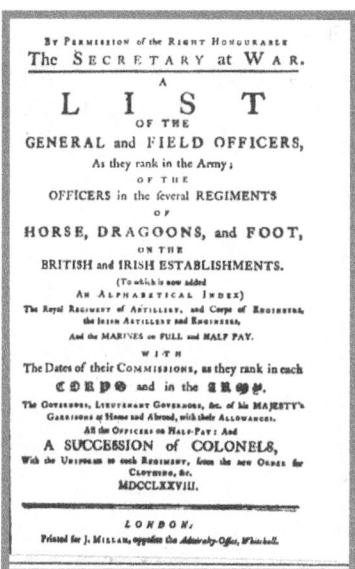

Fig. 43

line. Because of so many repetitions, the plain text was obtained by straightforward analysis by an officer recently on duty in NSA, Captain Edward W. Knepper, USN, to whom I am indebted for this interesting example. The plain text, once obtained, gave him clues as to what the key text might be, simply by placing the plaintext letters in their numerical-equivalent order in the putative key text. This done, Captain Knepper was quick to realize what the key text was – a British Army List. The date of the message enabled him to find the list without much difficulty in the Library of Congress (fig. 43).

There was an American who seems to have been the Revolution's one-man National Security Agency, for he was the one and only cryptologic expert Congress had, and, it is claimed, he managed to decipher nearly all, if not all, of the British code messages obtained in one way or another by the Americans. Of course, the chief way in which enemy messages could be obtained in those days was to capture couriers, knock them out or knock them off, and take the messages from them. This was very rough stuff, compared to getting the material by radio intercept, as we do nowadays.

I think you'll be interested to hear a bit more about that one-man NSA. His name was James Lovell, and besides being a self-trained cryptologist, he was also a member of the Continental Congress. There's on record a very interesting letter he wrote to General Nathaniel Greene, with a copy to General Washington. Here it is.

Philadelphia, Sept. 21, 1781

Sir:
You once sent some papers to Congress which no one about you could decypher. Should such be the Case with some you have lately forwarded I presume that the Result of my pains, here sent, will be useful to you. I took the Papers out of Congress, and I do not think it necessary to let it be known here what my success has been in the attempt. For it appears to me that the Enemy make only such Changes in their Cypher, when they meet with misfortune, as makes a difference of Position only to the same Alphabet, and therefore if no talk of Discovery is made by us here or by your Family, you may be in Chance to draw Benefit this Campaign from my last Night's Watching.
I am Sir with much respect,

Your Friend,
JAMES LOVELL

Maj. Genl. Greene
(With copy to Genl. Washington)

In telling you about Lovell, I should add to my account of that interesting era in cryptologic history an episode I learned about only recently. When a certain message of one of the generals in command of a rather large force of colonials came into Clinton's possession, he sent it off posthaste to London for solution. Of course, Clinton knew it was going to take a lot of time for the message to get to London, be solved and returned to America – and he was naturally a bit impatient. He felt he couldn't afford to wait that long. Now it happened that in his command were a couple of officers who fancied themselves to be cryptologists, and they undertook to solve the message, a copy of which had been made before sending the original off to London. Well, they gave Sir Henry their solution, and he acted upon it. The operation turned out to be a dismal failure, because the solution of the would-be cryptanalysts happened to be quite wrong! The record doesn't say what Clinton did to those two unfortunate cryptologists when the correct solution arrived from London some weeks later. By the way, you may be interested in learning that the British operated a regularly established cryptanalytic bureau as early as 1630, and it continued to operate until the end of July 1844. Then there was no such establishment until World War I. I wish there were time to tell you some of the details of that fascinating and little known bit of British history.

There's also an episode I learned about only very recently, which is so amusing I ought to share it with you. It seems that a certain British secret agent in America was sent a message in plain English, giving him instructions from his superior. But the poor fellow was illiterate, and there wasn't anything to do but call upon the good offices of a friend to read it to him. He found such a friend, who helped him read his instructions. What he didn't know, however, was that the friend who'd helped him was one of General Washington's secret agents!

The next illustration (fig. 44) is a picture of one of several syllabaries used by Thomas Jefferson. It is constructed on the so-called two-part principle, which was explained in the preceding lecture. Figure 44a is a portion of the encoding section, and figure 44b is a portion of the decoding section, in which the code equivalents are in numerical order accompanied by their meanings as assigned them in the encoding section. This sort of system, which, as I've already explained, was quite popular in colonial times as in the early days of Italian cryptography, is still in extensive use in some parts of the world.

A few minutes ago I mentioned Benjamin Franklin's cipher system, which, if used today, would be difficult to solve, especially if there were only a small amount of traffic in it. Let me show you what it was. Franklin took a rather lengthy passage from some book in French and numbered the let-

Fig. 44a

Fig. 44b

ters successively. These numbers then became equivalents for the same letters in a message to be sent. Because the key passage was in good French, naturally there were many variants for the letter E – in fact, there were as many as one would expect in normal plaintext French; the same applied to the other high-frequency letters such as R, N, S, I, etc. What this means, of course, is that the high-frequency letters in the plain text of any message to be enciphered could be represented by many different numbers, and a solution on the basis of frequency and repetitions would be very much hampered by the presence of many variant values for the same plaintext letter. In figure 45 you can see this very clearly.

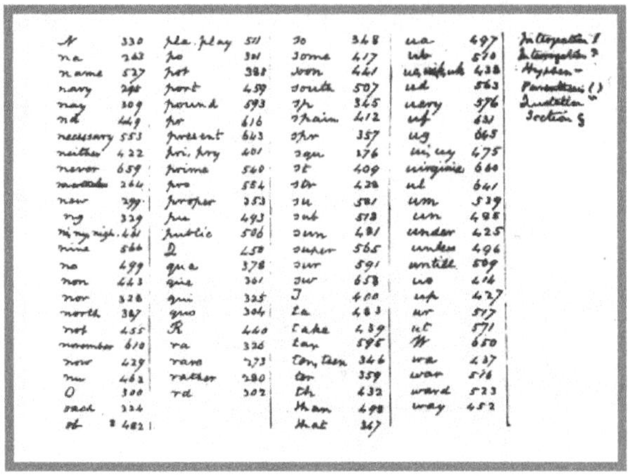

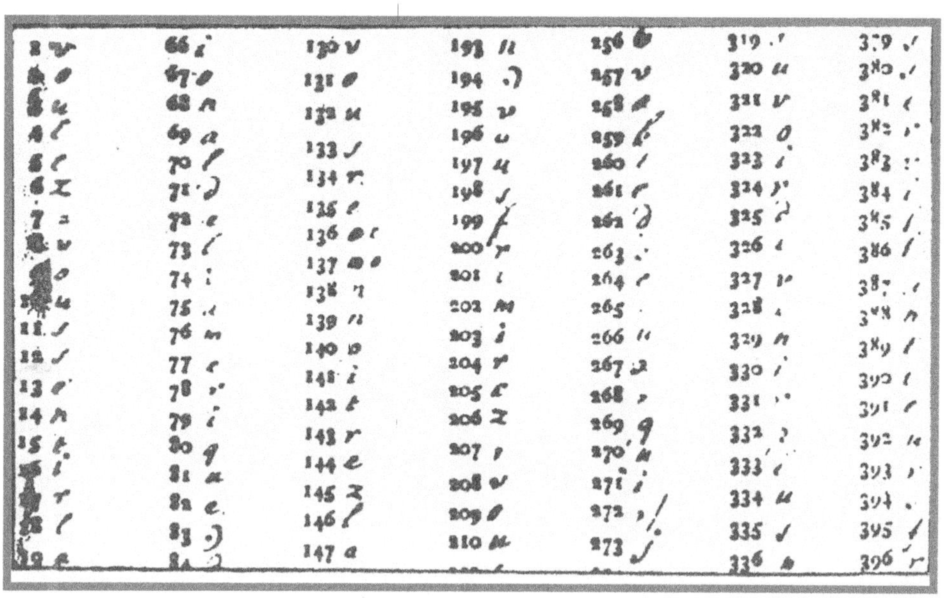

Fig. 45

I know of but one case in all U.S. history in which a resolution of Congress was put out in cryptographic form. It is shown in figure 46 – a resolution of the Revolutionary Congress dated 8 February 1782. I have in my collection not only a copy of the resolution but also a copy of the syllabary by which it can be deciphered.

Interest in cryptology in America seems to have died with the passing of Jefferson and Franklin. But if interest in cryptology in America wasn't very great, if it existed at all after the Revolution, this was not the case in Europe. Books on the subject were written, not by professionals, perhaps, but by learned amateurs, and I think you will find some of them in the NSA library if you're interested in the history of the science. The next illustration (fig. 47) is the frontispiece of a French book the title of which (translated) is *Counter-espionage, or keys for all secret communications*. It was published in Paris in 1793. In the picture, we see Dr. Cryppy himself, and perhaps a breadboard model of a GS-11 research analyst, or maybe an early model of a WAC.

I am now going to tell you something about the early steps in finding an answer to the age-old mystery presented by Egyptian hieroglyphics, not only because I think that the solution represents the next landmark in the history of cryptology, but also because the story is of general interest to any aspiring cryptologist. About 1821 a Frenchman, Champollion, startled the world by beginning to publish translations of Egyptian hieroglyphics, although in the budding new field of Egyptology much had already transpired and been published. In figure 48 we see the gentleman and in figure 49, a picture of the great Napoleonic find that certainly facilitated and perhaps made possible the solution of the Egyptian hieroglyphic writing – the Rosetta Stone. A The Rosetta Stone was found in 1799 at Rashid, or as the Europeans called it, Rosetta, a town in northern Egypt on the west bank of the Rosetta branch of the Nile.

Rosetta was in the vicinity of Napoleon's operations that ended in disaster. When the peace treaty was written, Article 16 of it required that the Rosetta Stone, the significance of which was quickly understood by both the conquered French and victorious British commanders, be shipped to London, together with certain other large antiquities. The Rosetta Stone still occupies a prominent place in the important exhibits at the British Museum. The Rosetta Stone is a bilingual inscription, because it is in Egyptian and also in Greek.

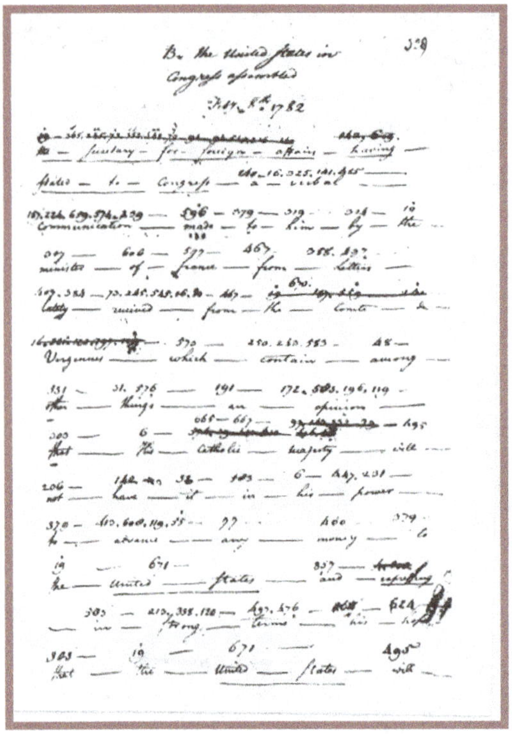

Fig. 46

Fig. 47

The Egyptian portion consists of two parts, the upper one in hieroglyphic form, the lower one in a sort of cursive script, also Egyptian, but called "Demotic." It was soon realized that all three texts were supposed to say the same thing, of course, and since the Greek could easily be read, it served as something called in cryptanalysis a "crib." Any time

you are lucky enough to find a crib, it saves you hours of work. It was by means of this bilingual inscription that the Egyptian hieroglyphic writing was finally solved, a feat that represented the successful solution to a problem the major part of

Fig. 48

which was linguistic in character. The cryptanalytic part of the task was relatively simple. Nevertheless, I think that anyone who aspires to become a professional cryptologist should have some idea as to what that cryptanalytic feat was, a feat that some professor (but not of cryptologic service; I think it was Professor Norbert Wiener of the Massachusetts Institute of Technology) said was the greatest cryptanalytic feat in history. We shall see how wrong the good professor was, because I'm going to demonstrate just what the feat really amounted to by showing you some simple pictures.

First, let me remind you that the Greek text served as an excellent crib for the solution of both Egyptian texts, the hieroglyphic and the Demotic, the latter merely being the conventional abbreviated and modified form of the Hieratic character or cursive form of hieroglyphic writing that was in use in the Ptolemaic Period.

The initial step was taken by a Reverend Stephen Weston, who made a translation of the Greek inscription, which he read in a paper delivered before the London Society of Antiquaries in April 1802.

In 1818 Dr. Thomas Young, the physicist who first proposed the wave theory of light, compiled for the fourth volume of *Encyclopaedia Britannica*, published in 1819, the results of his studies on the Rosetta Stone; among them was a list of several

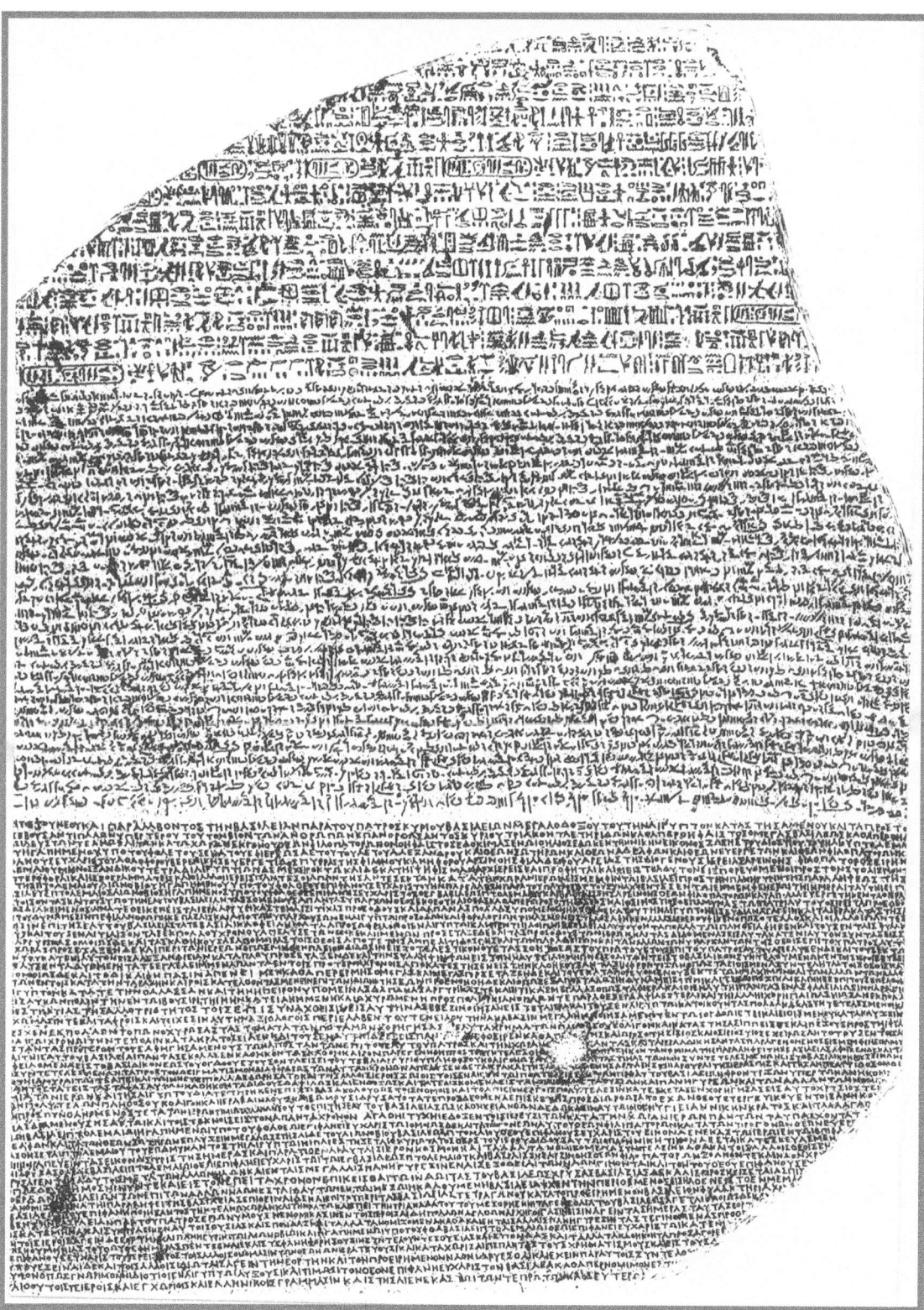

Fig. 49

Egyptian characters to which, in most cases, he had assigned correct phonetic values. *He was the first to grasp the idea of a phonetic principle in the Egyptian hieroglyphs, and he was the first to apply it to their decipherment.* He also proved something that others had only suspected, namely, that the hieroglyphs in ovals or cartouches were royal names. But Young's name is not associated in the public mind with the decipherment of Egyptian hieroglyphics – that of Champollion is very much so. Yet much of what Champollion did was based upon Young's work. Perhaps the greatest credit should go to Champollion for recognizing the major importance of an ancient language known as Coptic as a bridge that could lead to the decipherment of the Egyptian hieroglyphics. As a lad of seven, he'd made up his mind that he'd solve the hieroglyphic writing, and in the early years of the nineteenth century he began to study Coptic. In his studies of the Rosetta Stone, his knowledge of Coptic, a language the knowledge of which had never been lost, enabled him to deduce the phonetic value of many syllabic signs and to assign correct readings to many pictorial characters, the meanings of which became known to him from the Greek text on the Stone.

The following step-by-step account of the solution is taken from a little brochure entitled *The Rosetta Stone*, published by the Trustees of the British Museum. It was written in 1922 by E.A. Wallis Budge and was revised in 1950. I quote:

> The method by which the greater part of the Egyptian alphabet was recovered is this: It was assumed correctly that the oval, or 'cartouche' as it is called, always contained a royal name. There is only one cartouche (repeated six times with slight
>
>
>
> modifications) on the Rosetta Stone, and this was assumed to contain the name of Ptolemy, because it was certain from the

Greek text that the inscription concerned a Ptolemy. It was also assumed that if the cartouche did contain the name of Ptolemy, the characters in it would have the sounds of the Greek letters, and that all together they would represent the Greek form of the name of Ptolemy. Now on the obelisk which a certain Mr. Banks had brought from Philae there was also an inscription in two languages, Egyptian and Greek. In the Greek portion of it two royal names are mentioned, that is to say, Ptolemy and Cleopatra, and on the second face of the obelisk there are two cartouches, which occur close together, and are filled with hieroglyphs which, it was assumed, formed the Egyptian equivalents of these names. When these cartouches were compared with the cartouche on the Rosetta Stone it was found that one of them contained hieroglyphic characters that were almost identical with those which filled the cartouche on the Rosetta Stone. Thus there was good reason to believe that the cartouche on the Rosetta Stone contained the name of Ptolemy written in hieroglyphic characters. The forms of the cartouches are as follows:

On the Rosetta Stone:

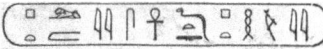

On the Obelisk from Philae:

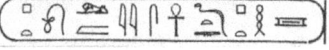

In the second of these cartouches a single sign takes the place of three signs at the end of the first cartouche. Now it has already been said that the name of Cleopatra was found in Greek on the Philae Obelisk, and the cartouche that was assumed to contain the Egyptian equivalent to this name appears in this form:

Taking the cartouches which were supposed to contain the names of Ptolemy and Cleopatra from the Philae Obelisk, and numbering the signs we have:

Ptolemy, A.

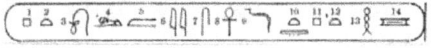

Cleopatra, B.

Now we see at a glance that No.1 in A and No.5 in B are identical, and judging only by their position in the names, they must represent the letter P. No.4 in A and No.2 in B are identical, and arguing as before from their position, they must represent the letter L. As L is the second letter in the name of Cleopatra, sign No.1 in B must represent K. In the cartouche of Cleopatra, we now know the values of Signs Nos. 1,2 and 5, so we may write them down thus:

In the Greek form of the name Cleopatra, there are two vowels between the land P, and in the hieroglyphic form there are two hieroglyphs,

this

and this,

so we may assume that the first is E and the other O. In some forms of the cartouche of Cleopatra, No. 7 (the hand) is replaced by a half circle, which is identical with No.2 in A and No. 10 in B. As T follows P in the name Ptolemy, and as there is a T in the Greek form of the name of Cleopatra, we may assume that the half circle and the hand have substantially the same sound, and that that sound is T. In the Greek form of the name Cleopatra, there are two A's, the position of which agree with No.6 and No.9, and we may assume that the bird has the value of A. Substituting these values for the hieroglyphs in B we may write it thus:

Thomas Young noticed that the two signs

and

always followed the name for a goddess, or queen, or princess. Other early decipherers regarded the two signs as a mere feminine termination. The only sign for which we have no phonetic equivalent is No.8, the lens, and it is obvious that this must represent R. Inserting this value in the cartouche, we have the name Cleopatra deciphered. Applying now the values that we have learned from the cartouche of Cleopatra to the cartouche of Ptolemy we may write it thus:

We now see that the cartouche must be that of Ptolemy, but it is also clear that there must be contained in it many other hieroglyphs which do not form part of his name. Other forms of the cartouche of Ptolemy are found, even on the stone, the simplest of them written thus:

It was therefore evident that these other signs were royal titles corresponding to those found in the Greek text on the Rosetta Stone meaning 'ever-living, beloved of Ptah.' Now the Greek form of the name Ptolemy, i.e., Ptolemaios, ends with S. We may assume therefore that the last sign in the simplest form of the cartouche given above has the phonetic value of S. The only hieroglyphs now doubtful are

and

and their position in the name of Ptolemy suggests that their phonetic values must be M and some vowel sound in which the I sound predominates. These values, which were arrived at by guessing and deduction, were applied by the early decipherers to other cartouches, e.g.:

Now in No.1, we can at once write down the values of all the signs, viz., P. I. L. A. T. R. A., which is obviously the Greek name Philotera. In No.2 we know only some of the hieroglyphs, and we write the cartouche thus:

It was known that the running water sign occurs in the name Berenice, and that it represents N, and that this sign is the last word of the transcript of the Greek title "Kaisaros," and therefore represent some S sound. Some of the forms of the cartouche of Cleopatra begin with , and it is clear that its phonetic value must be K. Inserting these values in the cartouche above we have:

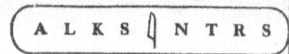

which is clearly meant to represent the name "Alexandros," or Alexander. The position of this sign shows that it represented some sound of E or A.

Well, I've shown you enough to make fairly clear what the problem was and how it was solved. As you may have already gathered, the cryptanalysis was of a very simple variety.

The grammar? Well, that's an entirely different story: there's where the difficult part lay. It was very fortunate that the first attacks on Egyptian hieroglyphics didn't have to deal with enciphered writing. Yes, the Egyptians also used cryptography; yes, there are "cryptographic hieroglyphics"! We'll get to these later, but at this point it may be of interest to many of you to learn something about what the Rosetta Stone had to say, as set forth by Dr. Budge:

> The opening lines are filled with a list of the titles of Ptolemy V, and a series of epithets which proclaim the king's piety towards the gods, and his love for the Egyptians and his country. In the second section of the inscription the priests enumerate the benefits which he had conferred upon Egypt and which may thus be summarized:
>
> 1. Gifts of money and corn to the temples.
> 2. Gifts of endowments to temples.
> 3. Remission of taxes due to the Crown.
> 4. Forgiveness of debts owed by the people to the Crown.
> ___
> 7. Reduction of fees payable by candidates for the priesthood.
> 8. Reduction of the dues payable by the temples to the Crown.
> ___
> 13. Forgiveness of the debts owed by the priests to the Crown.

Fig. 50a

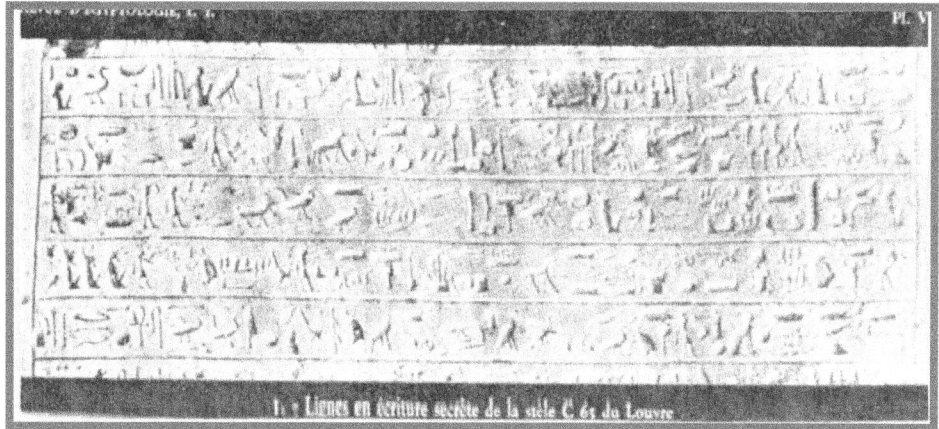

Fig. 50b

14. Reduction of the tax on byssus (a kind of flax or cotton fibre).
15. Reduction of the tax on corn lands.

Could it be that installment-plan buying was rampant in ancient Egypt too, so that people didn't have enough left to pay their taxes?

Now, let's go back to those cryptographic hieroglyphics mentioned a moment ago. Here, in figure 50a, for instance, is a picture of an inscription on a stela now in the Louvre, in Paris. Lines 6-10, inclusive, below the seated figures under the arch, contain secret writing in hieroglyphics; in figure 50b, these lines are seen enlarged. I won't attempt to explain the nature of the cryptography involved. It's pretty simple – something like the sort of cryptography involved in our own type of rebuses, and in our modern acronymic abbreviations, such as CARE (Cooperative for American Relief Everywhere) or NASA (National Aeronautics and Space Administration).

The following extracts, translated from a long article by Professor Étienne Drioton in "Revue D'Égyptologie," Paris, 1933, will be of interest (p. 1):

> From the time of the Middle Empire onwards, Egypt had, alongside the official and normal system of writing, a tradition of cryptographic writing, the oldest known examples of which are to be found in the tombs of Beni-Hassan, and the most recent in the inscriptions of the temples of the Greco-Roman epoch.
>
> * * * * * * *
>
> (p.32):
> It is necessary to add to the enumeration of the cryptographic procedures the variation in the appearance of the cryptographic signs themselves. . . . This variation, without however affecting their value, can (1) modify the appearance of the signs; (2) affect their position in various ways; and (3) combine these signs with others. . . . Finally. to note a last peculiarity of these inscriptions which, because of their fine form, deserve to be considered the classics of the cryptography of this period, the scribe has several times successfully carried out in them what was doubtless considered to be the triumph of the genre: the grouping of signs which offer a possible but fallacious meaning in clear, alongside a cryptographic meaning which is the only true one.

And now for the most intriguing explanation offered by Drioton as to why cryptography was incorporated in these inscriptions. You know quite well why cryptography is employed in military, diplomatic, banking, and industrial affairs; you also know perhaps that it is used for other purposes, in love affairs, for example, and in illicit enterprises of all sorts; and you probably also know that it is often used for purposes of amusement and diversion, in tales of mystery, in the sorts of things published in newspapers and literary journals – they are called "crypts." But none of these explanations will do for the employment of cryptography in Egyptian hieroglyphics. Here's what Drioton thinks:

> (p.50):
> There remains, therefore, the supposition that, far from seeking to prevent reading, the cryptography in certain passages of these inscriptions was intended to encourage their reading.
>
> The appeals which often introduce formulae of this type, and which are addressed to all visitors to the tombs, show in fact how much the Egyptians desired to have them read, but also, by the very fact of their existence, what an obstacle they encountered in the indifference, not to say satiety, produced by the repetition and the monotony of these formulae. To attempt to overcome this indifference by offering a text whose appearance would pique curiosity, based on the love, traditional in Egypt, for puzzles, to get people to decipher, with great

difficulty, what was desired they should read, such is perhaps, in last analysis, the reason why the three monuments of the period of Amenophis III here considered present certain passages in cryptography.

One must suppose, in this case, that the goal was not attained and that it was very quickly seen that the expedient produced, on the apathy of the visitors, an effect opposite to that intended: it removed even the slightest desire to read the inscriptions presented in this form. The new procedure was therefore – the monuments seem to prove it – abandoned as soon as it had been tried.

* * * * * *

Before leaving the story of Champollion's mastery of Egyptian hieroglyphic writing, I think I should reenact for you as best I can in words what he did when he felt he'd really reached the solution to the mystery. I'll preface it by recalling to you what Archimedes is alleged to have done when he solved a problem he'd been struggling with for some time. Archimedes was enjoying the pleasures of his bath and was just stepping out of the pool when the solution of the problem came to him like a flash. He was so overjoyed that he ran, naked, through the streets shouting, "Eureka! I've found it, I've found it." Well, likewise, when young Champollion one day had concluded he'd solved the mystery of the Egyptian hieroglyphics, he set out on a quick mile-run to the building where his lawyer brother worked, stumbled into his brother's office, shouting "Eugene, I did it!" and flopped down to the floor in a trance where he is said to have remained immobile and completely out for five days. "Champollion died on 4 March 1832, leaving behind the manuscript of an *Egyptian Grammar and of a Hieroglyphic Dictionary*, which, except for some errors of details inevitable in a gigantic work of decipherment and easily correctable, form the basis of the entire science of Egyptology."[1]

I shouldn't leave this brief story of the cryptanalytic phases of the solution of the Egyptian hieroglyphic writing without telling you that there remain plenty of other sorts of writings that some of you may want to try your hand at deciphering when you've learned some of the principles and procedures of the science of cryptology. A list of nineteen thus-far undeciphered writings was drawn up for me by Professor Alan C. Ross, of London University, in 1945. Since 1945 only two have been deciphered, Minoan Linear A and Linear B writing. The Easter Island writing is said to have very recently been solved, but I'm not sure of that. There are some, maybe just a very few, who think the hieroglyphic writing of the ancient Maya Indians of Central America may fall soon, but don't be too sanguine about that either.

Should any of you be persuaded to tackle any of the still undeciphered writings in the list drawn up by Professor Ross, be sure you have an authentic case of an undeciphered language before you. Figure 51 is one that was written on a parchment known as the Michigan Papyrus. It had baffled certain savants who had a knowledge of Egyptology and attempted to read it on the theory that it was some sort of variation – a much later modification – of Egyptian hieroglyphic writing. These old chaps gave it up as a bad job. Not too many years ago, it came to the attention of a young man who knew very little about Egyptian hieroglyphics. He saw it only as a simple substitution cipher on some old language. He tackled the Michigan Papyrus on that basis and solved it. He found the language to be early Greek. And what was the purport of the writing? Well, it was a wonderful old Greek beautician's secret formula for further beautifying lovely Greek young women – maybe the bathing beauties of those days, among whom possibly were "Miss Greece of 500 B.C." and "Miss Universe" of those days!

Fig. 51

The next period of importance in this brief account of the history of cryptology is the one that deals with the codes and ciphers used by the contestants in our Civil War, the period 1861-65. It is significant and important because for the first time in history, rapid and secure communications on a large scale became practicable in the conduct of organized warfare and worldwide diplomacy. They became practicable when cryptology and telegraphy were joined in happy, sometimes contentious, but long-lasting wedlock. There is one person I should mention, however, before coming to the Civil War. I refer here to Edgar Allan Poe, who in 1842 or thereabouts kindled an interest in cryptography in newspapers and journals of the period, both at home and abroad. For his day he was certainly the best informed person in this country on cryptologic matters outside of the regular employees of government departments interested in the subject.

In regard to Poe, one of our early columnists, there's an incident I'd like to tell you about in connection with a challenge he printed in one of his columns, in which he offered to solve any cipher submitted by his readers. He placed some limitations on his challenge, which amounted to this – that the challenge messages should involve but a single alphabet. In a later article Poe tells about the numerous challenge messages sent him and says: "Out of perhaps 100 ciphers altogether received, there was only one which we did not immediately succeed in resolving. This one we demonstrated to be an imposition – that is to say, we fully proved it a jargon of random characters, having no meaning whatever." I wish that cipher had been preserved for posterity because it would be interesting to see what there was about it that warranted Poe to say that "we fully proved it a jargon of random characters." Maybe I'm not warranted in saying of this episode that Poe reminds me of a ditty sung by a character in a play put on by some undergraduates of one of the colleges of Cambridge University in England. At a certain point in the play, the character steps to the front of the stage and sings

I am the Master of the College,
What I don't know ain't knowledge.

Thus, Poe. What he couldn't solve, he assumed wasn't a real cipher – a very easy out for any cryptologist up against something tough.

If any of you are interested sufficiently to wish to learn something about Poe's contributions to cryptology, I refer you to a very fine article by Professor W.K. Wimsatt, Jr., entitled "What Poe Knew About Cryptography," *Publications of the Modern Language Association of America*, New York, Vol. LVIII, No.3, September 1943, 754-79. In it you'll find references to what I have published on the same subject.

This completes the third lecture in this series. In the next one we shall come to that interesting period in cryptologic history in which codes and ciphers were used in this country in the War of the Rebellion, the War Between the States, the Civil War – you use your own pet designation for that terrible and costly struggle.

NOTES

1. Drioton, "Decipherment of Egyptian Hieroglyphics," *La Science Moderne*, August 1924, 423-32.

Lecture IV

A detailed account of the codes and ciphers of the Civil War of the United States of America can hardly be told without beginning with a bit of biography about the man who became the first signal officer in history and the first Chief Signal Officer of the United States Army, Albert J. Myer, the man in whose memory that lovely little U.S. Army post adjacent to Arlington Cemetery was named. Myer was born on 20 September 1827, and after an

Fig. 52. Brigadier General Albert J. Myer

apprenticeship in the then quite new science of electric telegraphy he entered Hobart College, Geneva, New York, from which he was graduated in 1847. From early youth he had exhibited a predilection for artistic and scientific studies, and upon leaving Hobart he entered Buffalo Medical College, receiving the M.D. degree four years later. His graduation thesis, "A Sign Language for Deaf Mutes," contained the germ of the idea he was to develop several years later, when in 1854 he was commissioned a first lieutenant in the regular army, made an assistant surgeon, and ordered to New Mexico for duty. He had plenty of time at this faraway outpost to think about developing an efficient system of military "aerial telegraphy," which was what visual signaling was then called. I emphasize the word "system" because, strange to say, although instances of the use of lights and other visual signals can be found throughout the history of warfare, and their use between ships at sea had been practiced by mariners for centuries, down to the middle of the nineteenth century surprisingly little progress had been made in developing methods and instruments for the systematic exchange of military information and instructions by means of signals of any kind. Morse's practical system of electric telegraphy, developed in the years 1832-35, served to focus attention within the military upon systems and methods of intercommunication by means of both visual and electrical signals. In the years immediately preceding the Civil War, the U.S. Army took steps to introduce and to develop a system of visual signaling for general use in the field. It was Assistant Surgeon Myer who furnished the initiative in this matter.

In 1856, two years after he was commissioned assistant surgeon, Myer drafted a memorandum on a new system of visual signaling and obtained a patent on it. Two years later, a board was appointed by the War Department to study Myer's system. It is interesting to note that one of the officers who served as an assistant to Myer in demonstrating his system before the board was a Lieutenant E.P. Alexander, Corps of Engineers. We shall hear more about him presently, but at the moment I will say that on the outbreak of war, Alexander organized the Confederate Signal Corps. After some successful demonstrations by Myer and his assistants, the War Department fostered a bill in Congress, which gave its approval to his ideas. But what is more to the point, Congress appropriated an initial amount of $2,000 to enable the Army and the War Department to develop the system. The money, as stated in the act, was to be used "for manufacture or purchase of apparatus and equipment for field signaling." The act also contained another provision: it authorized the appointment on the Army staff of one signal officer with the rank, pay, and allowances of a major of cavalry. On 2 July 1860, "Assistant Surgeon Albert J. Myer (was appointed) to be Signal Officer, with the rank of Major, 27 June 1860, to fill an original vacancy," and two weeks later Major Myer was ordered to report to the commanding general of the Department of New Mexico for signaling duty. The War Department also directed that two officers be detailed as his assistants. During a several months' campaign against hostile Navajos, an extensive test of Myer's new system, using both flags and torches, was conducted with much success. In October 1860, a Lieutenant J.E.B. Stuart, later to become famous as a Confederate cavalry leader, tendered his services to aid in signal instruction.

Less than a year after Major Myer was appointed as the first and, at that time, the only signal officer of the U.S. Army, Fort Sumter was attacked, and after a thirty-six-hour bombardment, it surrendered. The bloody four-year war between the North and the South had begun. The date was 14 April 1861. Myer's system of aerial telegraphy was soon to undergo its real baptism under fire, rather than by fire. But with the outbreak of war, another new system of military signal communication, signaling by the electric telegraph, began to undergo its first thorough test in combat operations. This in itself is very important in the history of cryptology. But far more significant in that history is a fact I mentioned at the close of the last lecture, *viz*, that for the first time in the conduct of organized warfare, *rapid and secret military communications on a large scale became practicable*, because cryptology and electric telegraphy were now to be joined in lasting wedlock. For when the war began, the electric telegraph had been in use for less than a quarter of a century. Although the first use of electric telegraphy in military operations was in the Crimean War in Europe (1854-56), its employment was restricted to communications exchanged among headquarters of the Allies, and some observers were very doubtful about its utility even for this limited usage. It may also be noted that in the annals of that war there is no record of the employment of electric telegraphy together with means for protecting the messages against their interception and solution by the enemy.

On the Union side in the Civil War, military signal operations began with Major Myer's arrival in Washington on 3 June 1861. His basic equipment consisted of kits containing a white flag with a red square in the center for use against a dark background, a red flag with a white square for use against a light background, and torches for night use. It is interesting to note that these are the elements that make up the familiar insignia of our Army Signal Corps. The most pressing need that faced Major Myer was to get officers and men detailed to him wherever signals might be required, and to train them in what had come to be called the "wig-wag system," the motions of which are depicted in figure 53. This training included learning something about codes and ciphers and gaining experience in their use.

But there was still no such separate entity as a Signal Corps of the Army. Officers and enlisted men were merely detailed for service with Major Myer for signaling duty. It was not until two years after the war started that the Signal Corps was officially established and organized as a separate branch of the Army, by appropriate congressional action.

In the meantime, another signaling organization was coming into being – an organization that was an outgrowth of the government's taking over control of the commercial telegraph companies in the United States on 25 February 1862. There were only three: the American, the Western Union, and the Southwestern. The telegraph lines generally followed the right-of-way of the railroads. The then

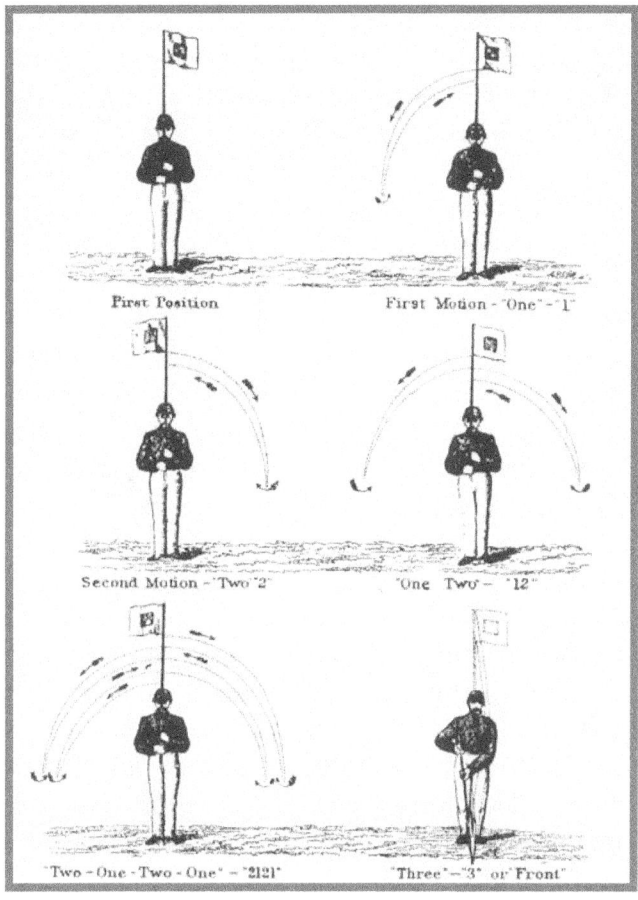

Fig. 53

secretary of war, Simon Cameron, sought the aid of Thomas A. Scott of the Pennsylvania Railroad, who brought some of his men to Washington for railroad and telegraphic duties with the federal government. From a nucleus of four young telegraph operators grew a rather large military telegraph organization that was not given formal status until on 28 October 1861 President Lincoln gave Secretary Cameron authority to set up a "U.S. Military Telegraph Department" under a man named Anson Stager, who, as a general superintendent of the Western Union, was called to Washington, commissioned a captain (later a colonel) in the Quartermaster Corps, and made superintendent of the Military Telegraph Department. Only about a dozen of the members of the department became commissioned officers, and they were made officers so that they could receive and disburse funds and property; all the rest were civilians. The U.S. Military Telegraph "Corps," as it soon came to be designated, without warrant, was technically under Quartermaster General Meigs, but for all practical purposes it was under the immediate and direct control of the secretary of war, a situation admittedly acceptable to Meigs. There were now two organizations for signaling in the Army, and it has hardly to be expected that no difficulties would ensue from the duality. In fact, the difficulties began very soon, as can be noted in the following extract from a lecture before the Washington Civil War Round Table, early in 1954, by Dr. George R. Thompson, Chief of the Historical Division of the Office of the Chief Signal Officer of the U.S. Army:

> The first need for military signals arose at the important Federal fortress in the lower Chesapeake Bay at Fort Monroe. Early in June, Myer arrived there, obtained a detail of officers and men and began schooling them. Soon his pupils were wig-wagging messages from a small boat, directing fire of Union batteries located on an islet in Hampton Roads against Confederate fortifications near Norfolk. Very soon, too, Myer began encountering trouble with commercial wire telegraphers in the area. General Ben Butler, commanding the Federal Department in southeast Virginia, ordered that wire telegraph facilities and their civilian workers be placed under the signal officer. The civilians, proud and jealous of their skills in electrical magic, objected in no uncertain terms and shortly an order arrived from the Secretary of War himself who countermanded Butler's instructions. The Army signal officer was to keep hands off the civilian telegraph even when it served the Army.

I have purposely selected this extract from Dr. Thompson's presentation because in it we can clearly hear the first rumblings of that lengthy and acrimonious feud between two signaling organizations whose uncoordinated operations and rivalry greatly reduced the efficiency of all signaling operations of the Federal army. As already indicated, one of these organizations was the U.S. Military Telegraph "Corps," hereinafter abbreviated as the USMTC, a civilian organization that operated the existing commercial telegraph systems for the War Department, under the direct supervision of the secretary of war, Edwin M. Stanton. The other organization was, of course, the infant Signal Corps of the United States Army, which was not yet even established as a separate branch, whereas the USMTC had been established in October 1861, as noted above. Indeed, the Signal Corps had to wait until March 1863, *two years after the outbreak of war*, before being established officially. In this connection it should be noted that the Confederate Signal Corps had been established a full year earlier, in April 1862. Until then, as I've said before, for signaling duty on both sides, there were only officers who were individually and specifically detailed for such duty from other branches of the respective armies of the North and the South. Trouble between the USMTC and the Signal Corps of the Union army began when the Signal Corps became interested in signaling by electric telegraphy and began to acquire facilities therefor.

As early as June 1861, Chief Signal Officer Myer had initiated action toward acquiring or obtaining electrical telegraph facilities for use in the field, but with one exception nothing happened. The exception was the episode in the military department in southeast Virginia, commanded by General Benjamin Butler, an episode that clearly foreshadowed the future road for the Signal Corps in regard to electrical signaling: the road was to be closed and barred. In August 1861 Colonel Myer tried again, and in November of the same year he recommended in his annual report that $30,000 be appropriated to establish an electric signaling branch in the Signal Corps. The proposal failed to meet the approval of the secretary of war. One telegraph train, however, that had been ordered by Myer many months before, was delivered in January 1862. The train was tried out in an experimental fashion, and under considerable difficulties, the most disheartening of which was the active opposition of persons of Washington, particularly the secretary of war. So, for practically the whole of the first two years of the war, signal officers on the Northern side had neither electrical telegraph facilities nor Morse operators – they had to rely entirely on the wig-wag system. However, by the middle of 1863 there were thirty "flying telegraph" trains in use in the Federal army. Here's a picture (fig. 54) of such a train. The normal length of field telegraph lines was five to eight miles, though in some cases the instruments had worked at distances as great as twenty miles. But even before the Signal Corps began to acquire these facilities, there had been agitation to have them, as well as their Signal Corps operating personnel, all turned over to the USMTC, which had grown into a tightly knit organization of over 1,000 men and had become very influential in Washington, especially by virtue of its support from Secretary of War Stanton. As a consequence, the USMTC had its way. In the fall of 1863, it took over all the electric telegraph facilities and telegraph operators of the Signal Corps. Colonel Myer sadly wrote: "With the loss of its electrical lines the Signal Corps was crippled."

So now there were two competing signal organizations on the Northern side: the U.S. Army's Signal Corps, which was composed entirely of military personnel with no electric telegraph facilities (but was equipped with means for visual signaling), and the USMTC, which was not a part of the Army, being staffed almost entirely with civilians, and that had electric telegraph facilities and skilled Morse operators (but no means or responsibilities for visual signaling or "aerial telegraphy" that, of course, was old stuff). "Electric telegraphy" was now *the* thing. The USMTC had no desire to share electric telegraphy with the Signal Corps, a determination in which it was most ably assisted by Secretary of War Stanton, for reasons that fall outside the scope of the present lecture.

However, from a technical point of view it is worth going into this rivalry just a bit, if only to note that the personnel of both organizations, the mili-

Fig. 54. A drawing from Myer's Manual of Signals *illustrating the field, or flying, telegraph. It shows the wagon with batteries and instruments. The wire (in this case presumably bare copper, since it is being strung on insulators on poles) is being run out from a reel carried by two men. The linemen are using a crowbar to open holes to receive the lance poles. Myer estimated that 2 ½ miles of such wire line could put up in an hour.*

tary and the civilian, were not merely signalmen and telegraph operators: they served also as cryptographers and were therefore entrusted with the necessary cipher books and cipher keys. Because of this, they naturally became privy to the important secrets conveyed in cryptographic communications, and they therefore enjoyed status as VIPs. This was particularly true of members of the USMTC, because they, and only they, were authorized to be custodians and users of the cipher books. Not even the commanders of the units they served had access to them. For instance, on the one and only occasion when General Grant forced his cipher operator, a civilian named Beckwith, to turn over the current cipher book to a colonel on Grant's staff, Beckwith was immediately discharged by the secretary of war, and Grant was reprimanded. A few days later Grant apologized, and Beckwith was restored to his position. But Grant never again demanded the cipher book held by his telegraph operator.

The Grant-Beckwith affair alone is sufficient to indicate the lengths to which Secretary of War Stanton went to retain control over the USMTC, including its cipher operators and its cipher books. In fact, so strong a position did he take that on 10 November 1863, following a disagreement over who should operate and control all the military telegraph lines, Myer, by then full colonel and bearing the imposing title "Chief Signal Officer of the United States Army," a title he had enjoyed for only two months, was peremptorily relieved from that position and put on the shelf. Not long afterward, and for a similar reason, Myer's successor, Lieutenant Colonel Nicodemus, was likewise summarily relieved as Chief Signal Officer by Secretary Stanton; indeed, he was not only removed from that position – he was "dismissed from the Service." Stanton gave "phony" reasons for dismissing Colonel Nicodemus, but I am glad to say that the latter was restored his commission in March 1865 by direction of the president; also by direction of the president, Colonel Myer was restored to his position as Chief Signal Officer of the U.S. Army on 25 February 1867.

When Colonel Myer was relieved from duty as Chief Signal Officer in November 1863, he was ordered to Cairo, Illinois, to await orders for a new assignment. Very soon thereafter he was either designated (or he may have himself decided) to prepare a field manual on signaling, and there soon appeared, with a prefatory note dated January 1864, a pamphlet of 148 pages, a copy of which is now in the Rare Book Room of the Library of Congress. The title page reads as follows:

A Manual of Signals: for the use of signal officers in the field. By Col. Albert J. Myer, Signal Officer of the Army, Washington, D.C., 1864.

Even in this first edition, printed on an Army press, Myer devoted nine pages to a reprint of an article from *Harper's Weekly* entitled "Curiosities of Cipher," and in the second edition, 1866, he expanded the section on cryptography to sixty pages. More editions followed, and I think we may well say that Myer's *Manual*, in its several editions, was the pioneer American text on military signaling. But I'm sorry to say that as regards cryptology it was rather a poor thing. Poe had done better twenty years before that in his essay entitled "A few words on secret writing."

Because of its historic nature, you may like to see what Myer's original "wig-wag code" was like. It was called a "two element code" because it employed only two digits, 1 and 2, in permutations of 1, 2, 3 and 4 groups. For example, A was represented by the permutation 22; B by 2122; and C, by 121, etc. In flag signaling, a "1" was indicated by a motion to the left, and a "2" by a motion to the right. Later these motions were reversed, for reasons that must have been good then but are now not obvious.[2] Myer's two-element code, which continued to be used until 1912, is shown in the figure below.

We must turn our attention now to the situation as regards the organization for signaling in the Confederate Army. It is of considerable interest to

A –	22	M –	1221	Y –	111
B –	2122	N –	11	Z –	2222
C –	121	O –	21	& –	1111
D –	222	P –	1212	ing –	2212
E –	12	Q –	1211	tion –	1112
F –	2221	R –	211		
G –	2211	S –	212	End of word	-3
H –	122	T –	2	End of sentence	-33
I –	1	U –	112	End of message	-333
J –	1122	V –	1222	Affirmative	-22.22.22.3
K –	2121	W –	1121	Repeat	-121.121.121
L –	221	X –	2122	Error	-212121

Note: No. 3 (end of word) was made by a forward downward motion, called "front." There were about a dozen more signals, for numerals, for frequently used short sentences, etc.

note that in the first great engagement of the war, the first Bull Run battle, the Confederate signal officer was that young lieutenant, E.P. Alexander, who had assisted in demonstrating the wig-wag system before a board appointed by the War Department to study Myer's system. Alexander, now a captain in grey, used Myer's system during the battle, which ended in disaster for the Union forces; it is said that Alexander's contribution by effective signaling was an important factor in the Confederate victory. Dr. Thompson, whom I have quoted before, says of this battle:

> Thus the fortunes of war in this battle saw Myer's system of signals succeed, ironically, on the side hostile to Myer. Because of general unpreparedness and also some disinterest and ignorance, the North has neither wig-wag nor balloon observations.

The only communication system that succeeded in signal work for the Union army was the infant USMTC. But the Confederate system under Alexander, off to a good start at Bull Run, throughout the war operated with both visual and electric telegraphy, and the Confederates thought highly enough of their signal service to establish it on an official basis on 19 April 1862, less than a year after that battle. Thus, although the Confederate Signal Corps never became a distinct and independent branch of the Army as did the Union Signal Corps, it received much earlier recognition from the Confederate government than did the Signal Corps of the federal government. Again quoting Dr. Thompson:

> The Confederate Signal Corps was thus established nearly a year earlier than its Federal counterpart. It was nearly as large, numbering some 1,500, most of the number, however, serving on detail. The Confederate Signal Corps used Myer's system of flags and torches. The men were trained in wire telegraph, too, and impressed wire facilities as needed. But there was nothing in Richmond or in the field comparable to the extensive and tightly controlled civilian military telegraph organization which Secretary Stanton ruled with an iron hand from Washington.

We come now to the codes and ciphers used by both sides in the war, and in doing so we must consider that on the Union side, there were, as I have indicated, two separate organizations for signal communications, one for visual signaling, the other for electric. We should therefore not be too astonished to find that the cryptosystems used by the two competing organizations were different. On the other hand, on the Confederate side, as just noted, there was only one organization for signal communications, the Signal Corps of the Confederate States Army, that used both visual and electric telegraphy, the latter facilities being taken over and employed when and where they were available. There were reasons for this marked difference between the way in which the Union and the Confederate signal operations were organized and administered, but I do not wish to go into them now. One reason, strange to say, had to do with the difference between the cryptocommunication arrangements in the Union and the Confederate armies.

We will discuss the cryptosystems used by both the Federal Signal Corps first and then those of the Confederate Signal Corps. Since both corps used visual signals as their primary means, we find them employing Myer's visual-signaling code shown above. At first both sides sent unenciphered messages; but soon after learning that their signals were being intercepted and read by the enemy, each side decided to do something to protect its messages. Initially both decided on the same artifice, viz, changing the visual signaling equivalents for the letters of the alphabet, so that, for instance, "22" was not always "A," etc. This sort of changing-about of values soon became impractical, since it prevented memorizing the wig-wag equivalents once and for all. The difficulty in the Union army's Signal Corps was solved by the introduction into usage of

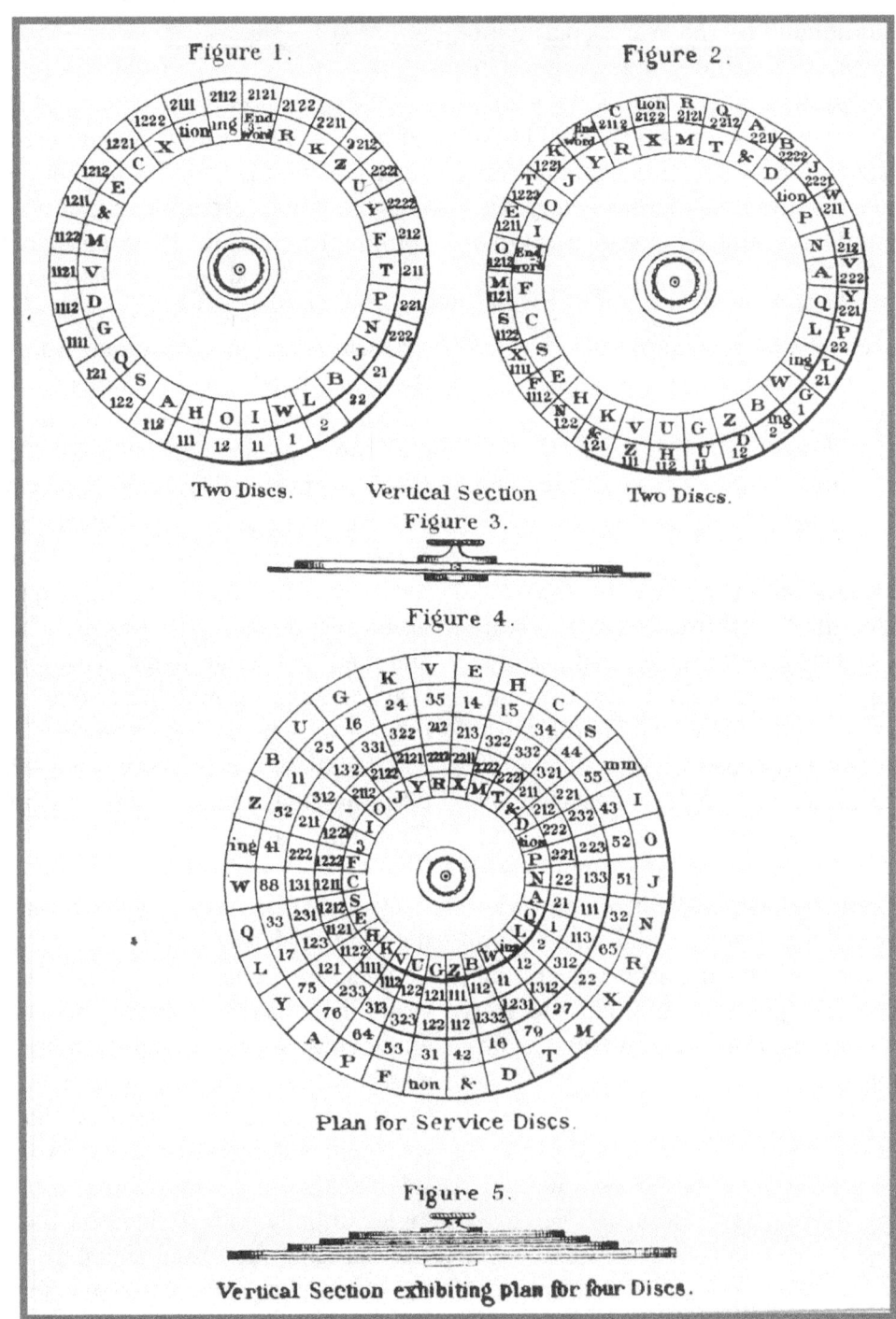

Fig. 55

a cipher disk invented by Myer himself. A full description of the disk in its various embodiments will be found in Myer's *Manual*, but here's a picture of three forms of it. You can see how readily the visual wig-wag equivalents for letters, figures, etc., can be changed according to some prearranged indicator for juxtaposing concentric disks. In my figure 55, the top left disks (fig. 1 of Myer's Plate XXVI) show that the letter A is represented by 112, B by 22, etc. By moving the two circles to a different juxtaposition, a new set of equivalents will be established. Of course, if the setting is kept fixed for a whole message, the encipherment is strictly monoalphabetic; but Myer recommends changing the setting in the middle of the message or, more specifically, at the end of each word, thus producing a sort of polyalphabetic cipher that would delay solution a bit. An alternative way, Myer states, would be to use what he called a "countersign word," but that we call a key word, each letter of which would determine the setting of the disk or for a single word or for two consecutive words, etc. Myer apparently did not realize that retaining or showing externally, that is, in the cipher text, the lengths of the words of the plain text very seriously impairs the security of the cipher message. A bit later we shall discuss the security afforded by the Myer disk in actual practice.

In the Confederate Signal Corps, the system used for encipherment of visual signals was apparently the same as that used for enciphering telegraphic messages, and we shall soon see what it was. Although Myer's cipher disk was captured a number of times, it was apparently disdained by the Confederates, who preferred to use a wholly different type of device, as will be described presently, for both visual and electric telegraphy.

So much for the cryptosystems used in connection with visual signals by the Signal Corps of both the North and the South, systems that we may designate as "tactical ciphers." We come now to the systems used for what we may call "strategic ciphers," because the latter were usually exchanged between the seat of government and field com-

manders, or among the latter. In the case of these communications, the cryptosystems employed by each side were quite different.

On the Northern side, the USMTC used a system based upon what we now call transposition, but in contemporary accounts they were called "route ciphers," and that name has stuck. The designation isn't too bad, because the processes of encipherment and decipherment, though dealing not with the individual letters of the message but with entire words, involves following the prescribed routes in a diagram in which the message is written. I know no simpler or more succinct description of the route cipher than that given by one of the USMTC operators, J.E. O'Brien, in an article in *Century Magazine*, XXXVIII, September 1889, entitled "Telegraphing in Battle":

> The principle of the cipher consisted in writing a message with an equal number of words in each line, then copying the words up and down the columns by various routes, throwing in an extra word at the end of each column, and substituting other words for important names and verbs.

A more detailed description in modern technical terms would be as follows: a system in which in encipherment the words of the plaintext message are inscribed within a matrix of a specified number of tows and columns, inscribing the words within the matrix from left. to right, in successive lines and rows downward as in ordinary writing, and taking the words out of the matrix, that is, transcribing them, according to a prearranged route to form the cipher message. The specific routes to be followed were set forth in numbered booklets, each being labeled "War Department Cipher" followed by a number. In referring to them hereinafter, I shall use the terms "cipher books" or, sometimes more simply, the term "ciphers," although the cryptosystem involves both cipher and code processes. It is true that the basic principle of the system, that of transposition, makes the system technically a cipher system as defined in our modern terminology; but the use of "arbitraries," as they were called, that is, words arbitrarily assigned to represent the names of persons, geographic points, important nouns, and verbs, etc., makes the system technically a code system as defined in our modern terminology.

There were in all about a dozen cipher books used by the USMTC throughout the war. For the most part they were employed consecutively, but it seems that sometimes two different ones were employed concurrently. They contained not only the specific routes to be used but also indicators for the routes and for the sizes of the matrices; and, of course, there were lists of code words, with their meanings. These route ciphers were supposed to have been the invention of Anson Stager, whom I have mentioned before in connection with the establishment of the USMTC, and who is said to have first devised such ciphers for General McClellan's use in West Virginia in the summer of 1861, before McClellan came to Washington to assume command of the Army of the Potomac.

Anson Stager and many others thought that he was the original inventor of the system, but such a belief was quite in error because word-transposition methods similar to Stager's were in use hundreds of years before his time. For instance, in 1685, in an unsuccessful attempt to invade Scotland, in a conspiracy to set the Duke of Monmouth on the throne, Archibald Campbell, 9th Earl of Argyll, suffered an unfortunate "accident": he was taken prisoner and beheaded by order of James the Second. The communications of the poor Earl were not secure, and when they fell into government hands they were soon deciphered. The method Argyll used was that of word transposition, and if you are interested in reading a contemporary account of how it was solved, look on pages 56-59 of that little book I mentioned before as being one of the very first books in English dealing with the subject of cryptology, that by James Falconer, entitled *Cryptomenysis Patefacta: Or the Art of Secret Information Disclosed Without a Key*, published in London in 1685. There you will find the progenitor of the route ciphers employed by the USMTC, 180 years after Argyll's abortive rebellion.

The route ciphers employed by the USMTC are fully described in a book entitled *The Military Telegraph during the Civil War*, by Colonel William R. Plum, published in Chicago in 1882. I think Plum's description of them is of considerable interest, and I recommend his book to those of you who may wish to learn more about them, but they are pretty much all alike. If I show you one example of an actual message and explain its encipherment and decipherment, I will have covered practically the entire gamut of the route ciphers used by the USMTC, so basically very simple and uniform were they. And yet, believe it or not, legend has it that the Southern signalmen were unable to solve any of the messages transmitted by the USMTC. This long-held legend I find hard to believe. In all the descriptions I have encountered in the literature, not one of them, save the one quoted above from O'Brien, tries to make these ciphers as simple as they really were; somehow, it seems to me, a subconscious realization on the part of Northern writers, usually ex-USMTC operators, of the system's simplicity prevented a presentation that would clearly show how utterly devoid it was of the degree of sophistication one would be warranted in expecting in the secret communications of a great modern army in the decade 1860-1870, three hundred years after the birth of modern cryptography in the papal states of Italy.

Let us take the plain text of a message that Plum (p. 58) used in an example of the procedure in encipherment. The cipher book involved is No.4, and I happen to have a copy of it so we can easily check Plum's work. Here's the message to be enciphered:

                        Washington, D.C.
                          July 15, 1863

For Simon Cameron

I would give much to be relieved of the impression that Meade, Couch, Smith and all, since the battle of Gettysburg, have striven only to get the enemy over the river without another fight. Please tell me if you know who was the one corps commander who was for fighting, in the council of war on Sunday night.

(Signed) A. Lincoln

Plum shows the word-for-word encipherment in a matrix of seven columns and eleven rows.[3] He fails to tell us why a matrix of those dimensions was selected; presumably the selection was made at random, which was certainly permissible. (See fig. 56.)

Note the seven "nulls" (nonsignificant, or "blind" words) at the tops and bottoms of certain columns, these being added to the cipher text in order to confuse a would-be decipherer. At least that was the theory, but how effective this subterfuge was can be surmised, once it became known that employing nulls was the usual practice. Note also the two nulls (*bless* and *him*) at the end of the last line to complete that line of the matrix. Words in italics are "arbitraries" or code words.

The cipher message is then copied down following the route prescribed by the indicator "BLONDE," as given on page 7 of Cipher Book No.4 for a message of eleven lines. The indicator could have also been "LINIMENT ."

To explain the diagram at the top of figure 57, I will show you the "Directions for Use" that appear on the reverse side of the title page of "War Department Cipher No.4," because I'm afraid you wouldn't believe me if I merely told you what they

1	2	3	4	5	6	7
(heavy)				(county)	(square)	
(null)				(null)	(null)	
Incubus	*Stewart*	*Brown*	*Norris*	*Knox*	*Madison*	
Wash., D.C.	July	15th	18	60	3	for
sigh	man	*Cammer*	on	flea	I	wood
Simon		*Cameron*		(period)	I	would
give	much	Toby	*trammeled*	*serenade*	impression	that
give	much	to be	relieved	of the	impression	that
Bunyan	*bear*	*ax*	*cat*	*children*	and	*awl*
Meade	,(comma)	Couch	,(comma)	Smith	and	all
bat	since	the	*knit*	of	get	ties
,(comma)	since	the	battle	of		
large	*ass*	have	striven	only	*Gettys*	get
burg	,(comma)	have	striven	only	to	get
village	*skeleton*	*turnip*	without	another	*optic*	*hound*
the enemy	over	the river	without	another	fight	(period)
Please	tell	me	if	you	no	who
Please	tell	me	if	you	know	who
was	the	*Harry*	*Madrid*	*locust*	who	was
was	the	one	corps	commander	who	was
for	*oppressing*	*bitch*	*quail*	*counsel*	of	war
for	fighting	,(comma)	in the	council	of	war
on	*Tyler*	*Rustle*	*upright*	*Adrian*	bless	him
on	Sunday	night	Signature	A. Lincoln	(null)	(null)
	(monkey)	(silk)	(martyr)		(suicide)	
	(null)	(null)	(null)		(null)	

Fig. 56

say. In figure 58 is a picture of the title page, and I follow it with figure 59, a photograph of what's on its reverse.

Do you imagine that the chap who was responsible for getting this cipher book approved ever thought about what he was doing when he caused those "Directions for Use" to be printed? It doesn't seem possible. All he would have had to ask himself was, "Why put this piece of information in the book itself? Cipher books before this have been captured. Suppose this one falls into enemy hands; can't he read, too, and at once learn about the intended deception? Why go to all the trouble of including "phony" routes, anyway? If the book doesn't fall into enemy hands, what good are the "phony" routes anyway? Why not just indicate the routes in a straightforward manner, as had been done before? Thus: "Up the 6th column (since "6" is the first number at the left of the diagram), down the 3rd, up the 5th, down the 7th. up the 1st, down the 4th, and down the 2nd." This matter is so incredibly fatuous that it is hard to understand how sensible men – and they were sensible – could be so illogical in their thinking processes. But there the "Directions for Use" stand for all the world to see and to judge.

Fig. 57

Now for the transposition step. The indicator "BI.ONDE" signifies a matrix of seven columns and eleven rows, with the route set forth above, viz, up the 6th column, down the 3rd, etc., so that the cipher text with a "phony" address and signature,[4] becomes as follows:

Washington, D.C

TO: A. HARPER CALDWELL,
Cipher Operator, Army of the Potomac:

Blonde bless of who no optic to get and impression I Madison square Brown cammer Toby ax the have turnip me Harry bitch rustle silk Adrian counsel locust you another only of children serenade flea Knox County for wood that awl ties get hound who was war him suicide on for was please village large bat Bunyan give sigh incubus heavy Norris on trammeled cat knit striven without if Madrid quail upright martyr Stewart man much bear since ass skeleton tell the oppressing Tyler monkey.

WAR DEPARTMENT CIPHER NO. 4.

Fig. 58

DIRECTIONS FOR USE.

To find the route, read the figures in the table at top of page from left to right in the order that they occur alternately in the upper and lower lines, the two intermediate lines of figures having no connection with the route, being introduced simply as a blind, the upper line of figures denoting the route *down* the column and the lower line *up*.

EXAMPLE.

See page 14; 7 columns.

Route—Up the 3d; down the 6th; up the 1st; down the 7th; up the 2d; down the 4th; up the 5th.

Commence a cipher with one of the "line indicators," taken from same page as route used, which word must indicate the number of lines in the message. Use two words for more than *twenty* lines.

Fig. 59

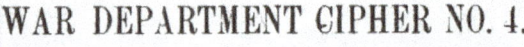

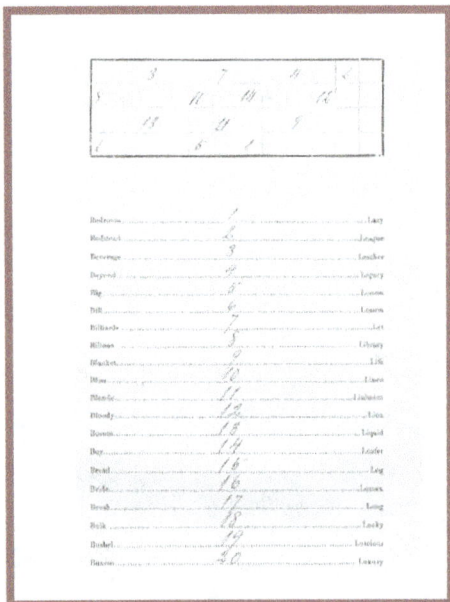

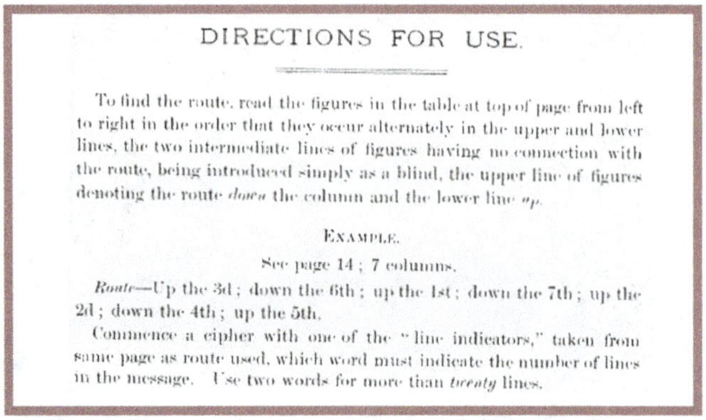

(Signed) D. HOMER BATES

Note that the text begins with the indicator "BLONDE." In decipherment the steps are simply reversed. The indicator tells which size matrix to outline; the words beginning "bless of who no optic. . ." are inscribed within the matrix: up the 6th column; then omitting the "check word" or "null" (which in this case is the word "square") down the 3rd column, etc. The final result should correspond to what is shown in figure 56. There then follows the step of interpreting orthographic deviations, such as interpreting "sigh," "man," "cammer ," and "on" as Simon Cameron; the word "wood" for "would," etc. The final step reproduces the original plain text.

Save for one exception, all the route ciphers used by the USMTC conformed to this basic pattern. The things that changed from one cipher book to the next were the indicators for the dimensions of the matrices and for the routes, and the "arbitraries" or code equivalents for the various items comprising the "vocabulary," the number of them increasing from one edition to the next, just as might be expected. The sole exception to this basic pattern is to be seen in Cipher Book No, 9 and on only one page of the book. I will show you that page. (See fig. 60.)

What we have here is a deviation from the straightforward route transposition, "up the column, . . .down the. . . column," etc. By introducing one diagonal path in the route (the 6th, 7th, 8th, 9th, 10th words in a message of five columns, and the 1st, 2nd, 3rd, 4th, 5th, and 6th words in a message of six columns) the simple up and down route no longer holds true. The words on the diagonal interrupt the normal up and down paths and introduce complexities in the method. In fact, the complexities seemed to be a bit too much for the USMTC cipher operators, because, as far as available records show, these complicated routes were never used.

I now wish to make a number of general and a few specific comments on Plum's description of the cryptosystems used by the USMTC.

First, we have learned that although Anson Stager has been credited with inventing the type of cipher under consideration in this study, he was anticipated in the invention by about 200 years. Also, he is given the lion's share of the credit for devising those ciphers, although he did have a number of collaborators. Plum names four of them, presumably because he thought them worthy of being singled out for particular attention. Plum and others tell us that copies of messages handled by the USMTC were sometimes intercepted by the enemy but not solved. He cites no authority for this last statement, merely saying that such intercepts were published in the newspapers of the Confederacy with the hope that somebody would come up with their solution. And it may be noted that none of the Confederate accounts of war activities cite instances of the solution of intercepted USMTC messages, although there are plenty of citations of instances of interception and solution of enciphered visual transmissions of the Federal army's signal corps.

Plum states that twelve different cipher books were employed by the Telegraph Corps, but I think there were actually only eleven. The first one was not numbered, and this is good evidence that a long war was not expected. This first cipher book had sixteen printed pages. But for some reason, now impossible to fathom, the sequence of numbered books thereafter was as follows: Nos. 6 and 7, which were much like the first (unnumbered) one; then came Nos. 12, 9, 10 – in that strange order; then came Nos. 1 and 2; finally came Nos. 3, 4, and 5. (Apparently there was no No.8 or No. 11 – at least they are never mentioned.) It would be ridiculous to think that the irregularity in numbering the successive books was for the purpose of communication security, but there are other things about the books and the cryptosystem that appear equally silly. There may have been good reasons for the erratic numbering of the books, but if so, what they

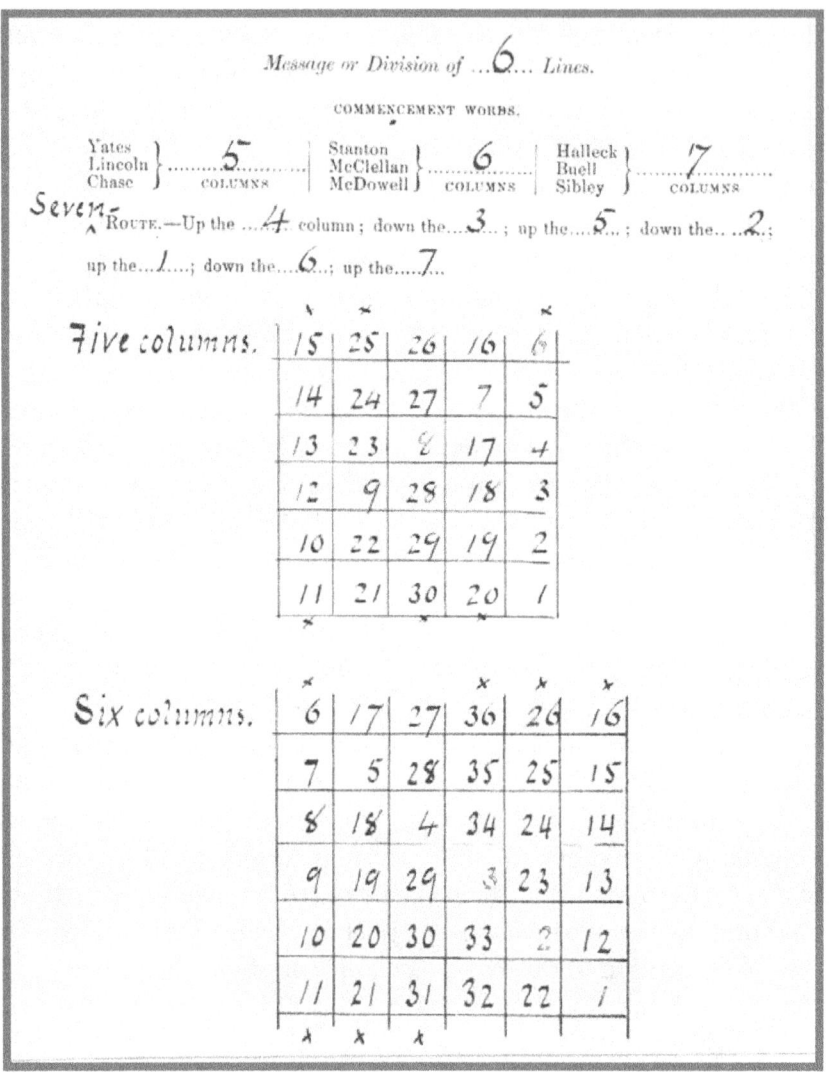

Fig. 60

were is now unknown. Plum states that No.4, the last one used in the war, was placed into effect on 23 March 1865, and that it and all other ciphers were discarded on 20 June 1865. However, as noted, there was a No.5, which Plum says was given a limited distribution. I have a copy of it, but whether it was actually put into use I do not know. Like No.4, it had forty pages. About twenty copies were sent to certain members of the USMTC, scattered among twelve states; and, of course, Washington must have had at least one copy.

We may assume with a fair amount of certainty that the first (the unnumbered) cipher book used by the USMTC was merely an elaboration of the one Stager produced for the communications of the governors of Ohio, Indiana, and Illinois, and of which a copy is given by only one of the writers who have told us about these ciphers, namely, David H. Bates. Bates, in his series of articles entitled "Lincoln in the Telegraph Office" (*The Century Magazine,* Vol. LXXIV, Nos 1-5, May-September, 1907)[5] shows a facsimile thereof (p. 292, June 1907 issue), and I have had as good a reproduction made of it as possible from rather poor photographic facsimile. The foregoing cipher is the prototype upon which all subsequent cipher books were based, the first of the War Department series being the one shown by Plum.

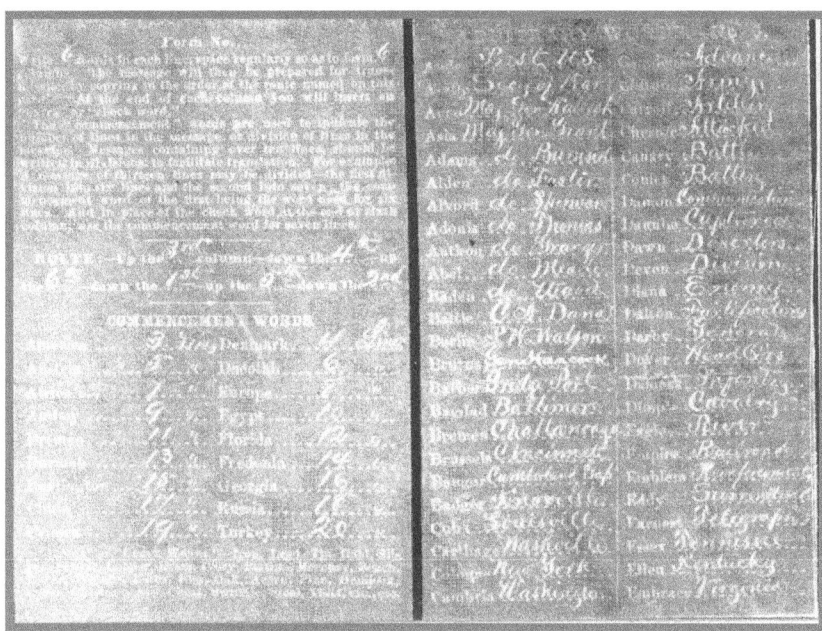
Fig. 61.

When these ciphers came into use, it was not the practice to misspell certain words intentionally; but as the members of the USMTC (who, as I've told you, served not only as telegraph operators but also as cipher clerks) developed expertness, the practice of using nonstandard orthography was frequently employed to make solution of messages more difficult. You have already seen examples of this practice, and one can find hundreds of other examples of this sort of artifice. Then, further to increase security, more and more code equivalents were added to represent such things as ordinal and cardinal numbers, months of the year, days of the week, hours of the day, punctuation, etc. As a last step, additional code equivalents for frequently used words and phrases were introduced. One good example of two typical pages from one of these books will characterize them all.

You will notice that the code equivalents are printed, but their meanings are written in by hand. This was usually the case, and the reason is obvious: for economy in printing costs, because the printed code equivalents of plaintext items in cipher books belonging to the same series are identical; only their meanings change from one book to another; and, of course, the transposition routes, their indicators, and other variables change from one book to another. I am fortunate in having six of these cipher books in my private collection, so that comparisons among them are readily made. The first feature to be noted is that the code equivalents are all good English dictionary words (or proper nouns) of not less than three nor more than seven (rarely eight) letters. A careful scrutiny shows that in the early editions the code equivalents are such as not very likely to appear as words in the plaintext messages; but in the later editions, beginning with No. 12, *more than 50 percent of the words used as code equivalents are such as might well appear in the plain text of messages*. For example, words such as AID, ALL, ARMY, ARTILLERY, JUNCTION, CONFEDERATE, etc., baptismal names of persons, and names of cities, rivers, bays, etc., appear as code equivalents. Among names used as code equivalents are SHERMAN, LINCOLN, THOMAS, STANTON, and those of many other prominent officers and officials of the Union army and the federal government, as well as of the Confederate army and government; and, even more intriguing, such names were employed as indicators for the number of columns and the routes used – the so-called "Commencement Words." It would seem that names and words such as those I've mentioned might occasionally have brought about instances where difficulty in deciphering messages arose from this source of confusion, but the literature doesn't mention them. I think you already realize why such commonly used proper names and words were not excluded. There was, indeed, method in this madness.

But what is indeed astonishing to note is that in the later editions of these cipher books, in a great majority of cases, the words used as "arbitraries" differ from one another by at least two letters (for example, LADY and LAMB, LARK and LAWN, ALBA and ASIA, LOCK and WICK, MILK and MINT) or by more than two (for example, MYRTLE and MYSTIC, CARBON and CANCER, ANDES and ATLAS). One has to search for cases in which two words differ by only one letter, but they can be found if you search long enough for them, for example, QUINCY and QUINCE, PINE and PIKE, NOSE and ROSE. Often there are words with the same initial trigraph or tetragraph, but then the rest of the letters are such that errors of transmission or reception would easily manifest themselves, for example, in the cases of MONSTER and MONARCH, MAGNET and MAGNOLIA. All in all, it is important to note that the compiler or compilers of these cipher books had adopted a principle known today as the "two-letter differential," a feature found only in codebooks of a much later date. In brief, the principle involves the use, in a given codebook, of code groups differing from one another by at least two letters. This principle is employed by knowledgeable code compilers to this very day, because it enables the recipient of a message not only to detect errors in transmission or reception, but also to correct them. This is made possible if the permutation tables used in constructing the codewords are printed in the codebooks, so that most errors can be corrected without calling for a repetition of the transmission. It is clear, therefore, that the compilers of these cipher books took into consideration the fact that errors are to be expected in Morse telegraphy, and by incorporating, but only to a limited extent, the principle of the two-letter differential, they tried to guard against the possibility that errors might go undetected. Had artificial five-letter groups been used as code equivalents, instead of dictionary words, possibly the cipher books would also have contained the permutation tables. But it must be noted that permutation tables made their first appearance only about a quarter of a century after the Civil War had ended, and then only in the most advanced types of commercial codes.

There is, however, another feature about the words the compilers of these books chose as code equivalents. It is a feature that manifests real perspicacity on their part, and you probably already have divined it. A few moments ago I said that I would explain why, in the later and improved editions of these books, words that might well be words in plaintext messages were not excluded from the lists of code equivalents: it involves the fact that the basic nature of the cryptosystem in which these code equivalents were to be used was clearly recognized by those who compiled the books. Since the cryptosystem was based upon *word* transposition, what could be more confusing to a would-be cryptanalyst working with messages in such a system than to find himself unable to decide whether a word in the cipher text of a message he is trying to solve is actually in the original plaintext message and has its normal meaning, or is a codeword with a secret significance – or even a null, a nonsignificant word, a "blind" or a "check word," as those elements were called in those days? That, no doubt, is why there are, in these books, so many code equivalents that might well be "good" words in the plaintext message. And in this connection I have already noted an additional interesting feature: at the top of each page devoted to indicators for signaling the number of columns or rows in the specific matrix for a message are printed the so-called "commencement words," or what we now call "indicators." Now there are nine such words, in sets of three, anyone of which *could* actually be a real word or name in the plaintext message. Such words when used as indicators could be very confusing to enemy cryptanalysts, especially after the transposition operation. Here, for example, are the "commencement words" on page 5 of cipher book

No.9: Army, Anson, Action, Astor, Advance, Artillery, Anderson, Ambush, Agree; on page 7 of No. 10: Cairo, Curtin, Cavalry, Congress, Childs, Calhoun, Church, Cobb, etc. Moreover, in Nos. 1, 3, 4, 5, and 10 the "line indicators," that is, the words indicating the number of horizontal rows in the matrix, are also words that could easily be words in the plaintext messages. For example, in No.1, page 3, the line indicators are as follows:

Address	1	Faith	Assume	6	Bend
Adjust	2	Favor	Awake	7	Avail
Answer	3	Confine	Encamp	8	Active
Appear	4	Bed	Enroll	9	Absent

Note two things in the foregoing list first, there are variants – there are two indicators for each case; and, second, the indicators are not in strict alphabetic sequence. This departure from strict alphabeticity is even more obvious in the pages devoted to vocabulary, a fact of much importance cryptanalytically. Note this feature, for example, in figure 62, that shows pages 14 and 15 of cipher book No. 12.

In this respect, therefore, these books partake somewhat of the nature of two-part or "randomized" codes or, in British terminology, "hatted" codes. In the second lecture of this series, the physical difference between one-part and two-part codes was briefly explained, but an indication of the technical cryptanalytic difference between these two types of codes may be useful at this point. Two-part codes are much more difficult to solve than one-part codes, in which both the plaintext elements and their code equivalents progress in parallel sequences. In the latter type, determination of the meaning of one code group quickly and rather easily leads to the determination of the meanings of other code groups above or below the one that has been solved. For example, in the following short but illustrative example, if the meaning of code group 1729 has been determined to be "then," the mean-

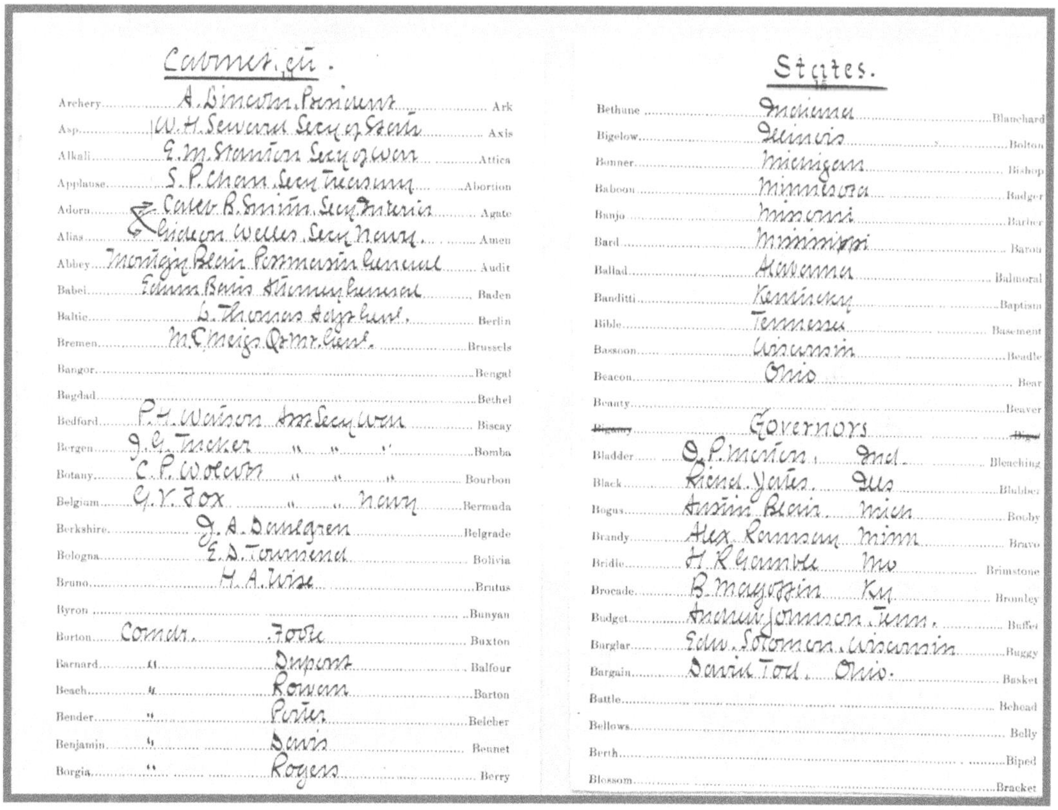

Cabinet, etc.

Archery	A. Lincoln, President	Ark
Asp	W. H. Seward Secy of State	Axis
Alkali	E. M. Stanton Secy of War	Attica
Applause	S. P. Chase Secy Treasury	Abortion
Adorn	Caleb B. Smith, Secy Interior	Agate
Alias	Gideon Welles, Secy Navy.	Amen
Abbey	Montgy Blair Postmaster General	Audit
Babel	Edward Bates Attorney General	Baden
Baltic	L. Thomas Adjt Genl.	Berlin
Bremen	M. C. Meigs Qr Mr. Genl.	Brussels
Bangor		Bengal
Bagdad		Bethel
Bedford	P. H. Watson Ass Secy War	Biscay
Bergen	J. G. Tucker " " "	Bomba
Botany	C. P. Wolcott " " "	Bourbon
Belgium	G. V. Fox " " Navy	Bermuda
Berkshire	J. A. Dahlgren	Belgrade
Bologna	E. D. Townsend	Bolivia
Bruno	H. A. Wise	Brutus
Byron		Bunyan
Burton	Comdr. Foote	Buxton
Barnard	" Dupont	Balfour
Beach	" Rowan	Barton
Bender	" Porter	Belcher
Benjamin	" Davis	Bennet
Borgia	" Rogers	Berry

States.

Bethune	Indiana	Blanchard
Bigelow	Illinois	Bolton
Bonner	Michigan	Bishop
Baboon	Minnesota	Badger
Banjo	Missouri	Barber
Bard	Mississippi	Baron
Ballad	Alabama	Balmoral
Banditti	Kentucky	Baptism
Bible	Tennessee	Basement
Bassoon	Wisconsin	Beadle
Beacon	Ohio	Bear
Beauty		Beaver
~~Bigamy~~	Governors	~~Bigot~~
Bladder	O. P. Morton, Ind.	Bleaching
Black	Richd. Yates. Ills	Blubber
Bogus	Austin Blair. Mich	Booby
Brandy	Alex Ramsey Minn	Bravo
Bridle	H. R. Gamble Mo	Brimstone
Brocade	B. Magoffin Ky	Bromley
Budget	Andrew Johnson Tenn.	Buffer
Burglar	Edw. Solomon. Wisconsin	Buggy
Bargain	David Tod. Ohio.	Basket
Battle		Behead
Bellows		Belly
Berth		Biped
Blossom		Bracket

Fig. 62

ing of the code group 1728 could well be "the" and that of the code group 1730, "there."

But in a two-part code, determining the meaning of the code group 0972 to be "then" gives no clue whatsoever to the meaning of the groups 7621 or 1548. For ease in decoding messages in such a code, there must be a section in which the code

1728 – the	7621 – the
1729 – then	0972 – then
1730 – there	1548 – there

groups are listed in numerical sequence and are accompanied by their meanings, which, of course, will be in a random sequence. The compilers of the USMTC code books must have had a very clear idea of what I have just explained, but they made a compromise of a practical nature between a strictly one-part and a strictly two-part code, because they realized that a code of latter sort is twice as bulky as one of the former sort, besides being much more the laborious to compile and check the contents for accuracy. The arrangement they chose wasn't too bad, so far as cryptosecurity was concerned. As a matter of fact, and speaking from personal experience, in decoding a rather long message addressed to General Grant, I had a difficult time in locating many of the code words in the book, because of the departure from strict alphabeticity. I came across that message in a workbook in my collection, the workbook of one of the important members of the USMTC – none other than our friend Plum, from whose book *The Military Telegraph during the Civil War* comes much of the data I've presented in this lecture. On the flyleaf of Plum's workbook appears, presumably in his own handwriting, the legend "W.R. Plum Chf Opr with Gen. G.H. Thomas." Here's one of the messages (fig. 63) he enciphered in cipher book No.1, the book in which, he says, more important telegrams were sent than in any other: Note how many "arbitraries" appear in the plaintext message, that is, before transposition. After transposition, the melange of plain text, codewords, indicators and nulls makes the cryptogram mystifying.[6] And yet, was the system as

Fig. 63

inscrutable as its users apparently thought? It is to be remembered, of course, that messages were then transmitted by wire telegraphy, not by radio, so that enemy messages could be obtained only by "tapping" telegraph lines or capturing couriers or headquarters with their files intact. Opportunities for these methods of acquiring enemy traffic were not frequent, but they did occur from time to time, and in one case a Confederate signalman hid in a swamp for several weeks and tapped a federal telegraph line, obtaining a good many messages. What success, if any, did Confederate cryptanalysts have in their attempts to solve such USMTC cryptograms as they did intercept? We shall try to answer this question in due time.

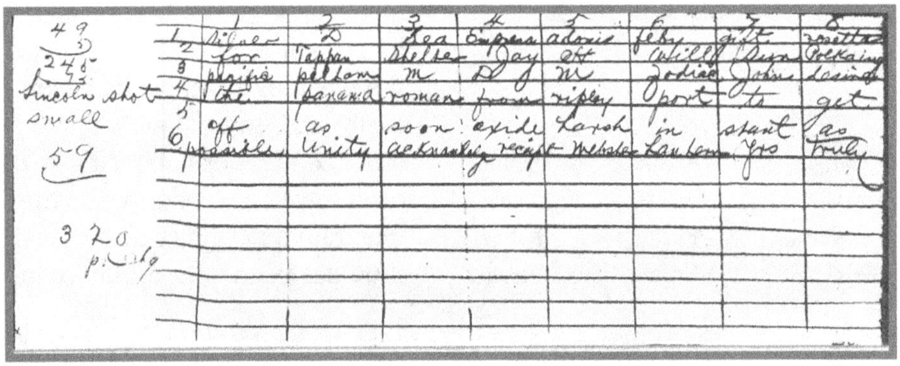

As indicated earlier, there were no competing signal organizations in the Confederacy as there were on the Union side. There was nothing at the center of government in Richmond or in the combat zone comparable to the extensive and tightly controlled civilian military telegraph organization that Secretary Stanton ruled with such an iron hand from Washington. Almost as a concomitant, it would seem, there was in the Confederacy, save for two exceptional cases, one and only one officially established cryptosystem to serve the need for protecting tactical as well as strategic communications, and that was the so-called Vigenère Cipher, which apparently was the cipher authorized in an official manual prepared by Captain J.H. Alexander as the partial equivalent of Myer's *Manual of Signals*. You won't find the name Vigenère in any of the writings of contemporary signal officers of either the North or the South. The signalmen of those days called it the "Court Cipher," this term referring to the system in common use for diplomatic or "court" secret communications about this period in history. It is that cipher that employs the so-called Vigenère Square with a repeating key.[7] In figure 64 is the square that Plum calls the "Confederate States Cipher Key" and that is followed by his description of its manner of employment.

There are certain comments to be made on the two sample messages given by Plum. In the first place, in one of the messages certain words are left unenciphered; in the second place, in both sample messages, the ciphers retain and clearly show the lengths of the words that have been enciphered. Both of these faulty practices greatly weaken the security of ciphers because they leave good clues to their contents and can easily result in facilitating solution of the messages. We know today that cipher messages must leave nothing in the clear. Even the address and the signature, the date, time and place of origin, etc., should if possible be hidden; and the cipher text should be in completely regular groupings, first, so as not to disclose the lengths of plaintext words, and, second, to promote accuracy in transmission and reception.

So far as my studies have gone, I have not found a single example of a Confederate Vigenère cipher that shows neither of these two fatal weaknesses. The second of the two examples is the only case I have found in which there are no unenciphered words in the text of the message. And the only example I have been able to find in which word lengths are not shown (save for one word) is in the case of the following message:

> Vicksburg, Dec. 26, 1862.
> GEN J.E.JOHNSTON, JACKSON:
>
> I prefer oaavvr, it has reference to xhvkjqchffabpzelreqpzwnyk to prevent anuzeyxswstpjw at that point, raeelpsghvelvtzfautlilaslt lhifnaigtsmmlfgccajd.
>
> (Signed) J.C. PEMBERTON
> Lt. Gen, Comdg.

Even in this case there are unenciphered words that afforded a clue enabling our man Plum to find the key and solve the message. It took some time, however, and the story is worth telling.

According to Plum, the foregoing cipher message was the very first one captured by USMTC operators, and it was obtained during the siege of Vicksburg, which surrendered on 4 July 1863. But note the date of the message: 26 December 1862. What was done with the captured message during the months from the end of December 1862 to July 1863? Apparently nothing. Here is what Plum reports:

> What efforts General Grant caused to be made to unravel this message, we know not. It was not until October, 1864, that it and others came into the hands of the telegraph cipherers, at New Orleans, for translation....
>
> The New Orleans operators who worked out this key (Manchester Bluff) were aided by the Pemberton cipher and the original telegram, which was found among the general's papers, after the surrender of Vicksburg; also by the following cipher dispatch, and one other.

Plum gives the messages involved, their solution, and the keys, the latter being the three cited above. It would seem that if the captured Pemberton message had been brought to General Grant's attention and he did nothing about it, he was not much interested in intelligence. Second, the solution of the Pemberton message and the others apparently took some time, even though there was one message with its plain text (the Pemberton message) and two messages not only with interspersed plaintext words but also with spaces showing word lengths. But Plum does not indicate how long it took for solution. Note that he merely says that the messages came into the hands of the telegraph cipherers in October 1864; he does not tell when solution was reached.

Confederate States Cipher Key.

	26	25	24	23	22	21	20	19	18	17	16	15	14	13	12	11	10	9	8	7	6	5	4	3	2	1
1	a	b	c	d	e	f	g	h	i	j	k	l	m	n	o	p	q	r	s	t	u	v	w	x	y	z
2	b	c	d	e	f	g	h	i	j	k	l	m	n	o	p	q	r	s	t	u	v	w	x	y	z	a
3	c	d	e	f	g	h	i	j	k	l	m	n	o	p	q	r	s	t	u	v	w	x	y	z	a	b
4	d	e	f	g	h	i	j	k	l	m	n	o	p	q	r	s	t	u	v	w	x	y	z	a	b	c
5	e	f	g	h	i	j	k	l	m	n	o	p	q	r	s	t	u	v	w	x	y	z	a	b	c	d
6	f	g	h	i	j	k	l	m	n	o	p	q	r	s	t	u	v	w	x	y	z	a	b	c	d	e
7	g	h	i	j	k	l	m	n	o	p	q	r	s	t	u	v	w	x	y	z	a	b	c	d	e	f
8	h	i	j	k	l	m	n	o	p	q	r	s	t	u	v	w	x	y	z	a	b	c	d	e	f	g
9	i	j	k	l	m	n	o	p	q	r	s	t	u	v	w	x	y	z	a	b	c	d	e	f	g	h
10	j	k	l	m	n	o	p	q	r	s	t	u	v	w	x	y	z	a	b	c	d	e	f	g	h	i
11	k	l	m	n	o	p	q	r	s	t	u	v	w	x	y	z	a	b	c	d	e	f	g	h	i	j
12	l	m	n	o	p	q	r	s	t	u	v	w	x	y	z	a	b	c	d	e	f	g	h	i	j	k
13	m	n	o	p	q	r	s	t	u	v	w	x	y	z	a	b	c	d	e	f	g	h	i	j	k	l
14	n	o	p	q	r	s	t	u	v	w	x	y	z	a	b	c	d	e	f	g	h	i	j	k	l	m
15	o	p	q	r	s	t	u	v	w	x	y	z	a	b	c	d	e	f	g	h	i	j	k	l	m	n
16	p	q	r	s	t	u	v	w	x	y	z	a	b	c	d	e	f	g	h	i	j	k	l	m	n	o
17	q	r	s	t	u	v	w	x	y	z	a	b	c	d	e	f	g	h	i	j	k	l	m	n	o	p
18	r	s	t	u	v	w	x	y	z	a	b	c	d	e	f	g	h	i	j	k	l	m	n	o	p	q
19	s	t	u	v	w	x	y	z	a	b	c	d	e	f	g	h	i	j	k	l	m	n	o	p	q	r
20	t	u	v	w	x	y	z	a	b	c	d	e	f	g	h	i	j	k	l	m	n	o	p	q	r	s
21	u	v	w	x	y	z	a	b	c	d	e	f	g	h	i	j	k	l	m	n	o	p	q	r	s	t
22	v	w	x	y	z	a	b	c	d	e	f	g	h	i	j	k	l	m	n	o	p	q	r	s	t	u
23	w	x	y	z	a	b	c	d	e	f	g	h	i	j	k	l	m	n	o	p	q	r	s	t	u	v
24	x	y	z	a	b	c	d	e	f	g	h	i	j	k	l	m	n	o	p	q	r	s	t	u	v	w
25	y	z	a	b	c	d	e	f	g	h	i	j	k	l	m	n	o	p	q	r	s	t	u	v	w	x
26	z	a	b	c	d	e	f	g	h	i	j	k	l	m	n	o	p	q	r	s	t	u	v	w	x	y

Fig. 64

In the various accounts of these Confederate ciphers, there is one and only one writer who makes a detailed comment on the two fatal practices to which I refer. A certain Dr. Charles E. Taylor, a Confederate veteran (in an article entitled "The Signal and Secret Service of the Confederate States," published in the *Confederate Veteran*, Vol. XL, August-September 1932), after giving an example of encipherment according to the "court cipher," says:

> It hardly needs to be said that the division between the words of the original message as given above was not retained in the cipher. Either the letters were run together continuously or breaks, as if for words, were made at random. Until the folly of the method was revealed by experience, only a few special words in a message were put into cipher, while the rest was sent in plain language. Thus... I think it may be said that it was impossible for well prepared cipher to be correctly read by anyone who did not know the key-word. Sometimes, in fact, we could not decipher our own messages

when they came over telegraph wires. As the operators had no meaning to guide them; letters easily became changed and portions, at least, of messages rendered unmeaningly [sic] thereby.

Frankly, I don't believe Dr. Taylor's comments are to be taken as characterizing the practices that were usually followed. No other ex-signalman who has written about the ciphers used by the Confederate Signal Corps makes such observations, and I think we must simply discount what Dr. Taylor says in this regard.

It would certainly be an unwarranted exaggeration to say that the two weaknesses in the Confederate cryptosystem cost the Confederacy the victory for which it fought so mightily, but I do feel warranted at this moment in saying that further research may well show that certain battles and campaigns were lost because of insecure cryptocommunications.

A few moments ago I said that, save for an exception or two, there was in the Confederacy one and only one cryptosystem to serve the need for secure tactical as well as strategic communications. One of these exceptions concerned the cipher used by General Beauregard after the battle of Shiloh (8 April 1862). This cipher was purely monoalphabetic in nature and was discarded as soon as the official cipher system was prescribed in Alexander's manual. It is interesting to note that this was done after the deciphered message came to the attention of Confederate authorities in Richmond via a Northern newspaper. It is also interesting to note that the Federal War Department had begun using the route cipher as the official system for USMTC messages very promptly after the outbreak of war, whereas not until 1862 did the Confederate States War Department prepare an official cryptosystem, and then it adopted the "court cipher."

The other exception involved a system used at least once before the official system was adopted, and it was so different from the latter that it should be mentioned. On 26 March 1862 the Confederate States president, Jefferson Davis, sent General Johnston by special messenger a dictionary with the following accompanying instruction:[8]

> I send you a dictionary of which I have the duplicate, so that you may communicate with me by cipher, telegraphic or written, as follows: First give the page by its number; second, the column by the letter L, M, or R, as it may be, in the left-hand, middle, or right-hand columns; third, the number of the word in the column, counting from the top. Thus, the word junction would be designated 146, L, 20.

The foregoing, as you no doubt have already realized, is one of the types of cryptosystems used by both sides during the American Revolutionary period almost a century before, except that in this case the dictionary had three columns to the page instead of two. I haven't tried to find the dictionary, but it shouldn't take long to locate it, since the code equivalent of the word "junction" was given: 146, L, 20. Moreover, there is extant at least one fairly long message, with its decode. How many other messages in this system there may be in the National Archives I don't know.

Coming back now to the "court cipher," you will probably find it just as hard to believe, as I find it, that according to all accounts three and only three keys were used by the Confederates during the three and a half years of warfare from 1862 to mid-1865. It is true that Southern signalmen mention frequent changes in key, but only the following three are specifically cited:

1) COMPLETE VICTORY

2) MANCHESTER BLUFF

3) COME RETRIBUTION

It seems that all were used concurrently. There may have been a fourth key, IN GOD WE TRUST, but I have seen it only once, and that is in a book explaining the "court cipher." Note that each of the three keys listed above consists of exactly fIfteen letters, but why this length was chosen is not clear. Had the rule been to make the cipher messages contain only five-letter groups, the explanation would be easy: 15 is a multiple of 5, and this would be of practical value in checking the cryptographic work. But, as has been clearly stated, disguising word lengths was apparently not the practice even if it was prescribed, so that there was no advantage in choosing keys that contain a multiple of five letters. And, by the way, doesn't the key COME RETRIBUTION sound rather ominous to you even these days?

Sooner or later a Confederate signal officer was bound to come up with a device to simplify enciphering operations, and a gadget devised by a Captain William N. Barker seemed to meet the need. In Myer's *Manual* there is a picture of one form of the device, shown here in figure 65. I don't think it was necessary to explain how it worked, for it is almost self-evident. Several of these devices were captured during the war, one of them being among the items in the NSA museum (fig. 66). This device was captured at Mobile in 1865. All it did was to mechanize, in a rather inefficient manner, the use of the Vigenère Cipher.

How many of these devices were in existence or use is unknown, for their construction was an individual matter – apparently it was not an item of regular issue to members of the corps.

In practically every account of the codes and ciphers of the Civil War, you will find references to ciphers used by Confederate secret service agents engaged in espionage in the North as well as in Canada. In particular, much attention is given to a set of letters in cipher, which were intercepted by the New York City postmaster and which were involved in a plot to print Confederate currency and bonds. Much ado was made about the solution of these ciphers by cipher operators of the USMTC in Washington and the consequent breaking up of the

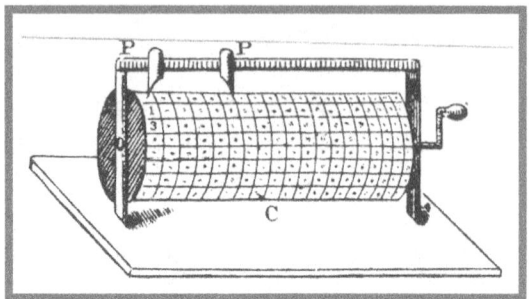

Fig. 65

plot. But I won't go into these ciphers for two reasons. First, the alphabets were all of the simple monoalphabetic type, a total of six altogether being used. Since they were composed of a different series of symbols for each alphabet, it was possible to compose a cipher word by jumping from one series to another without any external indication of the shift. However, good eyesight and a bit of patience were all that was required for solution in this case because of the inept manner in which the system was used: whole words, sometimes several successive words, were enciphered by the same alphabet. But the second reason for my not going into the story is that my friend and colleague of my NSA

Fig. 66

days, Edwin C. Fishel, has done some research among the records in our National Archives dealing with this case, and he has found something of great interest and that I feel bound to leave for him to tell at some future time, as that is his story, not mine.

So very fragmentary was the amount of cryptologic information known to the general public in these days that when there was found on John Wilkes Booth's body a cipher square that was almost identical with the cipher square that had been mounted on the cipher reel found in Confederate secretary of state Judah P. Benjamin's office in Richmond, the federal authorities in Washington attempted to prove that this necessarily meant the Confederate leaders were implicated in the plot to assassinate Lincoln and had been giving Booth instructions in cipher. Figure 67 is a picture of the cipher square found on Booth, and also in a trunk in his hotel room in Washington.

The following is quoted from Philip Van Doren Stern's book entitled *Secret Missions of the Civil War* (New York: Rand McNally and Co., 1951, 320):

> Everyone in the War Department who was familiar with cryptography knew that the Vigenére was the customary Confederate cipher and that for a Confederate agent (which Booth is known to have been) to possess a copy of a variation of it meant no more than if a telegraph operator was captured with a copy of the Morse Code. Hundreds – and perhaps thousands – of people were using the Vigenére. But the Government was desperately seeking evidence against the Confederate leaders so they took advantage of the atmosphere of mystery which has always surrounded cryptography and used it to confuse the public and the press. This shabby trick gained nothing, for the leaders of the Confederacy eventually had to be let go for lack of evidence.

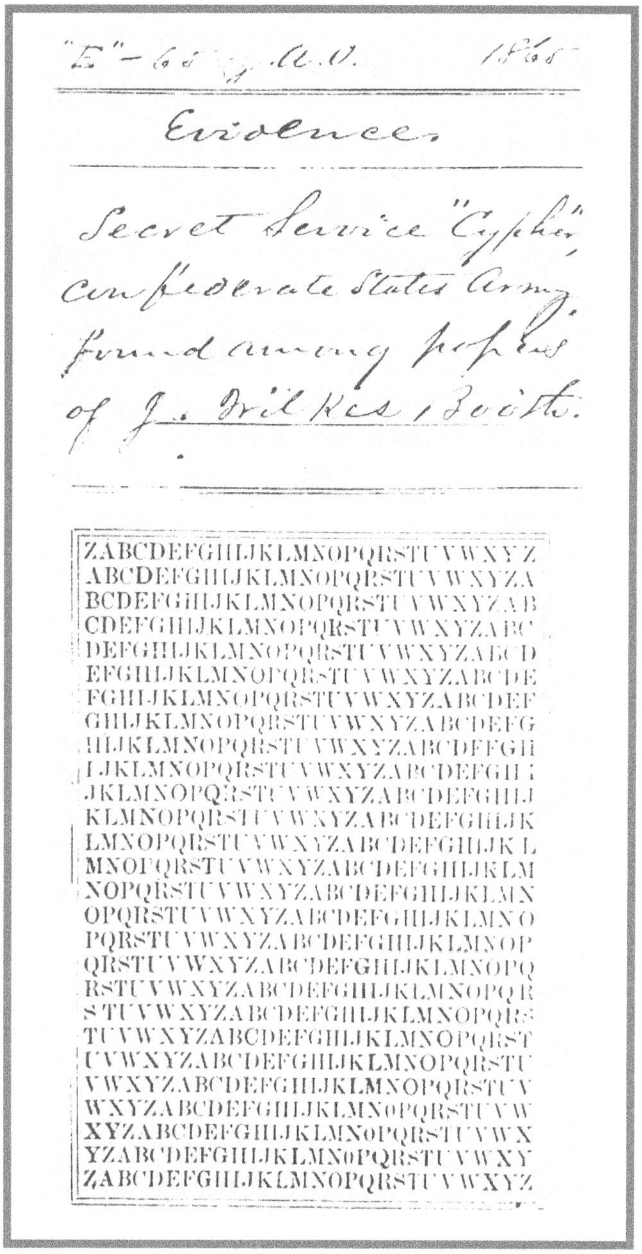

Evidence

Secret Service "Cipher"
Confederate States Army
found among papers
of J. Wilkes Booth.

ZABCDEFGHIJKLMNOPQRSTUVWXYZ
ABCDEFGHIJKLMNOPQRSTUVWXYZA
BCDEFGHIJKLMNOPQRSTUVWXYZAB
CDEFGHIJKLMNOPQRSTUVWXYZABC
DEFGHIJKLMNOPQRSTUVWXYZABCD
EFGHIJKLMNOPQRSTUVWXYZABCDE
FGHIJKLMNOPQRSTUVWXYZABCDEF
GHIJKLMNOPQRSTUVWXYZABCDEFG
HIJKLMNOPQRSTUVWXYZABCDEFGH
IJKLMNOPQRSTUVWXYZABCDEFGHI
JKLMNOPQRSTUVWXYZABCDEFGHIJ
KLMNOPQRSTUVWXYZABCDEFGHIJK
LMNOPQRSTUVWXYZABCDEFGHIJKL
MNOPQRSTUVWXYZABCDEFGHIJKLM
NOPQRSTUVWXYZABCDEFGHIJKLMN
OPQRSTUVWXYZABCDEFGHIJKLMNO
PQRSTUVWXYZABCDEFGHIJKLMNOP
QRSTUVWXYZABCDEFGHIJKLMNOPQ
RSTUVWXYZABCDEFGHIJKLMNOPQR
STUVWXYZABCDEFGHIJKLMNOPQRS
TUVWXYZABCDEFGHIJKLMNOPQRST
UVWXYZABCDEFGHIJKLMNOPQRSTU
VWXYZABCDEFGHIJKLMNOPQRSTUV
WXYZABCDEFGHIJKLMNOPQRSTUVW
XYZABCDEFGHIJKLMNOPQRSTUVWX
YZABCDEFGHIJKLMNOPQRSTUVWXY
ZABCDEFGHIJKLMNOPQRSTUVWXYZ

Fig. 67

To the foregoing I will comment that I doubt very much whether "everyone in the War Department who was familiar with cryptography knew that the Vigenère was the customary Confederate cipher." Probably not one of them had even heard the name Vigenère or had even seen a copy of the table, except those captured in operations. I doubt whether anyone on either side even knew that the cipher used by the Confederacy had a name; or least of all, that a German army reservist named Kasiski, in a book published in 1863, showed how the Vigenère cipher could be solved by a straightforward mathematical method.

I have devoted a good deal more attention to the methods and means for cryptocommunications in the Civil War than they deserve, because professional cryptologists of 1961 can hardly be impressed either by their efficacy from the point of view of ease and rapidity in the cryptographic processing, or by the degree of the technical security they imparted to the messages they were intended to protect. Not much can be said for the security of the visual signaling systems used in the combat zone by the Federal Signal Corps for tactical purposes, because they were practically all based upon simple monoalphabetic ciphers or variations thereof, as for instance, when whole words were enciphered by the same alphabet. There is plenty of evidence that Confederate signalmen were more or less regularly reading and solving those signals. What can be said about the security of the route ciphers used by the USMTC for strategic or high command communications in the zone of the interior? It has already been indicated that, according to accounts by ex-USMTC men, such ciphers were beyond the cryptanalytic abilities of Confederate cryptanalysts, but can we really believe that this was true? Considering the simplicity of these route ciphers and the undoubted intellectual capacities of Confederate officers and soldiers, why should messages in these systems have resisted cryptanalytic attack? In many cases the general subject matter of a message and perhaps a number of specific items of information could be detected by quick inspection of the message. Certainly, if it were not for the so-called "arbitraries," the general sense of the message could be found by a few minutes' work, since the basic system must have been known through the capture of cipher books, a fact mentioned several times in the literature. Capture of but one book (they were all generally alike) would have told Confederate signalmen exactly how the system worked, and this would naturally give away the basic secret of the superseding book. So we must see that whatever degree of protection these route ciphers afforded, message security depended almost entirely upon the number of "arbitraries" actually used in practice. A review of such messages as are available shows wide divergences in the use of "arbitraries." In any event, the number actually present in these books must have fallen far short of the number needed to give the real protection that a well-constructed code can give. Thus it seems to me that the application of native intelligence, with some patience, should have been sufficient to solve USMTC messages – or so it would be quite logical to assume. That such an assumption is well warranted is readily demonstrable.

It was, curiously enough, at about this point in preparing this lecture that Mr. Edwin C. Fishel, whom I have mentioned before, gave me just the right material for such a demonstration. In June of 1960, Mr. Fishel had given Mr. Phillip Bridges, who is also a member of NSA and who knew nothing about the route ciphers of the USMTC, the following authentic message sent on 1 July 1863 by General George G. Meade, at Harrisburg, Pennsylvania, to General Couch at Washington. (See fig. 68)

It took Mr. Bridges only a few hours, five or six, to solve the cryptogram, and he handed the following plain text to Mr. Fishel:

> Thomas been it-(Nulls)
> For Parson. I shall try and get to you by tomorrow morning a reliable gentleman and some scouts who are acquainted with a country you wish to know of, Rebels this way have all concentrated in direction of Gettysburg and Chambersburg. I occupy Carlisle. Signed Optic. Great battle very soon. tree mush deal- (Nulls)

The foregoing solution is correct, save for one pardonable error: "Thomas" is not a "null" but an indicator for the dimensions of the matrix and the route. "Parson" and "Optic" are codenames, and I imagine that Mr. Bridges recognized them as such, but of course, he had no way of interpreting them, except perhaps by making a careful study of the events and commanders involved in the impending action, a study he wasn't called upon to undertake.

The foregoing message was enciphered by Cipher Book No. 12, in which the indicator THOMAS specifies a "Message of 10 lines and 5 columns." The route was quite simple and straightforward: "Down the 1st (column), up the 3rd; down the 2nd; up the 5th down the 4th."

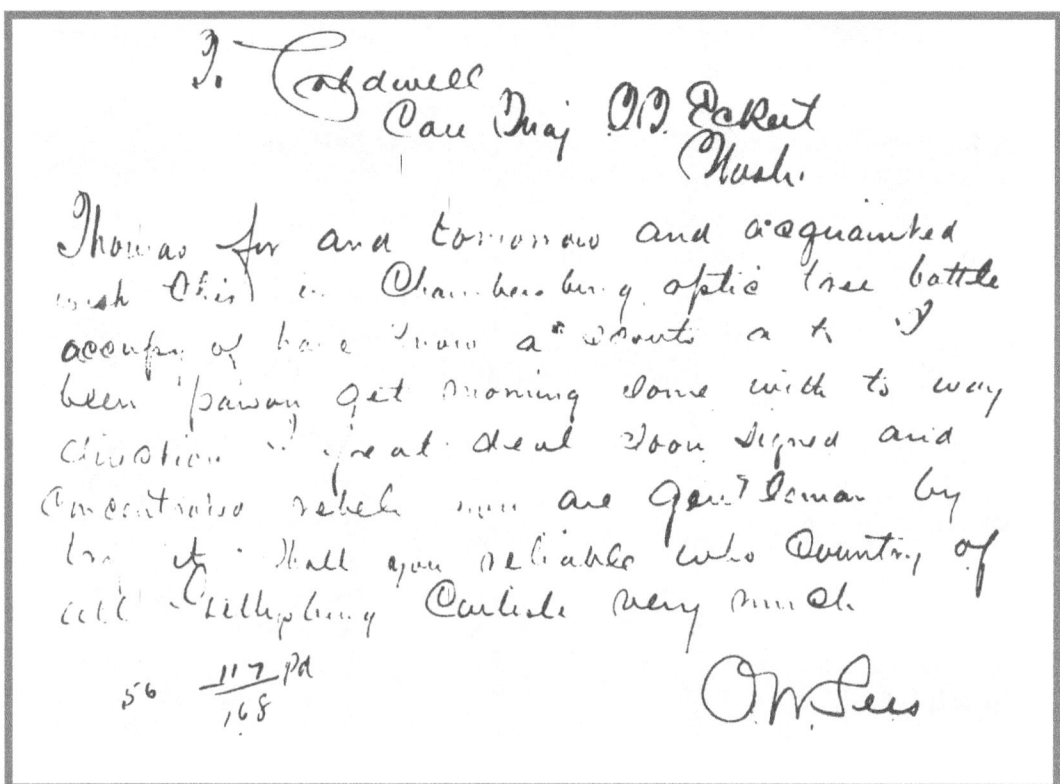

Fig. 68

It is obvious that in this example the absence of many "arbitraries" made solution a relatively easy matter. What Mr. Bridges would have been able to do with the cryptogram had there been many of them is problematical. Judging by his worksheets, it seemed to me that Mr. Bridges did not realize when he was solving the message that a transposition matrix was involved; and on questioning him on this point his answer was in the negative. He realized this only later.

A minor drama in the fortunes of Major General D.C. Buell, one of the high commanders of the Federal army, is quietly and tersely outlined in two cipher telegrams. The first one, sent on 29 September 1862 from Louisville, Kentucky, was in one of the USMTC cipher books and was externally addressed to Colonel Anson Stager, head of the USMTC, but the internal addressee was Major General H. W. Halleck, "General-in-Chief" [our present day "Chief of Staff"]. The message was externally signed by William H. Drake, Buell's cipher operator, but the name of the actual sender, Buell, was indicated internally. Here's the telegram.

COLONEL ANSON STAGER, Washington:

Austria await I in over to requiring orders olden rapture blissful for your instant command turned and instructions and rough looking further shall further the Camden me of ocean September poker twenty I the to I command obedience repair orders quickly pretty Indianapolis your him accordingly my fourth received 1862 wounded nine have twenty turn have to to to alvord hasty.

WILLIAM H. DRAKE

Rather than give you the plain text of this message, perhaps you would like to work it out for yourselves, for with the information you've already received the solution should not be difficult. The message contains one error, which was made in its original preparation: one word was omitted.

The second telegram, only one day later, was also from Major General Buell, to Major General Halleck, but it was in another cipher book – apparently the two books involved were used concurrently. Here it is:

GEORGE C. MAYNARD, Washington:

Regulars ordered of my to public out suspending received 1862 spoiled thirty I dispatch command of continue of best otherwise worst Arabia my command discharge duty of my last for Lincoln September period your from sense shall duties the until Seward ability to the I a removal evening Adam herald tribune.[9]

PHILIP BRUNER

As before, I will give you the opportunity to solve this message for yourselves. (At the end of the next lecture, I shall present the plain text of both messages.)

Figure 69 is a photograph of an important message that you may wish to solve yourself. It was sent by President Jefferson Davis to General Johnston, on a very significant date, 11 April 1865.[10] For ease in working on it, I give also a transcription below, since the photograph is very old and in a poor state. I believe that this message does not appear in any of the accounts I've read.

It is time now to tell you what I can about the success or lack of success that each side had with the cryptograms of the other side. I wish there were more information on this interesting subject than what I am about to present. Most of what sound information there is comes from a book by a man named J. Willard Brown, who served four full years in the Federal army's signal corps. The book is entitled *The Signal Corps, U.S.A., in the War of the Rebellion*, published in Boston in 1896 by the U.S.

> Greensboro N.C.
> April 11 1865
> Benaja 11   Hd Q near H.G.
> Genl J.E. Johnston
>
> A scout (reports?) that Genl Lee u i D v v s w v z F x – m q s – E G A z o x – H W – P J M – T z A T – near to appomattox Court house yesterday No official intelligence of the event D i F – x Y i k v – q T – F B B H Y G – F A S D – J H i – L P o u B – As to result Gen H. H. Walker is ordered Y W F T – W S K T M T – B X z S – G q – X A m E – C H T – i u – A K M S A u P u V F – Let me hear from you there – I will have need to see you to confer as to future action. The above is my telegram of yesterday which is repeated as requested.
>
> Jeffn Davis
> Official
> Burton Harrison
> Private Secy

Veteran Signal Corps Association. In his book Brown deals with the cryptanalytic success of both sides. First, let's see what the Union signalmen could do with rebel ciphers. Here are some statements he makes (p. 214):

> The first deciphering of a rebel signal code of which I find any record was that made by Capt. J.S. Hall and Capt. R.A. Taylor, reported Nov. 25, 1862. Four days later, Maj. Myer wrote to Capt. Cushing, Chief Signal Officer, Army of the Potomac, not to permit it to become public 'that we translate the signal messages of the rebel army'.
>
> April 9, 1863, Capt. Fisher, near Falmouth, reported that one of his officers had read a rebel message which proved that the rebels were in possession of our code. The next day he was informed that the rebel code taken (from) a rebel signal officer

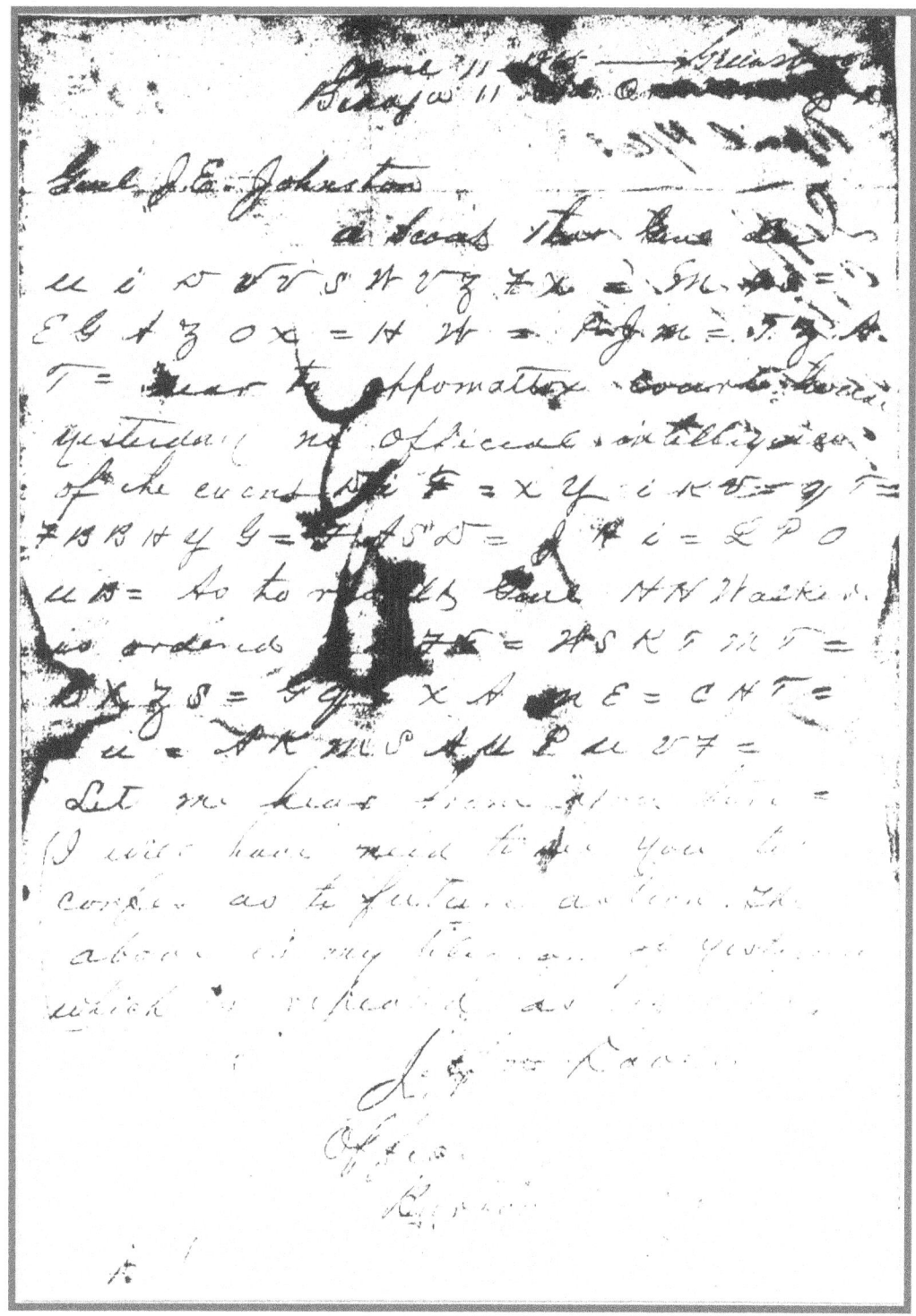

Fig. 69

was identical with one taken previously at Yorktown.

He received from Maj. Myer the following orders:

'Send over your lines, from time to time, messages which, if it is in the power of the enemy to decipher them, will lead them to believe that we cannot get any clew to their signals

Send also occasionally messages untrue, in reference to imaginary military movements, as for instance - 'The Sixth Corps is ordered to reinforce Keyes at Yorktown'.

Undoubtedly, what we have here are references to the general cipher system used by the Confederates in their electric-telegraph communications, for note the expression "Send over your lines." This could hardly refer to visual communications. Here we also have very early instances, in telegraphic communications, of what we call cover and deception, i.e., employing certain ruses to try to hide the fact that enemy signals could be read, and to try to deceive him by sending spurious messages for him to read, hoping the fraud will not be detected.

Brown's account of Union cryptanalytic successes continues (p. 215):

In October, 1863, Capt. Merril's party deciphered a code, and in November of the same year Capt. Thickstun and Capt. Marston deciphered another in Virginia. Lieut. Howgate and Lieut. Flook, in March, 1864, deciphered a code in the Western Army, and at the same time Lieut. Benner found one at Alexandria, Virginia.

Capt. Paul Babcock, Jr., then Chief Signal Officer, Department of the Cumberland, in a letter dated Chattanooga, Tennessee, April 26, 1864, transmitting a copy of the rebel signal code, says:

Capt Cole and Lieut. Howgate, acting Signal Officers, occupy a station of communication and observation on White Oak Ridge at Ringgold, Ga. . . . On the 22nd inst. the rebels changed their code to the one enclosed, and on the same day the above-mentioned officers by untiring zeal and energy succeeded in translating the new code, and these officers have been ever since reading every message sent over the rebel lines. Many of these messages have furnished valuable information to the general commanding the department.

The following is also from Brown (p. 279):

About the first of June (1864), Sergt. Colvin was stationed at Fort Strong, on Morris Island, with the several codes heretofore used by the rebels, for the purpose of reading the enemy signals if possible. For nearly two weeks nothing could be made out of their signals, but by persevering he finally succeeded in learning their codes. Messages were read by him from Beach Inlet, Battery Bee, and Fort Johnson. Gen. J .G. Foster, who had assumed command of the Department of the South, May 26th, was so much pleased with Sergt. Colvin's work, that in a letter addressed to Gen. Halleck, he recommended "that he be rewarded by promotion to Lieutenant in the Signal Corps, or by a brevet or medal of honor." This recommendation was subsequently acted upon, but, through congressional and official wrangling over appointments in the Corps, he was was not commissioned until May 13,1865, his commission dating from Feb 14,1865.

(p. 281):

During the month, Sergt. Colvin added additional laurels to the fame he had earned as a successful interpreter of rebel

> signals. The enemy had adopted a new cipher for the transmission of important messages, and the labor of deciphering it devolved upon the sergeant. Continued watchfulness at last secured the desired result, and he was again able to translate the important dispatches of the enemy for the benefit of our commandants. The information thus gained was frequently of special value in our operations, and the peculiar ability exhibited by the sergeant led Gen. Foster once more to recommend his promotion.

(p. 286):

> About the same time an expedition under Gen. Potter was organized to act in conjunction with the navy in the vicinity of Bull's Bay. Lieut. Fisher was with this command, and by maintaining communications between the land and naval forces facilitated greatly the conjoined action of the command. Meanwhile every means was employed to intercept rebel messages. Sergt. Colvin, assigned to this particular duty, read all the messages within sight, and when the evacuation of Charleston was determined upon by the enemy, the first notification of the fact I came in this way before the retreat had actually commenced. As a reward for conspicuous services rendered in this capacity, Capt. Merrill recommended that the sergeant be allowed a medal, his zeal, energy and labors fully warranting the honor.
> After the occupation of Charleston, communications was established by signals with Fort Strong, on Morris Island, Fort Johnson and James Island, Mount Pleasant, and Steynmeyer's Mills. A line was also opened with the position occupied by the troops on the south side of the Ashley river.

With regard to Confederate reading of Union visual signals, Brown makes the following observations of considerable interest (p. 274):

> The absolute necessity of using a cipher when signaling in the presence of the enemy was demonstrated during these autumn months by the ease with which the rebels read our messages. This led to the issuing of an order that all important messages should be sent in cipher. Among the multitude of messages intercepted by the enemy, the following were some of the more important . . .

Brown thereupon cites twenty-five such messages, but he gives no indication whatever as to the source from which he obtained these examples or how he knew they had been intercepted. They all appear to tactical messages sent by visual signals.

In many of the cases cited by Brown, it is difficult to tell whether wig-wag or electric telegraph messages were involved. But in one case (evacuation of Charleston), it is perfectly clear that visual messages were involved, when Brown says that Sergeant Colvin "read the messages within sight."

Further with regard to rebel cryptanalytic success with Union messages, Brown has this to say (p. 213):

> The reports of Lieut. Frank Markoe, Signal Officer at Charleston, show that during the siege thousands of messages were sent from one post to another, and from outposts to headquarters, most of which could have been sent in no other way, and many were of great importance to the Confederate authorities.
> Lieut. Markoe says that he read nearly every message we sent. He was forewarned of our attack on the 18th of July, 1863. He adds, regretfully, however, that through carelessness of the staff officers at headquarters it leaked out that he was

> reading our messages. Our officers then began to use the cipher disk. In August he intercepted the following message: "Send me a copy of rebel code immediately. if you have one in your possession." He therefore changed his code. . ... A little later our officers used a cipher which Lieut. Markoe says he was utterly unable to unravel.

It is unfortunate that neither Lieutenant Markoe, the Confederate cryptanalyst, nor Brown, the Union signalman, tell us what sort of cipher this was that couldn't be unraveled. I assume that it was the Myer disk used properly, with a key phrase of some length and with successive letters, not whole words, being enciphered by successive letters of the key. But this is only an assumption and may be entirely erroneous.

In the foregoing citations of cryptanalytic success, it is significant to note that visual messages were intercepted and read by both sides; second, that Confederate telegraphic messages protected by the Vigenère cipher were read by Union personnel whenever such messages were intercepted; and, third, that USMTC telegraph messages protected by the route cipher, apparently intercepted occasionally, were never solved. Later I shall make some comments on this last statement, but at the moment let us note that technically the Vigenère cipher is theoretically much stronger than the route cipher, so that we have here an interesting situation, *viz*, the users of a technically inferior cryptosystem were able to read enemy messages protected by a technically superior one, but the users of a technically superior cryptosystem were not able to read enemy messages protected by a technically inferior one – a curious situation indeed.

I can hardly close this lecture without citing a couple of messages that appear in nearly every account I've seen of the codes and ciphers of the Civil War. These are messages that were sent by President Lincoln under circumstances in which, allegedly, the usual cipher could not be, or at least was not, employed. The first of the two was sent on 25 November 1862 from the White House to Major General Burnside, Falmouth, Virginia. The circumstances are so bizarre that if I merely presented the cipher message to you without some background, I doubt if you would believe me. And even after I've presented the background, I'm sure you won't know what to think. I, myself, don't really know whether to take the incident seriously or not. Let me quote from an account of it in the book by David Homer Bates, one of the first members of the USMTC, in his *Lincoln in the Telegraph Office* (New York: Appleton-Century Co., 1939, 58-61):

> During Burnside's Fredericksburg campaign at the end of 1862, the War Department operators discovered indications of an interloper on the wire leading to his headquarters at Aquia Creek. These indications consisted of an occasional irregular opening and closing of the circuit and once in a while strange signals, evidently not made by our own operators. It is proper to note that the characteristics of each Morse operator's sending are just as pronounced and as easily recognized as those of ordinary handwriting, so that when a message is transmitted over a wire, the identity of the sender may readily be known to any other operator within hearing who has ever worked with him. A somewhat similar means of personal identification occurs every day in the use of the telephone.
> At the time referred to, therefore, we were certain that our wire had been tapped. In some way or other the Confederate operator learned that we were aware of his presence, and he then informed us that he was from Lee's army and had been on our wire for several days, and that, having learned all that he wanted to know, he was then about to cut out and run. We gossiped with him for a while and then ceased to hear his signals and believed he was gone.
> We had taken measures, however, to discover his whereabouts by sending out line-

men to patrol the line; but his tracks were well concealed, and it was only after the intruder had left, that we found the place where our wire had been tapped. He had made the secret connection by means of fine silk-covered magnet wire, in such a manner as to conceal the joint almost entirely. Meantime, Burnside's cipher-operator was temporarily absent from his post, and we had recourse to a crude plan for concealing the text of telegrams to the Army of the Potomac, which we had followed on other somewhat similar occasions when we believed the addressee or operator at the distant point (not provided with the cipher key) was particularly keen and alert. This plan consisted primarily of sending the message backward, the individual words being misspelled and otherwise garbled. We had practiced on one or two dispatches to Burnside before the Confederate operator was discovered to be on the wire, and were pleased to get his prompt answers, couched also in similar outlandish language, which was, however, intelligible to us after a short study of the text in each case. Burnside and ourselves soon became quite expert in this homemade cipher game, as we all strove hard to clothe the dispatches in strange, uncouth garb.

In order to deceive the Confederate operator, however, we sent to Burnside a number of cipher messages, easy of translation, and which contained all sorts of bogus information for the purpose of misleading the enemy. Burnside or his operator at once surmised our purpose, and the general thereupon sent us in reply a lot of balderdash also calculated to deceive the uninitiated. It was about this time that the following specially important dispatch from Lincoln was filed for transmission:

Executive Mansion, Washington, November 25, 1862. 11:30 AM.

MAJOR-GENERAL BURNSIDE, Falmouth, Virginia: If I should be in boat off Aquia Creek at dark tomorrow (Wednesday) evening, could you, without inconvenience, meet me and pass an hour or two with me?

A. Lincoln

Although the Confederate operator had said good-bye several days before, we were not sure he had actually left. We therefore put Lincoln's telegram in our homemade cipher, so that if the foreign operator were still on the wire, the message might not be readily made out by the enemy. I At the same time extra precautions were taken by the Washington authorities to guard against any incident to the President while on his visit to Burnside. No record is now found of the actual text of this cipher-despatch, as finally prepared for transmission, but going back over it word for word, I believe the following is so nearly like it as to be called a true copy:

Washington, D.C., November 25, 1862

BURNSIDE, Falmouth, Virginia: Can Inn Ale me withe 2 oar our Ann pass Ann me flesh ends N. V. Corn Inn out with U cud Inn heaven day nest Wed roe Moore Tom darkey hat Greek Why Hawk of Abbott Inn B chewed I if. BATES

This sort of subterfuge is hardly worthy of becoming embalmed in the official records of the war – and apparently it wasn't. But several years later, one of identical nature did become so embalmed, for the message appears on page 236, Vol. 45, of "Telegrams received by the Secretary of War":

> Hq. Armies of the U.S., City Point, Va.,
> 8:30 a.m., April 3, 1865
>
> TINKER, War Department: A. Lincoln its in fume a in hymn to start I army treating there possible if of cut too forward pushing is He is so all Richmond aunt confide is Andy evacuated Petersburg reports Grant morning this Washington Secretary War.
> BECKWITH

Both Plum and Bates cite the foregoing telegram, and their comments are interesting if not very illuminating. Plum says merely: "By reading the above backward with regard to the phonetics rather than the orthography, the meaning will be apparent." Bates says:

> The probable reason for adopting this crude form was to insure its reaching its destination without attracting the special attention of watchful operators on the route of the City Point-Washington wire, because at that crisis every one was on the *Qui vive* for news from Grant's advancing army, and if the message had been sent in plain language, the important information it conveyed might have been overheard in its transmission and perhaps would have reached the general public in advance of its receipt by the War Department.
>
> It is not necessary to give the translation of this cipher-message. To use a homely term, 'any one can read it with his eyes shut.' In fact, the easiest way would be for one to shut the eyes and let some one else read it backward, not too slowly. The real wording then becomes plain.

Can you imagine for one moment that a "cryptogram" of such simplicity could not be read at sight by any USMTC operator, even without having someone read it to him backward? Such a "cryptogram" is hardly worthy of a schoolboy's initial effort at preparing a secret message. But I assure you that I did not make this story up, nor did I compose the cryptogram.

Ruminating upon what I have shown and told you about the cryptosystems used by both sides in the Civil War, do you get the feeling, as I do, that the cryptologic achievements of neither side can be said to add luster to undoubtedly great accomplishments on the battlefield? Perhaps this is a good place to make an appraisal of the cryptologic efficiency of each side.

First, it is fair to say that we can hardly be impressed with the cryptosystems used by either side. The respective signal corps at first transmitted by visual signals messages wholly in plain language; such messages were often intercepted and read straight away. Then both sides began enciphering such messages, the signal corps of the Federal army using a cipher disk invented by the Chief Signal Officer, the signal corps of the Confederate army using the Vigenère cipher. In both cases the use of cryptography for tactical messages was quite inept, although it seems that from time to time the Federal signalmen had better success with the Vigenère-enciphered visual messages of the Confederate signalmen than the latter had with the disk-enciphered messages of the Union signalmen.

With regard to the cryptosystem used by the Confederate Signal Corps, although there may initially have been cases in which monoalphabetic substitution alphabets were used, such alphabets were probably drawn up by agreement with the signal officers concerned and changed from time to time. Nowhere have I come across a statement that the Myer disk or something similar was used. In any event, messages transmitted by visual signals were read from time to time by Union signalmen, the record showing a number of cases in which the latter "worked out the rebel signal code" – meaning, of course, that the substitution alphabet involved was solved. When did the Confederate Signal Corps begin using the Vigenère cipher? The answer seems to be quite clear. In a letter dated 6 June 1888 from General J.H. Alexander (brother of General E.P.) to J. Willard Brown [11] we find the following statements:

> At the first inauguration of the Signal Service in the Confederacy, I, having received in the first place the primary instruction from my brother, Gen. E.P .A., then a colonel on Beauregard's staff near the Stone Bridge at Manassas, was assigned the duty of preparing a confidential circular of instruction for the initiation of officers and men, in this branch. I did prepare it, in Richmond, in early spring, 1862, and surrendered the copy to Hon. James A. Seddon, the then Secretary of War at Richmond. It was issued in form of a small pamphlet. *I had attached a table for compiling cipher dispatches – which was printed with the rest of the matter – and the whole was issued confidentially to the officers newly appointed for signal duty.*[12]

I have italicized the last sentence because I think that the "table for compiling cipher dispatches" can refer only to the Vigenère square table, for that and only that sort of table is even mentioned in accounts of the ciphers used by the Confederacy. One could, of course, wish the writer had given some further details, but there are none. However, the statement about the table is sufficiently explicit to warrant the belief that it was General J.H. Alexander who officially introduced the Vigenère square into Confederate cryptography, although he may have obtained the idea from his brother, since he states that "he received in the first place the primary instruction from my brother."

In the Federal Signal Corps, it is quite possible that polyalphabetic methods Myer cites in his *Manual* for using his cipher disk (changing the setting with successive words of a message) were used in some cases, because there are found in the record several instances in which the Confederate signalmen, successful with monoalphabetic encipherments, were completely baffled. One is warranted in the belief that it was not so much the complexities introduced by using a key word to encipher successive words of the plain text as it was the lack of training and experience in cryptanalysis that hampered Confederate signalman who tried to solve such messages. In World War I a German army system of somewhat similar nature was regularly solved by Allied cryptanalysts, but it must be remembered, in the first place, that by 1914 the use of radio made it possible to intercept volumes of traffic entirely impossible to obtain before the advent of radiotelegraphy; and in the second place, would-be cryptanalysts of both sides in the Civil War had nothing but native wit and intelligence to guide them in their work on intercepted messages, for there were, so far as the record goes, no training courses in *cryptanalysis* on either side, though there were courses in cryptography and signaling. It would seem to cryptanalysts of 1961, a century later, that native wit and intelligence nevertheless should have been sufficient to solve practically every message intercepted by either side, so simple and inefficient in usage do the cryptosystems employed by both sides appear today.

No system employed by the Federals, either for tactical messages (Signal Corps transmissions) or strategic messages (USMTC transmissions), would long resist solution today, provided, of course, that a modicum of traffic was available for study. Although technically far less secure in actual practice than properly enciphered Vigenère messages, the route ciphers of the USMTC seem to have eluded the efforts of inexpert Confederate cryptanalysts. Ex-USMTC operators make the statement that none of their messages was ever solved, and that the Confederates published intercepted messages in Southern newspapers in the hope that somebody would come forward with a solution; yet it must be remembered that those operators were Northerners who were very naturally interested in making the achievements of the Union operators, both in cryptography and cryptanalysis, appear more spectacular than they really were. And it is probable that they wrote without having made a real effort to ascertain whether the Confederates did have any success. A "real effort" would have been a rather imposing undertaking then – as it still is, I fear. Now it must be presumed that if Confederate operators had succeeded in solving intercepted traffic of the USMTC, they would have recorded the facts to their own credit. But in his seven volumes on the campaigns of Lee and his lieutenants, Douglas S. Freeman does not mention a single instance of interception and solution of telegraphic messages of the Union. Perhaps Freeman was seeking 100 percent confirmation, which is too much to expect in a field of such great secrecy. This failure of the Confederate cryptanalysts is the more astonishing when we know that copies of the USMTC cipher books were captured and that, therefore, they must have become aware of the nature of the route ciphers used by the USMTC, unless there was a lack of appreciation of the value of such captures and a failure to forward the books to the proper authorities, who could hand them over to their experts. In those books the USMTC route ciphers would have been seen in their naive simplicity, complicated only by the use of "arbitraries" or code equivalents, but hardly to the degree where all messages would be impossible to solve. It seems to me that there can be only four possible explanations for this failure to solve the USMTC route ciphers. Let us examine them in turn.

First, it is possible that there was not enough intercept traffic to permit solution. But this is inadequate as an explanation. The route cipher is of such simplicity that "depth" is hardly an absolute requirement – a single message can be solved, and its intelligibility will be determined to a large degree by the number of "arbitraries" it contains. When there are many, only the dim outlines of what is being conveyed by the message may become visible; where there are few or even none, the meaning of the messages becomes fairly evident. But the abundant records, although they contain many references to intercepts, fail to disclose even one instance of solution of a USMTC message. Thus we are forced to conclude that it was not the lack of intercept traffic that accounts for lack of success by the Confederates with USMTC messages, but some other factor.

Second, the lack of training in cryptanalysis of Confederate cryptanalysts might have been the reason why Confederate signalmen failed to solve the messages. This sounds plausible until we look into the matter with a critical spirit. Solution of route ciphers requires little training; native wit and intelligence should have been sufficient. The degree of intelligence possessed by Confederate officers and men was certainly as high as that of their Union counterparts, who were up against a technically far superior cryptosystem, the Vigenère. We may safely conclude that it was not lack of native wit and intelligence that prevented them from solving messages enciphered by the USMTC route ciphers.

Third, it is possible that Confederate high commanders were not interested in communications intelligence operators or in gathering the fruits of such operations. Such an explanation seems on its face fatuous and wholly unacceptable. We know of the high estimate of value field commanders placed upon the interception and solution of tactical messages transmitted by visual signaling; but an appreciation of the extraordinary advantages of learning the contents of enemy communications on the strategic level may have been lacking. My colleague, Mr. Fishel, thinks that "intelligence consciousness" and "intelligence sophistication" were of a very low order in the Union army, and of a markedly lower order in the Confederate army. But to us, in 1961, to disregard the advantages of a possible reading of strategic messages seems almost incredible, and I am inclined to discount this sort of explanation.

Fourth, it is possible that Confederate cryptanalysts were far more successful in their efforts to solve USMTC transmissions than present publicly available records indicate; that Confederate commanders obtained great advantages from their communications intelligence operations; that they fully recognized the supreme necessity of keeping this fact and these advantages secret; and that the Confederate States government adopted and enforced strict communications intelligence security regulations, so that the truth concerning these matters has not yet emerged. Let it be noted in this connection that very little information can be found in the public domain today about Allied cryptanalytic successes during World War I; and were it not for the very intensive and extensive investigations in the matter of the Japanese attack on Pearl Harbor on 7 December 1941, very little, if any, information would be known to the public about British and American successes in communications intelligence during World War II. Immediately following the capture of Richmond and before Confederate records could be removed to a safe place, a great fire broke out and practically all those records were destroyed. It is possible that this is one of the reasons why the records of their communications intelligence successes have never come to light. But it is also possible that Confederate cryptanalysts kept their secrets to themselves. We know that the records possessed or taken by certain Confederate leaders have been gone over with great care and attention, but what happened to those retained by other Confederate leaders, such as Secretary of War Seddon or his predecessor Judah P. Benjamin, who later became secretary of state, and others? Here is a fascinating speculation and one that might well repay careful, painstaking research in the voluminous records of our National Archives. I shall leave the delving into those records to some of you young and aspiring professional cryptanalysts who may be interested in undertaking such a piece of research. With this thought I bring this lecture to a close.

NOTES

1. And, of course, the G.I.s of those days had a pet name for the users of the system. They called them "flag floppers."

2. This reversal can be seen in figure 53.

3. Ruled paper was provided to aid in accuracy. In the diagram the upper of each pair of lines of writing is the cipher, the lower one, the plain text. Simon Cameron was Lincoln's secretary of war until January 1862, when he was replaced by Edwin M. Stanton. If this message cited by Plum is authentic, and there is no reason to doubt this, then Cameron was still in friendly contact with Lincoln, possibly as a special observer.

4. It was the usual practice to use for address and signature the names of the USMTC operators concerned,

5. The series was then put out in book form under the same title by the Appleton-Century Company, New York, 1907, reprinted in 1939.

6. In searching for a good example, my eye caught the words "Lincoln shot" at the left of the matrix and I immediately thought that the message had to do with Booth's assassination of the president. But after hurriedly translating the message and finding nothing in it having anything to do with the shooting, it occurred to me to look up the indicators for a matrix of six rows and eight columns. They turned out to be LINCOLN (message of eight columns), SHOT (6 rows). The word SMALL beneath the "Lincoln shot" is a variant for SHOT, also meaning "6 rows."

7. A key word is employed to change the alphabets cyclically, thus making the cipher what is called today a periodic polyalphabetic cipher controlled by the individual letters of a key, which may consist of a word, a phrase, or even of a sentence, repeated as many times as necessary.

8. *Battles and Leaders of the Civil War* (New York: The Century Co., 1884), 581.

9. A curious coincidence – or was it fortuitous foreshadowing of an event far in the future? – can be seen in the sequence of the last two words of the cipher text. The message is dated September 30, 1862; the *New York Herald* and the *New York Tribune* combined to make the *New York Herald-Tribune* on March 19, 1924–62 years later!

10. I should warn you that it contains several errors!

11. Op. cit., 206.

12. My emphasis. W.F.F.

Lecture V

For a half century following the close of the Civil War, cryptology in the United States enjoyed a period of hibernation from which it awoke at long last about 1914, not refreshed, as did Rip Van Winkle, but weaker. This is perhaps understandable if we take into account that the United States was able to enjoy a long era of peace, broken only briefly by the short war with Spain in 1898. For over three decades there was little or no need for cryptology in the United States government, except for the communications of the Department of State. The military and naval services apparently felt that in time of peace there was no need for either cryptography or cryptanalysis, and since it looked as though the United States was going to enjoy peace for long, an indefinitely long time, those services did not think it necessary to engage in theoretical cryptologic studies. Of course, the War Department and the Army still had those route ciphers and cipher disks described in the preceding lecture; the Navy Department and the Navy had cipher disks for producing simple monoalphabetic ciphers; and the State Department had a code more or less specifically designed for its communications. Separated from Europe by the broad Atlantic, and mindful of General Washington's policy of noninvolvement in the problems of European diplomacy, America followed the traditional and easy course of isolationism. The quarrels among the countries in Europe were none of our business, and America turned its back to them for a half century, uninvolved and unconcerned.

There was, however, in this long hibernating period in U.S. cryptology one episode of particular interest. It concerned a presidential election in which the circumstances paralleled the election of 1960, when the very small popular-vote majority of the Democratic candidate suggested a possible upset in the electoral college voting. The episode to which I refer occurred nearly a century ago, in the presidential election of 1876, in which Democratic candidate Samuel J. Tilden was pitted against Republican candidate Rutherford B. Hayes. On the basis of early evening election returns, Tilden seemed to be easily the winner. Indeed, just before going to bed on election night, 8 November 1876, Hayes conceded the election to Tilden, and the newspapers the next morning followed this lead and reported a Tilden victory. But when final tallies began coming in, they showed that the closeness of the popular vote made Tilden's victory not as sure as his supporters had calculated, and they therefore began to become apprehensive about their candidate's victory. Their apprehensions were valid because of our peculiar system of electing a president, peculiar because it is the electoral and not the popular vote which determines who is to be the next occupant of the White House. Two days after the people had voted, it became clear that Tilden would have 184 electoral votes, just one short of insuring victory, whereas Hayes would have only 163, thus needing twenty-two more. The Tilden supporters began a frantic campaign to get that one additional vote they needed, and they didn't hesitate to try every possible ruse to obtain it, including bribery, a rather serious piece of business and one obviously requiring a good deal of secrecy, especially in communications. Of course, many telegrams had to be exchanged between the Tilden headquarters in New York City and confidential agents who had to be sent to certain states where one or more electoral votes could perhaps be purchased; telegrams also had to be exchanged among those secret agents in the field. About 400 telegrams were exchanged, and some 200 of these were in cryptographic form. Communication difficulties caused two almost consummated bribery deals to fall through; and a third deal failed because the electors proved to be honest Republicans not susceptible to monetary temptation. The existence of these telegrams, however, remained unknown to the public for months. We shall come to them later.

Despite the efforts of the Tilden supporters, the outcome of the election remained in doubt because four states – Florida, South Carolina, Louisiana, and Oregon – each sent two groups of electors, an event not foreseen or provided for in the Constitution. A crisis arose, and the country seemed to be on the verge of another civil war. By an act of 29 January 1877, Congress created a special electoral commission to investigate and decide upon the matter of the disputed electoral votes in the four states. Recounts of votes in certain election precincts were made, sometimes aided by soldiers of the Federal army. The commission voted in favor of the Hayes electors in each case, and having obtained the needed twenty-two electoral votes, Hayes entered the White House.

It was only some months afterward that the telegrams to which I have referred were brought to light, and a situation arose which Congress felt it had to look into. Somehow or other, in the summer of 1878, copies of those telegrams had come into the possession of a Republican newspaper in New York, *The Tribune*. Interested only in ascertaining the truth, the editor put two members of his staff on the job, and they succeeded in solving those telegrams that were in cipher.

Various books dealing with the political aspects of his intriguing story are available in public libraries, but those of you who are interested only in its cryptologic aspects will find excellent material in the following four documents:

[1] "The Cipher Dispatches," *The New York Tribune*, Extra No. 44, New York, (14 January) 1879.

[2] Hassard, John R.G., "Cryptography in Politics," *The North American Review*, Vol CXXVII, No. 268, March 1879, 315-25.

[3] Holden, Edward S., *The Cipher Dispatches*, New York, 1879.

[4] *U.S. House Miscellaneous Documents, Vol. 5, 45th Congress, 3rd Session, 1878-79*. The last-mentioned item, that put out by the congressional committee which had been designated to conduct the investigation (and which was named "The Select Committee on alleged frauds in the Presidential Election of 1876") is of special interest. In the course of the investigation, the committee solicited the technical assistance of Professor Edward S. Holden, of the United States Naval Observatory in Washington, the author of the third item listed above, who, I believe, was a captain in the navy and had specialized in mathematics. *The Tribune* had brought him into the picture by asking his help when solution seemed hopeless, but it turned out that Mr. John R.G. Hassard, the chief of *The Tribune* staff, and his colleague, Colonel William M. Grosvenor, also of that staff, solved the ciphers independently and, in fact, shortly before Professor Holden solved them, although it was the latter that the congressional committee called upon to explain matters, as would only be natural under the circumstances.

Professor Holden's testimony, in which he set forth his solution of the nearly 200 cryptograms entered in evidence, is presented in the form of a letter to the committee, dated 21 February 1879. In it he described and explained all the cryptosystems used, together with their keys and full details of their application. In that letter, Professor Holden makes the following statement: "By September 7, 1878, I was in possession of a rule by which any key to the most difficult and ingenious of these [ciphers] could infallibly be found." Most of the ciphers involved word transpositions and Holden worked out the keys, but in this he had been anticipated by the *Tribune* cryptanalysts. There were in all ten different keys, two for messages of 10, 15, . . words, up to and including two for messages of thirty words. On the following page will be found the complete "Table of Keys."

You may be wondering why there are two transposition keys for each pair of messages from ten to thirty words, in multiples of 5. The two keys constituting a pair are related to each other, that is, they bear a relationship that Mr. Hassard, one of the *Tribune* cryptanalysts, termed "correlative," but which we now would call an "encipher-decipher" or a "verse-inverse" relationship. Either sequence of a correlative pair of sequences may be used to encipher a message; the other can then be used to decipher the message. For example, key III consists of the following series of numbers: 8-4-1-7-13..., etc., and the correlative, key IV, is 3-7-12-2-6..., etc. A cipher message of fifteen words can be deciphered either by (1) numbering its words consecutively and then assembling the words in the other 8-4-1-7-13, or by (2) writing the sequence 3-7-12-2-6... above the words of the cipher message and then assembling the numbered words according to the sequence 1-2-3-4-5 .... Thus, there were, in reality, not ten different transposition keys but only five. In the case of each pair of keys, one of them must have been the basic sequence, the other the inverse of it, or at least some derivative thereof.

I suspect that the basic or "verse" sequences of numbers were not drawn up at random but were derived from words or phrases; and I think that they were the odd-numbered ones because, as you will notice, it is in the odd-numbered keys that the *positions of sequent digits* reflect the presence of an underlying key word or phrase; this is not true in the even-numbered keys. I have not seriously attempted to reconstruct the key words, but perhaps some of you may like to try and will succeed in doing so.

In addition to transposition, this system involved the use of "arbitraries" to represent certain words, the names of important persons and places, etc. There were also a few nulls.

Professor Holden adds some comments about this system that are worth quoting:

TABLE OF KEYS

10 Words		15 Words		20 Words		25 Words		30 Words	
I	II	III	IV	V	VI	VII	VIII	IX	X
9	4	8	3	6	12	6	18	17	4
3	7	4	7	9	18	12	12	30	26
6	2	1	12	3	3	23	6	26	23
1	9	7	2	5	5	18	25	1	15
10	6	13	6	4	4	10	14	11	8
5	3	5	8	13	1	3	1	20	27
2	8	2	4	14	20	17	16	25	16
7	10	6	1	20	16	20	11	5	30
4	1	11	11	19	2	15	21	10	24
8	5	14	15	12	19	19	5	29	9
		9	9	17	13	8	15	27	5
		3	14	1	10	2	2	19	19
		15	5	11	6	24	17	28	17
		12	10	15	7	5	24	24	25
		10	13	18	14	11	9	4	22
				8	17	7	22	7	28
				16	11	13	7	13	1
				2	15	1	4	18	18
				10	9	25	10	12	12
				7	8	22	8	22	6
						9	23	21	21
						16	20	15	20
						21	3	3	29
						14	13	9	14
						4	19	14	7
								2	3
								6	11
								16	13
								23	10
								8	2

Fig. 70

The essence of this ingenious and novel system consists in taking apart a sentence written in plain English (dismembering it, as it were) and again writing all the words in a new order, in which they make no sense. The problem of deciphering it consists in determining the order according to which the words of the cipher should be written in order to produce the original message.

There is one way, and only one way, in which the general problem can be solved, and that is to take two messages, A and B, of the same number of words, and to number the words in each; then to arrange message A with its words in an order which will make sense, and to arrange the words of message B in the same order. There will be one order – and only one – in which the two messages will simultaneously make sense. This is the key.

Here, in a nutshell, we find the basic theory of solving transposition ciphers by anagramming messages of the same length, explained in a most succinct manner.

It appears that Professor Holden, clever as he was, did not note the verse-inverse relation in each pair of sequences, or if he did, he failed to mention it in his testimony. However, Hassard [2] specifically points this out.

There were enough messages in this system to make it possible to solve codewords used, as well as to recognize a few nulls which were occasionally added to complicate matters. Hence, the most complicated of the cryptosystems involved in this bizarre political episode were solved.

Another system used by the conspirators employed a bilateral substitution, that is, one in which a pair of cipher letters represents a single letter. This substitution was based upon a 10 x 10 checkerboard. Apparently neither Professor Holden nor the *Tribune* cryptanalysts recognized the latter principle, nor did they find that the coordinates of the checkerboard employed a key phrase, nor did they realize that the same checkerboard, with numerical coordinates, was used for a numerical substitution alphabet in which pairs of digits represent letters of the alphabet.

Here are two of the messages exchanged by the conspirators, one in letter cipher, the other in the figure cipher The messages are long enough for solution. Try to solve them, reconstruct the matrix and find the key phrase from which the coordinates of the matrix were derived. It should amuse you by its appropriateness.

The message in letter cipher is as follows:

Jacksonville, Nov. 16 (1876)

Geo. R Raney, Tallahassee:

PP YY EM NS HY YY PI MA SH NS YY SS
IT EP AA EN SH NS SE US SH NS MM PI
YY SN PP YE AA PI EI SS YE SH AI NS SS
PE EI YY SH NY NS SS YE PI AA NY IT NS
SH YY SP YY PI NS YY SS IT EM EI PI MM
EI SS EI YY EI SS IT EI EP YY PE EI AA SS
IM AA YE SP NS YY IA NS SS EI SS MM PP
NS PI NS SN PI NS IM IM YY IT EM YY SS
PE YY MN NS YY SS IT SP YY PE EP PP
MA AA YY PI IT   L'Engle goes up tomorrow.

(Signed) Daniel

The example in figure cipher is as follows:

Jacksonville, Nov. 17 (1876)

S. Pasco and E. M. L'Engle:

84 55 84 25 93 34 82 31 31 75 93 82 77 33
55 52 93 20 90 66 77 65 33 84 63 31 31 93
20 82 33 66 52 48 44 55 42 82 48 89 42 93
31 82 66 75 31 93

(Signed) Daniel

There were several other systems involved in this episode of political skullduggery, but I am going to pass them by because they hardly deserve attention in this brief history. I do, however, want to call your attention to the very close resemblance between the word-transposition ciphers characterized by Professor Holden as the "most difficult and ingenious" of the ciphers he solved, and the USMTC route ciphers described in the preceding lecture. Yet, not only he but also the *Tribune* amateur cryptanalysts solved those ciphers without too much difficulty, even though they were technically more complex. I think their work on the Tilden ciphers clearly confirms my own appraisal of the weakness of the route ciphers used by the USMTC in the Civil War.

After this digression into the realm of what may be called political cryptology, let us now go on with our military cryptologic history. I have already told you that the Department of State used a code for cryptographic communications in the years following the Civil War, but I do not know what it was like. It may even have been an adaptation of some commercial code. But in an article entitled "Secret Writing," which appeared in *Century Magazine*, Vol. LXXXV, November 1912, No.1, a man named John H. Haswell, apparently at that time a code clerk in the Department, referred to a new code of the Department in the following terms:

> The cipher of the Department of State is the most modern of all in the service of the Government. It embraces the valuable features of its predecessors and the merits of the latest inventions. Being used for every species of diplomatic correspondence, it is necessarily copious and unrestricted in its capabilities, but at the same time it is economic in its terms of expression. It is simple and speedy in its operation, but so ingenious as to secure absolute secrecy. The construction of this cipher, like many ingenious devices whose operations appear to be simple to the eye but are difficult to explain in writing, would actually require the key to be furnished for the purpose of an intelligible description of it.

Only four years later a certain telegraph operator and code clerk of the State Department proved how vulnerable the Department's system of enciphered code really was. His name was Herbert O. Yardley (fig. 71), and many of you may know a bit about him as the author of a famous or infamous book (depending upon whose side you're on) entitled *The American Black Chamber*, published in Indianapolis by the Bobbs-Merrill Co. in 1931. So far as I know, it is the only book that cannot be legally reprinted in the United States because a special law passed in 1934 makes it a criminal offense to do so. That is quite a story in itself, but I cannot tell it now. If you happen to own a copy of the first and only American edition, don't let it get away from you, because you can obtain another copy of it only by a more or less "under the table" deal; but you may be able to purchase a British edition, or a translation in French, in Japanese, or in other languages, for the book was sensational. But to return to that State Department cryptosystem, which was considered by Haswell as giving absolute secrecy and which was readily solved by Yardley, here is what appears on the cover page of Yardley's twenty-one-page typewritten analysis and solution of the system:

Fig. 71

THEORY AND PRACTICE OF
ENCIPHERED CODE
State Department Problems
I, II, and III

Note: The following was written in March 1916 and, so far as I can learn, is the first successful attempt to solve a problem in enciphered code.

H.O. Yardley

Yardley was quite wrong in thinking that his was the first successful attempt to solve a problem in enciphered code, for in Europe more complicated cases were often solved, and I imagine that European cryptanalysts could have read, and perhaps did read, State Department messages as a more or less routine matter. I think I am warranted in assuming that what I have just said is true because, in Europe, cryptanalytic studies were going on apace during the years of American neglect of such studies. The turning point from neglect to a renaissance of interest in cryptographic studies in Europe is said by some authorities to have been about the year 1880; but we must confine ourselves for the most part to developments in America, in order to keep this lecture within bounds of what can be told in a limited time.

In our navy it seems that simple monoalphabetic ciphers continued in use until the middle of the eighties, when several naval officers were designated to prepare a more suitable system, based upon a code particularly designed for naval communications. The system they worked out was embodied in a very large codebook, 18" long, 12" wide, and 2" thick, which had the official title *The U.S. Navy Secret Code*. There was also an accompanying but separate cipher book, almost as large, designated as *The Book of Key Words*. In addition to these was a third large book called *General Geographical Tables*. The system was placed into effect on 1 December 1887. Later I will show you a most historic message sent in that system of secret communication, which today impresses one as being extraordinarily clumsy and slow.

In our army, in the middle of the eighties, a code was also prepared. It is no pleasure to have to tell you that its composition and format hardly shed laurels upon those responsible for its reproduction, because it was merely a simple and acknowledged adaptation of a commercially available small code for use by the general public, first published in 1870 with the title *Telegraphic Code to Ensure Secresy* [sic] *in the Transmission of Telegrams*. It had been compiled by the secretary of the French Trans-Atlantic Telegraph Company, a man named Robert Slater, and it became known everywhere as "Slater's Code." As to the nature of the code, I will quote from Slater's own "Short explanation of the mode of using this work," in a sort of preface to the 2nd Edition:

> It is a numbered Telegraphic Dictionary of the English language, of which each word bears a distinctive No. (from 00001 to 25000, with exactly 100 words per page), and the method of using it is by an interchange of Nos., in accordance with a private understanding between correspondents that a further No. is to be added to or deducted from the number in the code, of the word telegraphed or written, to indicate the real word intended, that a 'Symbolic' or 'Dummy Word' is telegraphed, the meaning of which can only be read by those who have the key to the secret of how many should be added to or deducted from the original number in the Code, of the 'Dummy Word' to find the word meant. (Punctuation as in the original)

Here we have a sentence of 116 words. Though it is rather long and a bit murky, I think you will gather its import. The system as thus far described is what we now call the additive or subtractive method. But in the detailed instructions Slater goes one step further and suggests that instead of telegraphing the code number resulting from addition or subtraction of a key number, the word standing alongside the sum (or difference) of the mathematical operation be sent as the telegraphic code. Slater's code must have met with popular acclaim because by 1906 it was in its fifth edition. A copy of the second edition (1870) is in my collection. As for a copy of the very first edition, not even the Library of Congress has one, it's that scarce.

To get on with the story, in 1885 the War Department published an adaptation of Slater's Code for its use and the use of the Army. Here is the picture of its title page, the only difference between it and that of Slater's Code being in the spelling of the word "secrecy," as you can easily see in the picture I. show you next (fig. 72). It would appear that the "compiler" of this code, Colonel Gregory, was just a bit deficient in imagination. Not only did he merely borrow the basic idea and format of Slater's Code, but even when it came to explaining and giving examples of enciphering the code groups, the colonel used not only the identical rules but also the very same wording and even the very same type of examples of transformations that are found in Slater's original. Let me show you an example of Slater's code side by side with the same example in Gregory's. (See fig 73.)

You will note that Colonel Gregory just couldn't use the same text for his examples of enciperment that Slater used, which was "The Queen is the supreme power in the Realm." Instead he used the enigmatic text "War is a punishment whereof death is the maximum."[1]

All the other methods and examples of enciperment in the two codes are practically identical. Colonel Gregory gives credit in the following terms to a civilian aide in his great work: "The labor of compiling the new vocabulary has been performed by Mr. W. G. Spottswood." What did the latter do? Well, Mr. Spottswood's work consisted of casting out from Slater's list such words as ABALIENATE and ABANDONEE and replacing them with such words as ABATEMENT and ABATIS. This sort of work must indeed have been arduous. I'm sorry to appear to be critical of the performance of my predecessors in the construction of codes and code systems for War Department and Army usage, but I feel sure you will agree that more imagination and

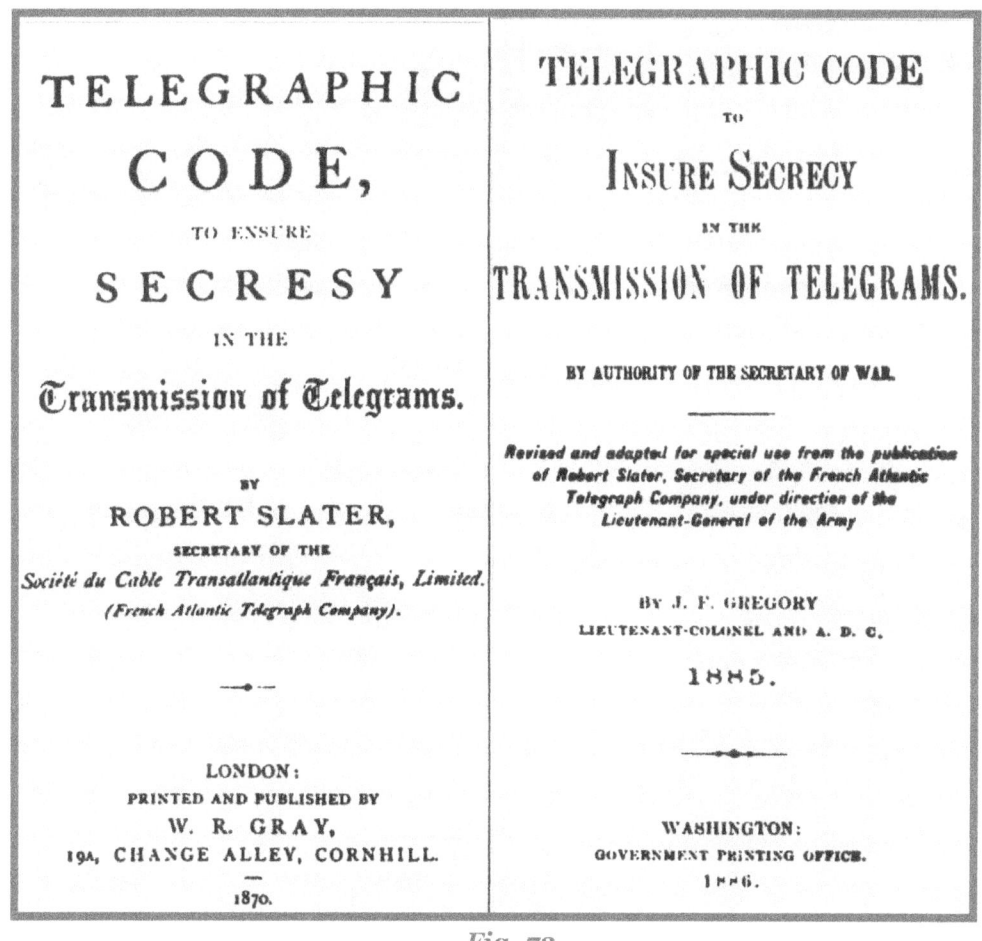

Fig. 72

EXAMPLES. vii

EXAMPLE I.

The Queen is the supreme power in the Realm.

Add any number below 25000 (say, for instance,) 5555 to the numbers opposite to those words it is desired to transmit. Where the result exceeds 25000, deduct that number, or, in other words, commence the alphabet again.

Word to be transmitted.	No. in Vocabulary.	Plus 5555.	Representing in Vocabulary.
The	22313	27868	Bounteous
Queen	18095	23650	wedge
is	12370	17925	purifying
the	22313	27868	bounteous
supreme	21953	27508	biography
power	17056	22611	transparent
in	11426	16981	posed
the	22313	27868	bounteous
Realm	18419	23974	yoke

The message being transmitted:—

Bounteous wedge purifying bounteous biography transparent posed bounteous yoke,

the receiver reverses the operation, adding 25000 to the number where it is below that to be deducted.

Word received.	No. in Vocabulary.	Minus 5555.	Representing in Vocabulary.
Bounteous	02868	22313	The
wedge	23650	18095	Queen
purifying	17925	12370	is
bounteous	02868	22313	the
biography	02508	21953	supreme
transparent	22611	17056	power
posed	16981	11426	in
bounteous	02868	22313	the
yoke	23974	18419	Realm

VI EXAMPLES.

EXAMPLE I.

War is a punishment whereof death is the maximum.

Add any number below 25000 (say, for instance, 3333) to the numbers opposite to those words it is desired to transmit. Where the result exceeds 25000, deduct that number, or, in other words, commence the alphabet again.

Word to be transmitted.	Number in vocabulary	Plus 3333.	Representing in vocabulary.
War	23724	27057	Barker
is	12373	15706	ovation
a	00001	03334	cairn
punishment	17893	21226	sousing
whereof	23887	27220	begetting
death	06202	09535	frequent
is	12373	15706	ovation
the	22327	25660	agape
maximum	14032	17365	priggish

The message being transmitted reads—

Barker ovation cairn sousing begetting frequent ovation agape priggish,

the receiver reverses the operation, adding 25000 to the number where it is below that to be deducted.

Word received.	Number in vocabulary.	Minus 3333.	Representing in vocabulary.
Barker	02057	23724	War
ovation	15706	12373	is
cairn	03334	00001	a
sousing	21226	17893	punishment
begetting	02220	23887	whereof
frequent	09535	06202	death
ovation	15706	12373	is
agape	00660	22327	the
priggish	17365	14032	maximum

Fig. 73

ingenuity could have been employed than were used by Colonel Gregory and Mr. Spottswood.

Colonel Gregory prepared a confidential letter addressed to Lieutenant General Sheridan, "Commanding Army of the United States," to explain the advantages of the new code. But in this letter Colonel Gregory quotes very largely from Holden's little brochure [3] and deals almost solely with the ways in which additional security may be gained by changing the additives to the code numbers in Slater's Code. For example, for all messages sent in January add 111; for all messages sent in February add 222, in March 333, etc. Another suggested way: "Send out a simple message in ordinary English: Add 1437 to all ciphers until further orders."

Believe it or not, this was the code that the War Department and the Army used during the Spanish-American War. It was apparently used with a simple additive, because in a copy in my collection the additive is written on the inside of the front cover. It is 777; perhaps it was the additive for the month of July, but the number 777 was written in ink, so it may have been the permanent additive for the whole of the war. In pages 41-42 of *The American Black Chamber*, the author throws an interesting sidelight on this code system:

> The compilation of codes and ciphers was, by General Orders, a Signal Corps function, but the war [1917] revealed the unpreparedness of this department in the United States. How much so is indicated by a talk I had with a high officer of the Signal Corps who had just been appointed a military

attaché to an Allied country. It was not intended that attachés should actually encode and decode their own telegrams, but as a part of an intelligence course they were required to have a superficial knowledge of both processes in order that they might appreciate the importance of certain precautions enforced in safeguarding our communications.

When the new attaché, a veteran of the old Army, appeared, I handed him a brochure and rapidly went over some of our methods of secret communications. To appreciate his attitude, the reader should understand that the so-called additive or subtractive method for garbling a code telegram (used during the Spanish-American War) is about as effective for maintaining secrecy as the simple substitution cipher which as children we read in Foe's 'The Gold Bug.'

He listened impatiently, then growled: 'That's a lot of nonsense. Whoever heard of going to all that trouble? During the Spanish-American War we didn't do all those things. We just added the figure 1898 to all our figure code words, and the Spaniards never did find out about it.'

Although *The American Black Chamber* abounds with exaggerations and distortions, what the author tells about the inadequacies of United States codes and ciphers in the years just before our entry into World War I is true enough, and Yardley's impatience and satiric comments in this regard, it grieves me to say, are unfortunately fully warranted.

During or perhaps shortly after the end of the Spanish-American War, the War Department must have begun to realize that there were shortcomings in the code based upon Slater's Code, the one which was in current usage and upon which I have already dwelt. On 16 January 1898 the publication of a new War Department Telegraphic Code was authorized by General Orders No.9. The code was to be prepared under the direction of General A. W. Greely, then Chief Signal Officer of the Army. The cited General Order makes it quite clear that the War Department version of Slater's Code was still in use, but the Western Union Telegraphic Code was to be used in connection with Slater's until the new War Department Code was completed; it apparently was ready in December 1899, when Slater's was withdrawn from use with this statement in General Orders No. 203: "By direction of the Secretary of War, the *Telegraphic Code to Insure Secrecy in the Transmission of Telegrams*, will on and after January 15, 1900, only be used for correspondence in such cases as may be specially ordered by the Secretary of War." On 12 December 1899 the new War Department Code was issued. Here is a picture of its title page (fig. 74). It comprised a specially compiled list of tables, words, phrases, and sentences to which code numbers and code words were assigned for specific use in War Department and Army communications. The code numbers began with 78201 and went to 95286; the accompanying code words were foreign, outlandishly unusual real words, and artificial words, beginning with KOPERKIES, KOPERKLEURS, KOPERMOLEN, etc., etc., down through the L's, M's and ending with words such as NAZWELGEN, NEANTHE, NEAPELGELB, etc., etc. You may wish to know why the code numbers didn't begin with 00000 and go to 99999; or why the code groups began with K and went for thousands and thousands of words down to N. The answer is that this brand new War Department Telegraphic Code was to be used, as Slater's Code was used, in conjunction with the Western Union Telegraphic Code, a code of 78,200 groups beginning with numerical code groups 00000 accompanied by literal code words beginning with BEERKAR, BEERKARREN, BEERMELD... and going to KOOT JONGEN, KOOTKRUID, KOOTSPEL. Here is a picture of a typical page in this code (fig. 75).

The introduction to this code explains this puzzling fact:

> Through lack of time it has been impossible to incorporate in the *War Department Telegraphic Code* all desirable phrases, and in consequence the first 471 pages of the *Western Union Telegraphic Code* now in use by the Army will continue in use as a supplementary code. This affords the Army the telegraphic use of 100,000 code words, of which numbers 1 to 78,201, inclusive, are in the *Western Union Telegraphic Code* and numbers 78,201 to 100,000 are in the *War Department Telegraphic Code.*

It thus becomes clear that for several years the new War Department Code was to be used in conjunction with the commercially available large *Western Union Telegraphic Code*. This was stated to be for the purpose of economy. For secrecy, the additive or subtractive method was to be used. The futility of such an old and simple method for achieving communications security needs no comment. I wish there were time to read you the instructions in that new *War Department Telegraphic Code* regarding the use of these ciphers for secrecy. They are practically the same as those in the 1885 version of Slater's Code and are unbelievably futile, but what else could be expected when cryptology is relegated to a position in military science far inferior to that of teaching the use of a rifle or bayonet, subjects which are taught, as a rule, by experts? Why was cryptology left to inexperienced amateurs during all those years? Was it stupidity? No, just a lack of appreciation of the importance of secure communications in military operations – and a lack of enough people with the requisite know-how.

How long this combination of two codes continued to be used I don't know, Sometime from 1900 to 1915 this absurd system must have proved itself entirely unsatisfactory, for in 1915 another brand new *War Department Telegraph Code* was put out, under direction of Brigadier General George P. Scriven, the Chief Signal Officer of the Army who succeeded Greeley. A picture of its title page can be seen on page 99. (fig. 76). The book bears no security classification, for even as late as 1915 there was no real or definite classification system for security purposes. The instructions recommended certain precautions. "The War Department Telegraph Code," says paragraph 5 of the instructions, "while not absolutely confidential, will be guarded with the greatest care and will never be out of the immediate possession or control of the officer to whom issued or of his confidential agent. Care will be taken to prevent theft, loss, use, or inspection except by

Fig. 74

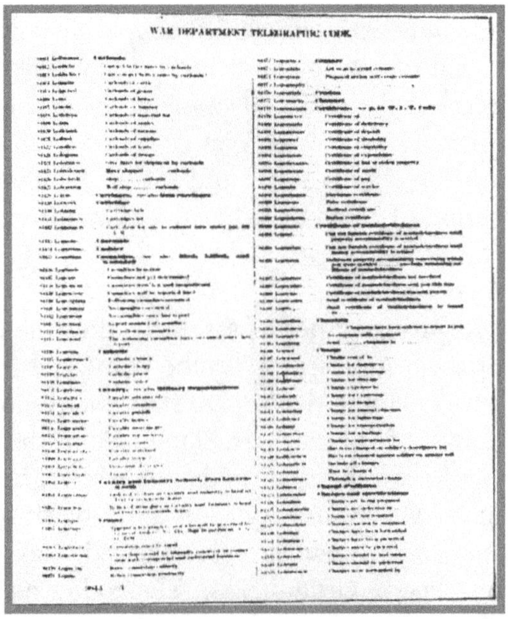

Fig. 75

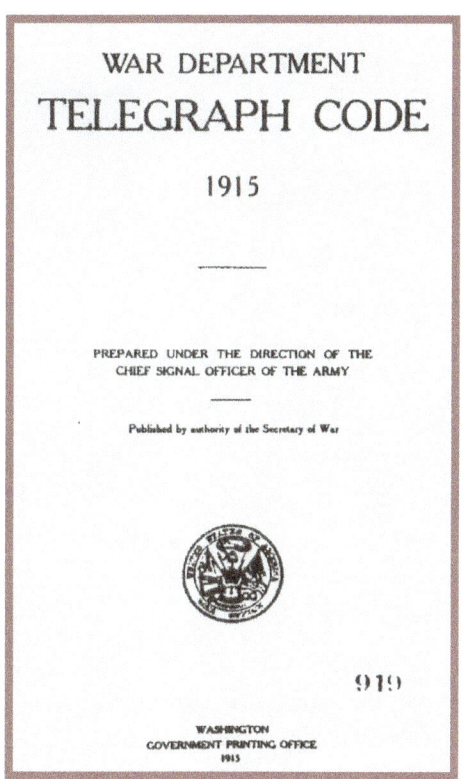

Fig. 76

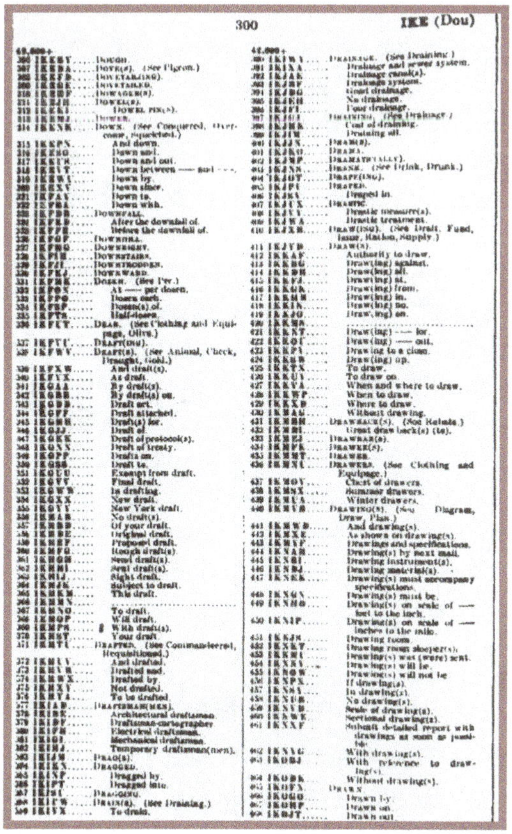

Fig. 77

those whose duties require them to employ the code. Special pains will be taken to prevent the code from falling into the hands of unauthorized persons or of the enemy."

This new code was intended, as was its predecessor, to serve two purposes: "First, secrecy and second, economy. When secrecy is desired it is to be used as a cipher code, as is explained in subsequent paragraphs under 'Enciphered Code'." But there are no subsequent paragraphs in which this is explained. Apparently some change in this regard was decided, because I have seen, as a separate pamphlet, a set of cipher tables for use with this code.

The code itself embodied some of the latest ideas of code compilation. It had over 113,000 code groups, and these were both five-figure groups and, for the first time, five-letter groups. The latter embodied the principle of the two-letter difference, but the instructions do not mention this fact, and no permutation table was included in the code itself. The book has a very extensive vocabulary of words, phrases, and sentences. Here is a picture of a typical page (fig. 77). I feel sure that a great deal of thought and effort went into the production of this code, but I must tell you two things about it. First, I must tell you that my immediate predecessor in the Office of the Chief Signal Officer told me, on my return from France in 1919, that that particular edition of the War Department Telegraph Code had been printed in Cleveland by a commercial printer, and, second, that when the United States became a belligerent in World War I, our British allies found it desirable to notify the U.S. government (through our G-2) that our War Department Telegraph Code was not safe to use, even with its superencipherment tables. The implications of this notification are rather obvious and hardly require comment. The compilation of a new code in 1917 was initiated, but this time the work was done within and under the direction of the Military Intelligence Division of the General Staff (G-2), and in particular within the section devoted to cryptanalysis. This undertaking, which indubitably was a direct affront to the Signal

Page 101

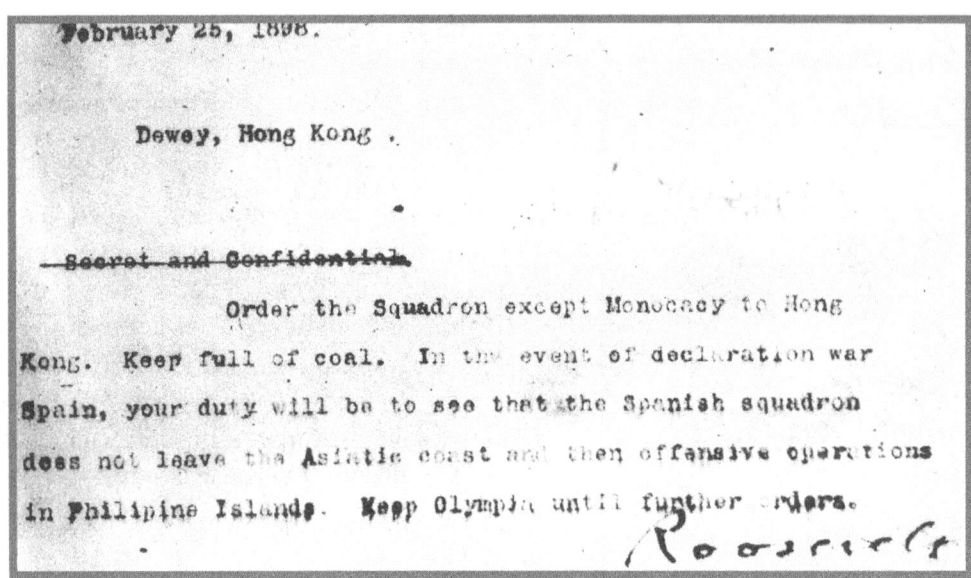

Fig. 78

Corps of the Army, met with no objection, it seems, from that group; perhaps it deserved the intended insult because of its long-standing neglect of its clear responsibilities for cryptography and cryptographic operations in and for the Army.

We have noted how inadequately the Army and the War Department were equipped for cryptocommunications from 1885 to 1915. Let us see how well equipped the Navy and the Navy Department were. For this purpose I have an excellent example and one of great historical significance and interest. You will recall my mention of the appointment of a board of navy officers to prepare a suitable cryptosystem for the Navy, and I told you about the large basic vocabulary and tabular contents of the codebook and its accompanying two large books, one for enciphering the code groups, the other for geographical names. For the story we go back to the time of President McKinley, whose election brought Theodore Roosevelt, a former member of the Civil Service Commission, back to Washington as assistant secretary of the navy. Teddy was an ardent advocate of military and naval preparedness. He forthrightly and frankly favored a strong foreign policy, backed by adequate military and naval strength – "speak softly but carry a big stick" was his now-famous motto. He was looking forward, in fact, to forcing the ultimate withdrawal of the European powers from the Western Hemisphere. With vigor, he set to work to make the Navy ready. When the battleship *Maine* was blown up in Havana harbor on 15 February 1898, Roosevelt sharpened his efforts. During a temporary absence of his chief, Navy Secretary John D. Long, he took it upon himself to initiate the preparations which he had in vain tried to persuade the secretary to make. He ordered great quantities of coal and ammunition, directed the assembling of the Fleet, and stirred the arsenals and navy yards into activity. On a miserably cold Saturday afternoon, ten days after the *Maine* was blown up, and still in the absence of Secretary Long, Teddy sat down and wrote out a cablegram to go to Commodore George Dewey at Hong Kong.You can see it above, with his bold signature at the bottom (fig. 78).

That is the now historic message that alerted Dewey and that resulted in our taking over the Philippine Islands under U.S. protection in the war with Spain, which was declared ten days later.

You will note that the message bears on its face a security classification, but the classification, "Secret and Confidential," was crossed out. That must have been many years later, for those three words appear in the plain text of the deciphered and decoded cablegram. Below is a picture of the code cablegram with its strange and outlandish code words, as it was received in Hong Kong (fig. 79).

And now I show you the deciphered and decoded text, which I was fortunate in being able to produce by courtesy of the chief of the Naval Security Group, who permitted me to consult and use the necessary codebooks that I found were still in Naval Security Group archives (fig. 80).

To translate a message in the code then in use, three steps are necessary. First, the cable words (the peculiar, outlandish words in line 2 – WASSERREIF, PAUSATURA, BADANADOS, etc.) are sought in the cipher book and their accompanying cable-word numbers set down. WASSERREIF yields 99055; PAUSATURA yields 62399, BADANADOS, 11005, etc. The next step is to append the first digit of the second cable-word number to the last digit of the first cable-word number to make the latter a six-digit number. Thus 99055 becomes 990556. The six-digit code group number 990556 is then sought in the basic codebook, and its meaning is found to be "Secret and Confidential." The transfer of the first digit, 6, of the second cable-word number, 62399, makes it become code-number 2399, to which must now be appended the first two digits of the third cable-word number, 11005, thus making the second code group of the code message 239911, which is sought in the basic codebook and yields the meaning "Order the squadron." And so on. It's painfully slow work, and I haven't told you about some of the difficulties I encountered in the process, including having to refer to the third book, the *General Geographical Tables*, It took me at least an hour to decipher and decode this relatively short Roosevelt message. I feel sure a naval operation in World War II or in World War I, for that matter, could never have been executed before a message even as brief as the Roosevelt one could be deciphered and decoded by this cumbersome system, even if all the digits had been transmitted and received correctly, Generally speaking, naval battles are fierce and quickly over. For instance, on 4 June 1942, between 10:24 and 10:26 a.m., the war with Japan was decided when the U.S, Pacific Fleet under Admirals Nimitz, Fletcher, and Spruance won the Battle of Midway, in which the Japanese lost four fast carriers, together with their entire complement of planes, and almost all their first-string aviators. When our navy entered World War I, a much more practical system was put into effect, using a cipher device known as the NCB, standing for "Navy Cipher Box," to encipher five-letter groups of a basic code.

We come now to European events of importance in this cryptologic history. During the decades from the end of the Civil War in America to the first decade of the twentieth century, there was some progress in cryptologic science in Europe, but it was not of a startling nature. German Army Major Kasiski's demonstration of a straightforward, mathematical method of solving the Vigenère

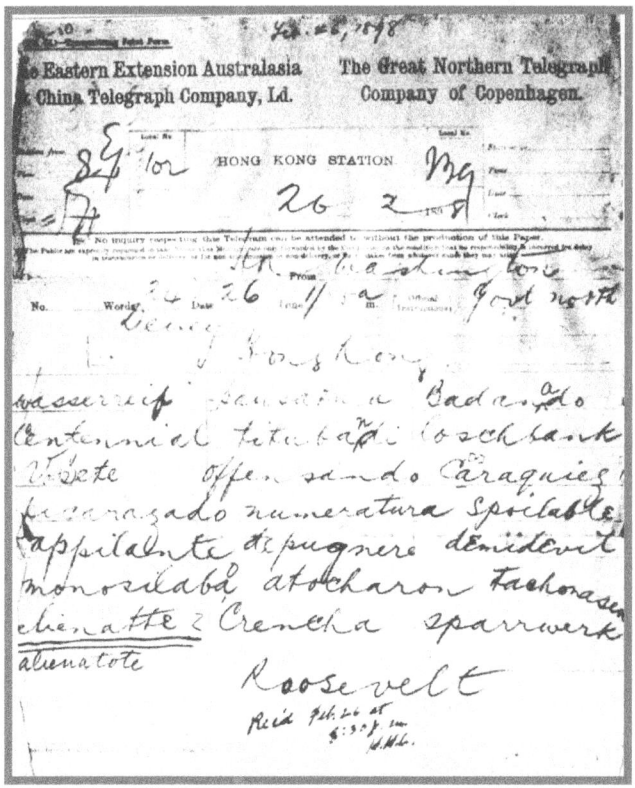

Fig. 79

Page 103

THEODORE ROOSEVELT, ASST. SECRETARY OF THE NAVY, TO ADMIRAL DEWEY, HONG KONG,
26 FEBRUARY 1898

1	1	2	3	4	5	6
2	WASSERREIF	PAUSATURA	BADANADOS	CENTENNIAL	TITUBANDI	LOSCHBANK
3	99055	62399	11005	16820	90000	52390
4	990.556	239.911	005.168	209.000	052.390	
5	SECRET AND CONFIDENTIAL	ORDER THE SQUADRON	EXCEPT	THE MONOCACY	TO HONGKONG, CHINA	

1	7	8	9	10	11	12
2	VOVETE	OFFNSADO	C(A)RAQUIEZ[a]	PICARZADO	NUMERATURA	SPOILABLE
3	98242	59841	21992	64004	58639	83607
4	982.425	984.121	992.640	045.863	983.607	
5	KEEP FULL OF COAL	IN THE EVENT OF	DECLARATION OF WAR	SPAIN	IT WILL BE YOUR DUTY TO SEE THAT	

1	13	14	15	16	17	18
2	APPILANTI	DEPUGNERE	DEMIDEVIL	MONOSILABO	ATOCHARON	TACHONASEN
3	07319	25545	24980	56346	09599	87782
4	073.192	554.524	980.563	460.959	987.782	
5	THE SPANISH SQUADRON	DOES NOT LEAVE	ASIATIC COAST	AND THEN	OFFENSIVE OPERATION(S)	

1	19	20	21
2	ALIENATOTE[b]	CRENCHA	SPARRWERKE
3	04665	22099	83000
4	046.653	209.983	000
5	IN PHILIPPINE ISLANDS	KEEP OLYMPIA UNTIL FURTHER ORDERS	

LEGEND:
1 — Group Number.
2 — Cable Word.
3 — Cable Word No.
4 — Code Number in Code.
5 — Meaning

(a) Correction necessary: The "A" is to be omitted
(b) Correction necessary: Group was received as ALIENATTE

Fig. 80

cipher was published in Berlin during the mid-period of the Civil War in America. If the book created an impression in Europe, it was altogether unspectacular; in America it remained unheard of until after the advent of the twentieth century. Although Kasiski's method is explained quite accurately in the first American text on cryptology,[2] the name Kasiski doesn't even appear in it. Other books on cryptologic subjects appeared in Europe during this period, and two of them deserve special attention. The first, by Commandant Bazeries, is a book notable not for its general contents, which are presented in a rather disorganized, illogical sequence, but for its presentation of a cipher device invented by the author, the so-called "cylindrical cipher device." But our own Thomas Jefferson anticipated Bazeries by a century, and the manuscript describing his "Wheel Cypher" is among the Jefferson Papers in the Library of Congress. The second book, which deserves special attention, is one by another French cryptologist, the Marquis de Viaris, in which he presents methods for solving cryptograms prepared by the Bazeries cipher cylinder, and although unknown to him, the ciphers of Jefferson's Wheel Cypher.[3] It was in the period during which books of the foregoing nature were written and published that the chanceries of European governments operated so-called "Black Chambers," organized for solving one another's secret communications. Intercept was unnecessary because the governments owned and operated the telegraph systems, and traffic could be obtained simply by making copies of messages arriving or departing from telegraph offices or passing in transit through them. This was true in the case of every country in Europe with one very important exception: Great Britain. The story, which is given in detail in a recently published and very fully documented book,[4] is highly interesting, but I must condense it to a few sentences.

In England, from about 1540 until 1844, a "black chamber" was in constant operation. It was composed of three collaborating organizations within the Post Office respectively called "The Secret Office," "The Private Office," and "The Deciphering Branch."

In the first of these carefully hidden secret organizations, letters were opened, copies of them were made, the letters replaced, the envelopes resealed, and if the wax seals were intact they were merely replaced. If the seals were not replaceable, duplicates were forged and affixed to the envelopes. Copies of letters in cipher were sent to the "Deciphering Branch" for solution and the results, if successful, were then sent to the Foreign Office. A famous mathematician, John Wallis, took part in the latter activities. The "Private Office" took care of similar activities, but only in connection with internal or domestic communications. In 1844, a scandal involving these secret offices caused Parliament to close them down completely, so that from 1844 until 1914 there was no black chamber at all in Britain. As a consequence, when World War I broke out on the first of August 1914, England's black chamber had to start from scratch. But within a few months British brains and ingenuity built a cryptologic organization known as "Room 40 O.B.," which contributed very greatly to the Allied victory in 1918. Although the British government has never issued a single official publication on the activities and accomplishments of "Room 40 O.B.," several books by private authors have pushed aside the curtain of secrecy to make a most fascinating story too long to tell in this lecture. But I must tell you at least something about what was perhaps the single greatest achievement of "Room 40 O.B.," an achievement which just in the nick of time brought this country into World War I as an active belligerent on the Allied side and saved England, as well as France, from possible destruction.

The operation involved the interception and solution of a message known as the Zimmermann Telegram, deservedly called the most important single cryptogram in all history. On 8 September 1958 I gave before an NSA audience a detailed account of this amazing cryptogram. I told about its interception and solution; I told how the solution was handed over to the United States; how it brought America into the war on the British side; and how all this was done without disclosing to the Germans that the plain text of the Zimmermann Telegram had been obtained by interception and solution by cryptanalysis, that is, by science and not by treason. My talk was given under the auspices of the NSA Crypto-Mathematics Institute, was recorded, and is on file so that, if you wish, you can hear it. It took two and a half hours to deliver, and at that I didn't quite succeed in telling the whole story. But you may read an excellent account of this episode, set forth in great detail in a book entitled *The Zimmermann Telegram*, by Barbara Tuchman, published in 1958 by the Viking Press, New York. Also, you should consult a book entitled *The Eyes of the Navy*, by Admiral Sir William James, published in 1955 by Methuen & Co., London. Both books deal at length with the Zimmermann Telegram and tell how astutely Sir William Reginald Hall, Director of British Naval Intelligence in World War I, managed the affair to get the maximum possible advantage from the feat accomplished by "Room 40 O.B." It was, indeed, astounding!

To summarize, as I must, this fascinating and true tale of a very important cryptanalytic conquest, let me show you again the telegram as it passed from Washington to Mexico City, for if you will remember, I showed it to you in the very first lecture of this series, and promised to tell you about it later. Here I show it to you once again [See Figure 86]. As you can easily see, the code groups are composed of three-, four-, and five-digit groups, mostly the latter. Here is the English decoded translation of the message as transmitted by Ambassador Page in London to President Wilson:

> Foreign Office Telegraphs Jan 16, No.1. Most secret. Decipher yourself.
>
> We intend to begin unrestricted submarine warfare on the first of February. We shall endeavour in spite of this to keep the United States of America neutral. In the event of this not succeeding, we make Mexico a proposal of alliance on the following basis. Make war together, make peace together, generous financial support and an understanding on our part that Mexico is to reconquer the lost territory in Texas, New Mexico and Arizona. The settlement in detail is left to you. You will inform the President (of Mexico) of the above most secretly as soon as the outbreak of war with the United States of America is certain, and add the suggestion that he should, on his own initiative, invite Japan to immediate adherence, and at the same time mediate between Japan and ourselves. Please call the President's attention to the fact that the ruthless employment of our submarines now offers the prospect of compelling England, in a few months, to make peace.
>
> ZIMMERMANN

From the day that Ambassador Page sent his cablegram to President Wilson, on 28 February 1917, quoting the English translation of the Zimmermann Telegram in the form in which had been forwarded by German ambassador von Bernstorff in Washington to German minister von Eckhardt in Mexico City, the entrance of the United States into the war as a belligerent on the side of the Allies became a certainty. Under big black headlines the English text appeared in our newspapers, because, after assuring himself of the authenticity of the telegram handed over by the British and that it had been decoded and checked by a member of Ambassador Page's own staff, President Wilson directed that the text of the message be released to the Associated Press. Its publication the next day was the first of a momentous and sensational series of reports and accounts of the Zimmermann Telegram and its contents.

There were plenty of members of Congress who disbelieved the story. But when Zimmermann himself foolishly acknowledged that he had indeed sent such a telegram, disbelief changed quickly into most vehement anger. Thus, it came about that

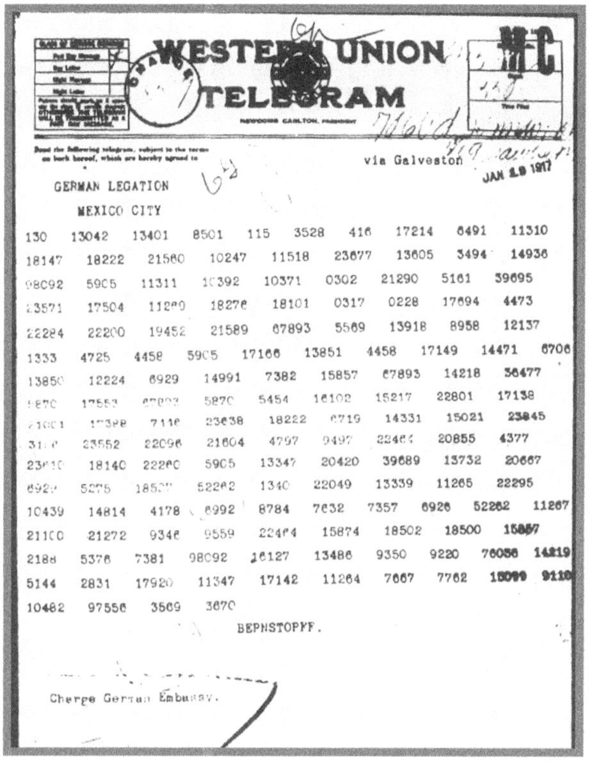

Fig. 81

Americans in the Middle West and Far West, who had thus far been quite unconcerned about a war that was going on in Europe, thousands of miles away, and wanted no part of it, suddenly awoke when they learned that a foreign power was making a deal to turn over some rather large slices of U.S. real estate to a then hostile neighbor across the southern border. They were aroused to the point where they, too, as well as millions of other Americans in the East, were ready to fight. Surely war would now be declared on Germany.

Notwithstanding all the furor that the disclosure of the Zimmermann Telegram created in America, President Wilson still hesitated. He was still determined that America would not, must not, fight. It was not until more than a month later, *and after several American ships were sunk without warning on 18 March*, that a now fully aroused President got Congress to declare war on Germany and her allies. The date was 6 April 1917.

In the War Department and in the Navy Department, the pace set for preparing for active war operations quickened. It is difficult to believe, but I assure you that it was true, there was at the moment in neither of those departments, nor in the Army or Navy, any organizations or technical groups whatever, either for intercepting enemy communications or for studying them, let alone solving such communications. There had been, it is true, since the autumn of 1916, a very small group of self-trained cryptanalysts, sponsored and supported by a private citizen named Colonel George Fabyan,[5] who operated the Riverbank Laboratories at Geneva, Illinois. I served as leader of the group, in addition to other duties as a geneticist of the Laboratories. Riverbank, through George Fabyan, had initiated and established an unofficial, or at most, a quasi-official relationship with the authorities in Washington, so that it received from time to time copies of cryptographic messages obtained by various and entirely surreptitious means from telegraph and cable offices in Washington and elsewhere in the United States. At that period in our history, diplomatic relations with Mexico were in a sad state, so that U.S. attention was directed southward, and not eastward across the Atlantic Ocean. Therefore, practically all the messages sent to Riverbank for solution were those of the Mexican government. Riverbank was successful in solving all or nearly all the Mexican cryptograms it was given, usually returning the solutions to Washington very promptly. The great majority of them were of the Vigenère type but using mixed sequences with relatively long key phrases. Riverbank was also successful with certain other cryptograms which were concerned with the war in Europe, but I cannot deal with them now because there just isn't time. Soon after the United States declared war on Germany, Colonel Fabyan established a school for training at Riverbank, and he invited the services to send him army and navy officers to learn something about cryptology in formal courses established for the purpose. Each course lasted about six weeks, full time.

You may like to know what we novices used for training ourselves for this unusual task and what we used later on for training the student officers

Page 107

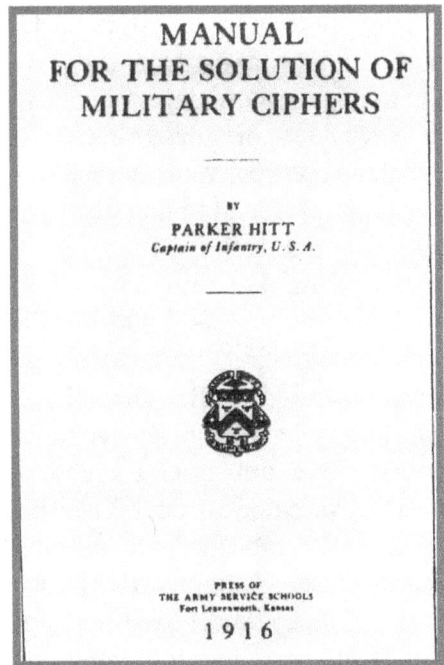

Fig. 82

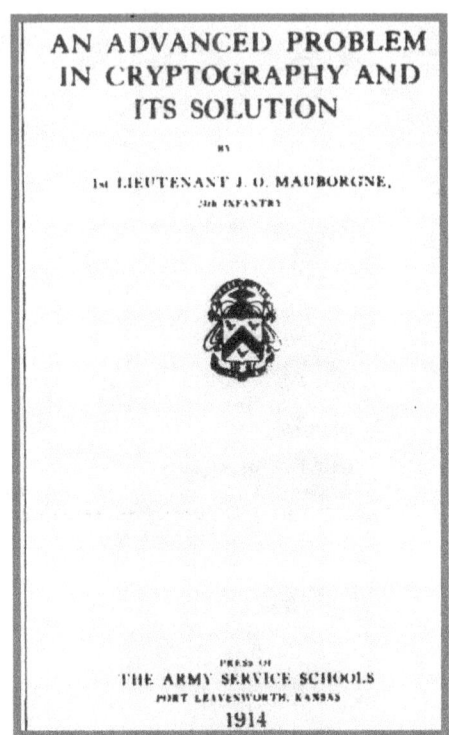

Fig. 84

Fig. 83

Fig. 85

sent to us for cryptologic instruction. As regards our self-instruction training material, there wasn't much available in English, but among the very sparse literature was that small book by Captain Parker Hitt, called *Manual for the Solution of Military Ciphers*, to which I referred earlier. Colonel Fabyan managed to get a copy of that manual for us to study. The Signal Corps School was then one of the army service schools, and there a few lectures were given by two or three officers who, when World War I broke out in August 1914, took an interest in the subject of military cryptography. They foresaw that sooner or later there would be a need for knowledge in that important branch of military technology. Captain Hitt's manual was then, and still is, a model of compactness and practicality. Let me show you the title page of the first edition (fig. 82).

It was the succinctness of Parker Hitt's manual that caused us much work and perspiration in our self-training at Riverbank, but we later came to know and admire its author, whose photograph I now show you as he looked when he became a colonel in the Signal Corps (fig. 83).

There was one other item of training literature which we also studied avidly. It was a very small pamphlet entitled *An Advanced Problem in Cryptography and its Solution*, and it too was put out by the Fort Leavenworth Press in 1914. Its title page is shown in figure 84. You will note that its author was then First Lieutenant J.O. Mauborgne; he advanced to become major general and Chief Signal Officer of the Army (fig. 85). The "advanced problem" dealt with in that pamphlet was the Playfair Cipher I about which I shall say only that at the time Mauborgne wrote about that particular cipher it was considered to be much more difficult than it is at present.

Returning now to what Riverbank's self-trained cryptanalytic group was able to do in a practical way in the training of others, there exist in NSA archives copies of the many exercises and problems prepared at Riverbank for this purpose. They are, I think, still of much interest as curiosities of U.S. cryptologic history.

In Lecture II, I showed you a picture of the last of the several classes sent by the Army to Riverbank for training. It should be noted, and it gives me considerable pleasure to tell you, that this instruction was conducted at Colonel Fabyan's own expense as his patriotic contribution to the U.S. war effort. I can't, in this lecture, say much more about this than it involved the expenditure of many thousands of dollars, never repaid by the government – not even by income-tax deduction or by some decoration or similar sort of recognition. Upon completion of the last training course, I was commissioned a first lieutenant in Military Intelligence, General Staff, and was ordered immediately to proceed to American General Headquarters in France, where I became a member of a group officially referred to as the Radio Intelligence Section. But it was the German Code and Cipher Solving Section of the General Staff, a designation that was abbreviated as G-2, A-6, GHQ-AEF. As the expanded designation implies, the operations were conducted in two principal sections, one devoted to working of German army field ciphers, the other, to working on German army field codes. There were also very small groups working on other material such as meteorologic messages, direction-finding (DF) bearings, and what we now call traffic analysis, that is, the detailed study of "the externals" of enemy messages in order to determine enemy order of battle and other vital intelligence from the study of DF bearings, the direction, ebb and flow of enemy traffic, and other data sent back from our intercept and radio direction-finding operations at or near the front line in the combat zone.

In connection with the last-mentioned operations, you will no doubt be interested to see what is probably one of the earliest, if not the very first, chart in cryptologic history that shows the intelligence that could be derived from a consideration of the results of traffic analysis. Its utility in deriving intelligence about enemy intentions from a mere study of the ebb and flow of enemy traffic, without being able to solve the traffic, was of unquestionable value. Here's that historic chart (fig. 86), which I must tell you was drawn up from data based solely upon the ebb and flow of traffic in what we called the ADFGVX cipher,[6] a clever cryptosystem that was devised by German cryptographers and which was restricted in its usage to German High Command communications, principally those between and among the headquarters of divisions and army corps. Its restriction to such high command messages made a study of its ebb and flow very important. Theoretically, that cipher was extremely secure. It combined both a good substitution and an excellent transposition principle in one system without being too complicated for cipher clerks. Below is a diagram which will give a

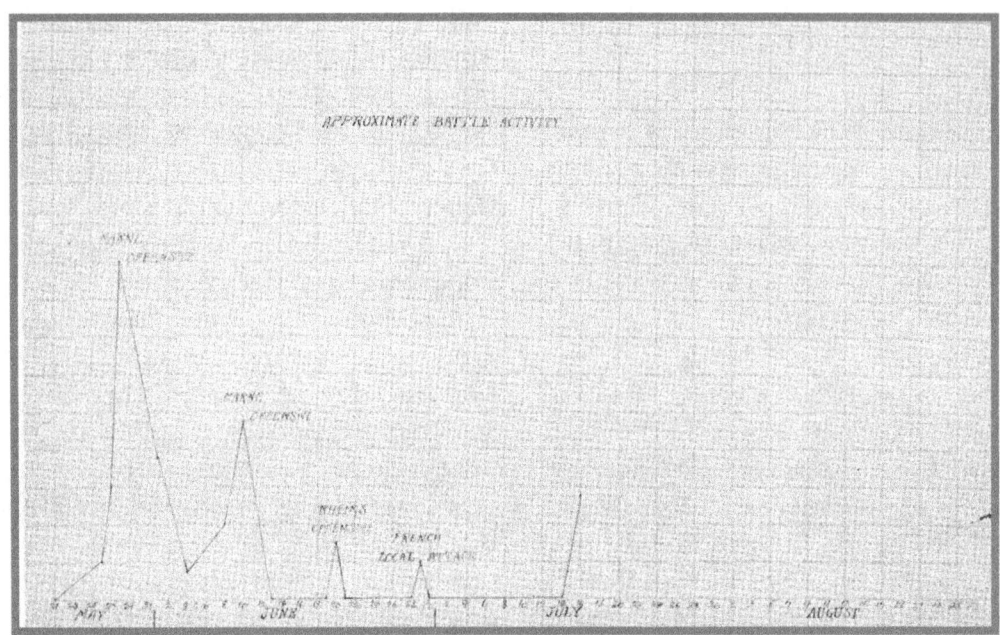
Fig. 86

clear understanding of its method of usage. [Regarding this system], in this lecture there is only time to tell you that although individual or isolated messages in the ADFGVX system then appeared to be absolutely impregnable against solution, a great many messages transmitted in it were read by the Allies.

You may be astonished by the foregoing statement and therefore may desire some enlightenment here and now on this point. In brief, there were in those days three and only three different methods of attacking that cipher. Under the first method, it was necessary to find, as the first step, two or more messages with identical plaintext beginnings because they could be used to uncover the transposition, which was the second step. Once this had been done, the cryptanalyst had then to deal with a substitution cipher in which two-letter combinations of the letters A, D, F, G, V, and x represented single plaintext letters. The messages were usually of sufficient length for this purpose. Under the second method, two or more messages with identical plaintext endings could be used to uncover the transposition. This was easier even than in the case of messages with identical beginnings. You might think that cases of messages with identical beginnings or endings would be rather rare, but the addiction to stereotypic phraseology was so prevalent in all German military communications that there were almost invariably found, in each day's traffic, messages with similar beginnings or endings, and sometimes both. Under the third method of solution it was necessary to find several messages with exactly the same number of letters. This happened, but not often. This system first came into use on 1 March 1918, three weeks before the last and greatest offensive by the German army. Its appearance was coincident with that of other new codes and ciphers. The number of messages in the ADFGVX cipher varied from about twenty-five a day, when the system first went into use, to as many as about 150 a day at the end of two months. It took about a month to figure out a method of solution, and this was first done by a very able cryptanalyst named Captain Georges Painvin of the French army's Cipher Bureau.

The ADFGVX cipher was used quite extensively on the Western Front with daily changing keys during May and June of 1918, but then, for reasons somewhat obscure, the number of messages dropped very considerably. How many different keys were solved by the Allies during the four

Plain text: REQUEST REENFORCEMENTS IMMEDIATELY

```
              Second Letter
              A  D  F  G  V  X
           A  Q  U  E  5  S  T
           D  I  9  0  N  A  1
           F  B  2  L  Y  F  3
           G  D  4  F  6  G  7
           V  H  8  J  O  K  M
           X  P  R  V  W  X  Z
```

Bilateral Substitution:

R E Q U E S T R E E N F O R C E
XD AF AA AD AF AV AX XD AF AF DG GF DF XD FV AF

M E N T S I M M E D I A T E L Y
VF AF DG AX AV DA VX VX AF GA DA DV AX AF FF FG

Key Word:

Q   U   I C K B R   O   W   N   F   O   X   J   U   M   P   E   D
14 16 6 2 8 1 15 11 18 10 5   12 19 7   17 9   13 4   3

Substituted Text:

```
Y  D  A  F  A  A  A  D  A  F  A  V  A  X  X  D  A  F  A
F  D  G  G  F  D  F  X  D  F  V  A  F  V  X  A  F  D  G
A  X  A  V  D  A  V  X  V  X  A  F  G  A  D  A  D  V  A
X  A  F  F  F  F  G
```

Transposed Text:

ADAFF GVFAG AFDVA VAAGA FXVAA FDFDA AFFXD XXVAF
AFDXF AXAFV GDDXA XXDAD VAFG

---

months from 1 March to the end of June? Not many – ten in all; that is, the keys for only ten different days were solved. Yet, because the traffic on those days was very heavy, about fIfty percent of all messages ever sent in that cipher, from its inception to its discard, were read, and a great deal of valuable intelligence was derived from them. On one occasion, solution was so rapid that an important German operation disclosed by one message was completely frustrated.

Although the ADFGVX cipher came into use first on the Western Front, it later began to be employed also on the Eastern Front, with keys that were first changed every two days but later every three days. On 2 November 1918 the key for that and the next day was solved within an hour and a half because two messages with identical endings were found. A thirteen-part message in that key gave the complete plan of the German retreat from Romania.

During the eight months of the life of the ADFGVX cipher, solution depended upon the three rather *special* cases I mentioned. No *general* solution for it was thought up by the Allies despite a great deal of study. However, members of our own Signal Intelligence Service, in 1933, devised a general solution and proved its efficacy. Pride in this achievement was not diminished when, in the course of writing up and describing the method, I happened to find a similar one in a book by French General Givierge (*Cours de Cryptographie*, published in 1925). Givierge was by then the head of the French Black Chamber, which was called the "Deuxieme Bureau," corresponding to our "G-2."

The ADFGVX cipher was not the only one used by the German army in World War I, but there will be time to mention very briefly only two others. The first of these was a polyalphabetic substitution cipher called the "Wilhelm," which used a cipher square with disarranged alphabets and with a set of thirty fairly lengthy key words. The cipher square is shown in figure 87. Just why the square contains only twenty-two rows instead of twenty-six is probably connected with the fact that German can get along very well with fewer than twenty-six letters. Certainly the rows within the square are not random sequences, as you can see, for the letters within them manifest permuted arrangements in sets of five letters. In figure 88 are shown the keys used – thirty of them. The key sequences seem to be composed of random letters, but underlying them is plain text. I leave it to you to try to reconstruct the real square, if possible. You should be able to reconstruct the real keys, for the latter problem should be relatively easy.

The other German army cipher to be mentioned is the double transposition, an example of which is shown below. The process consists in applying the same transposition key twice to the same matrix, once horizontally and once vertically, as seen in this slide. Solution of the true double matrix transposition usually depends upon finding two or more messages of identical length. (You will remember what I told you about Captain Holden in this connection.) No general solution was known to the Allies during World War I, and messages of identical length were few indeed. But it happened that occasionally a German operator would apply only the first transposition, and when this fortunate situation occurred solution was easy, because the key thus recovered from the single transposition could be used to decipher other messages which had been correctly enciphered by the double transposition. Again, the Signal Intelligence Service devised a general solution for the double transposition cipher, and during World War II we were able to prove that such ciphers could be solved without having to find two messages of identical length. I think the devising of a general solution for the true double transposition cipher represents a real landmark of progress in cryptanalysis.

We come now to the code systems used by the belligerents in World War I. First, let us differentiate those used for diplomatic communications from those used for military communications. What sorts did the German Foreign Office use? We have noted that the British Black Chamber, "Room 40 O.B.," enjoyed astonishing success with the code

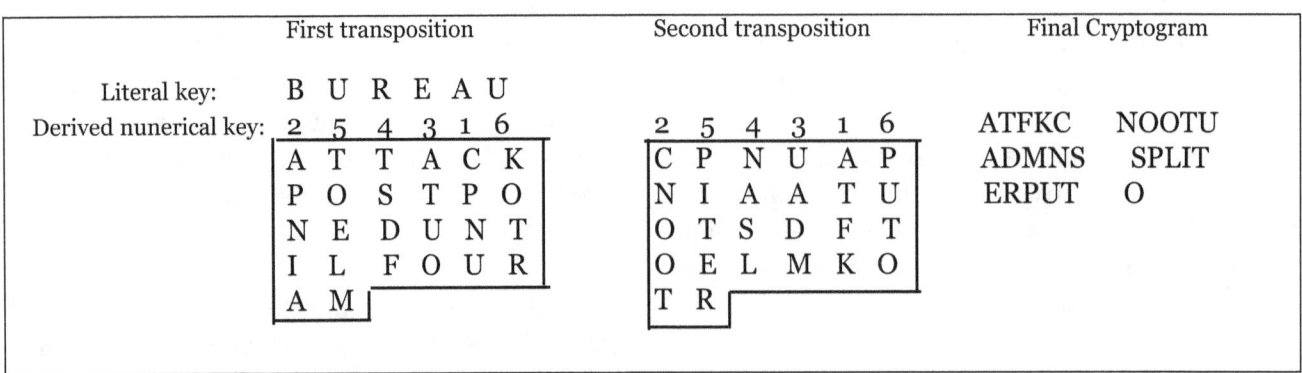

Double transposition

used for the transmission of the Zimmermann Telegram. Excessive pride in German achievements in science, a wholly unjustified confidence in their communication cryptosecurity, and a disdain for the prowess of enemy cryptanalysts laid German diplomatic communications open to solution by the Allies to the point where there came a time when nothing the German Foreign Office was telling its representatives abroad by telegraph, cable, or radio remained secret from their cryptologic antagonists. For those of you who would like to learn some details, I refer you to the following monograph on the subject by my late colleague, Captain Charles J. Mendelsohn: *Studies in German Diplomatic Codes Employed During the World War* (Government Printing Office, 1937). Says Dr. Mendelsohn:

> At the time of America's entrance into the war German Codes were an unexplored field in the United States. About a year later we received from the British a copy of a partial reconstruction of the German Code 13040 (about half of the vocabulary of 19,200 words and 800 of the possibly 7,600 proper names). This code and its variations of encipherment had been in

```
Table - 1. - THE ALPHABETS FOR THE "WILHELM" CIPHER

    A B C D E F G H I J K L M N O P Q R S T U V W X Y Z

A   S Q R Y V X U Z T W B D C A E J H K I F G P M O N L
B   L O P N M Q S R T U V Z X Y W C A B H E D G J F K I
C   P O N M R T S Q W Y U X Z V C A B E D F J G K H I L
D   I F H J G N K L M P O T S R Q V Y U X Z W D B C A E
E   X U V Z Y W A C B E D G I H J F K M O N L T R S Q P
F   U X Z W Y V A E B C F D I H G J N K M L S P O R T Q
G   A C D B H J F I G E M N L K O T R S T Q Y Z V U X W
H   B A D C F G E I H J N O K M L S R P T Q W X V Y U Z
I   T R S Q Y W X Z V U E B A C D K F J I G H M L P N O
J   L M O N T Q R P S Z X U Y V W B A C D E G J H F K I
K   M O K N L Q S R P W Z T V U X Y D B A C E F J G I H
L   I E H F G L O M J K N Q P T R S X V Y U Z V B A D C
M   H F I G N M J K O L Q P S R V T Z U W X Y B E D C A
N   C D A B G H E J F I K M P O L N T R Q S X U Z W V Y
O   E C D B A F J I G H L K O N M S P Q T R Z U X V W Y
P   R Q P S Z W T V U X Y D B C A G I E J H K F O N L M
Q   V Y X U Z W C A B E D I H G F L K N M J Q O T P S R
R   B A C H D J F E G I L O N P K M S Q R U Z T Y V W X
S   Q Y Z V X A B C E F D M J I G K A P L N S R O Y U T
T   E D I G H F L M K P O N R Q J S U X T Z W V Y C A B
U   R T S W V Y Z U X F A C B E D J K I G H O N M P Q L
V   M O L N P S R Q X T Y W Z U V A D C B H F I K E J G
```

Numbers were expressed by the following letters bracketed between "Q's":

1 2 3 4 5 6 7 8 9 0
H P J W D Y V R A F

The alphabet beginninng "SQRYV" was known as the "A" alphabet; that beginning "LOPNM" as "B" alphabet, etc.
Messages numbered 1, 31, 61, etc. were decipherable by the 13 alphabets in the order "JVCEPQHCMPQGP."
Messages numbered 2, 32, 62, etc. were decipherable by the 13 alphabets in the order "TBUULENFKEQGC."
The horizontal sequence above the table is the plain-text sequence. The vertical alphabet on the extreme left gives the arbitrary symbol by which the different alphabets were known in the 30 keys.
Attached is a list of these 30 keys:

Fig. 87

use between the German Foreign Office and the German Embassy in Washington up to the time of the rupture in relations, and our files contained a considerable number of messages, some of them of historical interest, which were now read with the aid of the code book.

The vocabulary of the German diplomatic codes comprised about 189 pages, each having 100 words or expressions to the page, arranged in two columns of fifty each, accompanied by numbers from 00 to 99. In each column the groups were in blocks of ten. In the left-hand column, for instance, were the five blocks from 00-99, 10-19, etc., to 40-49. Then 50-59, 60-69, etc., were in blocks often in the right-hand column. The pages in the basic code were numbered, and from this code several codes were made by the use of conversion tables. This enabled the original or basic code to serve as the framework for apparently unrelated and externally distinguishable codes for several different communication nets. What the number of the basic code was is unknown, but we do know that from the code designated as Code 13040 came codes 5950, 26040, and others, derived merely by means of tables for converting the page numbers in the basic code into different page numbers in the derived code. These conversions were systematic, in blocks of fours. Thus, for example, pages 15-18 in code 13040 became pages 65-68 in code 5950, etc. The there were tables for converting line numbers from one code into different line numbers in another version of the basic code, and this was done in blocks often. For example, the fifth block (penultimate figure 4) became the first (penultimate figure 0), and the 1st, 2nd, 3rd, and 4th blocks were moved down one place. The other five blocks (on the right hand side of the page) were rearranged in the same manner.

```
 1....J V C E P Q H C M P P G P
 2....T B U U L E N F K E Q G J
 3....V C B H E G C J K G E P
 4....I O C E B P G K K G P J V E G U G C
 5....H G J K E I I M P Q J B C K
 6....S O F C K M P K G C H C G N F M P Q
 7....L O Q G P L G N F J G U
 8....L B U U G P J E G S O F C G P
 9....P B N F G K L O J I E U N F
10....G J J N F I G N A K I E C
11....A B C A D E G F G C
12....D M N A G C D O P Q G
13....J N F L E G Q G C T O K G C
14....L E G U O P Q G R O M G C K G J
15....L E G T E G U A B J K G K G J
16....S C G I R G P H M N F
17....H G P G R E A K E P G C
18....J G U K G C L O J J G C
19....H G E L G I A O M S G P J E G
20....V O V E G C F O P R U M P Q
21....V S G C R G T G C I E G K G C
22....Q B U R O C H G E K G C
23....F O P R U M P Q J Q G F E U S G
24....F O P R J N F M F I O N F G C
25....E P J K C M I G P K G P I O N F G C
26....A O I G U K C G E H G C
27....C O R E G C Q M I I E
28....H G J B C Q G R E G V S G C R G
29....R M P A G U A O I I G C
30....C G N F K J O G U G F C K G C
```

It will be noticed that the same letter, as P, for instance, as in key no. 1, is repeated four different times. Again, the E and Q and G which occur in 1 also occur in 2. These facts pointed to the use in these 30 keys of intelligible German words. The arbitrary letters, which the keys in their present form contained, represented a simple substitution. This appeared from the frequency, for example, of G and the inseparable combinations NF and NA, N nevery appearing unless followed by F or A. It was therefore probable that these letters, arbitrarily chosen to represent the 22 different alphabets, in reality represented keywords in German text.

N was assumed to be the value of C, and F, H; and G, the most frequent letter which was never absent from any of the series, E. This simple substitution was continued until familiar German syllables began to appear and finally the complete key words themselves.

Fig. 88

It is obvious that codes derived in such a manner from a basic code by renumbering ages and shifting about the contents of pages in blocks can by no means be considered as being different and entirely unrelated codes, and once a relationship between two such codes was discovered, the two could be handled as equivalents of one another. Also to be mentioned is that in certain cases numbers were added to or subtracted from the code numbers of a message, and this gave rise to what seemed to be still different codes. It was not difficult to determine the additive or subtractive and thus get to the basic code numbers.

In none of the cases of codes mentioned thus far was there one that could be considered to be a randomized, "hatted," or true two-part code, since the same book served for both encoding and decoding. However, the German Foreign Office later on did compile and use real two-part, truly randomized codes of 10,000 groups numbered from 0000 to 9999. One such code had as its indicator the number 7500. And that there were several others like it I have no doubt.

When one reviews Dr. Mendelsohn's monograph, one becomes overwhelmed by the multiplicity of the codes and variants thereof used by the German Foreign Office. Some were basic codes, but many were derivatives or superencipherments thereof. It is even hard to ascertain the exact number of different codes and superencipherment methods. Yet a great deal of the traffic in these codes was read. Considering the rather small number of persons on the cryptanalytic staff of G-2 in Washington and in the British counterpart organization in London, the British Black Chamber, one can only be astonished by the remarkably great achievements of these two collaborating organizations that worked on German diplomatic codes during World War I.

So much for German diplomatic secret communications. What about German military cryptocommunications? I have already mentioned several systems used, but these were developed two or more years after the outbreak of World War I. When World War I commenced, the German army was very poorly prepared to meet the requirements for secure communications. It seems that up until the Battle of the Marne in 1914 several army radio stations went into the field without any provision having been made, or even foreseen, for the need for speedy and secure cryptocommunications. Numerous complaints were registered by German commanders concerning extensive loss of time occasioned by the far too complicated methods officially authorized for use and the consequent necessity for sending messages in the clear. Not only did this reveal intelligence of importance to their opponents, but, what is equally important, the practice permitted the British and the French to become thoroughly familiar with the German telegraphic procedures, methods of expression, terminology and style, and the knowledge gained about these items became of great importance in cryptanalysis when German cryptosystems improved. The German army learned by hard experience something about its shortcomings in this area of warfare and not only soon began to improve, but did so to the point where we must credit the Germans with being the initiators of new and important developments in field military cryptography. In fact, the developments and improvements began not long after the Battle of the Marne and continued steadily until the end of the war. When on 11 November the armistice ended active operations, German military cryptology had attained a remarkable high state of efficiency. The astonishing fact, however, is that, although very proficient in cryptographic inventions, they were apparently quite deficient in the science and practice of cryptanalysis. In all the years since the end of World War I, no books or articles telling of German successes with Allied radio traffic during that war have appeared; one Austrian cryptanalyst, a man named Figl, attempted to publish a book on cryptanalysis, but it seems to have been suppressed. One could, of course, assume that they kept their successes very well hidden, but the German archives taken at the end of World War II contained nothing significant in regard to cryptanalysis during World War I, although a great deal of important information in this field during World War II was found. A detailed account of the cryptologic war between the Allied and German forces in World War II would require scores of volumes, but there is one source of information that I can highly recommend to those of you who would like to know more details of the cryptologic warfare between the belligerents in World War I. That source is a book written and published in Stockholm in 1931 by a Swedish cryptanalyst, Yves Gylden, under the title *Chifferbråernas Insatser I Varldskriget Till Lands*, a translation of which, with some comments of my own in the form of footnotes, you will find under the title *The Contribution of the Cryptographic Bureaus in the World War* (Government Printing Office, 1936).

In this lecture, however, we are principally concerned with German military cryptology during World War I, and since I have already told you something about the cipher systems that were used, there remain to be discussed the field codes. It was the German army that first proved that the old idea that code books were impractical for use in the combat zone for tactical communications was wrong. They had two types of field codes: one they called the SCHLUESSELHEFT but that we called the "three-number code," the other that they called the SATZBUCH but that we called the "three-letter code." The former was a small, standardized code with a vocabulary of exactly 1,000 frequently used words and expressions, digits, letters and syllables, etc., for which the code equivalents were three-digit numbers. A cipher was applied only to the first two digits of the code numbers; this cipher consisted of two-digit groups taken from a 10 x 10 matrix for enciphering the numbers from 00 to 99. This table was called the GEHEIMKLAPPE or "Secret Key," and here's a picture of one (fig. 89). The last digit of a code group remained unenciphered. Thus, code group 479 would become 629. Each division compiled and issued its own secret key table, which was in two parts, or sections, of course, one for encipherment, the other for decipherment. The three-number code was intended for use in all forms of communication within, or to and from, a three-kilometer front-line danger zone. Although this code was completed by the end of January 1918, it was not distributed or put into use until the opening day of the last and greatest German offensive, 10 March 1918. Our code-solving section, through good fortune and careful attention, ascertained the nature of the new code, and a few groups in it were solved the very same day the code was put into

Verschlüsselungstafel.

	0	1	2	3	4	5	6	7	8	9
0	23	48	60	05	78	35	58	64	29	52
1	20	77	33	59	21	70	02	40	63	08
2	11	49	01	69	47	41	79	74	22	42
3	32	76	39	18	75	30	09	51	80	65
4	61	19	43	81	06	56	73	62	10	28
5	85	50	24	88	31	84	27	90	55	57
6	03	91	96	53	68	16	44	89	15	87
7	97	25	71	04	95	34	14	37	93	38
8	26	72	54	92	13	83	45	00	66	67
9	86	12	98	36	99	46	82	17	94	07

Entschlüsselungstafel.

	0	1	2	3	4	5	6	7	8	9
0	87	22	16	60	73	03	44	99	19	36
1	48	20	91	84	76	68	65	97	33	41
2	10	14	28	00	52	71	80	56	49	08
3	35	54	30	12	75	05	93	77	79	32
4	17	25	29	42	66	86	95	24	01	21
5	51	37	09	63	82	58	45	59	06	13
6	02	40	47	18	07	39	88	89	64	23
7	15	72	81	46	27	34	31	11	04	26
8	38	43	96	85	55	50	90	69	53	67
9	57	61	83	78	98	74	62	70	92	94

Fig. 89

effect, because a German cipher operator who was unable to translate a message in the new code requested and received a repetition in another code that had been solved to an extent that made it possible to identify homologous code groups in both messages. The three-number code proved rather easy to solve on a daily basis because only the encipher-decipher table was changed. Much useful intelligence was obtained from the daily solution of this key.

The solution of the SATZBUCH, or three-letter code, however, proved to be a much more difficult problem. In the first place, it had a much larger vocabulary, with nulls and many variants for frequently used words, letters, syllables, and numbers, in the second place, and what constituted the real stumbling block to solution, was that it was a true two-part randomized or "hatted" code; and in the third place, each sector of the front used a different edition of the code, so that not only did the traffic have to be identified as to the sector to which it belonged but also it was not possible to combine all the messages for the purpose of building up frequencies of usage code groups. Here is a typical page of one of these codes (fig. 90). Working with the sparse amount of traffic within a quiet sector of the front and trying to solve a few messages in this code was really a painfully slow, very difficult and generally discouraging experience. On my reporting for duty to Colonel Frank Moorman, who was chief of the whole unit, I was asked whether I wished to be assigned to the cipher section or to the code section Having had considerable experience with the solution of the former types of cryptosystems but none with the latter, and being desirous of gaining such experience, I asked to be assigned to the code-solving unit, in order to broaden my professional knowledge and practice in cryptology. Little did I realize what a painful and frustrating period of learning and training I had undertaken, but my choice turned out to be a very wise and useful one. If any of you would like to read about my experience in this area, let me refer you to my monograph, written in 1918-1919, entitled *Field Codes Used by the German Army During the World War*. I will quote the last two paragraphs from my "estimate of the three-letter code" (on p. 65 of that monograph) and will remind you that although they were written over forty years ago they are still applicable:

> In the light of this limited experience (of less than six months with the 3-letter code) it is impossible to say absolutely what the degree of security offered by such a highly developed system really is. There is no doubt but that it is very great. There is no doubt but that, with the proper precautions, careful supervision and control the employment of such a code by trained men offers the highest possible security for secret communication on the field of battle.
>
> But no code, no matter how carefully constructed, will be safe without tramed, intelligent personnel. A poorly constructed code may be in reality more safe when used by an expert than a very well constructed one when used by a careless operator, or one ignorant of the dangers of

Fig. 90

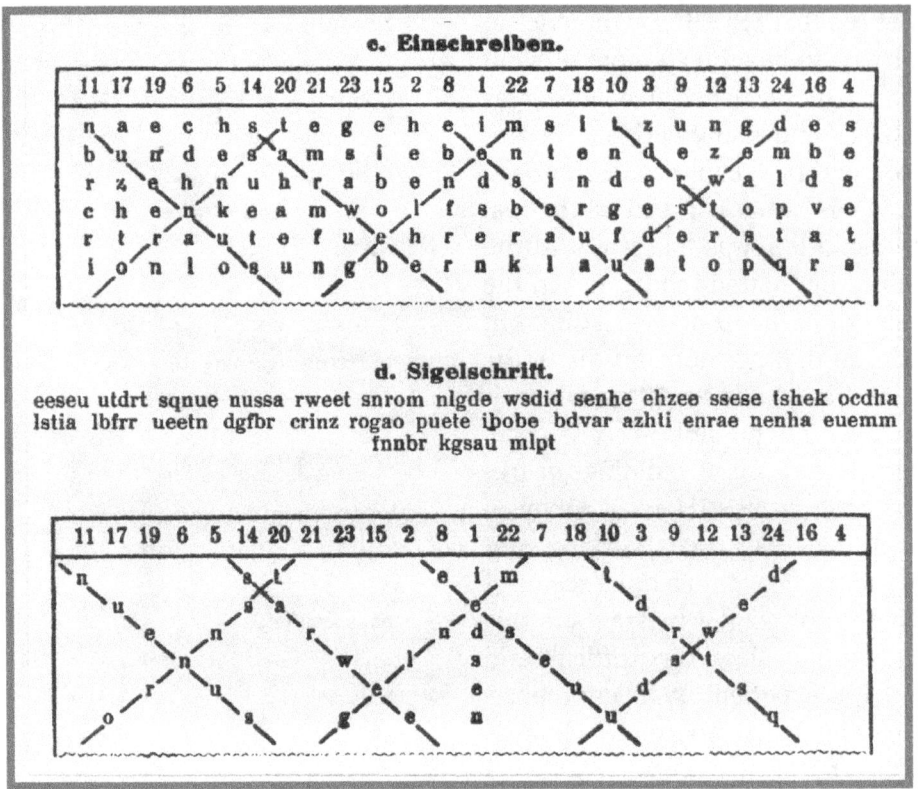

Fig. 91

improperly encoded messages. This point cannot be overemphasized. It is hardly necessary to point out, therefore, that the proper training of the personnel which is to be put in charge of the work of coding messages is an essential requisite to maintenance of secrecy of operations, and thus of success on the field of battle.

So much for the German army field codes, about which a great deal more could be said, but we must hurry on to the cryptosystems of some of the other armies of World War I.

What sorts of cryptosystems did the French army use? First, as for ciphers, they put much trust in transposition methods, and here is an example of one type (fig. 91). Perhaps you remember one of those special route ciphers I showed you in the preceding lecture, the one with the diagonal that produced complexities that made the use of that route much too difficult for the cipher operators of the USMTC. This French transposition cipher was much more complicated by those diagonals, and I wonder how much use was made of it by the French.

As for codes, like the Germans, they used a small, front-line booklet called a "Carnet Reduit," or an "Abbreviated Codebook." Various sectors of the front had different editions, and I show you now a picture of one of them (fig. 92). Then, in addition, there was a much more extensive code, which was not only a two-part, randomized book of 10,000 four-digit code groups but a superencipherment was applied to the code messages when transmitted by radio or by "TPS," that is "telegraphie par sol," or earth telegraphy. Here is one of the tables used for enciphering (and deciphering) the code groups (fig. 93), and here is the example of superencipherment given in the French code in my collection (fig. 94).

You will notice that the enciphering process breaks up the four-digit groups in a rather clever manner by enciphering the first digit of the first code group separately; the second and third digits of the first group are enciphered as a pair; then the last digit of the first group and the first digit of the second code group are enciphered as a pair, and so on. This procedure succeeds in breaking up the digital code groups in such a manner as to reduce very greatly the frequency of repetition of four-digit groups representing words, numbers, phrases, etc., of very common occurrence in military messages. My appraisal of this French army field cryptosystem is that, theoretically at least, it certainly was the most secure of all the field systems used by the belligerents. Now how about the cryptosystems used by the British army? First, they used the Playfair Cipher, a system of digraphic substitution considered in those days to be good enough for messages in the combat zone. But today, of course, its security is known to be so low that it hardly merits confidence for serious usage. The British also used a field code. It contained many common military expressions and sentences, grouped under various headings or categories, and, of course, a very small vocabulary of frequently used words, numbers, punctuation, etc. It was always used with superencipherment, the nature of which was not disclosed even to us, their allies, so I am not in a position

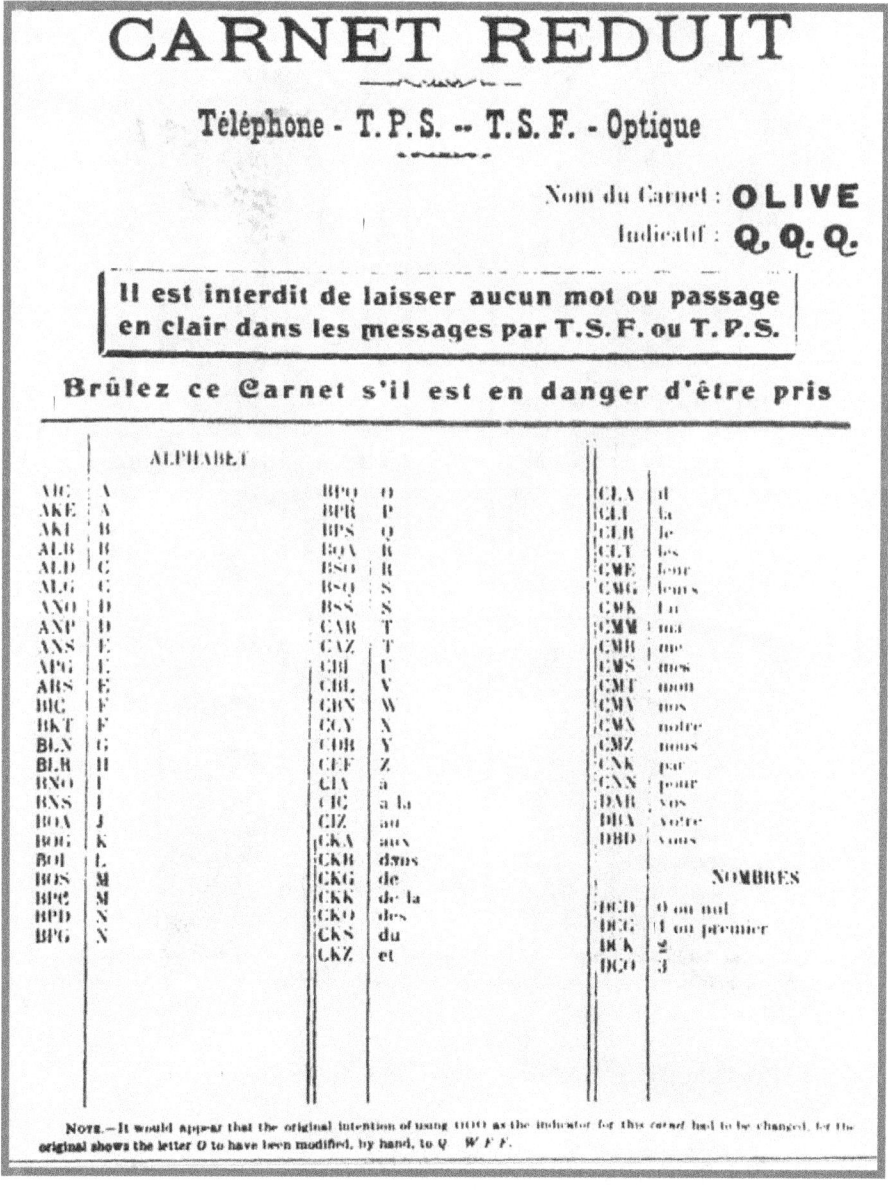

Fig. 92

CHIFFREMENT.			DECHIFFREMENT.		
0 – GS	30 – HR	70 – AN	AB – 09	EM – 49	ND – 13
1 – RH	31 – IA	71 – RB	AD – 82	ER – 88	NG – 66
2 – AM	32 – VS	72 – HN	AE – 39	ES – 20	NH – 34
3 – SI	33 – GU	73 – MH	AG – 14		NR – 81
4 – BH	34 – NH	74 – GD	AH – 60	GA – 01	NS – 5
5 – NS	35 – IS	75 – BU	AI – 78	GB – 54	NU – 27
6 – DA	36 – HD	76 – IE	AM – 2	GD – 74	
7 – TD	37 – TA	77 – DM	AN – 70	GH – 04	RB – 71
8 – EA	38 – IB	78 – AI	AR – 17	GI – 84	RD – 12
9 – UG	39 – AE	79 – RN	AS – 91	GM – 28	RH – 1
			AT – 00	GN – 99	RN – 79
00 – AT	40 – HT	80 – UH	AU – 50	GR – 46	RT – 21
01 – GA	41 – SD	81 – NR		GS – 0	
02 – IM	42 – US	82 – AD	BA – 11	GT – 98	SB – 18
03 – DN	43 – DI	83 – BM	BD – 93	GU – 33	SD – 41
04 – GH	44 – EI	84 – GI	BE – 25		SH – 67
05 – MN	45 – BS	85 – ED	BG – 63	HA – 22	SI – 3
06 – HI	46 – GR	86 – HB	BH – 4	HB – 86	SM – 51
07 – VG	47 – MD	87 – NA	BI – 57	HD – 36	SN – 90
08 – UR	48 – IR	88 – ER	BM – 83	HG – 89	SR – 24
09 – AB	49 – EM	89 – HG	BN – 19	HI – 06	
			BR – 65	HM – 96	TA – 37
10 – BT	50 – AU	90 – SN	BS – 45	HN – 72	TD – 7
11 – BA	51 – SM	91 – AS	BT – 10	HR – 30	TN – 62
12 – RD	52 – DB	92 – MS	BU – 75	HS – 53	TR – 58
13 – ND	53 – HS	93 – BD		HT – 40	TS – 15
14 – AG	54 – GB	94 – IN	DA – 6		
15 – TS	55 – UA	95 – DS	DB – 52	IA – 31	UA – 55
16 – EG	56 – DR	96 – HM	DG – 23	IB – 38	UG – 9
17 – AR	57 – BI	97 – EH	DH – 69	IE – 76	UH – 80
18 – SB	58 – TR	98 – GT	DI – 43	IM – 02	UM – 68
19 – BN	59 – EB	99 – GN	DM – 77	IN – 94	UR – 08
			DN – 03	IR – 48	US – 42
20 – ES	60 – AH		DR – 56	IS – 35	
21 – RT	61 – VN		DS – 95		VG – 07
22 – HA	62 – TN		DT – 26	MD – 47	VN – 61
23 – DG	63 – BG			MH – 73	VS – 32
24 – SR	64 – MU		EA – 8	MN – 05	
25 – BE	65 – BR		EB – 59	MS – 92	
26 – DT	66 – NG		ED – 85	MU – 64	
27 – NU	67 – SH		EG – 16		
28 – GM	68 – UM		EH – 97	NA – 87	
29 – NB	69 – DH		EI – 44	NB – 29	

Fig. 93

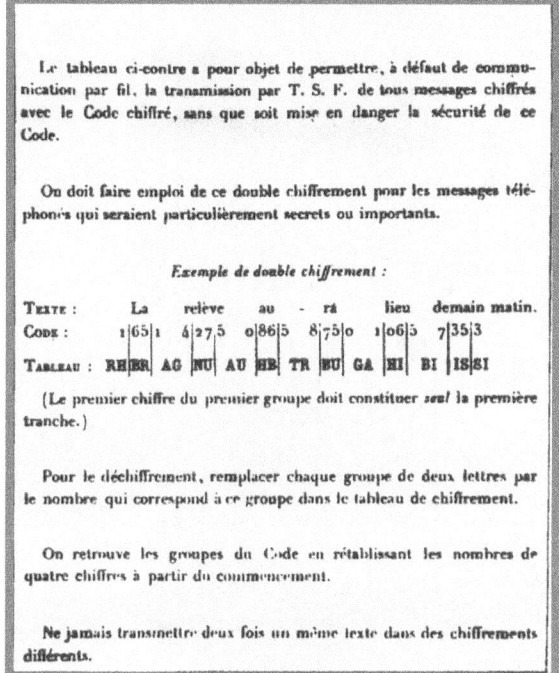

Fig. 94

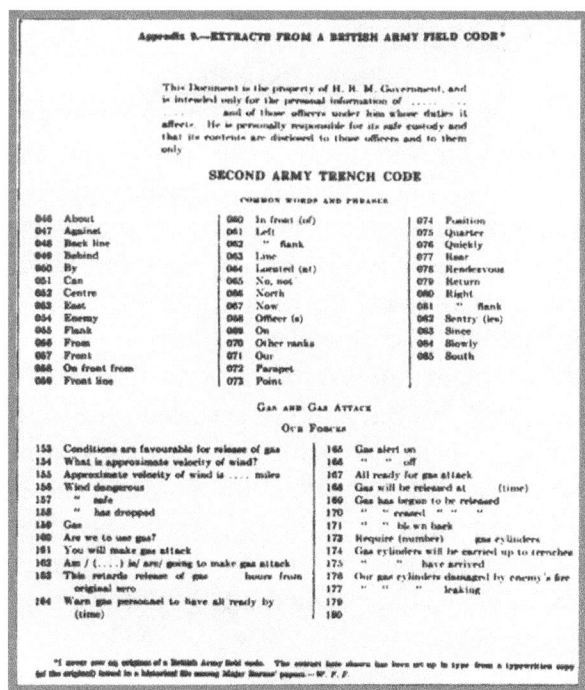

Fig. 95

to describe it. We did not even have a copy of their code – only a typewritten transcript which was furnished us quite reluctantly. This next slide was made by setting up in print a typical page thereof (fig. 95).

As for the Italians, the general level of cryptologic work in Italy during the period was quite low, a fact that is all the more remarkable when we consider that the birthplace of modern cryptology was in Italy several centuries before. There appears to have been in Italy a greater knowledge of cryptologic techniques in the fifteenth and sixteenth centuries than in the nineteenth, paradoxical as this may seem to us today. Perhaps this can be considered as one of the consequences of the need for secrecy that requires filing away in dusty archives records of cryptanalytic successes; but it is to be considered also that this prevents those who might have a flair for cryptologic work from profiting from the progress of predecessors who have been successful in such work. We should not be too astonished to learn, therefore, that when Italy entered World War I the Italian army put its trust in a very simple variation of the ancient Vigenère cipher, a system called the "cifrario militare tascabile," or the "pocket military cipher" (fig. 96). It, as well as several others devised by the same Italian "expert," was solved very easily by Austrian cryptanalysts during the war. The Italian army also used codes, no doubt, but since encipherment of such codes consisted in adding or subtracting a number from the page number on which a given code group appeared, the security of such systems was quite illusory. As late as 1927 the same Italian "expert" announced his invention of an absolutely indecipherable cipher system that, Gyldén says (p. 23), "still further demonstrates the astonishing lack of comprehension of modern cryptanalytic methods on his part."

As regards Russian cryptographic work, it is known that there was, during the era of the last of the Czarist rulers, an apparently well-organized and effective bureau for constructing and compiling diplomatic codes and ciphers, which had been organized by a Russian named Savinsky, formerly Russian minister to Stockholm. He saw to it that all codes and ciphers in use were improved; he intro-

1. Beispiel.

a. Cifrario tascabile.

•	a b c d e f g h i	•	j k l m n o p q r	•	s t u v w x y z	•	0 1 2 3 4 5 6 7 8 9	•
a	10 11 12 13 14 15 16 17 18	a	19 20 21 22 23 24 25 26 27	a	28 29 30 31 32 33 34 35	a	36 37 38 39 40 41 42 43 44 45	a
b	11 12 13 14 15 16 17 18 19	b	20 21 22 23 24 25 26 27 28	b	29 30 31 32 33 34 35 36	b	37 38 39 40 41 42 43 44 45 10	b
c	12 13 14 15 16 17 18 19 20	c	21 22 23 24 25 26 27 28 29	c	30 31 32 33 34 35 36 37	c	38 39 40 41 42 43 44 45 10 11	c
d	13 14 15 16 17 18 19 20 21	d	22 23 24 25 26 27 28 29 30	d	31 32 33 34 35 36 37 38	d	39 40 41 42 43 44 45 10 11 12	d
e	14 15 16 17 18 19 20 21 22	e	23 24 25 26 27 28 29 30 31	e	32 33 34 35 36 37 38 39	e	40 41 42 43 44 45 10 11 12 13	e
f	15 16 17 18 19 20 21 22 23	f	24 25 26 27 28 29 30 31 32	f	33 34 35 36 37 38 39 40	f	41 42 43 44 45 10 11 12 13 14	f
g	16 17 18 19 20 21 22 23 24	g	25 26 27 28 29 30 31 32 33	g	34 35 36 37 38 39 40 41	g	42 43 44 45 10 11 12 13 14 15	g
h	17 18 19 20 21 22 23 24 25	h	26 27 28 29 30 31 32 33 34	h	35 36 37 38 39 40 41 42	h	43 44 45 10 11 12 13 14 15 16	h
i	18 19 20 21 22 23 24 25 26	i	27 28 29 30 31 32 33 34 35	i	36 37 38 39 40 41 42 43	i	44 45 10 11 12 13 14 15 16 17	i
j	19 20 21 22 23 24 25 26 27	j	28 29 30 31 32 33 34 35 36	j	37 38 39 40 41 42 43 44	j	45 10 11 12 13 14 15 16 17 18	j
k	20 21 22 23 24 25 26 27 28	k	29 30 31 32 33 34 35 36 37	k	38 39 40 41 42 43 44 45	k	10 11 12 13 14 15 16 17 18 19	k
l	21 22 23 24 25 26 27 28 29	l	30 31 32 33 34 35 36 37 38	l	39 40 41 42 43 44 45 10	l	11 12 13 14 15 16 17 18 19 20	l
m	22 23 24 25 26 27 28 29 30	m	31 32 33 34 35 36 37 38 39	m	40 41 42 43 44 45 10 11	m	12 13 14 15 16 17 18 19 20 21	m
n	23 24 25 26 27 28 29 30 31	n	32 33 34 35 36 37 38 39 40	n	41 42 43 44 45 10 11 12	n	13 14 15 16 17 18 19 20 21 22	n
o	24 25 26 27 28 29 30 31 32	o	33 34 35 36 37 38 39 40 41	o	42 43 44 45 10 11 12 13	o	14 15 16 17 18 19 20 21 22 23	o
p	25 26 27 28 29 30 31 32 33	p	34 35 36 37 38 39 40 41 42	p	43 44 45 10 11 12 13 14	p	15 16 17 18 19 20 21 22 23 24	p
q	26 27 28 29 30 31 32 33 34	q	35 36 37 38 39 40 41 42 43	q	44 45 10 11 12 13 14 15	q	16 17 18 19 20 21 22 23 24 25	q
r	27 28 29 30 31 32 33 34 35	r	36 37 38 39 40 41 42 43 44	r	45 10 11 12 13 14 15 16	r	17 18 19 20 21 22 23 24 25 26	r
s	28 29 30 31 32 33 34 35 36	s	37 38 39 40 41 42 43 44 45	s	10 11 12 13 14 15 16 17	s	18 19 20 21 22 23 24 25 26 27	s
t	29 30 31 32 33 34 35 36 37	t	38 39 40 41 42 43 44 45 10	t	11 12 13 14 15 16 17 18	t	19 20 21 22 23 24 25 26 27 28	t
u	30 31 32 33 34 35 36 37 38	u	39 40 41 42 43 44 45 10 11	u	12 13 14 15 16 17 18 19	u	20 21 22 23 24 25 26 27 28 29	u
v	31 32 33 34 35 36 37 38 39	v	40 41 42 43 44 45 10 11 12	v	13 14 15 16 17 18 19 20	v	21 22 23 24 25 26 27 28 29 30	v
w	32 33 34 35 36 37 38 39 40	w	41 42 43 44 45 10 11 12 13	w	14 15 16 17 18 19 20 21	w	22 23 24 25 26 27 28 29 30 31	w
x	33 34 35 36 37 38 39 40 41	x	42 43 44 45 10 11 12 13 14	x	15 16 17 18 19 20 21 22	x	23 24 25 26 27 28 29 30 31 32	x
y	34 35 36 37 38 39 40 41 42	y	43 44 45 10 11 12 13 14 15	y	16 17 18 19 20 21 22 23	y	24 25 26 27 28 29 30 31 32 33	y
z	35 36 37 38 39 40 41 42 43	z	44 45 10 11 12 13 14 15 16	z	17 18 19 20 21 22 23 24	z	25 26 27 28 29 30 31 32 33 34	z
•	a b c d e f g h i	•	j k l m n o p q r	•	s t u v w x y z	•	0 1 2 3 4 5 6 7 8 9	•

b. Schlüsseln.

Klarschrift: D a s v i e r t e B a t a i l l o n h a t v o n s e i n e r S t e l l u n g a m . .

Schlüssel: i n m i t t e n m e i n e s l e b e n s w e g

Sigel: 39 31 26 35 12 33 15 23 41 14 26 34 25 42 34 32 30 18 34 39 16 27 22

c. Sigelschrift.

Das 3931 2635 1233 1523 4114 2634 2542 34 hat von seiner 3230 1834 3916 2722 am . . .

Fig. 96

duced strict regulations for their use; and he kept close watch over the cryptographic service. He also was head of a cryptanalytic activity, and it is known that Turkish, British, Austrian, and Swedish diplomatic messages were solved. After the Bolshevik revolution of 1916, some of the Russian cryptanalysts managed to escape from their homeland, and I had the pleasure of meeting and talking with one of the best of them during his service with one of our allies in World War II. He is no longer alive, but I vividly recall that he wore with great pride on the index finger of his right hand a ring in which was mounted a large ruby. When I showed interest in this unusual gem, he told me the ring had been presented him as a token of recognition and thanks for his cryptanalytic successes while in the service of Czar Nicholas, the last of the line.

But the story is altogether different as regards cryptology in the Russian army. The Military Cryptographic Service was poorly organized, and, besides, it had adopted a cryptographic system that proved to be too complicated for the poorly trained Russian cipher and radio operators to use when it was placed into effect toward the end of 1914. Here is a picture of that cipher (fig. 97), which was composed of two tables, one arranged for convenience in enciphering and the other arranged for convenience in deciphering. In the enciphering table the letters of the Russian alphabet (thirty-three in all) appwear in the topmost row of characters, the two-digit groups, in random order within each of the eight rows below the top row, are their cipher equivalents. These rows therefore constitute a set of eight cipher alphabets, these alphabets being preceded by key numbers from 1 to 8 in random order. Both the cipher equivalents and the indicators were subject to change. Indicators were used to tell how many letters were enciphered consecutively in each alphabet, the indicator consisting of one of the digits from 1 to 9 repeated five times. The alphabets were then used in key-number sequence, enciphering the first set of letters (5, 7, etc., according to the indicator) by alphabet I, the next set by alphabet 2, and so on. After the eighth set of letters, which was enciphered by cipher alphabet 8, one returned to

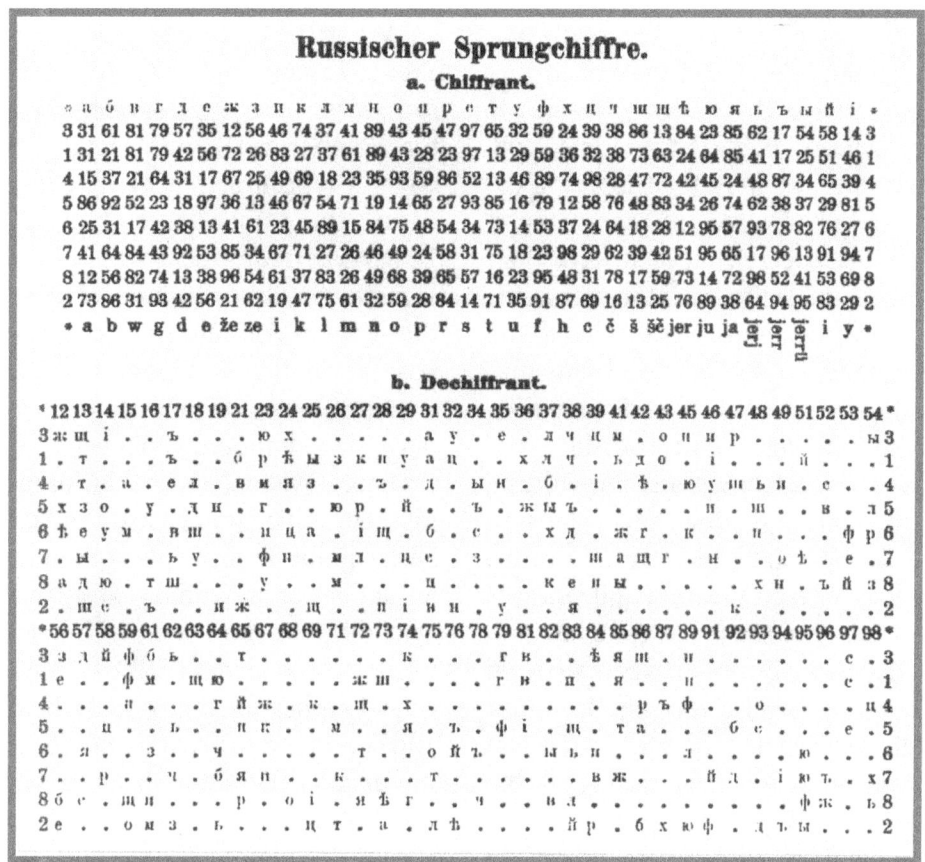

Fig. 97

cipher alphabet I, repeating the sequence in this manner until the entire message had been enciphered. In enciphering a long message, the cipher operator could change the number of letters enciphered consecutively by inserting another indicator digit repeated five times and then continuing with the next alphabet in the sequence of alphabets. The cipher text was then sent in five-digit groups. The use of the deciphering table hardly requires explanation, but this question may be in order: Why the aversion to the use of zero and to the use of double digits such as 11, 22, 33, etc.? This probably was thought to be helpful to the telegraph operators as well as to the cipher clerks in straightening out errors in transmission and reception.

I have told you that this cipher system proved too difficult for the Russians to use, and I think you can see why. It was so difficult that messages had to be repeated over and over, with great loss of time. It is well known to all historians by this time that the Russians lost the Battle of Tannenberg in the autumn of 1914 largely because of faulty communications. Poor cryptography and failure to properly use even the most simple ciphers on the field of battle, and not brilliant strategy on the part of the enemy, were the cause of Russia's defeat in that and in subsequent battles. The contents of Russian communications known to the German and Austrian High Commands within a few hours after transmission by radio. The disposition and movements of Russian troops and Russian strategic plans were no secrets to the enemy. The detailed and absolutely reliable information obtained by intercepting and reading the Russian communications made it very easy for the German and Austrian commanders not only to take proper countermeasures to prevent the execution of Russian plans but also to launch attacks on the weakest parts of the Russian front.

Although the Russian ciphers were really not complicated, their cipher clerks and radio operators found themselves unable to exchange messages with accuracy and speed. As a matter of fact, they were so inept that not only were their cipher messages easily solved but also they made so many errors that the intended recipients themselves had considerable difficulty in deciphering the messages, even with correct keys. In some cases this led to the use of plain language, so that the German and Austrian forces did not even have to do anything but intercept the messages and translate the Russian. To send out dispositions, impending movements, immediate and long-range plans in plain language was, of course, one cardinal error. Another was to encipher only words and phrases deemed the important ones, leaving the rest in clear. Another cardinal error, made when a cipher was superseded, was to send a message to a unit that had not yet received the new key, and, on learning this, to repeat the identical message in the old key. I suppose the Russians in World War I committed every major error in the catalog of crypto-criminology. No wonder they lost the Battle of Tannenberg, which one military critic said was not a battle but a massacre, because the Russians lost 100,000 men in the three-day engagement, on the last day of which the Russian commander in chief committed suicide. Three weeks later another high Russian commander followed suit, and the Russian army began to fall apart, completely disorganized, without leadership or plans. Russia itself began to go down in ruins when its army, navy, and government failed so completely, and this made way for the October revolution, ushering in a regime that was too weak to put things together again. The remnants were picked up by a small band of fanatics with military and administrative ability. By treachery, violence, and cunning, they welded together what has now become a mighty adversary of the Western world, the USSR.

I have left to be treated last in this lecture the cryptosystems used by the American Expeditionary Forces (AEF) in Europe during their participation in World War I.

When the first contingents of the AEF arrived in France in the summer of 1917, there were available for secret communications within the AEF but three authorized means. The first was the extensive code for administrative telegraphic correspondence, the 1915 edition of the *War Department Telegraph Code,* about which I've already told you something. Although it was fairly well adapted for that type of communication, it was not at all suitable for rapid and efficient strategic or tactical communications in the field, nor was it safe to use without a clumsy superencipherment. The second cryptosystem available was that known as the repeating-key cipher, which used the Signal Corps Cipher Disk, the basic principles of which were described as far back as about the year 1500. The third system available was the Playfair Cipher, which had been frankly copied from the British, who had used it as a field cipher for many years before World War I and continued to use it. In addition to these authorized means, there were from time to time current in the AEF apparently several – how many, no one knows – unauthorized, locally improvised "codes" of varying degrees of security, mostly nil. I show you one of these in this slide (fig. 98) and will let you assess its security yourself.

Seen in retrospect, when the AEF was first organized it was certainly unprepared for handling secret communications in the field; but it is certain that it was no more unprepared in this respect than any of the other belligerents upon their respective entries into World War I, as I've indicated previously in this lecture. This is rather strange because never before in the history of warfare had cryptology played so important a role as a consequence of advances in electrical communications technology. When measured by today's standards, it must be said that not only was the AEF on its arrival in Europe wholly unprepared as to secret communication means and methods and as to cryptanalysis, but for a limited time it seemed almost hopeless that the AEF could catch up with the technical advances both sides had made, because their British and French allies were at first most reluctant to disclose any of their hard-earned information about these vital matters.

Nevertheless, and despite so inauspicious a commencement, by the time of the armistice in November 1918, not only had the AEF caught up with their allies but they had surpassed them in the preparation of sound codes, as may be gathered from the fact that their allies had by then decided to adopt the AEF system of field codes and methods for their preparation, printing, distribution, and usage.

Just as the invention of Morse wire telegraphy had a remarkable effect upon military communications during the American Civil War, as related in the preceding lecture, so the invention of radio also played a very important role in field communications during World War I. Now, although it can hardly be said that all commanders from the very earliest days of the use of radio in military communications acutely recognized one of the most important disadvantages of radio – namely, that radio signals may be more or less easily intercepted by the enemy – it was not long before the consequences of a complete disregard of this obvious fact impressed themselves upon most commanders, with the result that the transmission of plain language became the exception rather than the rule. This gave the most momentous stimulus to the development and use of cryptology that this service had ever experienced.

Let us review some of the accomplishments of the Code Compilation Service under the Signal Corps, AEF. It was organized in January 1918, and consisted of one captain, three lieutenants, and one enlisted man. Until this service was organized, that is, from the summer of 1917 until the end of that year, the AEF had nothing for cryptocommunications except those three inadequate means which I've mentioned. When it had been determined that field codes were needed, little time was lost in getting on with the job that had to be done. Since I had no part in this effort, I can say, without danger of being charged with impropriety, that the Code Compilation Service executed the most remarkable job in the history of military cryptography up to the time of World War II.

The first work entrusted to it was the compilation of a so-called "Trench Code," of which 1,000 copies were printed, together with what were then called "distortion tables." These were simple monoalphabets for enciphering the two-letter groups of the code. I will show you a picture of a page of this code (fig. 99) and of one of the "distortion tables" (fig. 100). The danger of capture of these codes was recognized as being such that the books were not issued below battalions. Hence, to meet the needs of the front line, a much smaller book was prepared and printed, called the "Front Line Code." Distortion tables, thirty of them in all, were issued to accompany this code, of which an edition of 3,000 copies was printed. But the code was not distributed, because a study of its security showed defects. The truth is that AEF cryptographers with personnel inexperienced in cryptanalysis were groping in the dark, with little or no help from allies. Finally, the light broke through: the Code Compilation Service began to see the advantages of that German three-letter randomized two-part code I've told you about, the one called the *Satzbuch*. Here, then, was the origin of the Trench Codes that were finally adopted and used by the AEF ,when it was decided that copying and benefitting from the experience of German code compilers was no dishonor. But the AEF then went them one better, as you shall now learn. The first code of the new series of the AEF field codes was known as the "Potomac Code"; it was the first of the so-called" American River Series," and it appeared on 24 June 1918, in an edition of 2,000 copies (fig. 101). It contained approximately 1,700 words and phrases and, as the official report so succinctly states, "was made up with a coding and decoding section in order to reduce the work of the operators at the front." The designation "two-part," "randomized," or least of all, the British nomenclature, a "hatted" code, was still unknown – but the principle was there nonetheless. Let us see what the official report goes

Headquarters
52nd Infantry Brigade
26th Division
A.E.F.

France, 17 April 1918.

BULLETIN
No. 1

The following code for communications between Companies, Battalions, Regiments and Headquarters 52nd Infantry Brigade will be effective 18 April 1918, 12 o'clock.

CASUALTIES

KILLED	Strike out
SERIOUSLY WOUNDED	Base on balls
SLIGHTLY WOUNDED	Hit by pitched ball
ACCIDENTALLY WOUNDED	Balk
MISSING	Put outs
COMMISSIONED OFFICER	Major
ENLISTED MEN	Minors

CAPTURES

HAVE TAKEN (NO)_____ PRISONERS	Stolen Bases __(No)
HAVE LOST (NO)_____ PRISONERS	Left on base __(No)
HAVE LOST MACHINE GUNS	Errors
HAVE TAKEN MACHINE GUNS	Assists

ARTILLERY, TRENCH WEAPONS

WE WERE BOMBARDED WITH MINNENWERFERS	Johnson using spit ball
WE BOMBARDED WITH TRENCH MORTARS	Leonard using slow ball
WE BOMBARDED WITH STOKES MORTARS	Leonard using spit ball
WE BOMBARDED WITH 37 M.M. CANNON	Leonard using a curve
FIRED ON BY MACHINE GUNS	Johnson using fast ball
FIRED WITH MACHINE GUNS	Leonard using fast ball
WE WERE UNDER BOMBARDMENT	Wagner at bat
WE WERE UNDER HEAVY BOMBARDMENT	Wagner knocked a home run
WE WERE UNDER MODERATE BOMBARDMENT	Wagner tripled
WE WERE UNDER LIGHT BOMBARDMENT	Wagner doubled
WE WERE BOMBARDED WITH GAS	Wagner singled
ENEMY REGISTRATION FIRE	Wagner bunted
WE BOMBARDED	Cobb at bat
WE BOMBARDED HEAVILY	Cobb knocked a home run
WE BOMBARDED MODERATELY	Cobb tripled
WE BOMBARDED LIGHTLY	Cobb doubled
WE BOMBARDED WITH GAS	Cobb singled
REGISTRATION FIRE (OURS)	Cobb bunted
BARRAGE REQUESTED FROM <u>6666</u>	_____ fanned
OUR ARTILLERY LAID DOWN A BARRAGE	Sent in a pinch hitter

MISCELLANEOUS

NO UNUSUAL TRENCH EVENTS	Game called, rain
QUIET DAY	Game called, darkness
ACTIVE DAY	Extra inning game
THE ENEMY IS DOING TRENCH WORK AT _____	He is warming up
WE ARE DOING TRENCH WORK AT _____	We are warming up

Fig. 98

on to say on this point; let us listen to some sound and common sense:

> The main point of difference from other Army codes lay in the principle of reprinting these books at frequent intervals and depending largely upon the rapidity of the reissuance for the secrecy of the codes. This method did away with the double work at the front of ciphering and deciphering, and put the burden of work upon general headquarters, where it properly belonged. Under this system one issue of codes could be distributed down to regiments; another issue held at Army Headquarters; and a third issue held at General Headquarters. As a matter of record this first book, the Potomac, was captured by the enemy on July 20, just one month after issuance, but within two days, it had been replaced throughout the entire Army in the field.

The replacement code was the Suwanee, the next in the River Series, followed by the Wabash, the Allegheny and the Hudson, all for the American First Army. In October 1918 a departure in plan was made, and different codes were issued simultaneously to the First and Second Armies. This was done in order not to jeopardize unnecessarily the life of the codes by putting in the field at one time 5,000 or 6,000 copies of anyone issue. Thus the Champlain, the first of what came to be the "Lake Series," for the Second Army, was issued with the Colorado of the "River Series" for the First Army; these were followed by the Huron and the Osage, the Seneca and the Niagara, in editions of 2,500 each.

In addition to the foregoing series of codes were certain others that should be mentioned, for example, a short code of two-letter code groups to be used by frontline troops as an emergency code; a short code list for reporting casualties; a telephone code for disguising the names of commanding officers and their units, and so on. But there was in

```
13-C                                          1
 51 OB......Advance
 52 OC......Advance guard
 53 OD......Advancing
 54 OF......Advantage
 55 OG......Aeroplane (s)
 56 OK......Aeroplane observation
 57 OL......Aeroplane wireless
 58 OM......After
 59 ON......Afternoon
 60 OP......Again
 61 OR......Against
 62 OS......Age
 63 OT......Aim
 64 OV......Air
 65 OW......-Al
 66 OZ......Alert
 67 UB......All
 68 UC......All clear
 69 UD......All communication has been cut (with)
 70 UF......All is well
 71 UG......All of your messages have been received
 72 UH......All ready
 73 UK......All returned
 74 UL......All right
 75 UM......Alone
 76 UN......Along
 77 UP......Already
 78 UR......Also                     —ed—1721—HEG
 79 US......Alter                    —ing—1999—LYW
 80 UT......Altogether               —ly—2083—MUZ
 81 UV......Always                   —ment—2121—NEG
 82 UW......Am
 83 UZ......Am having
 84 YB......Am I
 85 YC......Am not
 86 YD......Ambulance (s)
 87 YF......Ambush
 88 YG......Ammunition
 89 YH......Ammunition depot (s)
 90 YK......Ammunition exhausted
 91 YL......Ammunition for 75 m.m. Field Gun, reduced
 92 YM......Among         [charge, explosive projectile
 93 YN......Amplifier
 94 YP......An
 95 YR......-Ance
 96 YS......And
 97 YT......Angle
 98 YV......Annihilate
 99 YW......Announce
 00 YZ......Annoy
                         (7)
```

Fig. 99

addition to all the foregoing one large code that must be mentioned, a code to meet the requirements for secure transmission of messages among the higher commands in the field and between these and GHQ. This was a task of considerable magnitude and required several months' study of messages, confidential papers concerning organizations, replacements, operations, and of military documents of all sorts. The code was to be known as the AEF Staff Code. In May 1918, the manuscript of this code was sent to press, and the printing job was

2-a

THIS TABLE MUST NOT FALL INTO THE HANDS OF THE ENEMY.

1. If destroyed to prevent capture, report will be made to the office to which its return is ordered.

2. This table will be used from 3 a. m.............................
to 3 a. m.........................., after which it will be returned in sealed envelope to ....

ENCIPHER

A	B	C	D	E	F	G	H	I	K	L	M	N	O	P	R	S	T	U	V	W	Y	Z
h	o	m	s	v	a	r	e	c	z	k	n	f	l	u	w	y	i	t	b	d	p	g

DECIPHER

a	b	c	d	e	f	g	h	i	k	l	m	n	o	p	r	s	t	u	v	w	y	z
F	V	I	W	H	N	Z	A	T	L	O	C	M	B	Y	G	D	U	P	E	R	S	K

Key word ....

Service message ....

Private message ....

Fig. 100

Decoding

ABE...Falling back
ABF....Heavy
ABG...Message received
ABK...Supply
ABM...Have you received
ABO...Bombardment
ABP...Barrage
ABS...Battalion
ABV...Automatic
ABW...Must be
ABX...Truck
ABY...Received
AFC...Cannot
AFD...One
AFJ...Turn
AFM...Machine gun emplacement
AFO...Enemy
AFR...7
AFV...18
AFX...Smoke
AFY...Stop
AGE...Diminish
AGF...-en
AGH...Picket
AGK...Stay
AGL...Field buzzer
AGN...In communication with
AGO...Question
AGU...Lieutenant
AGY...Emplacement
AMC...Further
AMG...Wounded
AMK...We are losing heavily
AMO...At close quarters
AMP...Confirm
AMS...Our first line
AMV...-ate
AMX...Might
AMY...Evident
AND...Battalion
ANF...During the night
ANG...Fifth
ANK...All stations
ANP...Observer
ANO...31
ANS...Consider
ANW...36
ANX...Your
ANY...Within
APB...Bombproof

APE...Relief completed
APF...Retire
APJ...Premature
APN...Impossible
APO...Withdraw
APU...Machine gun ammunition
APW...E
APX...Remove
APY...Moving
ASB...92
ASF...Shell
ASG...T
ASK...Has not been
ASM...Gas is being blown back
ASO...Control
ASP...Removed
ASV...Keep
ASX...Surprise
ASY...(Null)
AUB...Runner
AUF...Must have
AUG...Condition
AUK...Safety
AUM...Minute
AUP...Rescue
AUS...Point
AUW...V. B. rocket
AUX...On the right
AWB...Sometime
AWC...Require
AWE...Barricade
AWG...O'clock
AWK...Light Signal
AWO...Double
AWP...Still
AWS...Lengthen
AWX...Will signal by
AWY...Will not
AXB...Forcing
AXF...Magazine
AXG...Trenches
AXM...45
AXP...Send
AXS...Moment
AXV...Your
AXW...Last night
AXY...Going
BAD...Advance
BAF...Afternoon
BAG...Division headquarters

Fig. 101

done in one month by the printing facilities of the AEF Adjutant General. Considering that the code contained approximately 30,000 words and phrases, accompanied by code groups consisting of five-figure groups and four-letter groups, the task completed represents a remarkable achievement by a field printing organization, and I believe that this was the largest and most comprehensive code book ever compiled and printed by an army in the field. More than 50,000 telegraphic combinations were sent in tests in order to cast out combinations liable to error in transmission. One thousand copies of this code were printed and bound. With this code, as a superencipherment system, there were issued from time to time "distortion tables." There remains only to be said that the war was over before this code could be given a good workout, but I have no doubt that during the few months it was in effect it served a very useful purpose. Moreover, the excellent vocabulary was later used as a skeleton for a new War Department Telegraph Code to replace the edition of 1915.

One more code remains to be mentioned: a "Radio Service Code," the first of its kind in the American army. This was prepared in October, to be used instead of a French code of a similiar nature. Finally, anticipating the possible requirement for codes for use by the Army of Occupation, a series of three small codes, identical in format with the wartime trench codes of the River and Lake series, was prepared and printed. They were named simply Field Codes No.1, 2, and 3 but were never issued because there turned out to be no need for them in the quietude in Germany after the Army of Occupation marched into former enemy, but now very friendly, territory.

I will bring this lecture to a close now by referring those of you who might wish to learn more about the successes and exploits of the cryptographic organization of the American Expeditionary Forces in World War I to my monograph entitled American *Army Field Codes in the American Expeditionary Forces during the First World War* (Government Printing Office, 1942). In that monograph you will find many details of interest which I have had to omit in this talk, together with many photographs of the codes and ciphers produced and used not only by the AEF but also by our allies and enemies during that conflict.

In Lecture IV two USMTC cipher messages were given, and I said that their solutions would be presented at the conclusion of the next lecture. Here they are, both being from Major General Buell to General-in-Chief Halleck, relating to the relief and reinstatement of Buell.

Louisville, Ky., September 29,1862

Maj. Gen. Halleck, General-in-Chief:

I have received your orders of the 24th inst., requiring me to turn over my command to Maj. Gen. G. H. Thomas. I have accordingly turned over the command to him, and in further obedience to your instructions, I shall repair to Indianapolis and await further orders.

D. C. Buell,
Major-General

Louisville, Ky., September 30,1862
Gen. Halleck:
I received last evening your dispatch suspending my removal from command. Out of a sense of public duty, I shall continue to discharge the duties of my command to the best of my ability until otherwise ordered.
D. C. Buell,
Major-General

NOTES

1. I wonder what that sentence means. It sounds sort of "anti-American" to me. Punishment to whom? To the soldiers and sailors and airmen who defend our country? If not to them. then to whom? To the people of a whole nation fighting for liberty? I just don't understand the sentence. Do you?

2. Captain Parker Hitt's *Manual for the Solution of Military Ciphers*, (Fort Leavenworth, Kansas: Army Service Schools Press, 1916).

3. *L 'art de chiffrer et dechiffrer les depeches secretes*, (Paris, 1893).

4. Kenneth L. Ellis, *The Post Office in the Eighteenth Century: A Study in Administrative History.* (London: Oxford University Press, 1958), 176. In conjunction with this book one should by all means also read the following extremely interesting and revealing article by the same author: "British Communications and Diplomacy in the Eighteenth Century," *Bulletin of the Institute of Historical Research,* Vol. XXXI, No. 84, Nov. 1958, 159-67.

5. Honorary title conferred by the governor of Illinois for Fabyan's participation as a member of the Peace Commission that negotiated the Treaty of Portsmouth, which terminated the Russo-Japanese War in 1905.

6. Initially this cipher employed only the letters A, D, F, G, and X, for a matrix of 5 X 5; later, the letter V was added, for a matrix of 6 X 6, for the 26 letters of the alphabet plus the ten digits.

Lecture VI

This, the sixth and final lecture in this series on the history of cryptology, will be devoted to a presentation of the events of importance in that history from the end of World War I to the end of World War II. It would be entirely too ambitious a project even to attempt to compress within a lecture of only fIfty minutes all that should or could be told in that segment of our history. Briefly, however, it can be said that the most significant events during that quarter of a century were directly concerned, firstly, with the advances made in the production of more complex mechanical, electrical, and electronic cryptographic apparatus and, secondly, with the concomitant advances in the production of more sophisticated cryptanalytic apparatus in order to speed up or to make possible the solution of enemy communications produced by these increasingly complex cryptographic machines. These two phases are interrelated because, to use a simple analogy, cryptography and cryptanalysis represent the obverse and reverse faces of a single coin.

As to advances in the development and use of more effective cryptographic apparatus, I will only note at this point a comment that General Omar Bradley of World War II fame makes in his very interesting book, *A Soldier's Story*:[1]

> Signal Corps officers like to remind us that "although Congress can make a general, it takes communications to make him a commander."

It is presumptuous to amend General Bradley's remark, but this is how I wish he had worded it:

> Signal Corps officers like to remind us that "although Congress can make a general, it takes rapid and secure communications to make him a good .commander."

This will in fact be the keynote of this lecture. In other words, communications security, or COMSEC, will be its main theme and the one I wish to emphasize.

But before we take up the cryptographic history of the years between 1918 and 1946, perhaps a bit more attention must be devoted to events and developments of cryptanalytic significance or importance during this period. By far the most spectacular and interesting of these are the ones that were so fully and disastrously disclosed by the various investigations conducted by the Army and Navy very secretly while World War II was still in progress, and both secretly and openly after the close of hostilities. The investigations were intended to ascertain why our army and navy forces in Hawaii were caught by surprise by the sneak attack on Pearl Harbor by the Japanese on the morning of 7 December 1941. They were also intended to ascertain and pin the blame on whoever was responsible. I don't think I should even attempt to give you my personal opinion on these complex questions, which were studied by seven different boards within the services and fmally by the Joint Congressional Committee on the Investigation of the Pearl Harbor Attack. I mentioned the latter investigation in my first lecture and now will add to what I said then. The committee began its work early in September 1945 with secret hearings, but on seventy days between 15 November 1945 and 31 May 1946, open hearings were conducted, in the course of which some 15,000 pages of testimony were taken and a total of 183 exhibits received, incident to an examination of forty-three witnesses. In July 1946 the committee put out a final report of 580 pages containing its findings, conclusions and recommendations. The report was accompanied by a set of thirty-nine volumes of testimony and exhibits. The report was really not a single report:

there was one by the Majority (signed by six Democratic and two Republican members), and one by the Minority (signed by two Republican members). The Minority Report was not nearly as long as that of the Majority, but it brought into focus certain troublesome points that still form the subject of acrimonious discussions and writings by those who believe the attack was "engineered" by President Roosevelt and that certain authorities in Washington were as culpable as were the principal commanders in the Army and the Navy in Hawaii.

For this lecture, however, it is an interesting fact that both the Majority and Minority Reports contain glowing tributes to the role played by COMINT before and during our participation in World War II. In my first lecture, I presented a brief extract in this regard, taken from the Majority Report;[2] but here is what the Minority Report says on the subject:[3]

> Through the Army and Navy intelligence services extensive information was secured respecting Japanese war plans and designs, by intercepted and decoded Japanese secret messages, which indicated the growing danger of war and increasingly after November 26 the imminence of a Japanese attack.
>
> With extraordinary skill, zeal, and watchfulness the intelligence services of the Army Signal Corps and Navy Office of Naval Communications broke Japanese codes and intercepted messages between the Japanese Government and its spies and agents and ambassadors in all parts of the world and supplied the high authorities in Washington reliable secret information respecting Japanese designs, decisions, and operations at home, in the United States, and in other countries. Although there were delays in the translations of many intercepts, the intelligence services had furnished to those high authorities a large number of Japanese messages which clearly indicated the growing resolve of the Japanese Government on war before December 7, 1941.

Although references to COMINT abound in the Report of the Majority as well as in the Report of the Minority, there are also many references having to do with COMSEC in both reports, as well as in the thirty-nine accompanying volumes of testimony and exhibits. Some technical misconceptions with regard to those subjects are there, too, and it is quite comprehensible that there should be some on the part of laymen, but to encounter a serious one in a book by an experienced high-level commander in World War II is a bit disconcerting. Listen to this paragraph from a recent book by General Wedemeyer, who was one such commander:[4]

> The argument has been made that we could not afford to let the Japanese know we had broken their code. But this argument against a Presidential warning does not hold water. It was not a mere matter of having broken a specific code; what we had done was to devise a machine which could break any [author's emphasis] code provided it was fed the right combinations by our extremely able and gifted cryptographers. The Japanese kept changing their codes throughout the war anyway. And we kept breaking them almost as a matter of routine.

I don't know where General Wedemeyer obtained his information about that wonderful machine he mentions. I imagine that there are many other persons who think there is such a machine because of all they hear and see about those marvelous "electronic brains" which are capable of performing such amazing feats in solving all kinds of problems. I dare say I won't be wrong in assuming that many of you do indeed wish there were such a machine as that mentioned by General Wedemeyer. Nobody doubts that electronic digital computers can do lots of things in cryptologic research, and many persons speculate on the role they may play in their possible applications in connection with research in future wars.

But let's leave such speculations, interesting as they may be, and continue with our history of past applications. Let's first dispose of some comments in the COMINT area of that history, not only on the events preceding the Pearl Harbor attack, but also on the military, naval, and air operations which ensued in the Pacific as well as in the European Theater.

You will recall that in my first lecture I called to your attention an article that appeared in the 17 December 1945 issue of *Time* and that was based upon a letter the late General Marshall wrote to Governor Dewey, Republican candidate for president in the 1944 campaign. Here's how the two principals looked at that time (fig. 102). In the letter, which was written on 27 September 1944 and hand-carried by Colonel Carter W. Clarke, a high-level officer in Army G-2, to Governor Dewey, General Marshall begged the governor to say nothing during the campaign about a certain piece of very vital information which had become known to the governor, it having been "leaked" to him by persons unknown and unauthorized to disclose it. The information dealt with the fact that U.S. government authorities had been reading Japanese codes and ciphers *before* the attack on Pearl Harbor. The points which General Marshall wanted to convey were not only that the "leaked" information was true, but also that, much more important, (1) the war was still in progress; (2) the Japanese were still using certain of the pre-Pearl Harbor cryptosystems; and (3) the U.S. government was still reading highly secret Japanese messages in those systems, as well as highly secret messages of other enemy governments. Therefore, it was absolutely vital that Governor Dewey not use the top secret information as political ammunition in his campaign.

After merely glancing over the first two paragraphs of the letter, Governor Dewey handed it back to Colonel Clarke with the comment that he did not wish to read any further, whereupon there was nothing for Colonel Clarke to do but return immediately to Washington. General Marshall then made certain changes in the opening paragraphs of the letter, and again Colonel Clarke hand-carried it to the Governor, who then read the whole of it. In my first lecture I said that I might later give further extracts from *Time's* account of this episode, but there isn't time. Instead, however, I've put the whole account in Appendix I to the present lecture. The Marshall-Dewey correspondence is so important in cryptologic history that I have deemed it useful to put the whole of it in Appendix II.

Fig. 102

The information disclosed during the various official investigations of the attack on Pearl Harbor, so far as concerns the important COMINT achievements of the Army and the Navy before and after that attack, was classified information of the very highest security level, and the disclosures were highly detrimental to our national security. Much has been written about them since the end of hostilities, and although all of that formerly top secret information is now in the public domain, fortunately very few details of technical significance or value can be found therein. Hints and even blunt statements about the great role played by COMINT in U.S. military, naval, and air operations are found in books and articles published by U.S. government officials and American officers, as well as by officers of the beaten Japanese, German, and Italian armed forces. In the interests of brevity, I will cite only a few examples.[5]

As regards disclosures by U.S. government officials and officers, I can begin with those of the late Mr. Cordell Hull, who was secretary of state at the time of the Pearl Harbor attack. In his memoirs are many references (over a dozen) to the contents of intercepted and solved Japanese Foreign Office messages.[6] The late Mr. Henry L. Stimson, secretary of war at that time, makes clear references in his autobiography to COMINT successes and our failure to use them prior to the attack.[7] Dr. Herbert Feis, who was Mr. Hull's advisor on international economic affairs from 1937 to 1943, and who from 1944 to 1946 was Mr. Stimson's Special Consultant, has a good deal to say about the role played by "Magic" in a book written as a member of the Institute for Advanced Study, at Princeton[8] Admiral Kimmel, one of the two commanders in Hawaii at the time of the attack, in defending himself in his book, cites many "Magic" messages.[9] And Major General Sherman Miles, head of G-2 at the time of the attack, has much to say about "Magic" in an article published in 1948.[10] As regards disclosures by former enemy officers, the following are of particular interest because they concern the Battle of Midway, which is considered the one that turned the tide of war in the Pacific from a possible Japanese victory to one of ignominious defeat:

> If Admiral Yamamoto and his staff were vaguely disturbed by the persistent bad weather and by lack of information concerning the doings of the enemy, they would have been truly dismayed had they known the actual enemy situation. Postwar American accounts make it clear that the United States Pacific Fleet knew of the Japanese plan to invade Midway even before our forces had sortied from home waters. As a result of some amazing achievements by American intelligence, the enemy had succeeded in breaking the principal code then in use by the Japanese Navy. In this way the enemy was able to learn of our intentions almost as quickly as we had determined them ourselves.

* * * * * *

> The distinguished American Naval historian, Professor Samuel E. Morison, characterized the victory of United States forces at Midway as "a victory of intelligence." In this judgment the author fully concurs, for it is beyond the slightest possibility of doubt that the advance discovery of the Japanese plan to attack was the foremost single and immediate cause of Japan's defeat.
>
> Viewed from the Japanese side, this success of the enemy's intelligence translates itself into a failure on our part – a failure to take adequate precautions for guarding the secrecy of our plans. Had the secret of our intent to invade Midway been concealed with the same thoroughness as the plan to attack Pearl Harbor, the outcome of this battle might well have been different. But it was a victory of American intelligence in a much broader sense than just this. Equally as important as the positive achievements of the enemy's intelligence on this occasion was the negatively bad and ineffective functioning of Japanese intelligence.[11]

It is the second extract above which is of special interest to us at the moment, and, in particular, the portion that refers to "the negatively bad and ineffective functioning of Japanese intelligence." The author is, I think, a bit too severe on the Japanese intelligence organization. I say this because their cryptanalysts were up against much more sophisticated cryptosystems than they dreamt of, or were qualified to solve. In fact, even if they had been extremely adept in cryptanalysis, it would have been of no avail – U.S. high-level communications were protected by cryptosystems of very great security.

This brings us to a phase of cryptology that is of highest importance – the phase that deals with communications security, or COMSEC, and I shall confine myself largely to its development and historical background in our armed forces. The background is a very broad one because it should include the background of the developments of each of the three components of COMSEC, viz, (1) cryptosecurity, (2) transmission security, and (3) physical security of cryptomaterials. But since time is limited and because I think you would be more interested in the phases pertaining to cryptosecurity, I will omit further references to the other two components or to the history of their development. And even in limiting the data to cryptosecurity, I will have opportunity only to give some of the highlights of the development of the items that comprise our present cryptomaterials, omitting comments on the history of the development and improvement of our techniques, procedures, and practices, all of which are extremely important.

I shall begin the story with a definition that you will find in any good English dictionary, a definition of the word "accident." You will get the point of what may seem to you right now to be merely another of my frequent digressions from the main theme, but if it be a digression I think you will nevertheless find it of interest. The word "accident" in *Webster's Unabridged Dictionary* is defined as follows:

1. Literally, a befalling;

a. An event that takes place without one's foresight or expectation; an undesigned, sudden, and unexpected event.

b. Hence, often, an undesigned and unforeseen occurrence of an afflictive or unfortunate character; a mishap, resulting in injury to a person or damage to a thing; a casualty; as, to die by an accident.

There are further definitions of the word, but what I've given is sufficient for our purposes. But why define the word? What has it to do with COMSEC?

During our participation in World War II, the president of the United States, accompanied by many of his highest-level military, naval, and civilian assistants, journeyed several times half way around the world. He and they journeyed in safety; neither he nor they met with an "accident." Here's a picture taken at the Casablanca Conference in January 1943 (fig. 103). Imagine the disaster, it

Fig. 103

would have been if the plane carrying this distinguished group had been shot down and lost in the Atlantic or the Mediterranean. On the other hand, in April 1943 Admiral Isoroku Yamamoto, Commander in Chief of the Combined Fleet of the

Japanese Imperial Navy, started out on what was to be just an ordinary inspection trip but turned out to be a one-way trip for him. Here's a good picture of the admiral (fig. 104), who was the architect of the attack on Pearl Harbor. His death was announced in an official Japanese Navy communique stating that the admiral "had met a glorious end while directing operations in a naval engagement against superior enemy forces." But we know that this was simply not true; Admiral Yamamoto "met with an accident." Some bright person – I think it was the late Jimmy Walker, when mayor of New York City – has said that "accidents don't just happen – they are brought about." Jimmy Walker's comment was true in this case at least; Admiral Yamamoto did not die by accident; he died because our navy knew the schedule of his trip down to the very last detail so that it was possible to set up an ambush with high degree of success. Here is the story as told in an interesting manner by Fleet Admiral William F. Halsey, USN, in his book entitled *Admiral Halsey's Story*.[12]

Fig. 104

I returned to Noumea in time to sit in on an operation that was smaller but extremely gratifying. The Navy's code experts had hit a jackpot; they had discovered that Admiral Isoroku Yamamoto, the Commander-in-Chief of the Imperial Japanese Navy, was about to visit the Solomons. In fact, he was due to arrive at Ballale Island, just south of Bougainville, precisely at 0945 on April 18. Yamamoto, who had conceived and proposed the Pearl Harbor attack, had also been widely quoted as saying that he was ftlooking forward to dictating peace in the White House at Washington." I believe that this statement was subsequently proved a canard, but we accepted its authenticity then, and it was an additional reason for his being No.3 on my private list of public enemies, closely trailing Hirohito and Tojo.

Eighteen P-38's of the Army's 339th Fighter Squadron, based at Henderson Field, were assigned to make the interception over Buin, 35 miles short of Ballale. Yamamoto's plane, a Betty, accompanied by another Betty and covered by six Zekes, hove in sight exactly on schedule and Lt. Col. Thomas G. Lamphier, Jr., dove on it and shot it down in flames. The other Betty was also shot down for good measure, plus one of the Zekes. . . We bottled up the story, of course. One obvious reason was that we didn't want the Japs to know that we had broken their code. . . . Unfortunately, somebody took the story to Australia, whence it leaked into the papers, and no doubt eventually into Japan.... But the Japs evidently did not realize the implication any more than the tattletale; we continued to break their codes.

But lest you get the impression that enemy intelligence agencies had no success at all with secret communications of U.S. armed forces, let me tell you that they did have some success and, in certain instances, very significant success. There is not time to go into this somewhat disillusioning statement, but I can say that as a general rule the successes were attributable not to technical weakness in U.S. cryptosystems, but to their improper use in the case of certain low-level ones, by unskilled and improperly or insufficiently trained cryptographic clerks. I may as well tell you right now that this weakness in cryptocommunications has been true for a great many years, for centuries as a matter of fact, because as long ago as 1605 Francis Bacon, who wrote the first treatise in English on cryptology, made the following comment:[13]

> This Arte of *Cypheringe*, hath for Relative, an Art of Discypheringe; by supposition unprofitable; but, as things, are of great use. For suppose that Cyphars were well managed, there bee Multitudes of them which exclude the Discypherer. But in regarde of the rawnesse and unskillfulness of the handes, through which they passe, the greatest Matters, are many times carryed in the weakest Cyphars.

When electrical, particularly radio, transmission entered into the picture, additional hazards to communications security had to be taken into account, but many commanders failed to realize how much valuable intelligence can be obtained merely from a study of the procedures used in the transmission of messages as well as from a study of the direction and flow of radio traffic, the call signs of the transmitting and receiving stations, etc., all without solving the communications even if they were in cryptic form. Following are two paragraphs extracted from a document entitled *German Operational Intelligence*, published in April 1946 by the German Military Document Section, a Combined British, Canadian, and U.S. Staff:

> Signal intelligence (i.e., communication intelligence or COMINT) was a chief source of information in the German Army. In the eastern theater, where there was offensive warfare primarily, the signal intelligence service was well-organized with well-defined purposes, efficient personnel, and adequate equipment. In the course of the campaign, it was reorganized to exploit to the fullest the success already experienced, and, by 1943, there existed a complete and smoothly functioning machine sufficient to meet all demands. (p. 8.)

* * * * * * *

> Most of their signal intercept success came from low-echelon traffic. Armored and artillery radio nets passing operational traffic were followed closely and were one of the chief sources of signal intelligence. Artillery radio nets were given first coverage priority. Apart from messages intercepted in code or in clear, signal procedure, peculiarities of transmitting, and characteristics of Allied radio operators provided enormous assistance in helping to evaluate signal information. The Germans noticed that call signs were often the same for a unit over long periods and that even frequencies remained unchanged for weeks at a time. (p. 8.)

A great many examples of intercepted messages of tactical content are cited in the aforementioned document, which is replete with information of deep interest, although the document was originally issued with the lowest security classification then in use (U.S. "Restricted"; British-Canadian "FOR OFFICIAL USE ONLY"). I wish there were time to quote at greater length from this useful brochure.

Coming directly now to the history of the development of our cryptomaterials themselves, I hardly need reiterate what was pointed out in previous lectures as to the profound effect of the advances in the science and art of electrical communications in the twentieth century. Those advances had a direct effect upon military communications and an indirect effect upon military cryptology. Hand-operated ciphers and, of course, code books became almost obsolete because the need for greater and greater speed of cryptographic operations became obvious in order to match as much as possible the very great increase in the speed of communications brought about by inventions and improvements in electric wire and radiotelegraphy. The need for cryptographic apparatus and machines thus very soon became quite obvious, but it took quite some time to satisfy that need in a manner that could be considered to give adequate security for military communications.

The history of the invention and development of cryptographic devices, machines, and associated apparatus and material is long and interesting. Let us begin with a resumé of the earliest items of importance in that history.

Until the advent of electronic cipher machines, most cryptographic apparatus and devices were built upon or around concentric circular rotating members such as cipher wheels, cipher disks, etc. A very early, perhaps the earliest, picture of such a device appears in a treatise by an Italian cryptologist named Alberti, whose *Trattati in Cifra* was written in Rome about 1470. It is the oldest tract on cryptography the world now possesses. Here's a photo of Alberti's disk (fig. 105), but I won't take the time to explain it except to say that the digits 1, 2, 3, 4 were used to encipher code groups and to call your attention to the fact that the letters of the cipher or revolving alphabet were in mixed order. In Porta's book, first published in 1563 in Naples, there appear several cipher disks; in the copy which was given me as a gift by Colonel Fabyan, they are still in working condition. Here is a picture of one of them (fig. 106). In this version the device uses symbols as cipher characters. And apparently nobody thought up anything much better for a long, long time. It seems, in fact, that not only did no one think up anything new or even some improvements on the original Alberti or Porta disks, but those who did any thinking at all on the subject merely "invented" or "reinvented" the same thing again,

Fig. 105

Fig. 106

and that happened repeatedly in successive generations. For instance, in Lecture No. IV of this series you were shown a picture of the cipher disk "invented" by Major Albert Myer, the first Chief Signal Officer of the U.S. Army, who obtained a patent on his invention in 1865. Here's a picture of the patented disk (fig. 107) and the explanation of the invention (fig. 108). You may also remember that signalmen of the Confederate Signal Corps mechanized the old Vigenère Square and put it out in the form of a cylinder (see figures 65 and 66 of Lecture No.

IV). The cipher disk used by the Signal Corps of the U.S. Army from 1910 to 1920, that is, during the period including our participation as a belligerent in World War I, was nothing but a white celluloid variation of the original Alberti parchment disk of the vintage of 1470 (except that it was even simpler than its progenitor, because in the latter the cipher alphabets produced were mixed alphabets whereas in the Signal Corps disk, the cipher alphabets are simple reversed standard sequences (fig. 109). We all know that it generally takes a pretty long time to get a patent through the U.S. Patent Office, but the ancient device was patented in 1924 by S.H. Huntington (fig. 110): here you can see a great improvement over the Signal Corps version – a blank is added to both sequences so that the space between words could be enciphered. Indication of word space, as you have learned, is a fatal weakness if seen in the cipher text; in the Huntington device the spaces between words would be enciphered, but the cipher text would have space signs, although they would not correspond to the actual spaces between words in the plain text. In the Huntington device, the space signs in the cipher text would be a bit misleading but not to an experienced cryptanalyst, who would soon realize that they do not actually represent "word space" in the plain text.

It is interesting to note that in 1936, during the days when the German National Socialists were banned as an organization in Austria, the Nazis used this variation of the old disk – it had ten digits on both the outer and the inner sequences for enciphering digits (fig. 111).

The first significant improvement on the old cipher disk was that made by Sir Charles Wheatstone in 1867, when he invented a cipher device which he called *The Cryptograph*. He described it in a volume entitled *The Scientific Papers of Sir Charles Wheatstone*, published in 1879 by the Physical Society of London. Here is a picture of the Wheatstone device in my private collection (fig. 112). What Sir Charles did was to make the outer circle of letters (for the plain text) comprise the twenty-six letters of the alphabet, plus one additional character to represent "space." The inner circle, for cipher equivalents, contains only the twenty-six letters of the alphabet, which can be disarranged in a mixed sequence. Two hands, like the hour and minute hands of a clock, are provided, and they are under control of a differential gear mechanism, so that when the long or "minute hand" is advanced to make a complete circuit of the letters on the outer circle, the short or "hour hand" advances one space or segment on the inner circle. In figure 112, for example, the plaintext letter G is represented by the cipher letter A, that is, $G_p = A_c$. If the long hand is now advanced in a clockwise direction for one revolution, G_p will be represented no longer by A_c but by G_c, the letter immediately to the right of A_c on the inner circle. In encipherment the long hand is always moved in the same direction (clockwise, for example), and its aperture is placed successively over the letters on the outer circle according to the successive letters of the plaintext message, the cipher equivalents being recorded by hand to correspond with the letters to which the short hand points on each encipherment. In this way, identical letters of the plain text will be represented by different and varying letters in the cipher text, depending upon how many revolutions of the long hand intervene between the first and subsequent appearances of the same plaintext letter. Thus, with the alphabets shown in figure 112, and with the initial setting $G_p = A_c$, the word "reference" would be represented in cipher as follows:

REFERENCE

XZZZBGQAM,

in which it will be seen that repeated letters in the plain text are represented by different letters in the cipher text. Correspondents must naturally agree upon the mixed alphabet used in the inner circle and the initial positions of the two hands at the beginning of the encipherment of a message. In decipherment, the operator moves the long hand again clockwise, until the hour hand points to the cipher letter in the plaintext letter that is seen through the aperture at the end of the long hand on

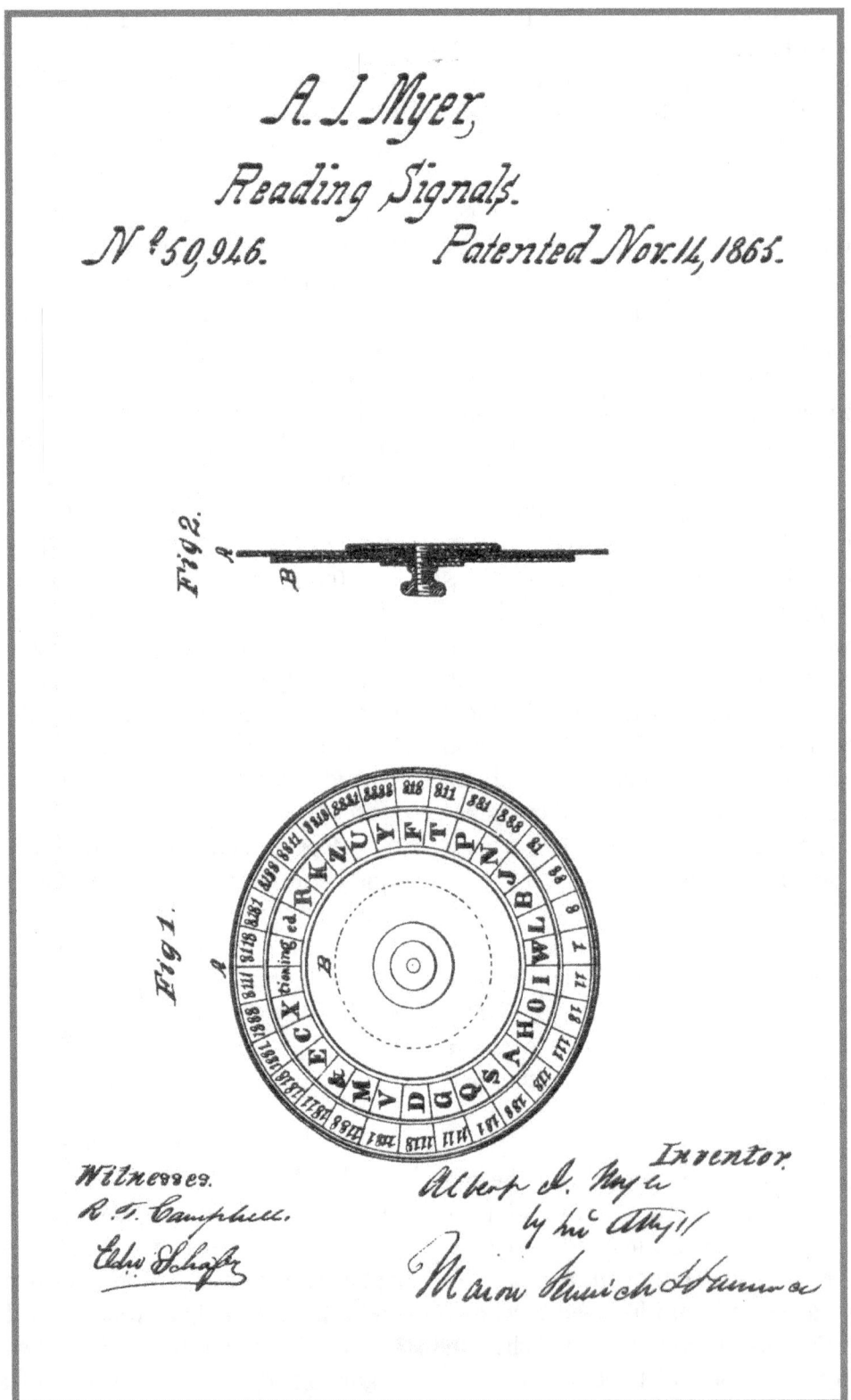

Fig. 107

UNITED STATES PATENT OFFICE.

ALBERT J. MYER, OF WASHINGTON, DISTRICT OF COLUMBIA.

IMPROVEMENT IN SIGNALS.

Specification forming part of Letters Patent No. **50,946**, dated November 14, 1865.

To all whom it may concern:

Be it known that I, ALBERT J. MYER, of Washington city, District of Columbia, have invented a new Mode of Communicating by Signals; and I do hereby declare that the following is a full, clear, and exact description thereof, reference being had to the accompanying drawings, making a part of this specification, in which—

Figure 1 is a front view of two disks having certain characters upon them to be used in communicating by signals. Fig. 2 is a diametrical section through the disks, showing the manner of attaching them together.

The object of this invention is to afford means whereby persons within signal distance of each other can communicate intelligibly by certain movements of flags or other objects, and a systematic arrangement of letters and numerals or other characters upon movable and stationary disks, without the possibility of having their messages detected by others.

To enable others skilled in the art to understand my invention I will describe my improved method of signaling.

In the accompanying drawings, A represents a disk having printed or engraved upon it in any sequence certain figures or characters, which indicate signals to be made or characters or words to be written. B is a smaller disk having upon it the letters of an alphabet in any desired sequence, which it may be desired to refer to in signaling. These two disks are pivoted together centrally by means of a clamp-screw, on loosening which the smaller disk may be turned in either direction, so as to bring different letters opposite to the numerals, after which, by tightening the screw a, the disks will be rigidly connected together.

Each person giving and receiving signals should be provided with one of these devices, and there should be a preconcerted understanding between such persons for moving the disk B and causing different signal combinations to stand at different times for different letters or messages, for the purpose of concealing the meaning of the signals.

The mode of signaling is as follows: Suppose two persons within signal distance of each other should desire to communicate the word "are," and by preconcerted signals have both adjusted their disks so that the letter A shall be opposite to the number 11. Now, to spell the word "are" the signals designated by the combination "11" for "A" are made, and this will indicate to the observer the letter "A." Then there should be made the signal indicated by the figures "8111" or "R," and this would indicate to the observer this letter. The signal or signals indicating the letter "E," which are "1181" on the disk, conclude the word are.

It may be desirable for purposes of concealment that the word "are," though often occurring, should not again be indicated in the same communication by the same signals. In this case let it be understood by preconcert that upon any given signal, such as the dropping of a flag or some peculiar wave of a flag, the smaller disk, or that which has upon it the letters of the alphabet, is to be moved upon the largest disk, or that which has upon it the numerals, turning to the right hand, say, the distance of four spaces, marked upon the disk. Now, without cessation of signaling, both persons, the transmitter and the receiver, would upon this signal each so change the position of the disks that in again signaling the word "are" "A" would stand opposite to and be designated by the combination "188," "R" would be designated by the combination "1188," and "E" by "1881." The letters "A R E" or the word "are" thus signaled would in no way resemble the same word before sent. In this way it can be so arranged by preconcerting that no word shall appear twice in the same manner in the same message.

There may be several disks joined together, having various figures and characters upon them, and by preconcert it may be understood that in certain messages some of them are to be used and not others, or there may be more than one row of figures or characters on any of the disks and the preconcerted arrangement for using may be changed infinitely, so that the uninstructed cannot discover in what manner the disks are to be moved or used.

Having thus described my invention, what I claim as new, and desire to secure by Letters Patent, is—

The within-described system of signaling, which is controlled by means of letters, numerals, or other characters upon disks that are put together in such manner that the relative positions of such characters can be changed at pleasure, substantially as set forth.

ALBERT J. MYER.

Witnesses:
R. T. CAMPBELL,
E. SCHAFER.

Fig. 108

the outer circle. Thus, in the case of the example given above, the cipher letters XZAABGQAM will be found to represent the word REFERENCE.

During World War I, sometime in 1917, the British army resuscitated Wheatstone's cryptograph and improved it both mechanically and cryptographically. Here's a picture of the device (fig. 113), in which it will be seen that there are now no longer the "minute" and "hour" hands but a single hand with an opening or window that simultaneously disclosed both the plain and the cipher letters.

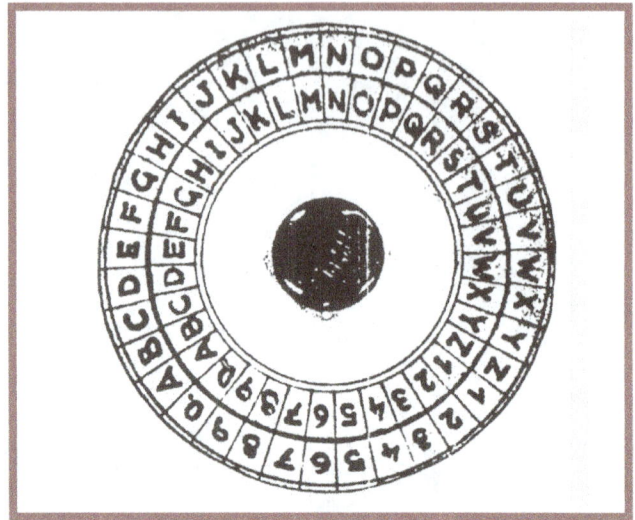

Fig. 111

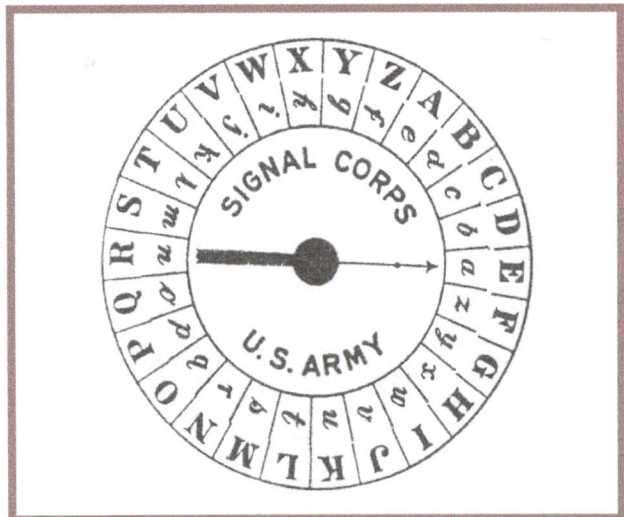

Fig. 109

Fig. 112

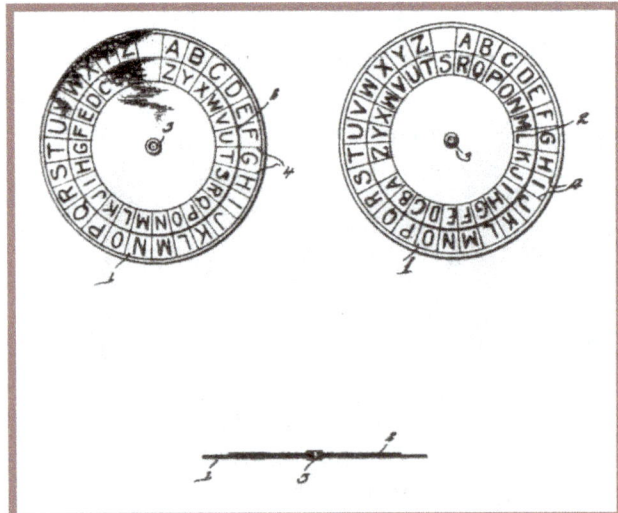

Fig. 110

When the single hand is turned, the inner circle of segments, which are made of a substance upon which letters may be written in pencil or in ink is advanced eccentrically and against a similarly made outer circle of segments. In this improvement on the original Wheatstone device, both sequences of letters are now mixed sequences. Making the outer circle also a mixed sequence added a considerable degree of security to the cipher. When it was proposed that all the Allied armies use this device for field cryptocommunications and its security had been approved by British, French, and American cryptologists (both at GHQ-AEF and at

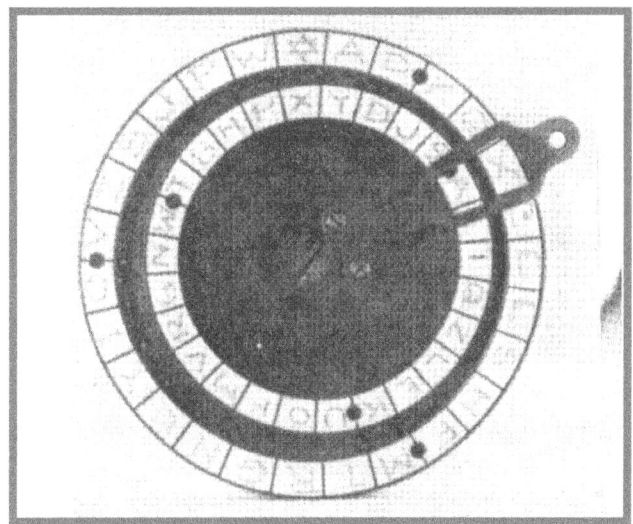

Fig. 113

Some years later, and almost by sheer good fortune, I learned that a cipher machine was in the museum of a small town in Connecticut named Hamden. I was interested and wrote to the curator of the museum, requesting that he lend the device for a short period to me as principal cryptanalyst of the War Department. Imagine my astonishment and pleasure when I unpacked the box upon its receipt and found a device, beautifully made and encased in a fine mahogany case, with its inventor's name, Decius Wadsworth, and the date, 1817, engraved on the face of the machine, which was nothing but another version of the Wheatstone Cryptograph. Here's a picture of it (fig. 114). There are good reasons to believe that the model was made by Eli Whitney. Mechanically, it was similar

Fig. 114

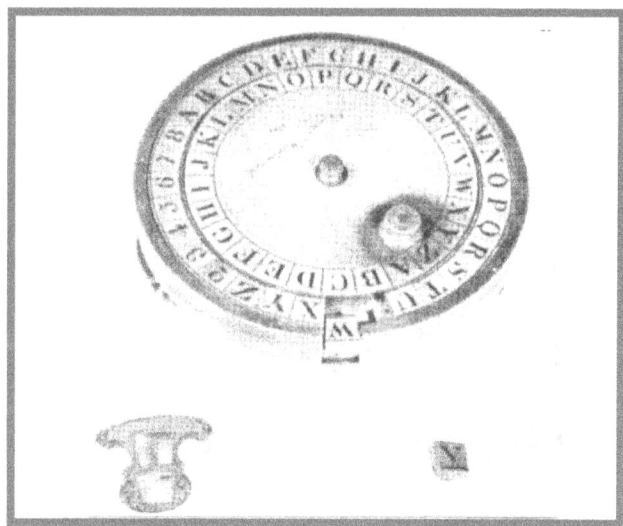

Fig. 115

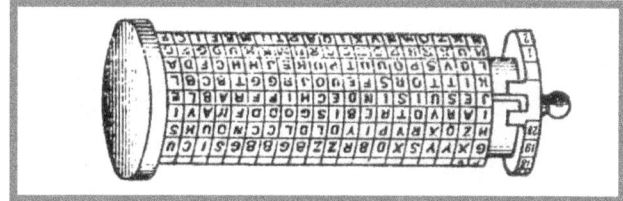

Fig. 116

Washington), an opportunity to agree or disagree with the assessment of these cryptologists was given me while still at Riverbank. I was able to show that the modified Wheatstone cryptograph was still insufficiently secure for military purposes, and the devices, thousands of which had been manufactured and issued, were withdrawn. If you are interested in the method of solution I used, you will find it in Riverbank Publication No. 20, entitled *Several Machine Ciphers and Methods for their Solution* (1918). A better method of solution was devised by me about 1923.

to the British modification, except that the outer sequence had thirty-three characters, the inner, twenty-six, so that the differential gear instead of operating on the ratio of 27 to 26 was now on the ratio 33 to 26. Thus, Colonel Decius Wadsworth, who was then the first Chief of Ordnance of the U.S. Army, had anticipated Wheatstone by over sixty years in this invention. He also anticipated the British army cryptologists of World War I by a whole century in their modification of Wheatstone's original, because in the Wadsworth device, too, there was only one hand and both alphabets could be made mixed sequences. This is very clearly shown in figure 115 as regards the outer sequence, and I believe the inner one could also be disarranged, but the picture does not clearly show this to be the case, so that I am not sure as to this point. I returned the device a good many years ago, and it is now on display in the Eli Whitney Room of the New Haven Historical Society's Museum.

The next device I bring to your attention is shown in figure 116, a device invented by a French army reservist, Commandant Bazeries, who for some ten years valiantly but unsuccessfully tried to get the French army to adopt it. He included a description of his device, which he called his "Cryptographe Cylindrique" or "cylindrical cryptograph," in a book published in 1901 in Paris.[14] He had, however, previously described his device in an article entitled "Cryptographe à 20 Rondelles - alphabets (25 lettres par alphabet)," published in 1891.[15] In this device there is a central shaft on which can be mounted twenty numbered disks on the peripheries of which are differently mixed alphabets of twenty-five letters each. The disks can be assembled in some prearranged or key sequence on the shaft, from left to right, but they can be revolved thereon and then locked into position on the shaft by pushing in the locking disk at the extreme left. The first twenty letters of the plain text of a message are first aligned, as seen in figure 116 (JE SUIS INDÉCHIFFRABLE = "I am indecipherable"); the disks are then locked into position so that the whole assembly can be turned; and as cipher text one may select anyone of the other twenty-four rows of letters, which are recorded then by hand on paper. Then the next twenty plaintext letters are aligned, one of the other twenty-four rows of letters selected and recorded, etc. To decipher a message, the disks having been assembled on the shaft in accordance with the prearranged or key sequence, one takes the first twenty cipher letters, aligns and then locks them into position, and then turns the whole cylinder, searching for a row of letters which form intelligible text. There will be one and only one such row, and the plaintext letters are recorded. Then the next twenty letters of cipher are aligned, etc.

Another French cryptologist, the Marquis de Viaris, soon showed how messages prepared by means of the Bazeries cylindrical cipher could be solved.[16] Maybe that is why Bazeries wasn't too successful in his attempt to get the French army to adopt his device. But in the United States there were apparently none who encountered either what Bazeries or de Viaris wrote on the subject. Captain Parker Hitt, U.S. Army, whom I have mentioned in a previous lecture, in 1915 invented a device based upon the Bazeries principle but not in the form of disks mounted upon a central shaft. Instead of disks, Hitt's device used sliding strips. Here is a picture of his very first model (fig. 117), which he presented to me sometime in 1923 or 1924. But I first learned about his device sometime in 1917 while still at Riverbank and solved one challenge message put up by Mrs. Hitt, a Riverbank guest for a day. In meeting the challenge successfully (which brought a box of chocolates for Mrs. Friedman from Mrs. Hitt), I didn't use anything like what I could or might have learned from de Viaris, because at that time I hadn't yet come across the de Viaris book. I solved the message by guessing the key Mrs. Hitt employed to arrange her strip alphabets. She wasn't wise to the quirks of inexperienced cryptographic clerks: she used RIVERBANK LABORATORIES as the key, just as I suspected she would. The device she brought with her was an improved model: the alphabets were on paper strips, and the latter were glued to strips of wood, as seen in figure 118.

Captain Hitt brought his device to the attention of the then Major Mauborgne, whom I have also mentioned in a previous lecture and who was then on duty in the Office of the Chief Signal Officer in Washington. There is some question as to whether it was Hitt who first brought his device to Mauborgne's attention; Mauborgne later told me that he had independently conceived the invention and, moreover, had made a model using disks instead of strips. I have that model, a present from General Mauborgne many years later. It is made of very heavy brass disks on the peripheries of which he had engraved the letters of his own specially devised alphabets. In 1919, after my return to Riverbank from my service in the AEF, Mauborgne sent Riverbank the beginnings (the first twenty-five letters) of a set of twenty-five messages enciphered

Fig. 118

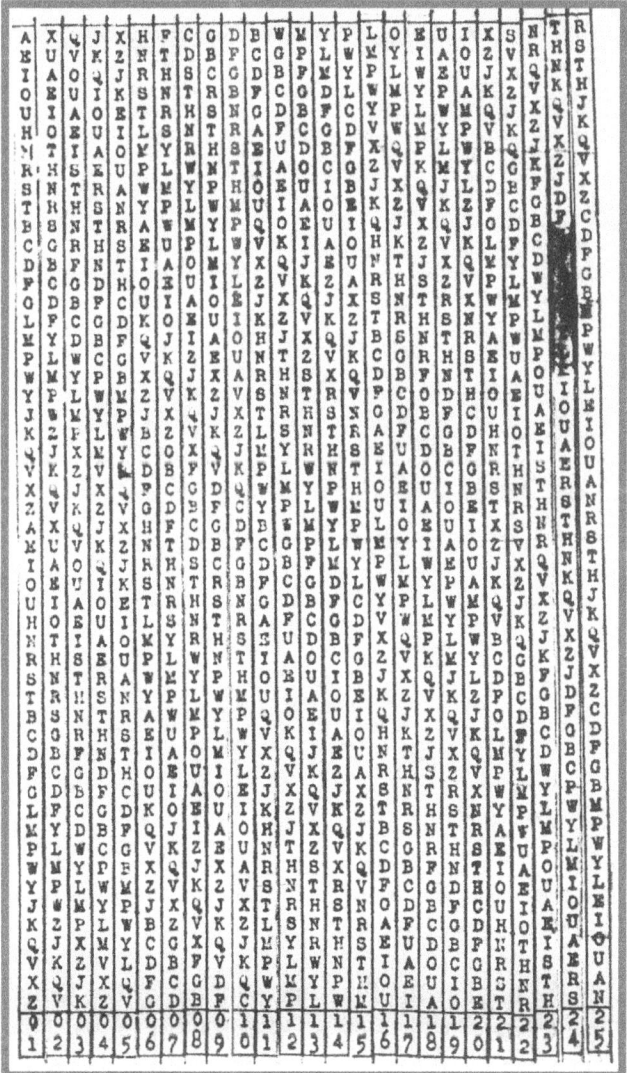

Fig. 117

by his device and alphabets. He also sent the same data to Major Yardley, in G-2. Nobody ever solved the messages, even after a good deal of work and even after Mauborgne told us that two consecutive words in one of the challenge messages were the words "are you." Many years later I found the reason for our complete lack of success, when I came across the plain texts of those messages in a dusty old file in one of the rooms occupied in the old Munitions Building by the Office of the Chief Signal Officer. Here is a picture of the beginnings of the first six messages (fig. 119). Mauborgne, when I chided him on the unfairness of his challenge messages, told me that he had not prepared them himself – he had an underling (Major Fowler was his name, I still remember it!) prepare them. In our struggles to solve the challenge messages, we had assumed they would contain the usual sorts of words found as initial words of military messages. It was the complete failure by Riverbank and G-2 to solve the challenge messages that induced

Mauborgne to go ahead with the development of his device. It culminated in what became known as Cipher Device, Type M-94. Here is a picture of it (fig. 120). That device was standardized and used for at least ten years in the United States by the Army, the Navy, the Marine Corps, the Coast Guard, the intelligence operations of the Treasury Department, and perhaps by other agencies.

In 1922, a wartime colleague, the late Captain John M. Manly (professor and head of the Department of English at the University of Chicago) brought to my attention a photostat of two pages of a holographic manuscript in the large collection of *Jefferson Papers* in the Library of

Fig. 119

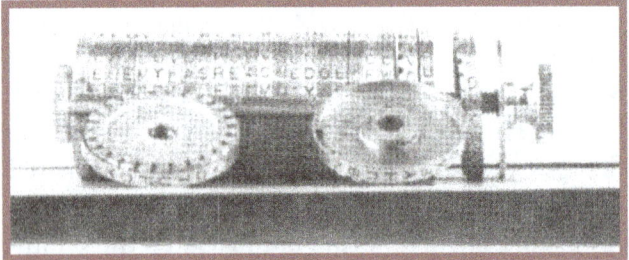

Fig. 120

Congress. It described his invention entitled "The Wheel Cypher," and figure 121 is a picture of the second page showing Jefferson's basis for calculating the number of permutations afforded by the set of thirty-six wheels of his device. He didn't attempt

to make the multiplication; he didn't have an electronic digital computer – for the total number is astronomical in size. Jefferson anticipated Bazeries by over a century, and the Hitt-Mauborgne combination by almost a century and a half.

It soon became apparent to both army and navy cryptologists that a great increase in cryptosecurity would be obtained if the alphabets of the M-94 device could be made variant instead of invariant. There began efforts in both services to develop a practical instrument based upon this principle. I won't take time to show all these developments but

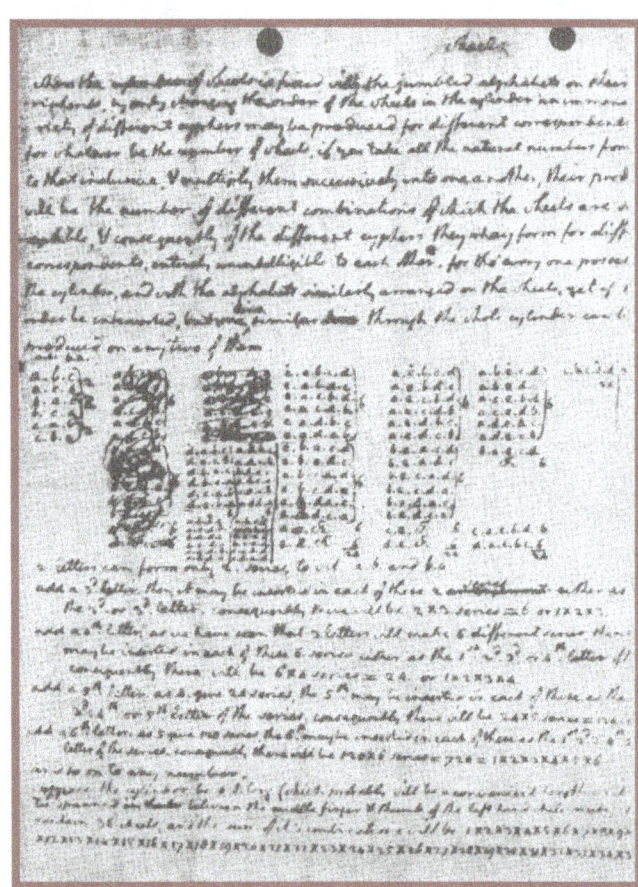

Fig. 121

only the final form of the one adopted by the Army, Strip Cipher Device Type, M-138A (fig. 122). This form used an aluminum base into which channels with overhanging edges were cut to hold cardboard strips of alphabets which could be slid easily within the channels. It may be of interest to you to learn that after I had given up in my attempts to find a

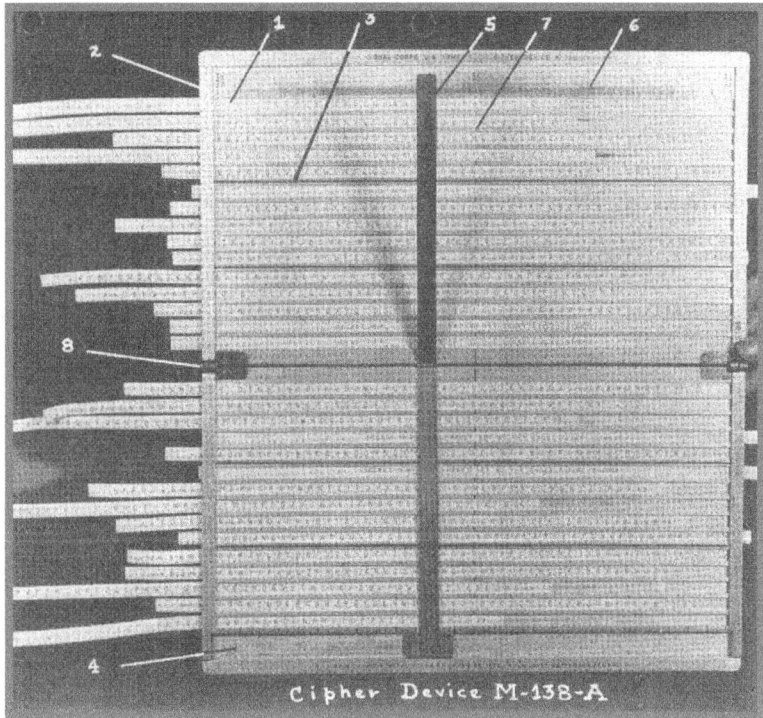

Fig. 122

firm that would or could make such aluminum grooved devices in quantity, Mrs. Friedman, by womanly wiles and cajolery on behalf of her own group in the Coast Guard, succeeded in inducing or enticing one firm to make them for her. And that's how the first models of strip cipher devices made of aluminum by the extrusion process came about, and how the U.S. Army, by administrative cooperation on an interservice level and technical cooperation on a marital level, found it practical to develop and produce in quantity its Strip Cipher Device, Type M-138A. This was used from 1935 to 1941 or 1942 by the Army, the Navy, the Marine Corps, the Coast Guard, et al., including the Treasury and State Departments. It was used as a back-up system even after the armed services as well as the Department of State began employing much better and more sophisticated cipher machines of high speed and security.

Thus far we have been dealing with cipher devices of the so-called "hand-operated" type. None of them can readily be considered as being "machines," that is, apparatus employing mechanically driven members upon which alphabetic sequences can be mounted so that constantly changing sequences of cipher alphabets are produced. We come now to types of apparatus that can be called machines, and one such machine is shown in figure 123. It is called the Kryha machine, after the name of its German inventor, who unfortunately committed suicide a few years ago, perhaps because the last model of his improved machine failed to impress professional cryptologists. The Kryha has a fixed semicircle of letters against which is juxtaposed a rotatable circle of letters. Both sequences of letters can be made mixed alphabets (the segments are removable and interchangeable on each sequence). The handle at the right serves to wind a rather powerful steel clock spring that drives the rotatable platform on which the letters of the inner circle are mounted. In figure 124 can be seen something of the inner mechanism. The large wheel at the right has segments that are open or closed, depending upon the "setting" or key. This wheel controls the angular displacement or "stepping" of the circular rotatable platform. The initial juxtaposition of the inner or movable alphabet against the

Fig. 123

Fig. 124

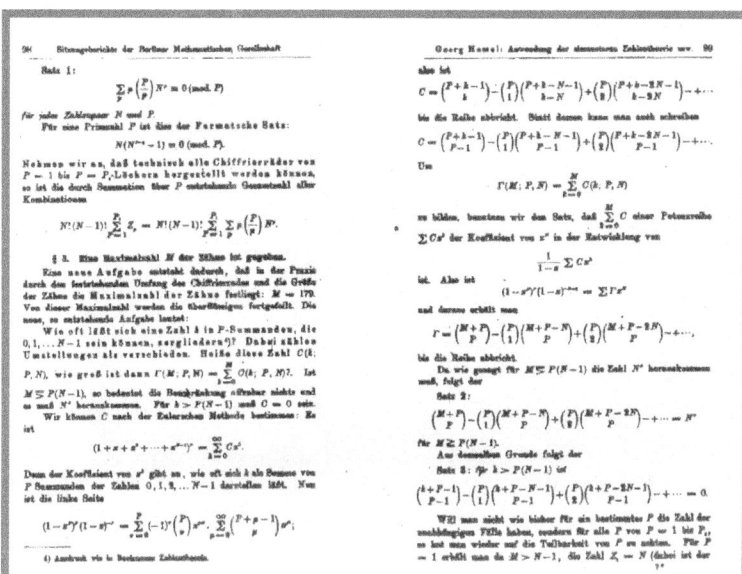

Fig. 125

Fig. 126

outer or fixed one, as well as the composition of these alphabets, is governed by some key or other prearrangement. The cipher equivalents must be recorded by hand. After each encipherment, the button you saw in the center of the panel in figure 123 is pushed down, the inner wheel is advanced 1, 2, 3, 4 ... steps, depending on the key, and the next letter is enciphered, etc. The pictures I've shown you apply to the latest model of the Kryha; as regards the first model, which came on the market sometime in the 1920s, a German mathematician produced an impressive brochure showing how many different permutations and combinations the machine afforded. Here's a picture of a couple of pages of his dissertation (fig. 125), but even in those days professional cryptanalysts were not too impressed by calculations of this sort. With modern electronic computers such calculations have become even less significant.

Let us now proceed with some more complex and more secure machines. In this next illustration (fig. 126), you see a machine that represents a rather marked improvement by a Swedish cryptographic firm upon the ones shown thus far. It is a mechanico-electrical machine designated as Cryptographe B-21. Here for the first time you see a cryptographic machine provided with a keyboard similar to that on an ordinary typewriter. Depressing a key on this keyboard causes a lamp to light under one of the letters on the indicating bank above the keyboard. At the top of this machine can be seen four wheels in front of two rear wheels. The four front wheels are the rotating elements that drive the two rear wheels; the latter are electrical commutators that serve as connection-changers to change the circuits between the keys of the keyboard and the lamps of the indicating board. There isn't time to discuss in detail the internal works that control the rotating elements and ciphering wheels, of which you'll see a glimpse later, but I must show you the next step in the improvement of such apparatus, which made it possible to eliminate the really tedious job of recording, by hand on paper, the results of operation. This was done by means of associating a type-

Fig. 127

writer with the cryptocomponent. Here is a picture (fig. 127) that shows the assembly – the B-21 connected to a Remington electric typewriter, modified to be actuated by impulses from the cryptomachine. Of course, it was natural that the next step would be to make the recording mechanism an integral part of the cryptomachine. This you can see in the next picture (fig. 128a), in which the four rotating members referred to in connection with figure 126 and which control the two commutators also mentioned in connection with that figure are seen. The slide-bar mechanism, in figure 128b, at the right, is called the "cage" or "barrel," and it controls the displacements of the printing wheel, causing the proper letter to be printed upon the moving tape seen at the front of the machine.

Fig. 128a

Now we come to some very important new types of electric cipher machines first conceived and developed in Europe but very soon thereafter, and probably independently, also in the United States. In the cryptocomponent of these machines, the electrical paths between the elements representing the plaintext characters and those representing their cipher equivalents are constantly varied by multiple connection-changers with the cryptocomponent. In early European models of this type of machine, the connection-changers consisted of a frame upon which insulated wires were mounted to connect in an arbitrary manner a series of contacts on one side of the frame to a similar number of contacts on the other side of the frame. This frame was slid between two fixed contactbearing members, one on each side of the frame. By sliding the frame between the two fixed members, the paths between the opposite contacts on the latter could be varied as a whole set with a single movement of the sliding frame. A connection-changer of this sort is shown in schematic form in figure 129a, where the sliding member 10 slides between fixed members 11 and 12, thus changing the electrical paths between the keyboard and the printing mechanism. The connection-changer 10 is moved to the left or right 1,2,3, . . . positions, as determined by a cam mechanism. We won't go into this type of machine any further because it wasn't

Fig. 128b

long before inventors saw the advantages of using, instead of slideable connection-changers, mechanisms performing a similar function but of a rotatable nature that we now call "electric-rotors," and that rotate, usually step-by-step, between circular, fixed, contact-bearing members called "stators." Rotors and stators of this type are shown in schematic form in figure 129b, there being a left-hand stator labeled 1, three rotors labeled 2a, 2b, 2c, and a right-hand stator labeled 3. The connections leading away from stator 1 toward the left go to the keys of the keyboard; those leading away from rotor 3 toward the right go to the magnets of the printer. About these elements we shall explain some details presently.

In Europe, the first machine using rotors and stators was that developed by a German firm, the Cipher-Machine Company of Berlin, and was appropriately named the ENIGMA. Here's a picture of it, figure 129c, in which you see a keyboard, a set of eight rotors juxtaposed in line, or, as we now generally say, "juxtaposed in cascade," and a printer. This machine was apparently too complicated for practical usage and was superseded by a second model, which also printed and was also unsuccessful. One of the difficulties with these two models was that a multiple switch with many contacts to be made simultaneously was required in order to establish an operative encipher-decipher relationship, so that if in enciphering the letter D_p, for example, the corresponding key on the keyboard is depressed, and a cipher letter, say F_e, is printed; then on deciphering the letter F_e, the corresponding key on the typewriter is depressed, and the plaintext letter D_p will be printed. In this machine this could be done only by making the current for decipherment traverse exactly the same path through the rotors and stators that it had traversed in encipherment. This was the function of the multiple switch shown schematically in figure 129d, in which a machine with only six characters (A to F) is depicted. In the left-hand circuit diagram, D_p is being enciphered and produces F_e; in the right hand circuit diagram F_e produces D_p. But the switching mechanisms 4 and 4' in figure 129d make things a bit complicated because they are within one switching member that operates in one of two positions, one for encipherment, the other for decipherment, and many contacts must be established in one fell swoop, so to speak. I won't go into further details as to its construction because a clever inventor of that German firm came up with a new idea which greatly simplified matters, in regard not only to the cryptocomponent but also to the indicating mechanism. We may quickly explain how the matter of simplifying the indicating mechanism was accomplished, namely, by eliminating the printer altogether and replacing it with a simple bank of flashlight-type lamps. We'll skip the third model of the ENIGMA, which was only a slightly simpler version of the fourth model, which is shown in figure 130a. This one comprised a keyboard, a bank of indicating lamps, and a set of rotors and stators, but no printer.

In figure 130a is seen the machine with its coverplate down. At the front is the keyboard; above it, the indicator board, consisting of twenty-six lamps beneath glass disks upon which letters have been inscribed. Above the indicator board are seen four oval apertures with covers, through which letters can be seen. To the right of each aperture can be seen the peripheries of four metal scalloped wheels, the first being unmarked but the next three being labeled 1. A switch lever seen at the right can be set to encipher, decipher, or neutral positions. In figure

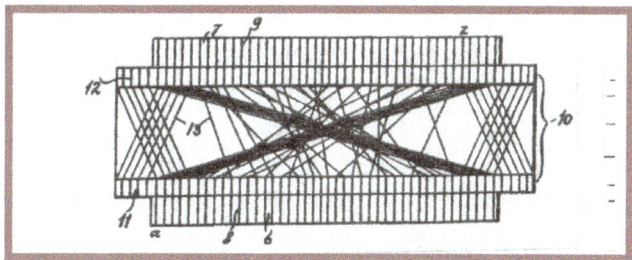

Fig. 129a

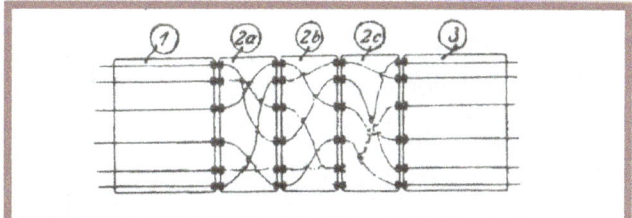

Fig. 129b

Fig. 129c

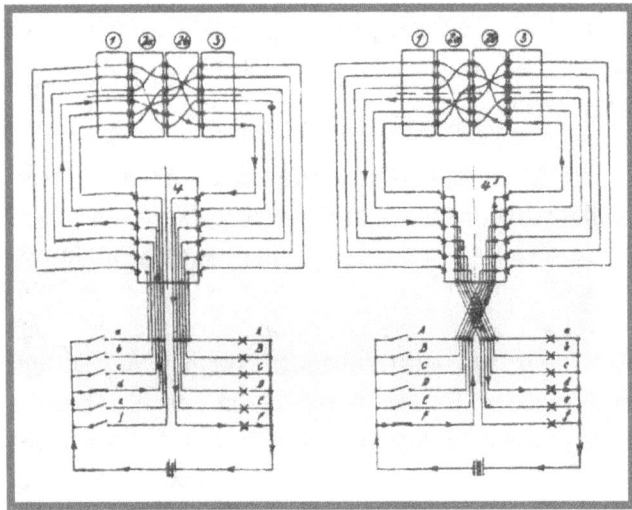

Fig. 129d

130b is seen the machine with the coverplate removed, exposing the internal cryptocomponent. Three rotors, labeled 4 in this figure, are seen, and affixed to them are the scalloped metal rings, which are not labeled. A fourth scalloped ring, labeled 11 in figure 130b, is affixed to another rotor-like member labeled 8 in that figure. This member looks like an ordinary rotor in this picture but is really a stator of special construction to be described presently.

Perhaps it would be useful at this point to show you what ENIGMA rotors look like and these can be seen in figures 131a-c. In each of these rotors is a circle of twenty-six equally spaced contact pins on one face of the rotor (fig. 131a) and a circle of twenty-six equally spaced contact surfaces on the other face (fig. 131b). Insulated wires connect the contact pins on one face to the contact surfaces on the other face, these connections being made in an arbitrary, systematic, or unsystematic manner, depending on certain circumstances into which we need not go. When the rotors are juxtaposed as seen in figure 131c, the contact pins on one rotor are brought against the contact surfaces on the adjacent rotor, so that an electric current will traverse all three rotors via a certain path. The large scalloped rings are for setting the rotors in alignment manually when they are juxtaposed and rotated to form a portion of the key setting (see E*Z*R in figure 131c).

The toothed metal ring seen in figure 131a is associated with a cam mechanism so that a rotor will be advanced one step when the preceding rotor has made a sufficient number of steps to permit a cam to fall into a notch in the ring. Sometimes a complete revolution will be necessary before this happens, depending on the initial keysetting. The first rotor immediately to the left of the stator at the extreme right in figure 131b, however, always makes one step with each depression of the key on the keyboard. The advance of the rotors is similar to that of the wheels of a counter like that of the odometer on your automobile.

We come now to the matter of simplifying the cryptocomponent of the ENIGMA shown in figure 130b to eliminate the multiple switching mechanism shown in figure 129d, without much loss in security (or so it would seem, at least). Let us see how this simplification was accomplished in the ENIGMA, by showing figure 129d, in connection with the first ENIGMA model. For this purpose I show you now figure 132, in which the encipher-decipher circuitry is clearly seen in a machine having, for illustrative purposes, only three rotors, labeled 1, 2, 3, rotatable between two stators, the one on the left labeled 4, that on the right labeled 5. Stator 4 is fixed or nonrotatable in this model, and it has twenty-six contacts on its left face, only two of which are shown. These contacts are connected fixedly to the keys of the keyboard and to the lamps of the lampboard. Stator 5 is rotatable, but only manually, and it has twenty-six contact surfaces on its right face, only two of which are shown. But in this stator the twenty-six contact surfaces are interconnected in pairs by thirteen insulated wires passing through the member. Thus, a current entering one of the twenty-six contact surfaces on the right face goes through the stator and returns to one of the remaining twenty-five contact surfaces. For this reason it is called a "reflector" and serves to return a current that has come from one of the twenty-six contacts on the fixed stator at the extreme right, then through the rotors and into the reflector via one path, returns through the rotors and back into the stator via a different path, emerging at one of

Fig. 130a

Fig. 130b

Fig. 131a

Fig. 131b

Fig. 131c

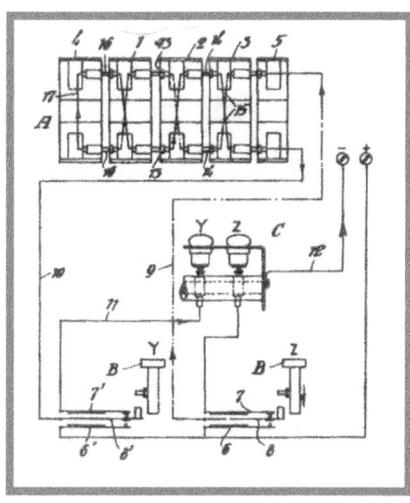

Fig. 132

the twenty-five other contacts on the left face of the stator at the extreme right. This circuitry assures that in a particular setting of the machine, if $Y_p = Z_c$, for example, then $Y_p = Z_c$, that is, the cipher is reciprocal. It also has as a consequence that no letter can be enciphered by itself, that is, Y_p, for example, cannot be represented by Y_c, no matter what the setting of the cryptocomponent is; this is true of all the other letters of the alphabet in regard to the ENIGMA.

If you like, you may trace the path traversed by the current in figure 132 in encipherment and decipherment, where $Z_p = Y_c$ and $Z_p = Y_c$, but Z_p cannot be represented by Z_p, nor can Y_p be represented by Y_c. I have already told you briefly about how the rotors are advanced. In the ENIGMA shown, the total number of encipherments that can be made before the key setting of the machine returns to its original setting, as seen through the windows I referred to a few moments ago when showing you the first picture of the fourth model ENIGMA, is 16,900, viz, $26^3 - 26^2$, and not 26^3, for technical reasons I won't go into now.

Power for the electrical circuits is provided by small dry cells in the machine. This model enjoyed a fair degree of financial success, but when Hitler came into power further promotion and sales of the ENIGMA were prohibited. Suffice it to say that it became the basis for machines used by the German

Fig. 133

armed forces in World War II.

In the United States, in about 1910, a California inventor named Edward H. Hebern (fig. 133) began to develop cipher machines, but he was merely traveling along roads that had this far led other inventors nowhere. In about 1918 he struck out along a new path in America. I don't know whether he independently conceived the idea of a machine using an electric rotor or had in his research come across patents covering very recently invented European electrical cipher machines. At any rate, Hebern's first application for a patent covering a rotor machine, which he called an "electric code," was filed on 31 March 1921, and a patent was issued on 30 September 1924. Figure 134 shows the first machine he had built. You will note that the cryptocomponent had but one rotor, and like the early models of the ENIGMA, it was associated with a printing mechanism, a typewriter operated electrically. Hebern's cipher system was also similar in nature with that of the first two ENIGMA models - a full reversing switch was essential since the electric current had to traverse exactly the same path in decipherment as it had in encipherment. I don't think he ever conceived the idea of using a reflector;

perhaps he was too late. At any rate, he never incorporated that idea in any of his machines. Moreover, I don't think he had any idea of the cryptologic advantages and disadvantages of a cryptocomponent using a "single traverse" or "straight through" system of rotors, as compared with one using a "double traverse" or "twice through" system of rotors with a reflector. But we won't go into that here, for it's a pretty involved piece of business.

But Hebern's rotors had a virtue not possessed by those of the ENIGMA machines, and not incorporated in the rotors of the latter, namely, the wirings of the rotors could be readily changed by the user of the Hebern machine, a feature of great importance in cryptosecurity (fig. 135). Hebern interested our navy in his three-rotor model (fig. 136) and as a result of conferences with navy cryptanalysts he built the five-rotor model, which is seen in figure 137. Another very important security feature I have thus far failed to mention about the Hebern rotors was that they could be inserted in a "right-side up" or in an "upside-down" position in the machine, which could not be done with the ENIGMA rotors. The navy liked the five-rotor model, even though it was not a printing machine, assuming properly that this could be added later on. Therefore, the navy placed a purchase order for two such machines on 30 July 1921 and was considering purchasing a rather large number of them later. Lieutenant Strubel, then chief of the Navy's Code and Signal Section of the Office of Naval Communications but now a retired vice admiral, asked me to study the machine for its cryptosecurity. The Navy had but two machines, neither of which could be made available, so I induced the Chief Signal Officer to buy a couple of them for Army study. The order was placed on 7 October 1924. The rotor wirings of the Army's machines were altogether different from those of the Navy, a fact I discovered simply by asking Strubel to encipher a few letters on his machine, using settings I specified. After some study I reported that in my opinion the security of the machine was not as great as the Navy thought. The result was a challenge, which I accepted. The Navy gave me ten messages

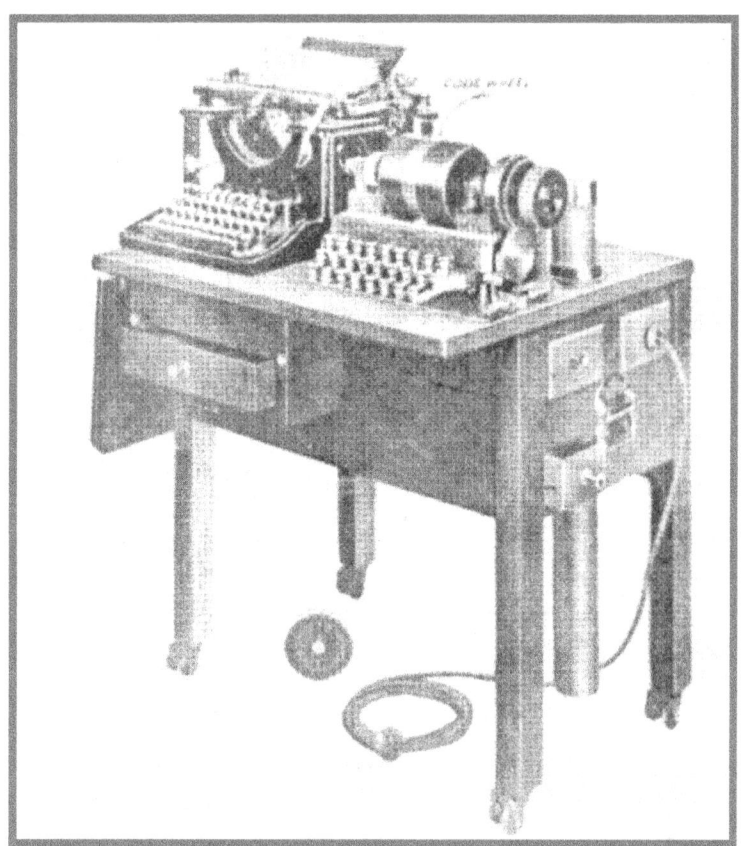

Fig. 134

Fig. 135

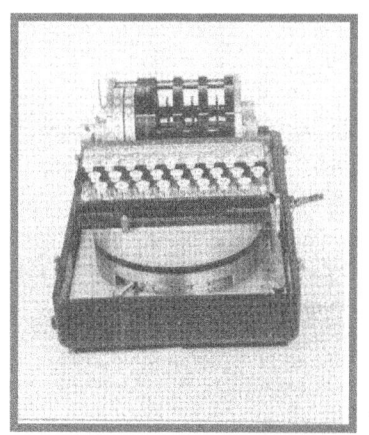

Fig. 136

Fig. 137

Fig. 138

put up on its machine, and I was successful in solving them. There isn't time to go into the methods used, but if you are interested you can find them described in my brochure entitled *Analysis of a Mechanico-Electrical Cryptograph, Part I* (1934), *Part II* (1935).

Hebern built several more models for Navy, and these had printing mechanisms associated with them, but Navy dropped negotiations with Hebern when it became obvious that he was not competent to build what Navy wanted and needed. Navy then established its own cryptographic research and development unit at what is now known as the Naval Weapons Plant in Washington. Army developed at the Signal Corps Laboratories at Fort Monmouth a machine known as Converter M-134, and here's an illustration (fig. 138) showing what it looked like. Army and Navy went separate ways in such work for a number of years, but finally, in 1938 or 1939, close collaborating brought as a result an excellent machine that was developed and produced in quantity by the Teletype Corporation in Chicago. This machine was distributed and used very successfully by all our armed forces from 1940 to the end of World War II and for some years thereafter. In accordance with Navy nomenclature, it was designated as the ECM Mark II, ECM standing for "electric cipher machine"; in the Army it was designated as the SIGABA, in accordance with a nomenclature in which items of Signal Corps cryptographic material were then given short titles with the initial trigraph SIG.

The ECM-SIGABA is a rather large machine requiring a considerable amount of electric power and much too heavy to be carried about by a signal operator performing field service. It was safeguarded with extreme care and under strictest security regulations during the whole period of World War II operations. None of our allies was permitted even to see the machine, let alone have it. The British had their own electric cipher machine, which they called TYPEX. In order to facilitate intercommunication between U.S. and British forces, adaptors were developed so that messages could be exchanged in cipher between American and British units. This system of intercommunication worked satisfactorily and securely.

Certain improvements in the method of usage and the development of special components, to be associated with the ECM-SIGABA for automatic decipherment by perforated tapes, were introduced during the wartime employment of these machines. But the ECM-SIGABA as originally developed and produced became obsolete some years after the close of hostilities when newer and better machines developed by NSA cryptologists and engineers replaced them, but not because there were ever any indications that messages enciphered on the machine had been deciphered by the enemy. As a matter of historical fact, it may be stated that all enemy efforts to solve such messages were fruitless, and it is also a fact that no machines were ever captured by the enemy; nor were there ever any suspicions that a machine had been exposed to enemy inspection at any time. Once and only once were there any apprehensions in this regard, when through a careless disregard of specific instructions, a truck and an attached trailer in which this machine and associated material were housed were stolen during the night when parked in front of the headquarters of the 28th Division during the Battle of the Bulge. A great search was instituted, during the course of which a river was diverted, and the trailer, with all its contents intact, was found resting on the former bed of the diverted stream. The episode terminated in court-martial proceedings, and there were no more incidents of this sort. Let me add that such apprehensions as were entertained at the time of this temporary loss of custody of the machine were based not upon the possibility that its usefulness was at an end but upon the fear that the Germans would make "Chinese copies" of it and thus be in a position to turn our very valuable weapon against us.

About five years before the SIGABA was put into service, the Army's need for a small cipher machine for field use became obvious. The strip cipher system was not suitable for this purpose, nor was the Army's first keyboard-operated electrical rotor machine, Converter M-134, suitable, for reasons already indicated in connection with the SIGABA. The sum of $2,000 was allotted by the Army to the Chief Signal Officer for the development of a cipher machine small enough to be suitable for field usage but also affording adequate security. The funds were naturally turned over to the Signal Corps Laboratories (SCL) at Fort Monmouth, New Jersey, for this development. The military director of the laboratories, spurning all proffered technical guidance or assistance from the Signal Intelligence Service (SIS) and deciding that his staff had sufficient know-how without outside assistance, developed a machine that required no electricity, being allmechanical. On its completion the model was sent to the Signal Intelligence Service for a cryptosecurity test. Two short messages were enciphered by the Chief of the SIS, using settings of his own selection. He then handed the messages and the model over to me as technical director, and I turned them over to two of my assistants. The reason for turning over the model with the messages was that it must be assumed that under field conditions machines will be captured. One of the two test messages was solved in about twenty minutes; the other took longer – thirty-five minutes. This test brought an ignominious end to the SCL development, brought about by the failure on the part of the military director of the SCL to recognize that cryptographic invention must be guided by technically qualified cryptanalytic personnel. Unfortunately, all the available funds had been expended on this unsuccessful attempt; none was left for a fresh start on a development with technical guidance from the SIS.

Fig. 139

It was about this time that a small mechanical machine which had been developed and produced in quantity by a Swedish engineer in Stockholm named Hagelin (fig. 139) was brought to the attention of the Chief Signal Officer (CSO) of the U.S. Army by a representative of the Hagelin firm. The SIS was asked to look into it, and as technical director, I turned in an unfavorable report on the machine for the reason that although its cryptosecurity was theoretically quite good, it had a low degree of cryptosecurity if improperly used – and practical experience had taught me that improper use could be expected to occur with sufficient frequency to jeopardize the security of all messages enciphered by the same setting of the machine, whether correctly enciphered or not. This was because the Hagelin machine operates on what is termed the key-generator principle, so that when two or more messages are enciphered by the same key stream or portions thereof, solution of those messages is a relatively simple matter. Such solution permits recovery of the settings of the keying elements so that the whole stream can be produced and used to solve messages that have been correctly enciphered by the same key settings, thus making a whole day's traffic readable by the enemy. I tried to assure the CSO that my opinion was not motivated by a factor commonly called "NIH" – "not invented here" but I was overruled by my military superiors, and properly so, because neither the SIS nor the SCL had developed anything that was better than the Hagelin machine, or even as good, with all its mechanical deficiencies and cryptographic weaknesses taken into consideration. Accepting, though somewhat reluctantly, the well-considered directive of the CSO, the SIS pointed out where improvements could be made, and the desired modifications were incorporated in the machine, which became known as the Converter M-209. Over 100,000 of them were manufactured in 1942-1944 by the Smith-Corona Typewriter Company at Groton, New York. Here's an illustration (fig. 140a) showing the machine, which was extensively used by all our armed forces during World War II, and here's another (fig. 140b) showing its internal mechanism. It turned out that under

Fig. 140a

Fig. 140b

field conditions the fears upon which I had based my personal rejection of the Hagelin machine proved to be fully justified – a great deal of traffic in it was solved by the Germans, Italians, and Japanese. If I was chagrined or suffered any remorse when I learned about the successful enemy attacks on M-209 traffic, those feelings were generated by my sense of having failed myself to think up something better than the M-209 despite the shortsighted attitude of the military director of the SCL.

With the introduction of printing telegraph or teleprinting machines for electrical communications, the need became pressing for a reliable and practical cryptographic mechanism to be associated or integrated with such machines. The first apparatus of this sort in the United States, shown in this photo (fig. 141), was that developed by the American Telephone and Telegraph Company in 1918, as a more or less simple but ingenious modification of its ordinary printing telegraph. First, a few explanatory words about the basic principles of the modern teleprinter may be useful. This principle employs what is called the "Baudot Code," that is, a system in which permutations of two different elements taken in groups of five are employed to represent characters of the alphabet. Curiously enough, Francis Bacon was the first to employ such a "code" way back in the early seventeenth century, and I showed you the one he used in Lecture No. II (see figure 31). These two elements in Bacon's "code" were *a*'s and *b*'s; he used but 24 of the 32 permutations available ($2^5=32$). For electrical communications the two elements may be positive and negative currents of electricity, or the presence and absence of current, the latter system often referred to as being composed of "marking'" and "spacing" elements, respectively. The illustration in figure 142 depicts the Baudot or "five-unit code" in the form of a paper tape in which there are holes in certain positions transverse to the length of the tape. The holes are produced by a perforating mechanism; the small holes running the length of the tape are "feed-holes" by means of which the tape is advanced step by step. You will note that there are five levels on which the perforations appear. The letter *A*, for example, is represented by a perforation only on the 1st and 2nd levels, the 3rd, 4th and 5th levels remaining unperforated; the letter *I* is represented by holes in positions 2 and 3, no holes on the other three levels, etc. The English alphabet uses twenty-six of the thirty-two permutations; the remaining six permutations are used to represent the so-called "stunt characters," which I will now explain. The third and fourth characters from the right-hand end of the tape are two permutations labeled "letters" and "figures," respectively. These are equivalent to the "shift and "unshift" keys on a typewriter keyboard, for "lower" and "upper" case. When the "letters" key is depressed, the characters printed are the twenty-six letters of the alphabet (all capital letters); when the "figures" key is depressed, the characters represented are similar to those printed on a typewriter when the "shift" key is depressed. The second, third, and fourth permutations at the left-hand end of the tape are also stunt characters and represent "line feed," "space," and "carriage return," and they perform electrically in a teleprinter what is done by hand on a typewriter: "line feed" causes the paper on which the message is printed to advance to the next line; "space" does exactly what depressing the space bar on a typewriter does, etc. When there are no holes anywhere across the taps, the character is called a "blank" or "idling" character – nothing happens: the printer does no printing, nor is there any "stunt" functioning by the printer, but the tape merely advances.

In modifying the standard printing telegraph machine to make it a printing telegraph cipher machine, or to put the matter in a slightly different way, in developing the printing telegraph cipher machine, the American Telephone and Telegraph Company was fortunate in having the services of a twenty-three-year old communications engineer named Gilbert S. Vernam (fig. 143), who conceived a brilliant principle and an automatic method for enciphering teleprinter communications. The principle and method turned out to be so useful and valuable, not only in the United States but also internationally, that it has come to bear his name and is often referred to as the "Vernam principle," the "Vernam rule," the "Vernam mod-2 addition," etc. Vernam saw that if in accordance with some general but invariant rule the marking and spacing elements of a five-unit code group were combined one by

Fig. 141

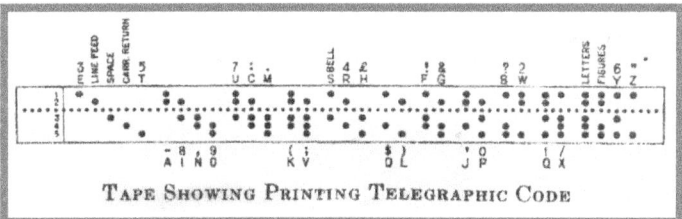

Fig. 142

one with those of another five-unit code group, which would serve as a keying group, and the resultant five-unit group transmitted over a circuit and combined at the receiver with the same keying group in accordance with the same general rule,[17] the final result would be the original character. Vernam conceived the idea early in 1918 or perhaps late in 1917. I have a copy of Vernam's circuit diagram, dated and witnessed on 27 February 1918, but the application for a patent thereon, with his name as inventor, was filed in the U.S. Patent Office on 13 September 1918, and Patent No. 1,310,719 was granted on 22 July 1919, covering the invention entitled a "Secret Signaling System."

The following more detailed description of Vernam's patent on the foregoing cipher system is extracted from a paper[18] written by one of the AT&T Company's engineers [R.D. Parker] who was associated with Mr. Vernam at the time the invention was conceived and who, a few years after retirement from that company, became one of NSA's consultants:

> This patent describes an "on-line" system, each character being enciphered, immediately transmitted, and in turn deciphered without delay at the receiving terminal. Thus, characters of a message in perforated tape form are automatically combined with other or key characters which are transmitted over the circuit. At the receiver an identical group of key characters is used to provide signals for combination with the arriving signals, character by character, to produce the original message. The combining rule for these operations disclosed in the patent was one in which like code elements produced "spaces" and unlike elements, "marks," as shown below.
>
> The cipher message tape prepared in this way is unintelligible in form and may be sent to the receiving station by messenger or by mail, or if desired, it may be transmitted by wire or radio and reproduced by another machine perforator at the receiving point. The cipher tape is there run through the message transmitter, where its characters combine with those of a duplicate key tape to reproduce the original message, which will be printed out in page form and in "plain text."

LENGTH OF KEY TAPE

With the system as described above, the key tape must be at least as long as the sum of all the message tapes used with it, as the messages will lose their secrecy to some extent if the key tape is used repeatedly. The use of a short repeating key may give sufficient secrecy for some uses, however.

A roll of tape 8 inches in diameter contains about 900 feet of tape and would serve to encipher about 18,000 words counting five printed characters and a space per word, without repeating the key. If sent at a average speed of 45 words per minute, this number of words would require 400 minutes or nearly 7 hours to transmit.

In order to reduce the amount of key tape required for handling large amounts of traffic, the "double key" system was devised.[19] In this system two key tapes are

Fig. 143

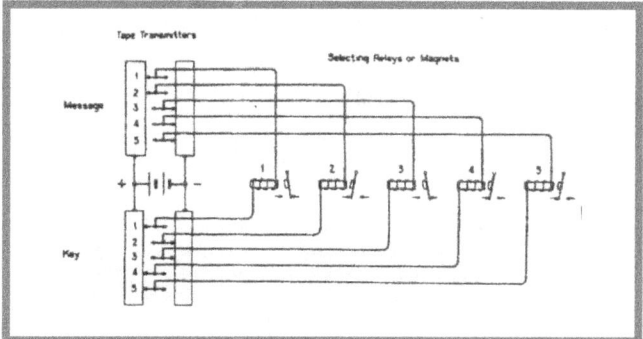

Fig. 144

used, the ends of each tape being glued together to form a loop preferably about seven feet in circumference. The tapes should differ in length by one character or by some number which is not a factor of the number of characters in either tape. A separate transmitter is used for each tape and the characters of the two key tapes are combined, by a method similar to that shown in [figure 144], with those of the message tape to form the cipher message.

The result is the same as though the two key tapes were first combined to produce a long single nonrepeating key, which was later combined with the message tape. This long, single key is not, strictly speaking, a purely random key throughout its length as it is made up of combinations of the two original and comparatively short key tapes. The characters in this key do not repeat in the same sequence at comparatively short regular intervals, however, as would be the case if only one key tape loop were used.

The number of characters in this equivalent single key is equal to the product of the number of characters in the two tape loops, and may easily exceed 600,000 before any part of the key begins to repeat. If proper care is taken to use the system so as to avoid giving information to the enemy regarding the lengths of the two key tape loops or their initial settings and to avoid the possibility of ever reusing any part of the resultant single key, this system is extremely difficult to break even by an expert cryptanalyst having a large number of messages and full knowledge of the construction of the machine and its method of operation.

The foregoing double-key-tape system was placed into operation in 1918 on three start-stop circuits that were used for intercommunication among four stations serving Washington, New York, Hoboken, and Norfolk, and that, according to Parker [see footnote 20 below], "continued in operation for many months, even after the end of the war." In addition, a Signal Corps Company was organized to go to Europe with new equipment for installation of printing-telegraph circuits in France. This Signal Company was about ready to sail when the armistice was signed on November 11, 1918.

On my return to Riverbank in April 1919 upon being demobilized, I became an interested party in a rather warm argument conducted by letters exchanged between Colonel Fabyan, the Chief Signal Officer, the Director of Military Intelligence, and the War Department, regarding the cryptosecurity of the cipher printing telegraph system as used by the Signal Corps. The argument ended by successfully meeting a challenge by the Signal Corps to prove Fabyan's contention. The challenge consisted in sending Fabyan on 6 October 1919, and requesting him to solve, the cipher tapes of about 150 messages selected from one day's traffic in the system. On 8 December 1919 Fabyan sent a telegram to the Chief Signal Officer notifying him that solution had been accomplished. In order to prove that this was true, I sent a perforated cipher-message tape to each of the officers named above. In order to decipher these messages, the Chief Signal Officer had to use his own key tapes, thus proving that Riverbank not only had solved the system but had recovered both key tapes that had been employed in enciphering the challenge messages, so that Riverbank was in a position to produce the plain text of any of the latter on request, if further proof of solution were needed or desired. I wrote a monograph on the solution, consisting of a basic paper of twenty-one typewritten pages, an Addendum 1 of ten pages, an Addendum 2 of twenty-five pages, and an Addendum 3 of six pages; a copy of each of these documents was sent to Washington. The solution was accepted with mixed feelings in Washington, especially on the part of Brigadier General Marlborough Churchill, the Director of Military Intelligence, who had signed a letter to the Chief Signal Officer, dated 8 August 1918, prepared by Captain Yardley to the effect that the cipher system in question "is considered by this office to be absolutely indecipherable."[20] General Churchill had the duty and courtesy to write a congratulatory letter to Colonel Fabyan, dated 24 March 1920, the Imal paragraph of which is as follows:

> *Your very brilliant scientific achievement reflects great credit upon you and your whole personnel. It would be impossible to exaggerate in paying you and Riverbank the deserved tribute for this very scholarly accomplishment.*

The paper by Mr. Parker (see footnote 18) closes with the following final paragraph:

> *Perhaps some day Mr. Friedman will tell of the part that he and the Riverbank Laboratories played in the cryptanalytic phase of this development.*

Mr. Parker was not aware that what he suggested had been done not only once but twice. The Ilrst time was immediately after the solution when copies of the writeup mentioned a moment ago had been sent to Washington where they had met the fate that often happens to documents of limited or special technical interest – complete disappearance in the voluminous files of bureaucracy. The second time was soon after the end of hostilities in World War II, when it was discovered that a certain outfit I won't name was using the double-tape keying system for its teleprinter communications. I rummaged through my own files and uncovered the handwritten manuscript of certain parts of what I had written at the close of the successful solution of that system while at Riverbank. My second writeup is a classified document, dated 21 July 1948, the subtitle of which is "Can Cryptologic History Repeat Itself?" It is possible that this writeup can be made available to those of you who are interested in reading it, ifproper authority grants permission.

Mr. Parker's paper (see footnote 18) devotes a good deal of space to the contention that the only reason why the double-tape keying method was adopted was that the Signal Corps and specifically its representative, Colonel Mauborgne, "complained about the difficulties that might be experienced in the preparation and distribution of one-time random key tapes and seemed inclined to disapprove of the proposed system because of these difficulties. Since the system, when properly used, seemed obviously to be one that gave absolute secrecy, a discussion arose on the value of the system and on methods that might be devised for the production and distribution oflong one-time key tapes having characters arranged at random." Parker points out that the original method of use contemplated the use oflong tapes ofthis nature and that he and his associates felt the problem of producing and distributing long tapes "while presenting a challenge, was not impractical." I am glad to admit they were right, because during World War II and for years afterward tapes of this nature were produced by special machinery (in some cases as many as five copies being perforated and the sections numbered automatically in a single operation.) Distribution of and accounting for the tapes proved practical, too, and aside from an occasional error involving the reuse of a once-used tape, absolutely secure intercommunication by radio printing telegraphy was assured and was used between and among large headquarters where the volume of traffic justified the use of this equipment. The principal advantage was the simplicity of crypto-operations – no rotors to be set, no setup of rotors to be enciphered, no checking of equipment by deciphering the message before transmission, etc.

The AT&T Company Printing Telegraph Cipher equipments purchased by the Signal Corps were withdrawn soon after Riverbank proved the double-key-tape system insecure. The machines went into storage, when in due course most of them were dismantled. But after I left Riverbank at the end of 1920 and had joined the Chief Signal Officer's staff in Washington, I induced the Chief Signal Officer to resuscitate two equipments. These I employed, believe it or not, in compiling codes, called Division Field Codes, for use in training or in an emergency. I won't undertake to explain how I performed this stunt, for it was a stunt, but it worked very successfully. The codes were duly printed, issued, and used until there was no longer any need for codes of this type.

Cipher printing telegraphy was placed upon the shelf and more or less forgotten by Signal Corps communications engineers from 1920 until soon after Pearl Harbor. However, the leading members of the SIS maintained a theoretical cryptanalytic interest in such equipment, and in 1931 there came an opportunity to test such theories as were developed by them when a machine produced by the International Telephone and Telegraph (IT&T) Company evoked the interest of the Department of State as a possible answer to the needs of that department for rapid and secure cryptocommunications by radio. The secretary of state requested the secretary of war to study the machine. which was to be associated with a standard teleprinter, and to study it only from the point of view of security. For this purpose messages enciphered by the chief of the Communications and Records Division of the Department of State were provided. Here are two pictures of the teleprinter attachment (figs. 145a and 145b). It is a source of satisfaction to be able to tell you that the SIS quickly solved the test messages and therefore reported that the machine was quite insecure; but it is with much regret that I must now tell you who invented and developed the machine. It was a retired officer of the Signal Corps,

Fig. 145a

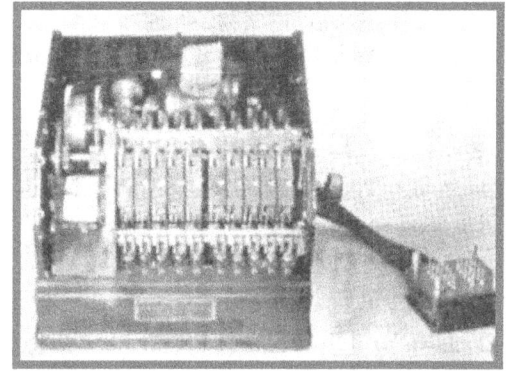

Fig. 145b

none other than my old friend Colonel Hitt. I was as embarrassed to tell him about the results of our test as he was to force himself to listen to what I had to say about the inadequacies of his brainchild. As is so often the case, when a competent technician has to neglect his technical studies because of the pressure of administrative duties, he unfortunately finds it very difficult to keep abreast of new developments and progress in a field in which he was at one time an expert. The IT&T Company, having spent a great deal of money on the development of a machine that hardly presented any room at all for improvement because the principles underlying it were so faulty, dropped further work on it. Colonel Hitt, I am glad to say, readily survived the disappointment and was well enough in 1942 to be able to return to active duty during World War II and retired a second time at the end of hostilities. He lives a quiet life now, on a small farm near Front Royal, Virginia.

Beginning about 1938, Mr. Frank B. Rowlett, one of my associates, and I kept urging that there was or would be real need for new and improved machines for protecting teleprinter communications. There was a complete lack of interest in such apparatus; but what was perhaps a more important factor in the failure to continue such work in this field was the lack of Signal Corps funds for research and development for such work.

Our more or less sudden entry into World War II after 7 December 1941 immediately brought a great need for cipher printing telegraphy, especially for radio communication, but there was no apparatus for it whatever – not a single one of those AT&T Company machines of 1918-1920 was in existence. But the SIS did have drawings in readiness, and the development of the machines was given as a priority task to the Teletype Corporation, because that firm had proved that it had the necessary know-how when it produced the SIGABA-ECMs for us. The Navy had less need for cipher printing telegraphy than the Army because the use of printing telegraphy by radio was then not practicable for ships at sea. However, the Navy did have a need for such apparatus for its land communications and joined the Army in the procurement thereof. The machines were produced with a remarkable speed by the Teletype Corporation. Most of them were allotted to the Army, a few to the Navy. The Army called the machine the SIGCUM, the Navy called it CSP-1515. Under heavy use in service, improvements were made in regard to both mechanical and electrical features and to methods of keying, the use of indicators, etc. But I must tell you that before those machines became available in quantity there was only one recourse: we went back to the use of double-key-tape method using standard teletype apparatus. The cipher was practically the same as it was in 1920, but we had safer methods of key-tape production and indicators for their use. The SIS and the equivalent unit in the Navy were not happy because operators' errors left messages open to solution, so that when the new cipher machines were ready they were pressed into service as soon as possible, priority given to circuits with heavy traffic.

Cryptographic equipments of the foregoing type fall in the category of apparatus for protecting *literal* cryptocommunications because the latter employ letters of the alphabet; but apparatus for protecting cifax transmissions, that is, picture or facsimile transmissions, and apparatus for protecting ciphony transmissions, that is, telephonic communications, were also developed. But there isn't time to go into details with regard to machines and apparatus for these last two categories of crypto-equipment, although the history of their development is rather fascinating and very important. I cannot refrain, however, from adding that, in every case except one, the apparatus was produced by commercial research and development firms with direct guidance from the cryptologists of the Army and the Navy. The one exception is, I believe, in the case of the extremely highsecurity ciphony system and equipment developed and built by the AT&T Company. It was called SIGSALY. There were six terminals, each of which cost over $1,000,000. But NSA cryptologists and engineers have produced smaller and better equipments based upon SIGSALY principles, and such equipments are bound to play extremely important roles in any wars in the future.

So much for the history of the developments and progress in cryptographic apparatus at this point. I shall return to that phase of cryptologic history before the close of this lecture. Right now I shall say a few words about the history of the developments and progress in cryptanalytic apparatus.

The solution of modern cryptocommunication systems has been facilitated and, in some cases, made possible only by the invention, development, and application of highly specialized cryptanalytic machinery, including apparatus for intercepting and recording certain types of transmission before cryptanalysis can even be undertaken. One must understand the basic nature of the problem that confronts the cryptanalyst when he attempts to solve one of these modern, very complex cryptosystems. First of all, he must be given the cryptocommunications in a form that makes them visible for

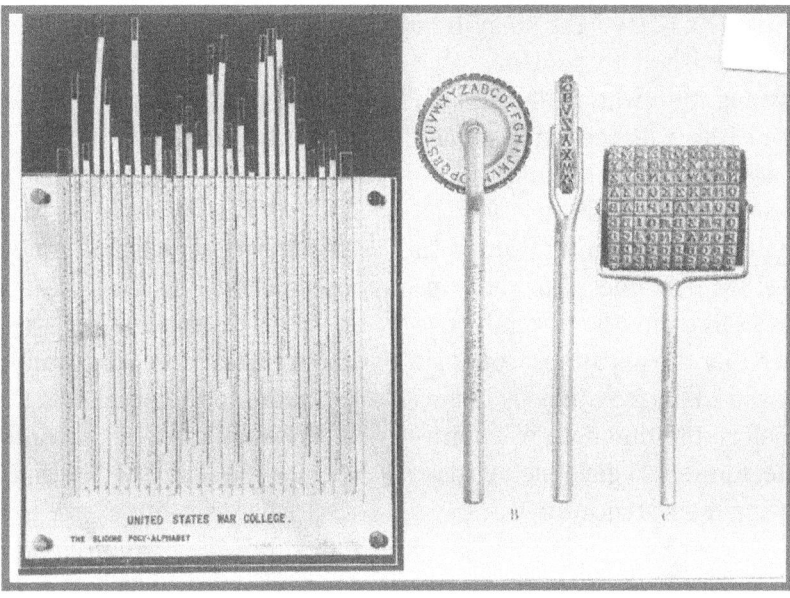

Fig. 146

inspection and study. Usually they are characters (letters or numbers) in the case of literal communications, or they are electrical signals of a recordable type in the case of cifax or ciphony communications. Next, he must have available to him instrumentalities that will assist him in his analytical work, such as machinery for making frequency counts, comparisons of sequences, etc., and this, in the case of complex systems, must be done at high speed. Cryptanalysis of modern cryptosystems requires testing a very great number of assumptions and hypotheses because sometimes astronomically large numbers of possibilities, i.e., permutations and combinations, must be tested one after the other until the correct answer is found. Since the advent of high-speed machinery for such purposes, including electronic digital computers about which so much is being heard and read nowadays, the cryptanalyst isn't discouraged by these astronomically great numbers of possibilities.

Perhaps long before my time, cryptanalysts in Europe discovered that the use of sliding strips of paper could sometimes facilitate reaching a solution to a cryptanalytic problem, but so far as I am aware the very first cryptanalytic aid made in the United States is the one shown in figure 146, which is a picture of what I made at Riverbank and which I called the *Polyalphabet*. It was useful in solving ciphers which today are regarded as being of the very simplest types. When I came to Washington after leaving Riverbank, I wasn't troubled by a plethora of ideas for cryptanalytic aids – I was preoccupied with devising and inventing cryptographic aids and machines. But I did now and then develop and tryout certain ideas for cryptanalytic aids, frequency counters, comparison or coincidence machinery, and the like. Why didn't I think of IBM machines? I did, but what good did that do? Did the Signal Officer have any such machines – or even one dollar for their rental? You know the answer to that without my spelling it out. There wasn't any use in even suggesting that IBM machines could be of assistance to me – remember, now, that I'm talking about the years from 1921 to 1933, and in the last-named year we were in the depths of a great economic depression. But one day in the summer of 1934 I learned by a devious route (the Army and the Navy were not then sharing secrets) that the Navy Code and Signal Section had an IBM machine or two, and my chagrin was almost unbearable.

Not long afterwards I learned that a certain division of the Office of the Quartermaster General in the Munitions Building had an IBM installation which had been used for accounting purposes in connection with the CCC – the Civilian Conservation Corps, established to provide work and subsistence for young men who could find no jobs in the depression. I also learned that a new officer had just been assigned to head that particular division – and that he just had no use for the newfangled ideas of his predecessor and wanted to get rid of those nasty IBM machines. But the contract with IBM still had some months to run before the lease expired, and either the machines would sit idle or the government would lose money by terminating the contract before the due date of expiration. This annoyed me, but it also gave me an idea, and I wrote the following memorandum:

> 30 October 1934
>
> Major Akin:
>
> In many years service here I have never once "set my heart on" getting something I felt desirable. But in this case I have set my heart on the matter because of the tremendous load it would lift off all our backs.
>
> The basic idea of using machinery for code compilation is mine and is of several years' standing. The details of the proposed system were developed in collaboration with Mr. Case of the Int. Bus. Machines Corp.
>
> I regard this as one of my most valuable contributions to the promotion of the work for which we are responsible.
>
> Please do your utmost to put this across for me. If you do, we can really begin to do worthwhile *cryptanalytic* work.

Attached to the memo was a brief explanation amounting to what I've told you about that IBM installation in the Office of the Quartermaster General. Note that I placed the emphasis upon the burden that would be lifted from cryptographic work by using the IBM machinery, thus leaving more time for cryptanalytic work. This was because the responsibilities of the SIS for cryptanalytic operations were at that time restricted purely to theoretical studies. Studies on cryptanalytic work on foreign cryptosystems had been a responsibility of G-2 of the General Staff until 1929, when that responsibility had been transferred to the Chief Signal Officer and the Signal Corps. But the Signal Officer had very little money to use for that purpose, and besides that, the army regulation applicable thereto specifically restricted cryptanalytic operations on foreign communications to wartime. And more to the point was that there was no material to work on even if funds had been available, because the Army had at that time no intercept stations whatever, anywhere in or outside the United States. But that's another story, and I'll proceed to the next point, which is that my memo to Major Akin produced results. Just a half month after I wrote and put it in his "in" basket, I got the machines moved from the Office of the Quartermaster General to my own warren in the Office of the Chief Signal Officer! That memo must have been potent magic.

Once having demonstrated the machines' utility to the Chief Signal Officer, the almost prematurely terminated contract with IBM was renewed – and soon expanded. I don't know how we could have managed without such machines during World War II.

We built or had built for us by IBM and other concerns adaptors to work with standard IBM machines; we constructed or had constructed for us by commercial firms highly specialized cryptanalytic apparatus, machines and complex assemblies of components. Under wartime pressures fantastic things were accomplished, and many were the thrills of gratifying achievement when things that just couldn't be done were done - and were of high importance in military, naval, and air operations against the enemy.

Even were time available, I couldn't show you pictures of some of the high-class gadgets we used; neither is it permissible to say more than I have already said about them, even though it is no longer a deep secret that electronic computers are highly useful in cryptologic work.

To the layman the exploits of professional cryptanalysts, when those exploits come to light, as, for example, in the various investigations of the attack on Pearl Harbor, are much more fascinating than those of cryptographers, whose achievements in their field appear in comparison to be dull or tedious to the layman. But long consideration of the military importance of COMSEC as against COMINT leads me to return to something I mentioned at the very beginning of this lecture, when I made a statement to the effect that cryptography and cryptanalysis represent the obverse and reverse faces of the same single coin. In closing this lecture, I will expand that statement a bit, and in doing so perhaps formulate a dictum which we may call the law governing the minting and usage of the cryptologic combat coin. It would run something like this:

When an officer is selected to command a fighting unit, an efficient appointing authority gives him and entrusts into his care a top secret, magic talisman of great potency, a coin which is called his cryptologic combat coin, and which, as is usual in the case of all but trick coins, has two faces, a COMINT face and a COMSEC face. When given to him that coin should be in mint condition; it should be bright and shiny on both faces, and he should strive his utmost to keep them both that way. If, to begin with, he is given a coin that is tarnished a bit on both faces, he is really starting out with a great handicap, no matter how good he and his forces are in respect to size, equipment, training, and ability. If he keeps both faces bright and shiny, he stands a good chance of winning a battle even if his forces are inferior in size, etc., compared with those of the enemy. But if he lets either face of his coin become dull from indifference, carelessness, or ignorance, he will almost surely lose the battle, even if his forces are superior in size, etc., compared with those of his enemy.

As a remarkable example of the validity of the foregoing dictum, an example that comes directly from the two Japanese navy officers who wrote *Midway: The Battle that Doomed Japan* (see footnote 11), let me quote the initial paragraphs of the Preface to their book (p.xiii):

> For Japan, the Battle of Midway was indeed a tragic defeat. The Japanese Combined Fleet, placing its faith in "quality rather than quantity," had long trained and prepared to defeat a numerically superior enemy. Yet at Midway a stronger Japanese force went down to defeat before a weaker enemy.
>
> Not only were our participating surface forces far superior in number to those of the enemy, but the initiative was in our hands. Nor were we inferior, qualitatively, in the crucial element of air strength, which played the major role throughout the Pacific War. In spite of this we suffered a decisive defeat such as the modern Japanese Navy had never before experienced or even dreamed possible.

Earlier in this lecture I quoted two other paragraphs from this same book, in which the Japanese authors make perfectly clear the reasons for the loss of the Battle of Midway, reasons which have also been stated by other writers. The cryptologic combat coin our navy entrusted to Admiral Nimitz was highly polished and bright on both sides; the one the Japanese navy entrusted to Admiral Yamamoto was dull on both sides to begin with. Admiral Yamamoto not only didn't know how tarnished it was, but lost his life because of his ignorance a couple of years later. Neither he or his superiors had the experience and knowledge that were necessary to polish up that coin. It took almost ten years for the truth of that dictum I formulated for you a moment ago to become clear to the Japanese navy. Had they taken quick and full advantage of the unfortunate leakage of the vital COMINT facts soon after the Battle for Midway, they could and perhaps would have come to the proper conclusions long before they did. Who knows what the results might have been, and the effect thereof, on the outcome of the war in the Pacific?

Hardly anything of importance in the cryptologic battles of World War II escaped the attention of Winston Churchill, who even way back in 1915, when he was First Sea Lord of the British Navy in World War I, had taken a great interest in cryptology. He made the following final comment on the Battle of Midway, a comment that is impressive in its guarded revelations and in its restraint:[21]

> One other lesson stands out. The American Intelligence system succeeded in penetrating the enemy's most closely guarded secrets well in advance of events. Thus Admiral Nimitz, albeit the weaker, was twice able to concentrate all the forces he had in sufficient strength at the right time and place. When the hour struck this proved decisive. The importance of secrecy and the consequences of leakage of information are here proclaimed.

It will probably seem to many of my listeners and readers that I have paid more tributes to the achievements of our navy cryptanalysts in World War II than to those of their army and air force opposite numbers. If I have done so, I can only say in extenuation that three factors are here involved. First, as regards my apparent overlooking of the contributions of the USAF, I need but remind you that it wasn't until after the war was all over that the Army Air Corps became autonomous; before then the technical achievements of cryptanalysts of that Corps were merged with those of the army. Second, as a member of the Army's Signal Intelligence Service, and then the Army Security Agency during World War II, it is fitting that somebody other than I blow the trumpets in celebration of our army's cryptanalytic achievements. All I will say is that they were as important as those of our navy, but for various reasons they have not received much publicity, which is just as well from the point of view of national security. As a matter of fact, the publicity regarding our navy's cryptologic successes comes very largely from former enemy officers and from the various official investigations into the attack on Pearl Harbor, and not from any U.S. Navy personnel. Third, there has been very little leakage with regard to the army's cryptanalytic successes except such as can also be traced back to those Pearl Harbor investigations. General Eisenhower's *Crusade in Europe* has not one word to say on the subjects of signal intelligence, cryptanalysis, codes, ciphers, or signal security, etc., although he does make a few rather caustic remarks about the failures and errors of his own intelligence staff. General Bradley's book is equally reticent on these subjects, but I cannot refrain from quoting one rather amusing episode having to do with COMSEC:

> To identify hills, road junctions, and towns without our giving our plans away in the event of an enemy tap on the wire, I had key features numbered on my war map and gave copies of those numbers to the division commanders. It was a makeshift private code, lax enough to cause Dickson [Bradley's G-2] to worry over the security of our plans.
>
> One morning when I called Major General Terry Allen, he referred to an obscure crossroad by its number in this private code.
>
> "Just a minute, Terry," I said. "I can't find that number on my map."
>
> "Well, listen carefully, Brad," he said. "The enemy may be listening in. I'll say the name of the place as fast as I can."
>
> Dickson overheard this conversation and threw up his hands. "Security wouldn't be much of a problem," he said, "if only there were fewer generals in the army."

General Hap Arnold's book I've mentioned before and have taken one extract from it. There are several others I might have used, but they are not too significant in revelations. One volume in the history of the U.S. Army in World War II, entitled "The Signal Corps," contains a few references to the achievements of the Signal Intelligence Service, but these, too, are not very illuminating. In only one book by a former U.S. army officer, Colonel Robert S. Allen, entitled *Lucky Forward: The History of Patton's Third Army*,[22] do I find a specific reference to the help SIS gave Patton. In telling about Patton's signal officer, Colonel Hammond, Allen writes:

> One of his ace units was the SIS. A radio-interception agency, commanded by Major Charles Flint, a young, trigger-smart expert, it worked closely with G-2 on a dual mission: maintaining a vigilant security check on friendly communications and intercepting enemy messages. The unit performed outstandingly in both fields.
> Its reports plugged up an unwitting leak from a Mechanized Cavalry source, capable of revealing important troop-movement information to the enemy. And at a critical period in the Battle of Bastogne, the unit broke a German coded message that enabled heavy losses to be inflicted upon the redoubtable 5 Para Division. The SIS was particularly fruitful in breakthroughs and fluid situations when the enemy was on the run and had to use radio.

The foregoing extract is, of course, far from spectacular. Indeed, I imagine that it will hardly bring forth more than a polite yawn from many members of an audience that has already learned about the sensational revelations made during the various Pearl Harbor investigations and about those famous letters that General Marshall wrote to Governor Dewey. But there remains this much more to be said: the achievements of our army's cryptologic units both in Washington and in the field, as well as certain still undisclosed top secret successes of our navy's units ashore and afloat, are locked away in archives, where they will probably remain for a long, long time. More than this I am not at liberty to tell you in this lecture.

With this statement I bring this series to a rather undramatic but I hope meaningful close. I will wind it up by paraphrasing the last sentence of the introduction to that important book *The Battle of Midway*, from which I have quoted at some length. The introduction was written by Admiral Nobutake Kondo, the senior living commander of the former Imperial Navy, who participated in that battle: I close this series with the hope that my lectures will serve as material for criticism and reflection.

NOTES

1. (New York: Henry Holt and Co., 1951), 474.
2. The 79th Congress, 2nd Session, Senate Document No. 244, (Washington: The Government Printing Office, 1946),232.
3. Ibid., 514.
4. General Albert Wedemeyer, *Wedemeyer Reports* (New York: Henry Holt and Company, 1958),430.
5. A good bibliographical survey of items concerning the attack up to the year 1955 will be found in the following: Louis Morton, *Pearl Harbor in Perspective*, U.S. Naval Institute Proceedings, Vol. 81, No.4, Whole No. 626, April 1955,461-8.
6. *The Memoirs of Cordell Hull* (New York: The MacMillan Co.), Vol. II, 998, 1013, 1035, 1055, 1056-7, 1060, 1063, 1068, 1074, 1077, 1087, 1092, 1095, 1096, 1099-100.
7. Henry L.Stimson and McGeorge Bundy, *On Active Service in Peace and War* (New York: Harper & Brothers, 1947),391-94, 454-5.
8. Herbert Feis, *The Road to Pearl Harbor* (Princeton: The Princeton University Press, 1950), vii, and 219-340, Passim. (See index: under "Magic" on 350.) 9. Husband E. Kimmel, *Admiral Kimmel's Story* (Chicago: Henry Regnery Co., 1954).
10. Sherman Miles, "Pearl Harbor in Retrospect," *The Atlantic Monthly*, Vol. 182, No. 1, July 1948,65-72.
11. *Midway, The Battle that Doomed Japan: The Japanese Navy's Story*, by Matsuo Fuchida and Matasake Okumiya (Annapolis: U.S. Naval Institute

Publication, 1955), 131, and 232. Admiral Morrison actually wrote:

"Midway was a victory of intelligence bravely and wisely applied." See Vol. IV of his *History of U.S. Navy Operations in the Pacific: Coral Sea, Midway, and Submarine Actions, May-August 1942.* (New York: Little, Brown, 1944), 185. It is interesting to note that Admiral Morrison, in an article entitled "Lessons of Pearl Harbor" published in the *Saturday Evening Post*, October 28, 1961, concludes, "It was the setup at Washington and at Pearl, not individual stupidity, which confused what was going on. No one person knew the intelligence picture; no one person was responsible for the defense of Pearl Harbor; too many people assumed that others were taking precautions that they failed to take."

12. *Admiral Halsey's Story* (New York: McGraw-Hill, 1947), 155-157.

13. *The Two Bookes of the proficience and advancement of Learning*, (London, 1605), 61. This book is commonly known as *The Advancement of Learning*. Some 18 years later Bacon saw no reason to change his comment in his *De Augmentis Scientiarum*, (London, 1623). In fact, he strengthened it by making it read: "... but the rawness and unskillfulness of Secretaries, and Clarks, in the Courts of Princes, is such that many times the greatest matters are committed to futile and weak Cyphers." (Gilbert Wats' translation, 1640, 270.)

14. *Les Chiffres secrets devoiles*.

15. *Comptes Rendus*, Marseilles, Vol. XX, 160-65.

16. *L'art de chiffrer et de dechiffrer les depeches secretes,* (Paris, 1893), 100.

17. In this system, which uses only two different symbols or elements, the so-called "binary code," the combining rule is its own inverse.

18. R. D. Parker, "Recollections Concerning the Birth of One-Time Tape and Printing-Telegraph Machine Cryptography," *NSA Technical Journal,* Vol. I, No.2, July 1956, 103-14.

19. By L.F. Morehouse, an A.T. & T. Company equipment engineer. See U.S. Patent No. 1,356,546, "Ciphering System," granted 26 October 1920-W.F.F.

20. The letter consisting of a single paragraph stated: "1. The mechanical means of enciphering messages with an arbitrary, meaningless running key of 999,000 letters, provided no two messages are enciphered at the same point on the tape as explained to Major Mauborgne, Signal Corps, and Captain Yardley, Military Intelligence Branch, by officials of the American Telegraph and Telephone Company, is considered by this office to be absolutely indecipherable."

21. *The Hinge of Fate*, Vol. IV (Boston: Houghton Mifflin Co., 1950), 252-53.

22. (New York: The Vanguard Press, Inc., 1957), 56. The author makes some quite caustic comments about the failure of the intelligence staffs to make use of the the intelligence they were furnished. They are worth reading.

Appendix I

From *Time*, 17 December 1945

MAGIC WAS THE WORD FOR IT

U.S. citizens discovered last week that perhaps their most potent secret weapon of World War II was not radar, not the VT fuse, not the atom bomb – but a harmless little machine that cryptographers painstakingly constructed in a hidden room at Fort Washington.

With this machine, built after years of trial and error, of inference and deduction, cryptographers had duplicated the decoding devices used in Tokyo. Testimony before the Pearl Harbor Committee had already shown that the machine – known in Army code as "Magic" – was in use long before December 7, 1941, had given ample warning of the Jap's sneak attack – if only U.S. brass hats had been smart enough to realize it (*Time*, December 10). Now General Marshall continued the story of "Magic's" magic. It had:

Enabled a relatively small U.S. force to intercept a Jap invasion fleet, win a decisive victory in the Battle of the Coral Sea, thus saving Australia and New Zealand.

Given the U.S. full advance information on the size of the Jap forces advancing on Midway, enabled the Navy to concentrate ships which otherwise might have been 3,000 miles away, thus set up an ambush which proved to be the turning-point victory of the Pacific war.

Directed U.S. submarines unerringly to the sea lanes where Japanese convoys would be passing.

By decoding messages from Japan's Ambassador Oshima in Berlin, often reporting interviews with Hitler, given our forces invaluable information on German war plans.

UNEASY SECRET

So priceless a possession was Magic that the U.S. high command lived in constant fear that the Japs would discover the secret, change their code machinery, force U.S. cryptographers to start all over again.

General Marshall had a long series of bad moments after U.S. flyers, showing a suspicious amount of foresight, shot down Admiral Yamamoto's plane at Bougainville in 1943. Gossip rustled through the Pacific and into Washington cocktail parties; General Marshall got to the point of asking the FBI to find an officer "who could be made an example of." (The FBI, fearful of looking like a Gestapo, refused.)

Once a decoder was caught in Boston trying to sell the secret. Once, well-meaning agents of the Office of Strategic Services ransacked the Japanese Embassy in Lisbon, whereupon the Japs adopted a new code for military attachés. This code remained unbroken more than a year later.[1] The worst scare of all came during the 1944 presidential campaign, when George Marshall heard that Thomas E. Dewey knew the secret and might refer to it in speeches (*see below*).

Yet for all these fears, the Japs never discovered that the United States was decoding their messages. Even after the surrender the Army still used Magic as a guide to occupation moves: though it had once been planned to send a whole army into Korea, Magic showed that a single regiment would be enough.

SECRET KEPT

The letter, on stationery of the Chief of Staffs Office, bore a bold heading: TOP SECRET. FOR MR. DEWEY'S EYES ONLY. Candidate Thomas E. Dewey, his curiosity piqued, read rapidly through the first two paragraphs:

> I am writing you without the knowledge of any other person except Admiral King (who concurs) because we are approaching a grave dilemma in the political reactions of Congress regarding Pearl Harbor. What I have to tell you below is of such a highly secret nature that I feel compelled to ask you either to accept it on the basis of your not communicating its contents to any other person and returning this letter or not reading any further and returning the letter to the bearer.

Tom Dewey looked up from the typewritten page. As he did, the word cryptograph, a few paragraphs below, flashed into his vision like a red traffic light. He made his decision quickly, folded the letter, handed it back. Colonel Carter W. Clarke (in mufti), who had flown from Washington to Tulsa to catch up with Tom Dewey's campaign, went back, his mission uncompleted.

YOU HAVE MY WORD

It was September 1944. The campaign train rolled up through the Midwest, returned to Albany. A few days later, Tom Dewey received another visit from Colonel Clarke.[2]

The Colonel, again in civilian clothes, handed over another letter from General Marshall. The General had changed his mind somewhat:

> I am quite willing to have you read what comes hereafter with the understanding that you are bound not to communicate to any other person any portions on which you do not now have or later receive factual knowledge from some other source than myself. . . . You have my word that neither the Secretary of War nor the President has any intimation whatsoever that such a letter has been addressed to you. . . .

THE LOCKED FILE

This time Tom Dewey read on. As he turned the pages, he became the first man outside the high command to know the full story of "Magic" and what it was accomplishing in the war against the Japs (see above). The letter closed with a plea:

> I am presenting this matter to you, for your secret information, in the hope that you will see your way clear to avoid the tragic results with which we are threatened in the present political campaign.

Tom Dewey locked the letter in his files, went back to his electioneering. Though he had known before that the United States had cracked the Jap code, had suspected that this information cast grave doubts on Franklin Roosevelt's role before Pearl Harbor, he held his tongue. The War Department's most valuable secret was kept out of the campaign.

MEETING AT A FUNERAL

Recounting this story at the Pearl Harbor hearing last week, General Marshall recalled that he and Tom Dewey had never discussed the matter in person until they met at Franklin Roosevelt's funeral last April: "I asked Mr. Dewey to come with me to the War Department and I showed him current Magic showing Japanese movements. His attitude was friendly and gracious."

Had Marshall ever told Franklin Roosevelt of the letters to Dewey? Said Marshall: "The President died without knowing of it."

SECRET LOST

The Pearl Harbor Committee blithely tossed away one still-secret U.S. weapon. George Marshall's letters to Governor Dewey (see above) mentioned that the United States, with the help of the British, had decoded German as well as Japanese messages. George Marshall begged the Committee to cut out these references. The Committee refused.

Publication of the letters thus gave the Germans their first knowledge that their code had been broken. It was also a breach of diplomatic confidence with the British, who had let the United States in on the secret on the understanding that it would be kept.

ANATOMY OF A CONFUSION

Up to the witness stand stepped Lieut. General Leonard T. Gerow, chief of the Army's War Plans Division in 1941, to accept full blame for one of Pearl Harbor's most egregious errors. On November 27, a sharp warning of impending hostilities had gone out from General Marshall to Lieut. General Walter C. Short in Hawaii. On November 28, General Short replied that he had ordered an alert against sabotage – which was like saying he had a butterfly net ready for a tiger. Yet his reply was never challenged by Washington. Why?

Explained General Gerow: he thought the Short message was an answer to other communications. Said he: "If there is any responsibility in the War Department for failure. . . I accept that responsibility."

Then up stepped General Marshall himself to take part of the blame. He didn't recall seeing the Short message; he should have. "That was my opportunity to intervene and I didn't take it," he confessed. "Just why, I do not know."

FOURTEEN POINTS

The week's testimony also shed light on the warning that came too late – the message Walter Short received on December 7 at 2:58 p.m. Hawaii time informing him that the Japs were on the way.

On the night of December 6, Major General Sherman Miles, Chief of Intelligence, received from "Magic" decoders the first thirteen points of the strongly worded, final Jap diplomatic note being sent from Tokyo to its envoys in Washington. Next morning, some time between 7 and 8 o'clock, an assistant telephoned that he had "important" information. General Miles reached his office at 9 o'clock.

General Marshall had risen early, breakfasted at 8, looked over the Sunday papers, gone out for a horseback ride. (He usually rode for 50 minutes.) He was in the shower when an urgent message arrived by telephone from General Miles' assistant. He finished his bath, dressed quickly and went straight to the War Department. The time: 11:25 a.m.

WHO'S CONFUSED?

A hastily gathered staff meeting decided that the Jap note meant war, that a warning should go immediately to Hawaii, the Philippines, the West Coast, the Canal. General Marshall called Admiral Harold R. ("Betty") Stark, then Chief of Naval Operations. "Betty" Stark thought by some obscure reasoning that further warnings would "only confuse" field commanders.

General Marshall wrote out a warning anyway, called Admiral Stark again to read it. Stark decided on second thought that the warning might as well go to Navy commanders as well. General Marshall sent it on to the Signal Corps that promised, according to General Miles, that it would be delivered in 20 minutes. It was then 11:50 a.m.; the attack was one hour and ten minutes away.

Instead of 20 minutes, the Signal Corps took eight hours and 28 minutes to get the message to Short (by commercial cable instead of Army radio). Nobody had bothered to check up on the Signal Corps; the General Staff took for granted that the message was going full speed ahead.

Why hadn't General Marshall used the telephone? His explanation: he knew that many phone calls – including transatlantic talks between Franklin Roosevelt and Winston Churchill – had been tapped; he feared that the Japs would intercept his call and label it an "overt act." Anyway, he said, even if he had phoned he would first have called the Philippines, where he thought the real danger lay.

Said George Marshall: "We thought Hawaii was the most improbable [target] of all. . . . I was inclined to feel the hazards were too great and they would not risk it."

Appendix II

The Letters from General Marshall to Governor Dewey, 25 and 27 September 1944

The Marshall-Dewey correspondence is so important in cryptologic history that I feel the whole of it should be included even in this brief history. When the letter was written, it was, of course, TOP SECRET and it was only under great pressure from certain members of the Joint Congressional Committee that General Marshall revealed its contents.[3] Thus, it came into the public domain not only on the very day that General Marshall was forced to place it in evidence – its publication caused a great sensation in the newspapers – but also when the forty volumes of the hearings of that committee were published and put on sale by the Superintendent of Documents of the Government Printing Office. The disclosure of the contents of the Marshall-Dewey correspondence was indeed such a sensation that *Life* printed the whole of it in its issue of 17 December 1945, with the following introduction:

MARSHALL-DEWEY LETTERS

General Told Candidate We Had Broken Jap Code

During the 1944 election campaign General George C. Marshall wrote two letters to Republican candidate Thomas E. Dewey, telling him that Army cryptographers had broken the Japanese "ultra" code. This fact was first revealed in a story by *Life* Editor John Chamberlain, which appeared in *Life*, Sept. 24. Marshall's purpose, Chamberlain wrote, was to forestall Dewey's revelation of that fact in a possible attack on the Roosevelt administration's Japanese policy before Pearl Harbor. The actual text of the letters emained secret until last week, when General Marshall appeared before the Congressional committee investigating Pearl Harbor and made the letters public. They appear below.

When he had finished reading the first two paragraphs of the first letter, Governor Dewey stopped because, as the Chamberlain article reported, "the letter might possibly contain material which had already come from other sources, and that anyway, a candidate for President was in no position to make blind promises." General Marshall sent the letter back again with an introduction which relieved the governor of binding conditions. This time Dewey read the letter and after much thought and discussion decided not to make use during the campaign of any information he previously had.

First Letter

> TOP SECRET
> (FOR MR. DEWEY'S EYES ONLY)
> 25 September 1944
>
> My Dear Governor:
>
> I am writing you without the knowledge of any other person except Admiral King (who concurs) because we are approaching a grave dilemma in the political reactions of Congress regarding Pearl Harbor.
>
> What I have to tell you below is of such a highly secret nature that I feel compelled to ask you either to accept it on the basis of your not communicating its contents to any other person and returning the letter or not reading it any further and returning the letter to the bearer.

I should have preferred to talk to you in person but I could not devise a method that would not be subject to press and radio reactions as to why the Chief of Staff of the Army would be seeking an interview with you at this particular moment. Therefore, I have turned to the method of this letter, to be delivered by hand to you by Colonel Carter Clarke, who incidentally has charge of the most secret documents of the War and Navy Departments.

In brief, the military dilemma resulting from Congressional political battles of the political campaign is this:

The most vital evidence in the Pearl Harbor matter consists of our intercepts of the Japanese diplomatic communications. Over a period of years our cryptograph people analyzed the character of the machine the Japanese were using for encoding their diplomatic messages. Based on this, a corresponding machine was built by us which deciphers their messages.

Therefore, we possessed a wealth of information regarding their moves in the Pacific, which in turn was furnished the State Department – rather than, as is popularly supposed, the State Department providing us with information – but which unfortunately made no reference whatever to intentions toward Hawaii until the last message before Dec. 7, which did not reach our hands until the following day, Dec. 8.

Now the point to the present dilemma is that we have gone ahead with this business of deciphering their codes until we possess other codes, German as well as Japanese, but our main basis of information regarding Hitler's intentions in Europe is obtained from Baron Oshima's message from Berlin reporting his interviews with Hitler and other officials to the Japanese Government. These are still in the codes involved in the Pearl Harbor events.

To explain further the critical nature of this setup which would be wiped out almost in an instant if the least suspicion were aroused regarding it, the Battle of the Coral Sea was based on deciphered messages and therefore our ships were in the right place at the right time. Further, we were able to concentrate our limited forces to meet their advances on Midway when otherwise we almost certainly would have been some 3,000 miles out of place.[4]

We had full information of the strength of their forces in that advance and also of the smaller force directed against the Aleutians which finally landed troops on Attu and Kiska.

Operations in the Pacific are largely guided by the information we obtain of Japanese deployments. We know their strength in various garrisons, the rations and other stores continuing available to them and what is of vast importance, we check their fleet movements and the movements of their convoys.

The heavy losses reported from time to time which they sustain by reason of our submarine action largely results from the fact that we know the sailing dates and the routes of their convoys and can notify out submarines to lie in wait at the proper point.

The current raids by Admiral Halsey's carrier forces on Japanese shipping in Manila Bay and elsewhere were largely based in timing on the known movements on Japanese convoys, two of which were caught, as anticipated, in his destructive attacks.

You will understand from the foregoing the utter tragic consequences if the present political debates regarding Pearl Harbor disclose to the enemy, German or Jap, any suspicion of the vital sources of information we now possess.

The Roberts report on Pearl Harbor had to have withdrawn from it all reference to this highly secret matter, therefore in portions it necessarily appeared incomplete. The same reason which dictated that course is even more important today because our sources have been greatly elaborated.

As a further example of the delicacy of the situation, some of Donovan's people (the OSS), without telling us, instituted a secret search of the Japanese Embassy offices in Portugal. As a result the entire military attaché Japanese code all over the world was changed, and though this occurred over a year ago, we have not yet been able to break the new code and have thus lost this invaluable information source, particularly regarding the European situation.

A recent speech in Congress by Representative Harness would clearly suggest to the Japanese that we have been reading their codes though Mr. Harness and the American public would probably not draw any such conclusion.

The conduct of General Eisenhower's campaign and of all operations in the Pacific are closely related in conception and timing to the information we secretly obtain through these intercepted codes. They contribute greatly to the victory and tremendously to the saving of American lives, both in the conduct of current operations and in looking toward the early termination of the war.

I am presenting this matter to you, for your secret information, in the hope that you will see your way clear to avoid the tragic results with which we are now threatened in the present political campaign. I might add that the recent action of Congress in requiring Army and Navy investigations for action before certain dates has compelled me to bring back the corps commander, General Gerow, whose troops are fighting at Trier, to testify here while the Germans are counterattacking his forces there. This, however, is a very minor matter compared to the loss of our code information.[5]

Please return this letter by bearer. I will hold it in my secret file subject to your reference should you so desire.

Faithfully yours,
G.C. Marshall

Second Letter

TOP SECRET
(FOR MR. DEWEY'S EYES ONLY)
27 September 1944

My Dear Governor:

Colonel Clarke, my messenger to you of yesterday, Sept. 26, has reported the result of his delivery of my letter dated Sept. 25. As I understand him you (A) were unwilling to commit yourself to any agreement regarding "not communicating its contents to any other person" in view of the fact that you felt you already knew certain of the things probably already referred to in the letter, as suggested to you by seeing the word "cryptograph," and (B) you could not feel that such a letter as this to a Presidential candidate could have been addressed to you by an officer in my position without the knowledge of the President.

As to (A) above I am quite willing to have you read what comes hereafter with the understanding that you are bound not to communicate to any other person any portions on which you do not now have or later receive factual information from some other source than myself. As to (B) above you have my word that neither the Secretary of War nor the President has any intimation whatsoever that such a letter has been addressed to you or that the preparation or sending of such a communication was being considered.

I assure you that the only persons who saw or know of the existence of either this letter or my letter to you dated Sept. 25 are Admiral King, seven key officers responsible for security of military communications, and my secretary who typed these letters.

I am trying my best to make plain to you that this letter is being addressed to you solely on my initiative, Admiral King having been consulted only after the letter was drafted, and I am persisting in the matter because the military hazards involved are so serious that I feel some action is necessary to protect the interests of our armed forces.

(The second letter then repeated substantially the text of the first letter except for the first two paragraphs.)

Life failed to note that the last two sentences in the penultimate paragraph of the "First Letter" were omitted from that paragraph in the "Second Letter," but there is no explanation for the omission.[6] Perhaps it was simply for the sake of brevity, but this seems improbable.

In my first lecture I called attention to the fact that the account given in the *Time* article gives credit to Army cryptanalysts for providing the secret intelligence "which enabled our navy to win such spectacular battles as those of the Coral Sea and Midway, and to waylay Japanese convoys," whereas the credit for the communications intelligence which enabled our navy to win those battles was produced by Navy cryptanalysts. One cannot blame the editors of Time for making such a bad error because the source of the error can be traced directly to General Marshall's letter itself. Several years ago I asked my friend Colonel Clarke, who, you will recall, carried General Marshall's letter to Governor Dewey, how such an error had crept into General Marshall's letter and was told that the letter that had been prepared for General Marshall's signature did not meet with the General's wholehearted approval and that the General himself had modified it. Perhaps that is how the error to which I have referred crept into it. One could hardly expect General Marshall to be entirely familiar with the technical cryptanalytic details involved in what he wanted to tell Governor Dewey, nor should one criticize him for not being able, in his very busy days and under very heavy pressure of events, to bear in mind or even to know about the differences between the enemy systems worked upon by the respective and separate Army and Navy cryptanalytic organizations. It is of course possible, indeed it may be, that in the cases of certain important naval operations valuable COMINT came from messages read by Army cryptanalysts, and this may be what confused General Marshall in implying that all the credit belonged to them because of their solution of the Japanese highest-level diplomatic cryptosystems, the one that used the so called "Purple Code," which wasn't a code but a cipher machine.

Since the period during which the disclosures of the joint congressional investigation were made, disclosures which were disastrous so far as the important accomplishments of the two services before and after the Pearl Harbor attack in the field of communications intelligence, much has been written and is now in the public domain regarding those accomplishments, but fortunately no technical details of significance have been disclosed.

NOTES

1. While I have no recollection of the Boston business. I shall never forget the Lisbon incident. – W.F.F.

2. "A few days later..." But note that the first letter is dated 25 September 1944, the second, 27 September. It is possible that Colonel Clarke was unable to deliver the letter, but my recollection is that he did deliver it the very next day.- W.F.F.

3. So far as I am aware it has neither been ascertained nor disclosed, if known, who gave Governor Dewey the information. But it is a fact that as a patriotic citizen, he acceded to General Marshall's request – he made no use whatever of the vital secret information during the campaign or after it. *Time's* account specifically states that Dewey "held his tongue. The War Department's most valuable secret was kept out of the campaign". I know this to be true.- W.F.F.

4. In regard to this and the succeeding four paragraphs, see my comment below (p.129).

5. The last two sentences in this paragraph were omitted from the Second Letter. See footnote 6.

6. The sentence beginning "I might add. . ." and the one beginning "This, however is. . ." were omitted.

BIBLIOGRAPHY
[for Friedman Lectures]

Allen, Robert S. *Lucky Forward: The History of Patton's Third Army*. New York: The Vanguard Press, Inc., 1957.

Bacon, Sir Francis. *Advancement of Learning*. London, 1604.

Bacon, Sir Francis. *The Advancement of Learning*. (Translated by Gilbert Wats, 1640).

Bacon, Sir Francis. *De Augmentis Scientiarum*. London, 1623.

Bakeless, Colonel. John. *Turncoats, Traitors and Heroes*. Lippincott, 1959.

Bates, David H. "Lincoln in the Telegraph Office," *Century Magazine*. Vol. LXXIV, Nos. 1-5, May-September, 1907.

Bates, David H. *Lincoln in the Telegraph Office*. New York: Appleton-Century Company, 1907, reprinted 1939.

Battles and Leaders of the Civil War. New York: The Century Co., 1884, 581.

Bazeries. *Les Chiffres secrets dévoilés*. Paris, 1901.

Bazeries. "Cryptographe à 20 Rondelles - alphabets (25 lettres par alphabet)," *Comptes Rendus*. Marseilles, Vol. XX, 1891.

Bradley, General Omar. *A Soldier's Story*. New York: Henry Holt and Co., 1951.

Brown, J. Willard. *The Signal Corps, U.S.A., in the War of the Rebellion*. Boston: U.S. Veteran Signal Corps Association, 1896.

Budge, Dr. E.A. Wallis. *The Rosetta Stone*. Trustees of the British Museum, 1922.

Champollion, Jean Francois. *Hieroglyphic Dictionary*.

Champollion, Jean Francois. *Egyptian Grammar*.

Churchill, Winston. *The Hinge of Fate*, Vol. IV. Boston: Houghton Mifflin Co., 1950.

"The Cipher Dispatches." *The New York Tribune*. Extra No. 44, New York, (14 January) 1879. [Tilden scandal]

Counter-espionage, or keys for all secret communications. Paris 1793.

Drioton, Prof. Étienne. *Revue D'Égyptologié*, Paris, 1933.

Drioton, Prof. Étienne. "Decipherment of Egyptian Hieroglyphics," *La Science Moderne*. August 1924.

Ellis, Kenneth L. *The Post Office in the Eighteenth Century: A Study in Administrative History*. London: Oxford University Press, 1958.

Falconer, James. *Cryptomenysis Patefacta: Or the Art of Secret Information Disclosed Without a Key*. London, 1685.

Feis, Herbert. *The Road to Pearl Harbor*. Princeton: The Princeton University Press, 1950.

Friedman, William F. *American Army Field Codes in the American Expeditionary Forces during the First World War*. Government Printing Office, 1942.

Friedman, William F. *Analysis of a Mechanico-Electrical Cryptograph, Part I* (1934), *Part II*, 1935.

Friedman, William F. *Field Codes Used by the German Army During the World War*. 1919.

Friedman, William F., and Elizabeth S. *The Shakespearean Ciphers Examined*. Cambridge University Press, 1957.

Fuchida, Matsuo, and Matasake Okumiya. *Midway, The Battle that Doomed Japan: The Japanese Navy's Story*. Annapolis: U.S. Naval Institute Publication, 1955.

Giverge, General. *Cours de Cryptographie*. 1925.

Gregory, Lieutenant Colonel J.F. *Telegraphic Code to Insure Secrecy in the Transmission of Telegrams*. Government Printing Office, 1886.

Gylden, Yves. *Chifferbråernas Insatser I Världskriget Till Lands*. [Translation by William F. Friedman, *The Contribution of the Cryptographic Bureaus in the World War*. Government Printing Office, 1936.]

Halsey, Fleet Admiral William F. *Admiral Halsey's Story*. New York: McGraw-Hill, 1947.

Hassard, John R.G. "Cryptography in Politics," *The North American Review*. Vol. CXXVIII, No. 268, March 1879. [Tilden scandal]

Haswell, John H. "Secret Writing," *Century Magazine*, Vol. LXXXV, November 1912.

Hitt, Captain Parker. *Manual for the Solution of Military Ciphers*. Fort Leavenworth, Kansas: Army Service Schools Press, 1916.

Holden, Edward S. *The Cipher Dispatches*. New York, 1879. [Tilden scandal]

Hull, Cordell. *The Memoirs of Cordell Hull*. New York: The MacMillan Co.,1948.

James, Admiral Sir William. T*he Eyes of the Navy*. London: Methuen & Co., 1955.

Kimmel, Husband E. *Admiral Kimmel's Story*. Chicago: Henry Regnery Co., 1954.

Mauborgne, 1st Lieutenant. J.O. *An Advanced Problem in Cryptography and its Solution*. Fort Leavenworth, Kansas: Army Service Schools Press, 1914.

Mendelsohn, Captain Charles J. *Studies in German Diplomatic Codes Employed During the World War*. Government Printing Office, 1937.

Miles, Sherman. "Pearl Harbor in Retrospect," *The Atlantic Monthly*. Vol. 182, No.1, July 1948.

Morison, Admiral Samuel E. *History of U.S. Navy Operations in the Pacific*. Vol. IV: "Coral Sea, Midway, and Submarine Actions, May-August 1942." New York: Little, Brown, 1944.

Morton, Louis. *Pearl Harbor in Perspective*. U.S. Naval Institute Proceedings, Vol. 81, No. 4, Whole No. 626, April 1955.

Myer, Colonel. Albert J. *A Manual of Signals: for the use of signal officers in the field*. Washington, D.C.: Signal Officer of the Army, 1864.

O'Brien, J .E. "Telegraphing in Battle," *Century Magazine*. XXXVIII, September 1889.

Parker, R.D. "Recollections Concerning the Birth of One-Time Tape and Printing-Telegraph Machine Cryptography." *NSA Technical Journal*. Vol. 1, No.2, July 1956.

Plum, Colonel William R. *The Military Telegraph during the Civil War*. Chicago, 1882.

Poe, Edgar Allan. "The Gold Bug."

Several Machine Ciphers and Methods for their Solution. Riverbank Publication No. 20, 1918.

Slater, Robert. *Telegraphic Code to Ensure Secresy* [sic] *in the Transmission of Telegrams*. 1870. [a.k.a. *Slater's Code*]

Stern, Philip Van Doren. *Secret Missions of the Civil War*. New York: Rand McNally and Co., 1951

Stimson, Henry L., and McGeorge Bundy. *On Active Service in Peace and War*. New York: Harper & Brothers, 1947.

Taylor, Dr. Charles E. "The Signal and Secret Service of the Confederate States," *Confederate Veteran*, Vol. XL, August-September 1932.

Time, 17 December 1945.

Tuchman, Barbara. *The Zimmermann Telegram*. New York: Viking Press, 1958.

U.S. House Miscellaneous Documents, Vol. 5, 45th Congress, 3rd Session, 1878-79. [Tilden scandal]

Viaris, Marquis de. *L 'art de chiffrer et déchiffrer les dépêches secrètes*. Paris, 1893.

Wedemeyer, General Albert C. *Wedemeyer Reports*. New York: Henry Holt and Company,1958.

Wheatstone, Sir Charles. *The Scientific Papers of Sir Charles Wheatstone*. London: Physical Society of London, 1879.

Wimsatt, Professor W.K. "What Poe Knew About Cryptography," *Publications of the Modern Language Association of America*. New York, Vol. LVIII, No.3, September 1943.

Yardley, Herbert O. *The American Black Chamber*. Indianapolis: Bobbs-Merrill Co., 1931.

Young, Dr. Thomas. "Studies on the Rosetta Stone," *Encyclopaedia Britannica*. Vol. 4, 1819.

The Legendary William F. Friedman

LAMBROS D. CALLMAHOS

Editor's Note: From a reprint in *Cryptologic Spectrum* (Vol. 4, No.1), Winter 1974.

PROLOGUE

When I joined the U.S. Army to enter the cryptologic service of my adopted country on February 11, 1941, William F. Friedman was already a legendary figure in my eyes. I had read two early papers of his, *"L'indice de coincidence et ses applications en cryptographie"* and *"Application des méthodes de la statisque à la cryptographie,"* when I was living in Paris in 1934, concertizing as a flute soloist throughout Europe while privately pursuing an active hobby of cryptology, which I felt would be my niche when the time came for me to enter the army. (Besides the U.S. Army, I was also liable for service in the Greek, Egyptian, and Turkish armies, and barely missed being in one of the latter.) As a member of the original group of twenty-eight students in the Cryptographic School at Fort Monmouth, New Jersey, I was overjoyed when I found that Mr. Friedman's texts on military cryptanalysis were to be our Old and New Testaments combined.[1]

I did not meet William Friedman until after our school moved in October of 1942 to Vint Hill Farms Station, Warrenton, Virginia. The previous summer I had been promised a direct commission by the Headquarters staff of Fort Monmouth. At that time I was, as a senior private first class – I had the rank that went with the job – head of the language department and taught Italian and cryptanalysis and, since I was presumably indispensable on weekdays, pulled KP only on Saturdays and Sundays. Tired of waiting, I went to Officer Candidate School and graduated with my class in August 1942.

It was at Vint Hill that Mr. Friedman first paid us a visit, and we were all properly impressed at the dapper figure with the Adolphe Menjou moustache, the characteristic bow tie, and the two-tone black-and-white shoes – the cryptologic giant who asked the most searching questions and understood our answers even before we had finished our explanations. Having been at Vint Hill for fourteen months and, thinking that I might be stuck there for the duration of the war (I was Chief Instructor in cryptanalytics, with several hundred students in the school), I seized the opportunity, when Mr. Friedman again visited us, to ask him to get me out of there. In two weeks I was transferred to Arlington Hall Station, where I was to have been assigned to Mr. Friedman for four months to write a course in operational cryptanalysis and then to have been sent to Europe. The army, though, has a wonderful way of working. The officer to whom I was to have reported was on leave; I reported to the wrong officer, was sent to the wrong building, found myself two weeks later enrolled in a Japanese course, and it was made perfectly clear that my destiny was eventual service in the Far East. Mr. Friedman discovered my predicament too late to do anything about it, so after a year at Arlington Hall I went to New Delhi as an Assistant Signal Intelligence Officer for the China-Burma-India Theater. When the war was over, I was sent as a junior captain to Leavenworth (to the Command and General Staff College – not to that other place). When I graduated in February 1946, Mr. Friedman requested my assignment to the Army Security Agency (ASA), and I was detailed as his technical assistant.

FRIEDMAN THE MAN

My respect and admiration for the man for whom I worked increased with every contact and discussion. At first, our relationship was most formal – "Captain C." and "Mr. Friedman." Later on it became "Cal" and finally "Lambros," but it was always "Mr. Friedman." It took Mark Rhoads, his administrative assistant and colleague of long standing, a dozen years to call him "Bill"; and Mr. Friedman was "Bill" only to his friend and respected colleague Brigadier John H. Tiltman, to the Chief, ASA, and to a handful of senior military officers. To the rest, including his closest associates of the early '30s – Solomon Kullback, Frank Rowlett, and Abraham Sinkov – he was always "Mr. Friedman" – even when they were not in his presence.

I used to speak of him affectionately as "Uncle Willie" when not within earshot; the sobriquet caught on and became widespread at Arlington Hall, and when he learned of the appellation he was amused. But once, at an Agency party when the two of us were by ourselves at the canape table and I called him "Uncle Willie," I was made aware of my impertinence. One simply did not take liberties with WFF.

Mr. Friedman's desk in his private office in Headquarters Building at Arlington Hall was about fifteen feet from mine in the outer office, but much of our daily contact was in the form of written notes. I would screen incoming technical papers and pass on to him those meriting his personal attention, with a buck slip on top. He would buck notes back and forth to me, sometimes exchanging six or seven notes: Mr. Friedman was fond of written records. Since he did superior work himself, he expected that all those around him would also do the same, without question. Compliments were hard to come by. Once, when I did something evidently worthy of particular notice, he wrote on a note, "Capt. C. – Good!" I poked my head into his door and inquired solicitously, "Are you ill, Mr. Friedman?" "No, why?" he replied. I answered, "You wrote 'Good' on your note." He laughed, and from then on he allowed himself an occasional complimentary adjective that greatly added to the psychic income that was already mine in having the privilege of working with him. On another occasion when I outlined what I thought was an especially good idea, he listened patiently and, when I had finished, said: "That's fine. I have a patent on that." At another time I received his compliments on an original procedure, until I found out a couple of weeks later that he had already written about it and had forgotten about it, so I embarrassedly brought it to his attention. *Homerus nutat*.

As an army captain, I was very proud to work for Mr. Friedman, in view of what he had done and was doing for his country. Always a stickler for *le mot juste*, he abhorred imprecise or inelegant language. Once, when I did not use the term "repetition" when he felt that I should have, he said: "Don't ever use 'repeat' as a noun again!" When I found that the dictionary recognized the use of "repeat" as a noun, I was a bit miffed, but I swallowed my pride and was very careful in the future how I expressed myself to the Great One. On another occasion, when he came across the cover name ICKY in a technical report he blew his top, exclaiming that this word made him puke [*sic*].

Mr. Friedman had complete faith in his subordinates – otherwise, he felt, they wouldn't be working for him. He took for granted that I knew all that was necessary to know about cryptanalysis – a most flattering compliment, but unrealistic. One day a paper came through on a most complicated and abstruse phase of a technical matter about which I comprehended not even the title. I shrugged my shoulders and bucked the paper to him, feeling that this certainly was one matter with which I should have absolutely nothing to do, especially since three leading technicians of the Agency differed among themselves as to the merits of technical points. To my horror, Mr. Friedman bucked the paper back to me with a note, "Captain C.: please study and prepare comments for me." I was frantic. But I spent the next three days working eighteen hours a day, did some historical research on the problem, spoke with technicians on the project, fortunately came up with a refutation of points held by the author of the paper, discovered a new approach, and drafted a substantive reply worthy of William Friedman. It wasn't until many years later that I told Mr. Friedman how that one paper made me sweat blood – he of course had blithely assumed that I was versed in all matters of cryptanalysis, including that one.

When I was first assigned to Mr. Friedman's office, I was living in a room on the third floor of Headquarters Building: my family was still in New Jersey, where they had been while I was overseas, as apartments were almost impossible to obtain in the immediate postwar years in Washington. I was working two shifts: the day shift for Mr. Friedman, the swing shift for me. With Mr. Friedman's knowledge and permission, I went systematically through all his files, reading hundreds of technical reports over a period of many months, trying to remember all I could in this unparalleled opportunity for acquiring a comprehensive technical education. The effort paid off when my boss asked me about things I had already digested and on which I was now knowledgeable: my ready answers strengthened his conviction of the extent of my cryptanalytic knowledge. Mr. Friedman was meticulous in his work habits, whether on staff policy papers or in technical exposition. He would first think out the problem or situation in broad outlines, and then would map out points *a, b, c, ...n* in logical progression, with clarity of exposition and the greatest attention to detail. He wasted but little time or motion, and especially on technical matters he knew instinctively when he was on the wrong track – a splendid attribute for any cryptanalyst. He had immense drive, and knew how to organize his colleagues for the most effective teamwork to achieve the maximum efficiency of effort.

In his technical writings, Mr. Friedman was a man of punctilio. In the first book that he wrote for the U.S. government, *Elements of Cryptanalysis*, a little gem of 157 pages published in May 1923 by the Office of the Chief Signal Officer, he brought order into the chaos of cryptologic exposition of previous authors in the public domain. This work he expanded in the late 1930s into his classic textbooks, *Military Cryptanalysis, Parts I-IV*. He had a flair for the dramatic, as witnessed by the following extract from one of his technical papers[2] in which he not only had two successive sentences ending with exclamation marks, but threw in some italics for good measure:

> A set of fifty test messages, each twenty-five letters in length and beginning at the same initial enciphering juxtaposition, was submitted by Mr. Burdick. By superimposing the messages the writer solved them and completely reconstructed both basic alphabets *by applying and extending the principles of indirect symmetry of position that were discovered by Mr. Burdick himself!* It is not often that a cryptanalyst unknowingly discovers the very weapon that deals the deathblow to his own brainchild!

It's too bad that not many tellers of cryptologic tales emulate the patterns set by the Master.

On a couple of occasions in the early 1950s, I received brief handwritten notes from Mr. Friedman asking me to do something or other which I felt really wasn't necessary. So I just let the notes go by, hoping he would forget about them. Several weeks later, he asked me what I had done about the items, and I lost no time in doing what he asked me to do in the first place, marvelling at his memory. Much later I found out his secret: he kept *carbon copies* of everything he wrote in longhand, no matter how brief! I was shocked: I never really got over what I considered to be a very unethical and underhanded way of doing business. After he retired in 1955, I was bold enough to tell him of my feelings, and he got a kick out of my reaction to his craftiness.

Mr. Friedman had a fine sense of humor, but his was a passive one, enjoying others' overt actions. He was particularly fond of me and enjoyed my company, considering me a character (this proves that Mr. Friedman was not always infallible in his judgment), and after he retired and we became fast friends I was able to pull his leg (in private, of course!) and treat him more irreverently than anyone else dared. Only once, however, did I overstep my bounds. He never liked to think of eventual death, and I had the temerity to suggest to him that after he passed on to the Great Beyond he should will his body to NSA so we could stuff him and prop him up in a corner of the cafeteria. Needless to say, *that* went over like a lead balloon.

I used to smoke Roi Tan Golfers, little cigars about 3 1/2" long. Once in the late '50s when I was visiting Mr. Friedman at his home, he asked, "Why do you smoke those little cigars?" I replied that I liked their taste and convenient size. "You know, somebody might think that's an affectation," he said, as he dipped into his engraved silver snuff box. I asked him if I might try some of his snuff, gingerly placed some in each nostril, sneezed, blew my nose (into a handkerchief), and found that it was a pleasant sensation. So for the next dozen years I gave up smoking in favor of snuff, and I collected over 170 varieties from all over the world. What bothered me, though, was that as soon as I had gotten hooked on snuff, he quit. Now *that's* no way for a pusher to act, I thought. (I myself quit in 1971, one less vice in my repertoire.)

In the years after his retirement, Mr. Friedman used to call me several times a week. The phone would ring, I'd pick up the receiver, and a voice would say "Cal?" I would reply, "Yes, Mr. Friedman." At other times the voice would say, "Professor?" and again I would reply, "Yes, Mr. Friedman." Once, however, when I picked up the phone and all I heard was someone clearing his throat, I said, "Yes, Mr. Friedman," and he was too startled for words: he never got over it. How could I explain to him that a musician's ear could recognize the "harrumph" of a particular speaker? This is closely correlated with linguistic talent, and Mr. Friedman was not conversant with any language other than English; but that did not prevent him from achieving significant successes with cipher messages in Japanese and other languages.

Mr. Friedman often relived his earlier years, and he found mine a willing ear as he recounted his early triumphs and successes. His career was rich in experiences, richer perhaps than anyone in the cryptologic world has had, before or since. I would ask him about technical points, and he would outline for me a particular solution that he had accomplished years before. I sincerely regret not taking notes of our discussions, for somebody should have been a Boswell to his Johnson.

During the last several years of his life, I was Mr. Friedman's close confidant. There were times when he felt depressed, that the world was no damned good, and that he really hadn't done anything to make it a better place to live in. Of course I vehemently disagreed, pointing out all he had done for his country (as if he didn't know!). He often asked my advice on various matters, technical and nontechnical, so I proposed that he retain me as an advisor for a dollar a year: after all, he didn't have to take my advice, but if he paid me he would respect me more. Several months ago Mrs. Friedman found among her husband's effects a note reading "Pay Cal a dollar a year."

Mr. Friedman always had a very inquiring and discerning mind. He was a bibliophile, a gentleman, and a true scholar. He was astute in judging character, and he could read his adversaries like a book. He was, as I have indicated before, very sensitive on interpersonal relationships, and he relished the friendship and acquaintance with high persons in the government and in industry, both here and abroad. He was an elegant dresser, prided himself on his ability as a ballroom dancer, and was a golfer of no mean stature.

FRIEDMAN THE CRYPTOLOGIST

William Friedman was blessed by phenomenal luck throughout his entire career as a cryptanalyst – everything he touched turned to plain text, a sort of latter-day Midas. But since this luck was so consistent it couldn't have been luck; on the other hand, it must have been luck. He was a young man when he started, and therefore had the courage of his convictions and the boldness of youth. He started young enough not to be scared of the magnitude of the problems facing him: had he been a Ph.D. with three or four years' postgraduate training, he could have been ruined. His definition of a cryptogram was simply a secret message that was meant to be solved, just that. Time and again he *shouldn't* have been able to solve a particular message or a cryptosystem, but he did: the odds were against him, but luck was with him. That is, luck tempered by logical insight and remarkable intuition. Some of his early solutions may seem almost childish by present-day standards, but William Friedman was the first child of any age to arrive at those solutions.

He wasn't disturbed by the apparent odds against him: after all, even a simple substitution cipher in a literal system involves 26! (= 4.03 X 10^{26}) possible alphabets, and it can be demonstrated that, if there existed a computer capable of testing one million alphabets per second, even if we have a thousand of these computers it would take over one billion years to run the gamut of all the alphabets. He might have countered that, since there is a .5 probability of success halfway through, he would expect results after only 500 million years.

There is no least common denominator of what makes a brilliant cryptanalyst: he can be a mathematician, but he may just as likely be an archaeologist, a chemist, a biologist, a musician, a gambler, a painter, or a cook – in short, just about anything. Now Mr. Friedman's background in mathematics was slight: college freshman mathematics. Even if he computed odds incorrectly, it didn't make any difference because he would forge ahead in his blissful ignorance and solve the problem anyway. On several occasions he told me that if he had had more of a mathematical background, he might not have been able to solve some of the things he did. Mr. Friedman may not have been a mathematician, but he had superb mathematical feeling and insight, inventing techniques that were missed by mathematicians working on the problem. A classic example of his innovative abilities was in his solutions of the Hebern machine in 1923, the first solution in history of a wired-rotor cipher machine. He postulated that there were ninety-one billion alphabets involved when there were really only forty-five billion, and – in spite of his modest mathematical background – originated an important theory of coincidence and, with only ten messages, arrived at a solution of the machine.

I told Mr. Friedman of an anecdote I used to relate to the students in my classes as an example of his lack of mathematical profundity, but stressing to them that this had absolutely no bearing on his prowess as a cryptologist. In his 1923 work, *Elements of Cryptanalysi*s, he gave on p.105 three 72-letter transposition messages with the following footnote:

> As an example of a most remarkable coincidence, note the appearance of the word CIPHER in the cipher text of the third message. Theoretically, such an event will happen, as a result of chance, once in 266 (= 308,916,776) times. The word CIPHER does not appear in the plaintext message at all!

What Mr. Friedman did not note was (1) that the cipher texts did not approach the appearance of random text but were composed of a good assortment of letters as found in English plain text; (2) that, in calculating probabilities, he did not take into account in which message, nor at what position in that message, the word should be; and (3) that he was not even looking for that particular word in the first place. Mr. Friedman always got a charge when I related this anecdote. To offset this mathematical lapse, though, it must be remembered that his paper written in 1920, *The Index of Coincidence and Its Applications in Cryptography*, was the pioneer paper in cryptomathematics.

As a simple example of the perpetual luck which plagued him, a case may be cited of a 443-letter cryptogram submitted to the War Department for solution.[3] The cipher text factored to ten alphabets, and Mr. Friedman unerringly selected equivalents for plaintext E in some of the alphabets when the next highest cipher values were only one or two tallies less than the supposed E plain, and he derived five other values scattered sporadically in the cipher message. At this point he focused his attention on the beginning of the text, which he had thus far deciphered as _ _TTH_ _ _ _. It must begin, said Friedman, with the words BUT THOUGH – and it did. Well, I assure you, dear reader, that this will be the first and last time you will ever encounter a message beginning with BUT THOUGH: the Friedman luck paid off again.

Another unbelievable piece of luck occurred in 1917 when Mr. Friedman was at Riverbank Laboratories in Geneva, Illinois, where he was employed as a geneticist mating fruit flies (or rather, helping them to mate). The British knew of a geared disk cipher device invented much earlier by Sir Charles Wheatstone that was regarded as absolutely indecipherable if the sequences for both plain and cipher components were unknown. The British did not dare use it earlier in World War I, because if the Germans captured it they too would have the indecipherable cipher. But now, since the United States had entered the war, the British decided to use this device for joint U.S.-British communications since its indecipherability was acknowledged by both London and Washington. But somebody in Washington suggested that perhaps it might be wise to have the device tested by William Friedman at the Riverbanks Laboratories, which were operated by a wealthy eccentric named Colonel George Fabyan, who had a quasi-official relationship with the government.[4] Accordingly, five very short test messages – a most unrealistic test – were sent to Friedman, and by a process that remains a mystery to this day he was able to scrounge out from the cipher texts the sequence for the cipher component, a numerical-key columnar transposition-mixed sequence based on the word CIPHER. But now he was stumped, since he didn't quite know what to do next (it wasn't until 1923 that he discovered the principle of reduction to monoalphabetic terms, which would have made the problem a very simple one). But he called in one member of his staff, his wife Elizabeth, told her to give him the first word that occurred to her. He said "cipher," and she replied "machine." Sure enough, the plain component was a numerical-key columnar transposition-mixed sequence based on MACHINE. And one of the messages read, "This cipher is absolutely undecipherable." The solution went back to the British and, although 11,000 of the devices had been manufactured, they were never used.

Mr. Friedman returned to Riverbank Laboratories after the war: he had been in France as a member of the Code and Cipher Solving Section, G2 General Headquarters, American Expeditionary Forces. At Riverbank occurred a third example of how he was hounded by incredible luck. The AT&T Corporation had devised a very complicated cipher teleprinter, adjudged to be beyond the realm of solvability. But though (there, I did it!) the system was good indeed, there was still a Friedman to be reckoned with. Accordingly, a set of 150 cipher tapes was dispatched to Riverbank, and for six weeks, sometimes working twelve hours a day, Friedman and his staff of six studied the traffic. His staff was disheartened: this was the first time they had spent such a length of time on a system without solving it, and they wanted to quit. Friedman, though, was sure that his methods were correct — therefore was it not possible that either he or one of his assistants had made an error in transcribing the punched tapes into characters on paper? He asked them to hang on for one more week to review their work. Sure enough, in checking, he discovered that one character had indeed been omitted accidentally in transcribing one of the tapes – but that character was at a very crucial point. Within minutes, he made an entry into the plain text, and the system was solved.[5] To make the solution even more convincing, a punched tape was laboriously prepared by hand and sent to Washington with the proper indicators: when the tape was set on their machine and the message read, it gave the proof of the solution.

All of these wonders William Friedman accomplished without the benefit of any machine aids whatsoever. In fact, during Riverbank days he invented the very first mechanical cryptanalytic aid made in the U.S. It was called the "polyalphabetic wheel" and consisted of the twenty-six letters A through Z on a rubber-faced wheel that, when inked, could be used for running down the alphabet from a predesignated initial letter. The device was improved by assembling ten such wheels together so that the plain-component sequences could be completed on ten letters at a time, but this required the services of a muscular cryptanalyst to bear down on the roller.

On January 1, 1921, Mr. Friedman began a six-month contract with the U.S. Army Signal Corps to prepare cryptographic systems, and the contract was renewed for another six months. In 1922 he was hired as the sole cryptanalyst in the Signal Corps, with a cauliflower-eared ex-professional boxer as a secretary. Until April 1, 1930, the entire cryptologic organization of the U.S. Army consisted of only Mr. Friedman and one clerk typist. During that first week in April, the Signal Intelligence Section was expanded by the addition of three young high school mathematics teachers recruited by Mr. Friedman as junior cryptanalysts: Solomon Kullback, Frank Rowlett, and Abraham Sinkov, who were to remain in cryptologic work, making notable contributions for over three decades and rising to high positions in NSA and its predecessor organizations.[6]

An amusing story is connected with a challenge message submitted to the Signal Corps in 1933 by a New York lawyer representing his client, a poor devil who had bought, for $100,000, the North American rights to a cipher machine invented by Alexander von Kryha of Germany. The machine was touted by the inventor as absolutely indecipherable, and a German mathematician had demonstrated that the number of ways in which a message could be enciphered was 2.29×10^{82}, a figure 100 million times as large as the number of atoms in the universe. Friedman had studied the machine earlier, and had demolished it along with everything he studied. After an exchange of correspondence with the lawyer, Friedman told his superior that it might be a profitable training exercise for his subordinates if the 200-word challenge were accepted. Accordingly, the lawyer prepared a message enciphered on the machine, the alphabets and initial setting being secret. The message, in triplicate as requested, was on February 24, and date-stamped "Feb 24 AM 11:12," with the notation in Friedman's handwriting, "Commenced work. W.F.F ." And then over the date-time stamp "Feb 24 PM 2:43," was the cryptic notation, "Solved. W.F.F." Elapsed time: 3 hours and 31 minutes, less 50 minutes for lunch – 2 hours and 41 minutes! A letter with the decipherment and the keys was sent to the lawyer that afternoon. This solution in 2 hours and 41 minutes is remarkable not only because of the absence of any machine aids at that time,[7] but particularly so for the light it throws on Mr. Friedman's direction and organization of the cryptologic effort of his three assistants. As a result of this solution, the Signal Intelligence Section gained renewed respect and – far more important – recognition at the highest army levels and increased fiscal support.[8]

Cryptologic literature in the 1930s was woefully inadequate.[9] Mr. Friedman therefore embarked on a program of translating foreign works in the public domain, and of publishing technical reports of the solution of cryptosystems studied, in order to begin collecting a body of literature for training cryptanalysts in the years to come. As a consequence, during an eight-year period in the 1930s the members of the Signal Intelligence Section (numbering not more than eight at any one time, including student officers) wrote over sixteen books of expository technical works in cryptanalysis.[10] Friedman systematized the art, and unfolded the science in his classic four volumes, *Military Cryptanalysis, Parts I-IV*. When Kullback, Rowlett, and Sinkov were recruited, they spent their first two years with Mr. Friedman in a course of study, consisting of a series of cryptanalytic problems prepared by the latter; the textbook was

Elements of Cryptanalysis, then the finest work extant. In 1931 1st Lieutenant Mark Rhoads was assigned to Mr. Friedman for one year to learn all there was to know about cryptography and cryptanalysis. Towards the end of his year, Lieutenant Rhoads wrote a memo to the Chief Signal Officer saying that one year was insufficient to learn all there was to know about cryptology: it would take two years. Consequently, Rhoads was kept on for a second year and became the instructor for 1st Lieutenant W. Preston Corderman, who was assigned for a two-year tour. The Signal Intelligence School was formally established, and Lieutenant Corderman (later to become Chief, Army Security Agency) was the instructor for the next student, and so on for a number of student bodies consisting of two each. Thus was established the groundwork of scientific cryptanalytic training.

Friedman studied many proposals for cryptographic systems, embracing both manual and machine methods, demolishing everything that came his way. Good cryptographic ideas were hard to come by, as requirements were stiff and standards high. One machine that was studied, the IT&T cipher machine with ten large cam wheels for teleprinter encipherment, had a period of 8.65×10^{14}: the inventor and his sponsors claimed that cryptograms produced by the machine were practically, if not absolutely, indecipherable without the key. It took almost four years to construct the machine, at a cost of approximately $100,000 – but it took Friedman and his staff less than three hours to break it. In another case, an ingenious machine fractionated a plaintext letter into two parts, subjected these fractional parts to a complex substitution, and finally recombined the parts to produce a single cipher letter: this was a brilliant idea that did not long withstand Friedman's scrutiny. In addition to his ability to destroy everyone else's ciphers, Friedman was able to invent a number of cryptographic systems for his country that would withstand sophisticated attack by enemy cryptanalysts. For his inventions Congress in 1956 awarded him $100,000 in compensation for profits he might have realized if the patents had not been held secret by the government.

Because of Mr. Friedman's foresight and pioneering efforts in cryptanalysis, cryptanalytic training, data processing machine utilization, and cryptanalytic organization, the U.S. Army was fully prepared to meet the cryptologic challenges of World War II. Friedman took part in all these aspects during the war and continued to make notable contributions. After the war a most spectacular role of cryptanalysis was revealed in the hearings held by the joint congressional committee on the investigation of the Pearl Harbor attack. At that time it was made public that shortly before the war the United States, in a brilliant stroke of cryptanalysis, had been able to reconstruct the Japanese cipher machine which was used for the highest-level diplomatic communications, enabling this traffic to be read throughout the war. The successful solution of this machine, known by its cover name as the PURPLE machine, represented eighteen months of intensive study by a group of U.S. Army cryptanalysts under the direction of William F. Friedman.

Mr. Friedman continued after the war as Director, Communications Research, under whom I was privileged to work as an army officer. With the establishment of the Armed Forces Security Agency in 1949, he became Chief of the Technical Division, and I was once again working for him, but this time in civilian clothes. In 1952 the National Security Agency was created; he was now Technical Consultant to the Director, and two years later was named Special Assistant to the Director, the post he held until his retirement in 1955, after over thirty-five years of service with United States cryptologic activities.

EPILOGUE

His inventions and many achievements won for Mr. Friedman the nation's highest awards and a reputation as one of the world's leading cryptologists. In 1944 he was presented the War Department's highest decoration, the Exceptional

Civilian Service Award; in 1946 he was awarded the Presidential Medal for Merit; and in 1955 Mr. Allen Dulles, then Director of Central Intelligence, presented him the National Security Medal, the country's highest award for contributions to the national security. He was the author of many classified publications and training texts, of articles in scholarly journals, and of the articles on cryptology in the 1927 and 1954 editions of the *Encyclopaedia Britannica*. With his wife (who was for years a cryptologist with the Treasury Department), he wrote the book *The Shakespearean Ciphers Examined,* for which they were awarded the Folger Shakespeare Literary Prize and the Fifth Annual Award of the American Shakespeare Festival Theater and Academy.

On Sunday, November 2, 1969, William Frederick Friedman died quietly at his home in Washington, D.C., and was buried with full military honors in Arlington Cemetery. The legendary figure is with us still – in the works he left behind, in the science he created, and in the inspiration he bequeathed to his colleagues and friends.

NOTES

1. The way I got into the Cryptographic School was no accident. I paid a courtesy call on my New York City draft board complete with waxed mustache, goatee, big black hat, Chesterfield coat, spats, gloves, and cane, like something out of a Dumas novel. When I showed them the list of 40-some works on cryptology I had read in preparation for eventual military service, the board sent me to Army Headquarters in Church Street, and they in turn sent me to Governor's Island, where G-2 arranged for what I thought was to be Army service of one year in the Cryptographic School.

2. ."The Principles of Indirect Symmetry of Position in Secondary Alphabets and Their Application in the Solution of Poly alphabetic Substitution Ciphers," Office of the Chief Signal Officer, Washington, 1935.

3. L.D. Callimahos and W.F. Friedman, *Military Cryptanalytics, Part II*, 108-113.

4. Fabyan's title was an honorary colonelcy conferred by the governor of Illinois for Fabyan's participation as member of the Peace Commission that negotiated the Treaty of Portsmouth, which terminated the Russo-Japanese War in 1905. One of Fabyan's fields of interest was cryptography, and in the latter part of 1916 he established a Department of Ciphers at Riverbank, first headed by Miss Elizebeth Smith and later by Mr. Friedman, who took over both the Department and Miss Smith. The Department of Ciphers conducted cryptanalytic work for the State, War, Navy, and Justice Departments, since at the time none of these organizations had any cryptanalytic units whatsoever until the Army established a unit (under Herbert O. Yardley) in the latter part of 1917.

5. For Mr. Friedman's own account of this solution, see "Can Cryptologic History Repeat Itself?" *NSA Technical Journal*, Vol. XVIII, No.3, Summer 1973.

6. In selecting his personnel, Mr. Friedman picked the three persons from the civil service list who had made the highest scores on the mathematics examination.

7. It was not until 1936, after Mr. Friedman's continued insistence, that the Army obtained its first IBM data processing machines for cryptologic purposes.

8. For the story of this solution in detail, see L.D. Callimahos, "Q.E.D. – 2 Hours, 41 Minutes," *NSA Technical Journal*, Vol. XVIII, No.4, Fall 1973..

9. Cryptologic literature in the 1970s is woefully inadequate.

10. In a memorandum that I sent on June 14, 1960, to the Director of Training, NSA, I pointed out that by comparison NSA should have published 3,200 books in the last eight years, but that the true figure was less than sixteen, or one-half of one percent of the productivity of the early Army effort.

Lambros Callimahos won world renown as a flute virtuoso before serving in the Army cryptologic unit in World War II. He was technical assistant to Mr. Friedman, with whom he collaborated on the classic texts, *Military Cryptanalytics, Parts I-II*. He was the author of many monographs, studies, and articles, including one on cryptology in the *Encyclopaedia Britannica*. For over twenty years Mr. Callimahos taught the Agency's most advanced course in cryptanalysis, Intensive Study Program in General Cryptanalysis. At the time of his death in October 1977, Mr. Callimahos had taught 32 classes and over 270 students.

Breaking Codes Was This Couple's Lifetime Career

JAMES R. CHILES

[Editor's Note: This article, published in the *Smithsonian* magazine of June 1987, is republished with the permission of the author.]

Toward the end of World War I, the British Army began manufacturing thousands of small cipher machines, "Pletts Cryptographs," for use by the Allied forces. The British asked the American forces to use them as well. No one in the French, British, or American military had been able to break the ciphers; the machine had a mechanism that regularly altered the ciphering scheme, so the first *a* might be turned into an *f* and the next *a* into an *r*.

Just to be sure that it was safe from enemy codebreakers, the American military passed it on to a remarkable husband-and-wife team in Illinois for testing. William and Elizabeth Friedman received a package with five telegram-length messages. It took them all of three hours to break the lot, after which they returned them to London, solved. The first of the five messages read: "This cipher is absolutely indecipherable."

Few ciphers were ever indecipherable to the Friedmans. By the end of his life, William Friedman was recognized as the greatest maker and breaker of secret messages in history – the Harry Houdini of codes and ciphers. Repeatedly, he accepted challenges to solve "unbreakable" ciphers, and succeeded. The papers he wrote brought cryptology, an ancient skill as obscure as witchcraft, into the scientific age. The team he trained and supervised broke into Japan's highest diplomatic cipher just before World War II; not only did the group penetrate the secret, it built a deciphering machine that worked as well as Japan's cipher machine. Elizabeth Friedman provided exceptional assistance to the U.S. Coast Guard and Navy, unraveling secret messages from rumrunners during Prohibition, narcotics traffickers during the 1930s, and enemy agents during wartime. True to the shadowy world of intelligence work, the pair shunned publicity and avoided discussing their work – even with each other.

Neither had planned a career of codebreaking. In keeping with the strangeness of their profession, it all began at a peculiar place called Riverbank Laboratories. The Riverbank estate, located on the Fox River in a small suburb west of Chicago, was the magnificent hobby of Colonel George Fabyan, an eccentric millionaire who had retired from cotton trading early in the century. Here, on 600 well-kept acres, Fabyan's stable of hired scientists pursued whatever he found interesting or worthwhile, from sound waves to cryptology to plant genetics. In the evenings, they enjoyed the genteel life of the "minor idle rich," in Elizabeth's words. Other employees tended his greenhouses, livestock-breeding operation, Dutch windmill, Japanese garden, and caged vegetarian bears. A monkey and other pets had free access to Fabyan's house, which was also notable for its furniture hung from the ceiling by chains.

Eccentric millionaire George Fabyan built up a brain trust at Riverbank. [Photo as in file]

Fabyan, a large and loud man with iron-gray hair who wore frayed formal clothes in the city and a sort of horseman's outfit in the country, "had great natural gifts of energy and dynamism," the Friedmans wrote later. "He also had the trick of parroting other people's jargon; his conversation was usually impressive – superficially, anyway."

In the spring of 1915, Fabyan went hunting for a geneticist to improve crop strains. A professor at Cornell suggested William Friedman, a graduate student in genetics. Friedman, who had been born to a Russian Jewish family in 1891 and brought to America as an infant, was preparing for a future in biology. When Fabyan offered him the job, Friedman asked him what he raised on his estate. "I raise hell," Fabyan replied. Friedman signed on at a hundred dollars a month as head of Riverbank's Department of Genetics and began work the following September, taking up quarters in an upper floor of the windmill. In a short time Fabyan had him planting oats by the light of the moon, to see whether the phases made any difference.

The other half of the Friedman team, Elizabeth Smith, graduated from Hillsdale College in Michigan in 1915 with an English degree, and a year later sought work in Chicago. At the Newberry Library, a staff member mentioned to her that a George Fabyan was looking for somebody to study Shakespeare and offered to call him at his Chicago office. Fabyan arrived in his chauffeured limousine and insisted that Elizabeth come to the estate immediately. "He was the kind of man who did not take 'no' for an answer," she would reminisce. That evening she met Elizabeth Wells Gallup, a woman who had convinced Fabyan that Francis Bacon was the real author of Shakespeare's plays and sonnets and that Bacon had hidden a number of secret messages inside the original printed copies. Elizabeth agreed to assist Mrs. Gallup in this unusual project.

And so began the Friedmans' long involvement in the esoteric world of ciphers and codes. For most of the rest of us, here's the difference between the two: in a typical cipher (such as the Pletts Cryptograph solved by the Friedmans in 1918) each letter of the original message is changed into another letter or symbol according to some orderly scheme. To decipher the message, it helps to know that e is the most frequently used letter in English. With additional knowledge of the language and guesses based on the context of the emerging message, the rest of the alphabet follows.

Most ciphers, however, are vastly more complicated than a single substitution: e will be represented by different symbols at different points in the message. A basic way to accomplish this is to assign each letter of the alphabet a number: a is 1, b is 2, and so on. Then we add a key, a regularly repeating group of characters or words superimposed onto the message. Say we want to send the word "trouble," and our key is "fast." It works like this:

Message:

20(T)   18(R)   15(O)   21(U)   2(B)   12(L)   5(E)

Key:

6(F)   1(A)   19(S)   20(T)   6(F)   1(A)   19(S)

Total them:

26   19   34   41   8   13   24

. . . and you have a cipher that your nosiest neighbor probably couldn't break. Your cousin on the other end will know the key, subtract it, and then distill the message. But it wouldn't even make lunchtime recreation for a cryptologist, who would aim a barrage of statistics at it and solve it in minutes.

A code is different. A typical code takes ideas in the message – words or even whole phrases – and changes them into something else, usually groups of numbers taken out of a codebook resembling a small dictionary. To compose a coded message, the sender first writes what he intends to say ("Attack is imminent") and then looks up the words in his code book. "Attack" is 1140, and "imminent" is 4539. And that's his message: 11404539. To further confound the enemy, the sender might scramble the signal by using a key to encipher those numbers, by switching around the order, or both. The receiver must have an identical code book and know anything extra the sender has done to scramble the number groups.

Codes and ciphers go back many centuries. Ancient Greek commanders scrambled messages by wrapping a strip of parchment or leather around a tapered staff in a tight spiral and writing their message down the length of the staff; unwound, the strip displayed a jumble of illegible letter fragments. A few centuries later, Julius Caesar wrote to associates in a simple cipher that took each letter of the message and substituted the letter three places farther down in the alphabet. Islamic people were the first to figure out how to attack ciphers in an organized way. During the Renaissance many European countries began setting up full-time codebreaking bureaus, called black chambers, to try to read each other's messages.

In 1623 Francis Bacon contributed a new kind of cipher to this busy scene, one that used only the letters *a* and *b* to represent the entire alphabet. In the table he set out, *aaaaa* stood for A, *aaaab* for B, *aaaba* for C, and so on. He called it the biliteral alphabet, and described how it could be disguised in an ordinary paragraph by using two different type-faces: one typeface representing *a*, and the other *b*.

Which brings us to Elizabeth Wells Gallup's Bacon-as-Shakespeare theory. It rested on two piers: Bacon had indeed invented the biliteral cipher, and the original printed folios of Shakespeare's plays employed an odd variety of typefaces.

Mrs. Gallup believed herself able to take printed lines from the plays and identify each character as either an *a* or a *b* typeface. Consulting the table that Bacon had published in 1623, she transformed each group of five *a*'s and *b*'s into a letter of the alphabet. The revelations she concocted were voluminous – one-fifth the length of the plays themselves – and sensational. Bacon, she claimed, not only wrote the plays but also was an illegitimate son of Queen Elizabeth I and the rightful heir to the throne. She convinced Fabyan to spend thousands of dollars digging holes around London, hunting for buried manuscripts. (Decades later, the Friedmans presented evidence that demolished the hidden-message theory. The peculiar typefaces were due to the economical habits of English printers, who preferred to repair old type rather than replace it.)

William Friedman spent time on the Bacon project as a photographer, taking close-up pictures of typefaces. Then, over the winter of 1916-17, with the approach of war, he turned over his genetics work to an assistant and joined Elizebeth in studying everything they could find on secret writings. Not much was available: the American literature, for example, consisted of a couple of short works by military men, and two articles and a story by Edgar Allan Poe. "We had a lot of pioneering to do," Elizebeth wrote later. "Literary ciphers may give you the swing of the thing, but they are in no sense scientific. There were no precedents for us to follow." In May 1917 the two married.

Meanwhile, Fabyan was bringing in coded diplomatic messages from unfriendly powers; he had offered his services free to the government, which had accepted. For almost a year, until the creation of the Army's Cipher Bureau, Riverbank was the only organization in the country capable of working out secret messages.

Among the most interesting problems to arrive at the large cottage where the Riverbank codebreakers worked were the cases involving the Hindu plotters. The first case was delivered personally by an official of Scotland Yard, who carried an attaché case packed with dozens of intercepted letters. For several years the Germans had been encouraging the aspirations of independence held by Indian citizens, on the theory that any trouble

Indian radicals could stir up would siphon British strength from the war. Some of these radicals lived in the United States, and they had been passing cryptic messages around regarding arms shipments and internal politics.

One of the Hindu systems the couple broke into was a code that used numbers to indicate words and letters from a book that both sender and receiver had available. The cryptic number groups came in clusters of three, and the middle section always contained a 1 or a 2; that indicated a two-column page, probably a dictionary. The frequent use of some number groups indicated certain common words like "the" and "of." The first break was 99-2-14 in the code – page 99, the second column, the 14th word – which they concluded from context was "you." That led to 99-2-17, which the couple guessed was near enough in the dictionary to be "your." Eventually they managed to make out nearly every word without having the actual dictionary at hand. Still, it was important to somehow obtain the dictionary for the upcoming trial of 135 Hindus in San Francisco. The Riverbank group polled large numbers of booksellers without results. Finally, having arrived in San Francisco to testify at the trial, William went into a university bookstore in Berkeley. He described what he was seeking (which must have been quite interesting in itself), and an employee dug around and produced the second volume of a German-English dictionary published in 1880. A quick check of the pages showed that this was, indeed, the book.

By late 1917 the Army had created its own Cipher Bureau, and the flow of intercepts to Riverbank ended. Fabyan, determined to stay in the center of the action, arranged for the Friedmans to conduct classes in cryptography for Army officers.

Soon after the classes ended, William accepted a first lieutenant's commission in the Army and left for France. He spent the first five months of the war with General Pershing's staff, concentrating on breaking into the German codebooks. It was enough time to learn some important things about how armies employed codes and ciphers in wartime, and what could go wrong. For example, he observed that the German messages often began and ended with ritualized phrases, and that when a new code or cipher was introduced, the enemy's clerks were most likely to make a serious error (called a "bust" in the trade), exposing the system.

The following spring, William and Elizabeth returned to Riverbank. There William returned to the studies he had started before he left for Europe, which Fabyan issued as individual volumes in his Riverbank Publications series. In 1920 Friedman finished No. 22, titled *The Index of Coincidence and Its Applications in Cryptography*. This booklet, says David Kahn, author of *The Codebreakers*, "must be regarded as the most important single publication in cryptology. It took the science into a new world." Friedman went beyond simple counts of letter frequency to discover techniques for applying statistical methods to cryptanalysis.

If you take any two lines of English text and place one above the other, so that each letter lines up with the one above or below it, there will occasionally be places where the same two letters appear in a vertical column. Friedman found that, for English, this coincidence consistently occurs in 6.67 columns out of every 100, or about seven percent of the time. He also found that this rate, the Index of Coincidence, is unique for each language. Such information can be very useful to a cryptanalyst with several enciphered messages from the same source. Usually these ciphers would be created using the same key, but the sender will have enciphered each message by starting at a different place in the key, according to some rule previously arranged between him and the receiver. Using the Index of Coincidence, the cryptanalyst can place the messages one above the other and, by sliding them back and forth, find the right "fit" – an indication that the key in the top message is vertically aligned with the same key in all the messages below it. Once the messages are aligned according to their key, he can work from message to message knowing that each letter in a vertical column has been enciphered with the same key letter as all the other letters in that column.

Shortly after this breakthrough, the Army offered to employ the Friedmans as civilian "code experts" for a six-month trial period. With a few wary glances backward at Fabyan, wondering whether his tenacious grasp would reach to Washington, they left Riverbank for good and started military contract work in Washington, D.C., early in 1921.

In 1922, the War Department hired William permanently as chief codebreaker. Over the next few years he solved several "unbeatable" ciphers produced by machines. One of these, developed by Edward Hebern, foretold the hellish complicated cipher machines that would dominate the next two decades. It used five movable rotors to scramble electrical signals between a keyboard and a set of glow lamps showing the enciphered letters. William had to determine the ciphering scheme and then reconstruct much of the internal wiring. "He was discouraged to the point of blackout," Elizabeth said later. "Probably he sat for six weeks before he thought of a way to attack it... It was all resolved in the end by the Index of Coincidence."

The Hebern solution was particularly important, says Louis Kruh, coauthor of *Machine Cryptography and Modern Cryptanalysis*, because that machine "introduced a whole new concept of encipherment. It was the forerunner of any decent cipher machine between then and beyond World War II. Some of the report that he wrote on the solution is still classified today."

The best way to appreciate the codebreaker's trade is to attack a secret message. The following cipher uses letter-for-letter substitution, and all punctuation and word spacing have been preserved. You will have to tabulate the cipher letters by how often they occur, and then guess at the plaintext letters they stand for. The way to do this is to compare the frequency of the cipher letters to the frequency of letters in common English. On average, the most common letter in English is E, followed by T, O, A, N, I, R, S, H, D, L, U, C, M, P, F, Y, W, G, B, V, K, J, X, Z and finally Q. Try to identify the most common letters first, then fill in the rest by context.

```
ZSOU OU D UDEGVF KA KLPOCDLX FCYVOUS.
___  __ _ _____ __ _____ _____
RBZ PKC'Z DUUBEF ZSDZ DVV FCYVOUS EBUZ
___ _____ _____ ____ ___ _____ ____
AKVVKI ZSF VFZZFL - ALFMBFCNX NKBCZU.
_____ ___ _____ _ _____ _____
AKL OCUZDCNF, DC DBZSKL CDEFP FLCFUZ
___ _____, __ _____ _____ _____
JOCNFCZ ILOYSZ ILKZF D ABVV - VFCYZS
_____ _____ _____ _ ____ _ _____
CKJFV ZOZVFP YDPURX IOZSKBZ BUOCY ZSF
_____ _____ _____ _____ _____ ___
VFZZFL F DUOCYVF ZOEF. ZSOU OCNLFPORVF
_____ _ _____ ____  ____ _____
AFDZ SDU CKZ RFFC PBGVONDZFP. ZK
____ ___ ___ ____ _____. __
DGGLFNODZF ILOYSZ'U DNSOFJFEFCZ, ZLX
_____ _____ _____, ___
ILOZOCY D CKZF ZK D ALOFCP IOZSKBZ
_____ _ ____ __ _ _____ _____
BUOCY ZSF VFZZFL F.
_____ ___ _____ _.
```

(For the solution, see page 201)

The latter part of that decade was exciting for Elizebeth. Her code breaking began in earnest in 1927 as a "special agent" on loan from the Department of Justice to the Coast Guard, which was struggling to enforce the Volstead Act against a flood of smuggled shipborne liquor from the Bahamas, Canada, and elsewhere.

The rumrunners' system required radio communications for rendezvous points, warnings, and prices. It was this encoded and enciphered radio traffic that Elizebeth attacked. The early messages were elementary and quick to break. But as time went on and profits climbed, larger and more sophisticated syndicates took over the distribution network, and coding systems became more and more elaborate. In the first three years she and her assistants solved 12,000 messages using dozens of different schemes. In 1934 her decoding, and the detective work it inspired, cleared up a major diplomatic problem between the United States and Canada dating to 1929. She proved from old telegrams that the *I'm Alone*, a Canadian-flag schooner shelled and sunk by the Coast Guard in the Gulf of Mexico, had been secretly owned by an American smuggling ring.

Elizebeth, now working for the Treasury Department, was a star witness in a large and expensive trial in New Orleans of top officials of a Canadian outfit that controlled most of the liquor smuggling via the Gulf of Mexico and the Pacific She deciphered and decoded cryptic radio messages that made prosecution possible.

The Friedman family, which by now included a son and a daughter, was aware that their mother's contact with organized crime had its dangers. Recalls daughter Barbara Atchison, "I remember Dad jesting once, when Mother was late getting home, that she might have been taken for a ride." And, in fact, while the *I'm Alone* case was under way, agents of the Treasury Department kept her under constant protection. Elizebeth broke open the code-ciphers used by narcotics smugglers. Her contributions to several sensational trials, and the associated convictions, earned her much unwanted attention from the press: "U.S. Woman Helps Smash Drug Ring" and "Key Woman of the T-Men," read two headlines.

War came and her work changed again. She devised a code system for William (Wild Bill) Donovan as he was organizing the Office of Strategic Services, and deciphered messages from German spies in Allied lands.

All this time William had been equally busy, but his work was well hidden from public view. In 1930 his responsibilities changed abruptly from the bookish work of composing codes. It was prompted by the closing of the Black Chamber, a cooperative codebreaking effort of the State Department and the Army that had evolved from the Army's old Cipher Bureau. The Black Chamber had decoded messages between Tokyo and the Japanese embassy, and in early 1929 Herbert Hoover's new secretary of state, Henry Stimson, had removed his department's funding upon hearing about it. Years later, in his autobiography, he justified his action by saying that diplomats should not engage in such activities because "gentlemen do not read each other's mail." The Army quietly transferred the activities from the State Department to a new unit in the War Department, the Signal Intelligence

Elizebeth leaves D.C. home to testify against smugglers whose codes she cracked.

Service (SIS). Friedman took charge as chief civilian cryptanalyst.

One of William's principal tasks was to train a new generation of experts to make and break codes, because all of the Black Chamber's personnel had dispersed. He started in the spring of 1930 with four spaces. He selected Frank Rowlett, a teacher from a small town in Virginia; Solomon Kullback and Abraham Sinkov, mathematicians from New York City; and John Hurt, the nephew of a congressman and an expert in Japanese.

The new team combed the files of the Black Chamber for useful information on Japanese cryptology. They read Friedman's booklets and worked through problems he concocted. He gave them assignments such as solving the Hebern cipher machine. "His teaching was such that we developed on our own," recalls Abraham Sinkov. "He just looked in from time to time to see how we were doing."

They operated on slim budgets – bringing their own pencils and writing on the back of old weather reports to save paper – but within two years they had progressed enough for Friedman to present them with the real thing: encrypted radio communications between Japanese diplomats.

By this time the Japanese knew that America had been reading secret diplomatic radio traffic. To protect its highest-level communications, Japan quickly switched to the new electromechanical cipher machine, "Angooki Taipu A," or "Red" to the Americans. It used a combination of wheels, rings, and a rotor to scramble clear messages into a complex cipher. In 1935 the Army ordered Friedman's group to concentrate on breaking the system; by 1936 they were able to read the messages.

The passion for cryptology spilled over into the Friedmans' home life. William created a cipher game for children called "The Game of Secrecy" and tried it out on his son, John. He printed holiday greeting cards with cipher messages.

The most inventive of these pastimes were the progressive dinner parties hosted by the Friedmans. They divided their guests – a unique blend of codebreakers, newspapermen and scientists – into teams, and held the first course at one restaurant. "While they were eating, the restaurant owner gave them a piece of paper containing a clue about the next place to go," recalls John Friedman. "They'd go to five or six restaurants. . . The first team to return home, won a prize."

William amused his children with enigmatic behavior. "He would come down to Sunday breakfast with six different ties on," remembers his daughter, Barbara, "He had a terrific sense of humor and whimsy, and women absolutely adored him."

Friedman had to leave most of his social life behind, however, when the Japanese decided to replace the the Red machine with something much more secure. Labeled "Purple" by the SIS, the machine first contributed messages to Japan's radio circuits in February 1939. Unlike its predecessors, Purple used a type of switch identical to those used in automatic telephone exchanges to accomplish the main work of the encipherment.

While dozens of others did the detailed statistical analysis necessary, William labored alone in his office on portions of the problem. He worked obsessively. The fear of failure – of what the Japanese were up to behind the screen of Purple – followed him home every night. "He'd be up until two or three in the morning," Elizabeth recalled later. "Sometimes I'd awaken and find him down in the kitchen making a Dagwood sandwich in the middle of the night." She remembered that her husband never discussed his difficulties with Purple, not even on the day in the fall of 1940 when the deciphering first succeeded. (For years, all he would tell his son, John, about his job was that he "worked for the Army.")

The team spent a total of eighteen months puzzling out the mechanism and the nest of wiring from their calculations on how the original machine converted plaintext to cipher. Then, out of $684.65 worth of parts, they went ahead and built their own reconstruction of the Purple machine.

The Purple disclosures (codenamed "Magic") proved extremely valuable during the war. Ironically, says David Kahn, Magic "had its greatest effect on the war against Germany, not Japan, became we were getting a great deal of information that the Japanese ambassador in Berlin was sending back to Tokyo." For example, the ambassador, Baron Oshima, described Germany's new jet fighters in detail, and he listed German troop strength in the Balkans. Oshima even cabled a close description of the Normandy defenses in late 1943. Unfortunately, Magic did not clearly reveal the Japanese intention to attack Pearl Harbor – signals only indicated an impending crisis between America and Japan.

Codebreaking definitely changed the course of the war. The Allies made three major breakthroughs in all: the Japanese diplomatic cipher, Purple; the main German military cipher called "Enigma," which was broken by the Polish and British; and the Japanese fleet code, broken by the U.S. Navy, which made possible many American victories including the Battle of Midway. What made the breaking of Purple so extraordinary, says author Louis Kruh, is that the SIS had no pieces of the machine to study. When the team studied genuine Purple components after the war; he adds, they found that, out of all the thousands of soldered connections, "only two wiring connections turned out to have been interchanged."

Due largely to overwork on Purple, William suffered a mental breakdown at the turn of the year, and spent the next three months recovering in Walter Reed Hospital. Though the hospital recommended he return to duty, shortly afterward the Army discharged him from service. He served out the war as a civilian, organizing attacks on new cipher systems and rapidly training more cipher personnel.

"The war years were horrendous," recalls his daughter. "He was very, very involved in his work. I remember being worried to death about Dad." Attacks of depression severe enough to require psychiatric treatment or hospitalization would return again.

Wartime associates remember William as demanding and brilliant. "When working on a problem," recalls Frank Rowlett, "he was inclined to develop a plan of attack which he usually followed meticulously until the problem was either solved or it could be established that the attack would not be successful. His memory was excellent and he had a most unusual ability to grasp the complexity of a problem." Lambros Callimahos, a concert flutist who became a codebreaker in 1942, remembered Friedman as the "dapper figure with the Adolphe Menjou mustache, the characteristic bow tie, and the two-tone black-and-white shoes." Friedman was notoriously meticulous, even to the point of keeping carbon copies of handwritten notes. Judy Friedman, his daughter-in-law, remembers her first weekend visit with the family. John had forewarned her that if his father failed to criticize her language, that meant she hadn't made the grade. Throughout the weekend, there was not a single comment from William about her speech. Judy was crushed. Then, upon leaving the house, he leaned close and whispered, "My dear, you made five grammatical errors this weekend," and proceeded to elaborate on them. Nothing could have pleased her more.

After the war, the Army restored William's rank and he served as a top-ranking cryptanalyst in the various agencies leading up to the present National Security Agency (NSA). In 1956 Congress awarded him $100,000, partly in compensation for many of his inventions that were so sensitive and useful that the military had kept them off the market. One of these, a mechanism he had developed with Frank Rowlett, was the basis of the SIGABA machine, which the U.S. military used as its top-level enciphering device during World War II. The Axis never penetrated its messages.

William retired officially from the NSA in 1955 but continued to undertake various special and highly secret missions. His relations with the NSA were stormy at times; he believed the Agency sometimes mistreated him and that it snooped excessively into citizens' communications. The NSA, in turn, occasionally saw him as a security risk; in 1958 three NSA employees appeared at his Capitol Hill house and carried off a stack of papers.

Elizabeth finished her professional career as a consultant for the International Monetary Fund, setting up a secure communications system there.

Toward the end of their careers (William died in 1969 and Elizebeth in 1980), the couple returned to the unlikely project that had first seduced them into the world of cryptography – the Shakespeare problem. Their incisive book, titled *The Shakespearean Ciphers Examined*, won them a Folger Shakespeare Library award in 1955. And in a classic demonstration of their life's work, Elizebeth and William Friedman included a hidden biliteral cipher on page 257 of the book. Buried in an italicized phrase, using two different typefaces, is their final verdict about the whole controversy: "I did not write the plays. F. Bacon."

Solution to cipher on page 197:

This is a sample of ordinary English. But don't assume that all English must follow the letter-frequency counts. For instance, an author named Ernest Vincent Wright wrote a full-length novel titled *Gadsby* without using the letter E a single time. This incredible feat has not been duplicated. To appreciate Wright's achievement, try writing a note to a friend without using the letter E.

Elizebeth Smith Friedman
1892-1980

Editor's Note: Reprinted from the Special Issue of *Cryptologic Spectrum*, December 1980.

Elizebeth Smith Friedman, the widow of William F. Friedman and herself a pioneer in U.S. cryptology, died on 31 October 1980 in Plainfield, New Jersey, at the age of 88. Coauthor (with her husband) of *The Shakespearean Ciphers Examined* and author of many technical papers, she was employed at various times by the U.S. Treasury Department, the U.S. Army, the U.S. Navy, the Canadian government, and the International Monetary Fund. Mrs. Friedman served the U.S. as a cryptologist in both World Wars, and in the period between she won distinction for her work on international drug and liquor smuggling cases.

The youngest of nine children of John M. Smith, a Quaker dairyman and banker, and his wife Sopha Strock Smith, Mrs. Friedman was born in Huntington, Indiana, in 1892.[1] She attended Wooster College briefly and graduated from Hillsdale College in Michigan, where she majored in English.

While working at the Newberry Library in Chicago in 1916, Mrs. Friedman was recruited by George Fabyan to work on his 500-acre estate – Riverbank – at Geneva, Illinois, to aid Mrs. Elizabeth Wells Gallup in her attempt to prove that Sir Francis Bacon wrote Shakespeare's plays and sonnets. Fabyan, a wealthy textile merchant who maintained laboratories in acoustics, chemistry, and genetics, had established a Department of Ciphers, which consisted of a staff of fifteen who lived on the estate.

It was at Riverbank that Elizebeth Smith met William F. Friedman, head of Fabyan's Department of Genetics at the time. They were married in May 1917 and worked together at Geneva, the only cryptologic laboratory in the country, solving messages that government agencies sent from Washington. During World War I, they developed courses in cryptology and trained U.S. Army officers and civilians.

After William Friedman's service with the American Expeditionary Force in Europe, the Friedmans returned to Riverbank, but in 1921 they moved to Washington where they both were employed by the War Department.

It was Elizebeth Friedman's own work for various branches of the government that brought her to prominence, first as assistant cryptanalyst for the War Department in 1921-22 and then as cryptanalyst for the U.S. Navy in 1923, which led to her work for the U.S. Treasury Bureau of Prohibition and Bureau of Customs. Most of her professional career was spent working against such international enterprises as smuggling and drug running. She broke up criminal syndicates and interrupted millions of dollars worth of illegal business. Although her work itself was not dangerous, on several occasions when she was called to testify, the government supplied her with bodyguards.

Her early career began during the era of Prohibition, when rumrunners turned to radio and encoded messages to control their offshore operations. Mrs. Friedman was established in the Coast Guard office in Washington, D.C., to work on rumrunners' traffic. In her first three years she solved 12,000 messages as special agent of the Bureau of Foreign Control, originally in the Department of Justice. In 1928 she was transferred to the Customs Investigative Service in the Bureau of Customs,

Treasury Department, which eventually became the Bureau of Narcotics.

During 1928-30 her cases centered on smuggling operations in the Gulf of Mexico and on the Pacific Coast. She appeared as an expert witness in several cases in Galveston and Houston, Texas, and in New Orleans, Louisiana. In 1933 she was the star prosecution witness in the New Orleans Federal Court as cryptanalyst for the Coast Guard, testifying to her solutions of messages from the Consolidated Exporters Company, Prohibition's largest and most powerful bootlegging ring – messages that connected ringleaders to the actual operations of the rum-running vessels. Her evidence at the trial indicted thirty-five rumrunners for conspiracy to violate the National Prohibition Act.

Her arguments for the establishment of a seven-man cryptanalytic section at headquarters was approved by Congress in 1931, and in the following years she solved not only bootlegging messages but also those of other highly organized smuggling gangs.

Another outstanding case involved messages of opium dealers. In 1937 the Canadian government sought her help. She went to Vancouver to testify in the trial of Gordon Lim and several other Chinese. Their secret messages dealing with opium smuggling were cast in a complicated system involving a code she solved without knowing Chinese. They were convicted and sentenced to seven years' imprisonment, where, as a Pacific Coast columnist observed, they would have plenty of time "to devise a code that a woman couldn't break."

In 1934 some of her solutions helped to extricate the United States from an embarrassing diplomatic tangle in the *I'm Alone* case, establishing a point of international law. The ship, built in Canada for the liquor trade, was sighted by a Coast Guard cutter on 23 March 1929, near the Louisiana coast. When the *I'm Alone* refused to honor the "heave to and be searched" signals, the cutter chased it into international waters and sank it with its Canadian flag still flying. Members of the crew were rescued, but for the loss of the vessel and its cargo, the Canadian government filed a claim against the United States for $365,000, based on the presumption that vessel and cargo were Canadian owned. American officials contended that the *I'm Alone* belonged to New Yorkers. International sentiments were aroused, and the U.S. embassy in Paris was stormed as a result of what was considered American high-handedness. However, with Elizebeth Friedman's decryption of twenty-three coded messages subpoenaed from telegraph company files addressed from Belize, British Honduras, to an unregistered code address in New York, the mystery was solved, the owner of the ship captured, and American ownership fully established.

Another case in which Mrs. Friedman's solutions proved crucial was the Doll Woman Case, solved in 1944. Mrs. Velvalee Dickinson, an antique doll dealer in New York City, was eventually found guilty of spying for the Japanese government. Suspicion of her activities while a member of the Japanese-American Society arose from a letter containing coded information hidden in obscure phrases about naval vessel movement in Pearl Harbor.

After her service as a cryptologist with the government in World War II, Mrs. Friedman, working as a consultant, created communications security systems for the International Monetary Fund.

The Friedmans' earlier interest in Shakespeare led to a lifelong battle against the doctrine supported by invalid decipherments of Shakespeare's plays, which others used to attempt to prove that Bacon was the author. They collaborated on a manuscript entitled "The Cryptologist Looks at Shakespeare," subsequently published as *The Shakespearean Ciphers Examined*, which won awards from the Folger Shakespeare Library (1955) and the American Shakespeare Theater and Academy. In this work, the Friedmans dismissed such Baconians as Mrs. Gallup and Mr. Ignatius Donnelly with a combination of technical skill and literary grace that won the book recognition far beyond those interested in the subject. It is generally regarded as the definitive work on the subject, if not the final word.

In 1938 Mrs. Friedman received an honorary LL.D. from Hillsdale College.

After her husband's death in 1969, Mrs. Friedman spent her retirement compiling a bibliography of his work and library for presentation to the George C. Marshall Research Library in Lexington, Virginia. It is considered the most extensive private collection of cryptologic material in the world.

NOTES

1. The spelling of Mrs. Friedman's first name was chosen by her mother, who wanted no one to call her daughter "Eliza."

Index

ADFGVX Cipher: 109-112
Advancement of Learning, The: 29, 172, 183
AEF Staff Code: 127
Aeneas Taciticus: 20
Alberti, Leon Battista: 140-141
Alexander, General E. P.: 25, 48, 55, 61, 73, 75, 86-87, 191
Alexander, General J. H.: 87
Alfred the Great: 21
American Black Chamber, The: 95, 98-99, 184
American Expeditionary Forces (AEF) cryptosystems, WW I: 124
American Lake Series (codes): 125
American River Series (codes): 125
American Shakespeare Theater and Academy Award: 206
American Telephone and Telegraph (AT&T) Company: 162, 165-166, 190
Andre, Major John: 38
Archbishop of Naples: 22
Arlington Hall Station: 185
Armed Forces Security Agency: 192
Army Cipher Bureau (See Cipher Bureau)
Army Security Agency: 170, 185, 192
Army Signal Corps: 56, 134, 191
Arnold, Benedict: 38-39
Arnold, General Hap: 170
Atchison, Barbara Friedman: 200
AT&T (See American Telephone and Telegraph Company)
Bacon, Sir Francis: 14, 29-33, 139, 160, 183, 196-197, 203, 205-206
Bakeless, Colonel John: 35-39, 183
Barker, Captain William N.: 76
Bates, David Homer: 67-68, 84-86, 183
Battle of Tannenberg: 25, 123-124
Baudot Code: 160
Bazeries, Commandant: 105, 146, 148, 183
Beckwith: 59, 86
Bell Telephone Laboratories: 17

Benjamin, Judah P.: 35, 42, 58, 77
Biblical ciphers: 20
Bi-literaire Alphabet: 31
Biliteral cipher (Bacon): 32, 197
Blackstone, Sir William: 35
Booth, John Wilkes: 77
Bradley, General Omar: 133, 170, 183
Breasted, James Henry: 17
Bridges, Philip: 78-79
British Black Chamber: 112, 115
Brown, J. Willard: 66, 80-84, 87, 183-184
Budge, Dr. E.A. Wallis: 46, 48, 183
Buell, Major General D.C.: 79-80, 130
Bureau of Customs: 205
Bureau of Foreign Control: 205
Bureau of Narcotics: 206
Bureau of Prohibition: 205
Burnside, Major General Ambrose E.: 84-85
Byrd, William: 13
Caesar, Julius: 21, 197
Caesar, Augustus: 30-31
Callimahos, Lambros: 194, 202
Cameron, Simon: 57, 64, 67
Carnet Reduit: 118
Cartouches: 46-48
Casablanca Conference: 137
Chamberlin, General: 6
Champollion, Jean Francois: 43, 46, 51, 183
Charlemagne: 21
Charles the First: 21, 29
Church, Dr. Benjamin: 35
Churchill, Brigadier General Marlborough: 164
Churchill, Winston: 170, 176
Cicero: 21
Cifax: 11, 166-167
Cifrario Militare Tascabile: 121
Cipher Bureau: 27, 110, 197-198, 200
Cipher Device, Type M-94: 148
Cipher-Machine Company of Berlin: 153

Ciphers: 7-9, 19, 22-24, 26, 28, 30, 33, 35-36, 52, 55-56, 61, 63-64, 67-69, 73-76, 80, 84, 87, 91-92, 94-96, 98-100, 105, 108, 108-110, 112, 118, 121, 123, 130, 135, 140, 145, 167, 170, 183-184, 192-193, 195-200, 203, 205-206
Ciphony: 11, 166-167
Civision: 11
Clarke, Colonel Carter W.: 135, 174, 178-181
Cleopatra: 46-48
Clinton, Sir Henry: 35-42
Clock Cipher: 21
Coast Guard: 148-149, 195, 200, 205-206
Code and Cipher Solving Section: 109, 190
Code and Cipher Systems, Revolutionary War: 35-36
Code and Signal Section (Navy): 167
Code Compilation Service: 125
Codes: 4, 6-9, 9, 25, 27, 35, 52, 55-56, 61, 70-71, 76, 82, 84, 97-100, 109-110, 113-118, 121, 124-125, 127, 130, 134-135, 138, 165, 170, 178-179, 183-184, 188, 195-198, 200-201
COMINT: 6, 10-11, 134-136, 139, 169, 180
Communications and Records Division (Department of State): 9, 91, 95, 149, 165
COMSEC: 10-11, 133-134, 137, 169-170
Confederate cipher systems: 74-75
Confederate Signal Corps: 55, 58, 61, 63, 75, 86, 140
Confederate States Cipher Key: 73
Converter M-134: 158-159
Converter M-209: 160
Coral Sea, Battle of: 5, 173, 178, 180, 184
Corderman, W. Preston: 192
Court Ciphers: 24
Cryppy, Dr.: 3, 43
Cryptanalysis: 6, 10, 13, 15, 17, 23, 44, 48, 87, 81, 101, 106, 112, 115, 124-125, 133, 137, 166-167, 169, 170, 185-187, 189, 191-192, 194, 198-199
Cryptogram: 3, 7-10, 13, 15, 72, 78-79, 85, 105, 112, 189
Cryptographe B-21: 151
Cryptographe Cylindrique: 146
Cryptographer: 7
Cryptographic Clerk: 7-8
Cryptographic devices, history and development: 25, 133, 140
Cryptography: 3, 6-8, 13, 15, 17, 19-25, 27, 37, 42, 48, 50-52, 60, 64, 77, 86-87, 91-92, 99, 102, 108-109, 115, 123, 125, 133, 140, 169, 183-184, 189, 192, 198-199, 203
"Cryptologist Looks at Shakespeare, The": 206

Cryptology: 1-7, 9-11, 14-15, 17, 22-23, 27, 29, 33, 36, 43, 51-52, 56, 60, 64, 91, 95, 100, 105, 107, 115-117, 121-122, 124-125, 133, 137, 139-140, 170, 185, 192-195, 198, 201, 205
CSP-1515: 166
Davis, President Jefferson: 75, 80
De Augmentis Scientiarum (Bacon): 31, 183
Deciphering: 4, 7-8, 13, 20, 24, 51, 67, 70, 80, 83, 93, 105, 118, 122-124, 127, 153, 164, 178, 195, 201
Decrypt: 7, 17
Demotic Script: 44
Deuxieme Bureau: 112
Dewey, Admiral George: 4, 102, 135, 171, 173-175, 177, 179-180
Dewey, Governor Thomas E.: 173-174, 177
Dickinson, Velvalee: 206
Division Field Codes: 165
Doll Woman Case: 206
Donnelly, Ignatius: 206
Donovan, William: 179, 200
Drioton, Prof. Étienne: 50, 52, 54, 183
ECM (Electric Cipher Machine) Mark II: 158
ECM-SIGABA: 158-159, 166, 202
Egyptian Hieroglyphics: 43, 46, 48, 50-51, 183
Elements of Cryptanalysis: 187, 189, 192
ELINT: 10-11
Encoder: 8
Encoding: 8, 24, 42, 115, 178
Enciphering: 7-8, 14, 24, 63, 76, 86, 97, 102, 116, 118, 122, 125, 141, 153, 161, 163, 187, 202
Encrypt: 7-8
ENIGMA: 153-156, 202
Fabyan, Colonel George: 107-109, 140, 163-164, 190, 195-199, 205
Falconer, James: 64, 183
Federal Signal Corps: 61, 78, 87
Feis, Dr. Herbert: 136
Field Codes No.1, 2, 3: 109, 116-118, 125, 130, 165, 183
"Field Codes used by the German Army During the World War": 109, 118
Fishel, Edwin C.: 76, 78
Folger Shakespeare Library Award: 203
Franklin, Benjamin (cipher system): 35, 42
French Army Cipher Bureau: 110, 118-119, 146
French Black Chamber (See Deuxieme Bureau)

French cryptosystems, WWI: 24-25, 28, 42-43, 95-96, 105, 110, 112, 115, 118-119, 124, 130, 144, 146, 195
Freeman, Douglas S.: 83
Friedman, Barbara (See Atchison, Barbara Friedman)
Friedman, John: 201
Friedman, Judy: 202
Front Line Code: 125
Galileo: 13
Gallup, Elizabeth Wells: 196-197, 205-206
Garamond: 32
GEHEIMKLAPPE: 116
George C. Marshall Research Library: 207
George III: 29
German Code and Cipher Solving Section: 109
German diplomatic codes, WWI: 113-115, 184
German military cryptocommunications, WW I: 115
Gerow, Lieutenant General Leonard T.: 175, 179
Givierge, General: 112
Grant, General Ulysses S.: 59, 72-74
Greely, General A.W.: 99
Greene, Major General Nathaniel: 41
Gregory, Colonel J. F.: 97-98, 183
Gripsholm Castle: 21
Grosvenor, Colonel William M.: 92
Gylden, Yves: 115
Hagelin, Boris: 159-160
Halleck, Major General H. W.: 79-80, 82, 130
Halsey, Fleet Admiral William F.: 138
Hassard, John R.G.: 92-94, 183
Haswell, John H.: 93, 182
Hatted Code: 71, 115, 117, 125
Hayes-Tilden election: 91-92
Hebern, Edward H.: 199
Hebern Cipher Machine: 201
Hitt, Captain Parker: 108-109, 146-148, 165, 184
Holden, Professor Edward S.: 92-94, 98, 112, 184
House, Colonel Edward M.: 9
Howe, General William: 35
Hull, Cordell: 136, 184
Huntington, S.H.: 141, 205
Hurt, John: 201
Huygens: 13
I'm Alone Case: 200, 206
Imprint: 33
Index of Coincidence and Its Applications in Cryptography, The: 189, 198

International Business Machines (IBM): 167-168
International Monetary Fund: 203, 205-206
International Telephone and Telegraph (IT&T) Company: 165
Jefferson Papers: 105, 148
Jefferson's Wheel Cypher: 105
Jefferson, Thomas: 42, 105
Johnston, J.E., General: 80
Joint Congressional Committee on the Investigation of the Pearl Harbor Attack: 5, 133, 173, 175, 192
Kahn, David: 198, 202
Kaiski, Major: 103, 105
Key: 7, 9-10, 28-29, 31, 35, 39, 41-42, 63-64, 73, 75-76, 84-85, 87, 92-96, 107, 111-112, 114, 116, 122, 124, 146, 149, 151, 153-155, 160-166, 170, 180, 185, 190, 192, 196, 198, 200
Kimmel, Admiral Husband E.: 136, 184
King, Admiral Ernest J.: 174, 177, 180
King's General Cipher: 24
Knepper, Captain Edward W.: USN: 41
Kruh, Louis: 199, 202
Kryha Machine: 149
Kullback, Solomon: 186, 191, 201
Lake Series (See American Lake Series)
Lavinde, Gabriele: 22
Lim, Gordon: 206
Lincoln, President Abraham: 75, 84
Louis XIII: 24
Louis XIV: 25
Louis XV: 25
Louis XVI: 25
Lovell, James: 41
M-94 (See Cipher Device Type M-94)
M-134 (See Converter M-134)
M-138A (See Strip Cipher Device Type, M-138A)
MacArthur, General Douglas: 6
MAGIC: 5-6, 10, 57, 136, 168-169, 173-175, 203
Majority Report (See Joint Congressional Committee on the Investigation of the Pearl Harbor Attack)
Maltese Inquisitor: 26
Manly, Captain John M.: 148
Mark II (See ECM Mark II)
Marshall-Dewey Letters: 177
Marshall, General George C.: 4, 177, 207
Mary, Queen of Scots: 27
Masonic Cipher: 38

Mauborgne, Major General J. O.: 109, 146-148, 164, 184
McClellan, General: 64
Mendelsohn, Captain Charles J.: 113
Michigan Papyrus: 51
Midway, Battle of: 103, 136, 169-171, 202
Miles, Major General Sherman: 136, 175
Military Cryptanalysis, Parts I-IV: 187, 191
Military Cryptographic Service (Russian WWI): 25, 121-124, 196
Military Telegraph Corps (See USMTC)
Minority Report (See Joint Congressional Committee on the Investigation of the Pearl Harbor Attack)
Monoalphabetic substitution: 23, 35-36, 86
Morehouse, L.F.: 172
Moorman, Colonel Frank: 117
Morison, Admiral Samuel Eliot: 136, 184
Myer, Brigadier General Albert J.: 55-56, 60
Naples, Archbishop of: 22
Napoleon: 25, 43
Napoleonic Code: 7
Naval Security Group: 103
NCB (Navy Cipher Box): 103
Nicodemus, Lieutenant Colonel: 59
O'Brien, J.E.: 63-64, 184
Ogam Writing: 21
One-part code: 24
Oshima, Ambassador Baron: 5, 173, 178, 202
Page, Ambassador: 9, 106
Painvin, Captain Georges: 110
Papal states' ciphers: 22, 24, 65
Parker, R.D.: 162-164, 172
Pearl Harbor Committee (See Joint Congressional Committee on the Investigation of the Pearl Harbor Attack)
Pemberton, Lieutenant General J.C.: 73-74
Pepys, Samuel: 13
Philae Obelisk: 46-47
Philip II: 28
Pigpen Cipher: 37-38
Playfair Cipher: 109, 119, 124
Pletts Cryptographs: 195
Plum, Colonel William R.: 64
Pocket Military Cipher: 121
Poe, Edgar Allan: 13, 23, 26, 52, 175
Polyalphabetic Cipher: 63
Polyalphabetic Wheel: 191
Porta: 28-29, 140
Porta's Alphabets: 28
Porta Table: 28
Ptolemaic Period: 44
PURPLE: 180, 192, 201-202
Radio Intelligence Section: 109
Radio Service Code: 130
Rebus: 17-18
Red Cipher Machine: 3, 38, 54, 174, 201
Revolutionary Congress: 43
Rhoads, Lieutenant Mark: 186, 192
Richelieu, Cardinal de: 24, 27
River Series (See American River Series)
Riverbank Laboratories: 107, 109, 145-147, 163-165, 167, 184, 190-191, 195-199, 205
Room 40 O.B.: 105-106, 112
Roosevelt, President Franklin D.: 174, 176
Roosevelt, President Theodore: 102
Rosetta Stone: 43-44, 46, 48, 183-184
Rossignol, Antonio: 24-25
Ross, Professor Alan C.: 51
Rowlett, Frank. B.: 2, 165, 186, 191, 201-202
Satzbuch Code: 116, 125
Savinsky: 121
SCHLUESSELHEFT Code: 116
SCL (See Signal Corps Laboratories)
Scriven, Brigadier General George P.: 100
Scytale: 20-21
Second Army Trench Code: 125, 127
Secret Inks: 11, 36
Secret Signaling System: 162
Secret Writing: 11, 20, 50, 60, 95, 184
Shakespearean Ciphers Examined, The: 33, 183, 193, 203, 205-206
Shakespeare, William: 33, 193, 196-197, 203, 205-206
Short, Lieutenant General Walter C.: 175
SIGABA (See ECM-SIGABA)
SIGCUM: 166
SIGINT: 10
Signal Corps (See Army Signal Corps)
Signal Corps Cipher Disk: 124
Signal Corps Laboratories (SCL), Ft. Monmouth: 158-159
Signal Intelligence School: 192
Signal Intelligence Section: 191

Signal Intelligence Service (SIS): 111-112, 139, 159-160, 163-166, 168, 171, 200-202
SIGSALY: 166
Simonetta, Sicco: 23
Sinkov, Abraham: 186, 191, 201
Slater, Robert: 96
Slater's Code: 96-100, 184
Smith-Corona Typewriter Company: 160
SPARTAN Dispatch: 32
Stager, Colonel Anson: 57, 64, 67-68, 79
Spottswood, W.G.: 97-98
Stanton, Edwin M.: 57-59, 61, 69, 73
Stark, Admiral Harold R.: 175
Stern, Philip Van Doren: 77
Stimson, Henry L.: 136, 184, 200
Strategic Ciphers: 63
Strip Cipher Device Type M-138A: 149
Substitution Cipher: 8, 35-37, 51, 99, 110, 112
Sullivan, General John: 38
Syllabary/repertory: 22, 24, 35, 43
Taciticus, Aeneas: 20
Tactical Ciphers: 63
Tannenberg, Battle of: 25, 123-124
Taylor, Dr. Charles E.: 75
Taylor, Daniel: 39
Teletype Corporation: 158, 166
Thomas, General G.H.: 62
Thompson, Dr. George R.: 57, 61
Tilden, Samuel J.: 91-92, 95, 183-184
Tiltman, Brigadier John H.: 186
Tiro: 21
Transposition Cipher: 8, 35, 63-64, 66-67, 69-72, 79, 93-94, 109-110, 112, 118, 189-190
Trench Code: 125
Trithemius: 27
TSEC/KL-7 Cipher Machine: 10
Two-letter differential: 70
Two-part codes: 71
TYPEX: 158
Union cipher systems: 56-58
Union Signal Corps: 61
USMTC (United States Military Telegraph Corps): 58-59, 61, 63-64, 67-69, 72-73, 75-76, 78-79, 84, 86, 94-95, 118, 130
U.S. Navy Secret Code, 1880s: 96
Vatican: 22-23, 27

Vatican Codex: 23
Vernam, Gilbert S.: 161-162
Viaris, Marquis de: 105, 146, 184
Vieta: 28
Vigenère Cipher: 35, 73, 86-87
Vigenère Square: 29, 73, 140
Vigenère Table (Tableau): 29
Vint Hill Farms: 185
Wadsworth, Colonel Decius: 145-146
Wallis, John: 25, 46, 105, 183
War Department Cipher: 63, 65
War Department Telegraphic Code: 99-100
Wats, Gilbert: 29, 31, 183
Wedemeyer, General Albert C.: 135, 184
Western Union Telegraphic Code: 99-100
Weston, Reverend Stephen: 44
Wheatstone, Sir Charles: 141, 144-146, 184, 190
Wheel Cypher, The: 105, 148
Whitney, Eli: 145-146
Wiener, Professor Norbert: 44
Wig-wag (two element) Code: 56, 58, 60-62, 83
Wilhelm Cipher: 112
Wilson, President Woodrow: 9, 106-107
Wimsatt, Professor W.K.: 52, 184
Wolsey, Cardinal Thomas: 21
Worcester, Marquis of: 21
Writing, History of: 25-47
Yamamoto, Admiral Isoroku: 136-138, 169, 173
Yardley, Herbert O.: 95-96, 99, 147, 164, 184
Young, Dr. Thomas: 44
Zimmermann Telegram: 7, 105-107, 112, 184

www.ingramcontent.com/pod-product-compliance
Lightning Source LLC
Chambersburg PA
CBHW082119230426
43671CB00015B/2737